# Political Philosophy and Public Purpose

Series Editor

Michael J. Thompson
William Paterson University
Wayne, New Jersey, USA

This series offers books that seek to explore new perspectives in social and political criticism. Seeing contemporary academic political theory and philosophy as largely dominated by hyper-academic and overly-technical debates, the books in this series seek to connect the politically engaged traditions of philosophical thought with contemporary social and political life. The idea of philosophy emphasized here is not as an aloof enterprise, but rather a publicly-oriented activity that emphasizes rational reflection as well as informed praxis.

More information about this series at
http://www.springer.com/series/14542

Daniel Krier • Mark P. Worrell
Editors

# The Social Ontology of Capitalism

*Editors*
Daniel Krier
Sociology
Iowa State University
Ames, Iowa, USA

Mark P. Worrell
SUNY Cortland
Cortland, New York, USA

Political Philosophy and Public Purpose
ISBN 978-1-349-95061-4      ISBN 978-1-137-59952-0   (eBook)
DOI 10.1057/978-1-137-59952-0

Library of Congress Control Number: 2016959442

© The Editor(s) (if applicable) and The Author(s) 2017
This work is subject to copyright. All rights are solely and exclusively licensed by the Publisher, whether the whole or part of the material is concerned, specifically the rights of translation, reprinting, reuse of illustrations, recitation, broadcasting, reproduction on microfilms or in any other physical way, and transmission or information storage and retrieval, electronic adaptation, computer software, or by similar or dissimilar methodology now known or hereafter developed.
The use of general descriptive names, registered names, trademarks, service marks, etc. in this publication does not imply, even in the absence of a specific statement, that such names are exempt from the relevant protective laws and regulations and therefore free for general use.
The publisher, the authors and the editors are safe to assume that the advice and information in this book are believed to be true and accurate at the date of publication. Neither the publisher nor the authors or the editors give a warranty, express or implied, with respect to the material contained herein or for any errors or omissions that may have been made.

Cover illustration: © Elisabeth Eide, from Cox's Bazaar, Bangladesh, January 2013.

Printed on acid-free paper

This Palgrave Macmillan imprint is published by Springer Nature
The registered company is Nature America Inc.
The registered company address is: 1 New York Plaza, New York, NY 10004, U.S.A.

# Series Editor's Foreword to Daniel Krier and Mark P. Worrell: *The Social Ontology of Capitalism*

The social sciences and social philosophy have consistently operated under assumptions about what defines its subject matter no less than what defines the core concepts that they both take as their objects of inquiry such as the individual, society, institutions, norms, and so on. What this means is that the core concepts that have historically commanded the attention of those who study society and human affairs have largely gone without thorough inquiry into the nature of existence of society itself. Indeed, the distinction between antiquity and modernity is largely understood as breaking along this central issue. Whereas classical and medieval political and social philosophy saw a particular kind of social ontology as the ground for their investigations into law, state, citizenship, and justice, modernity sought a break with this "communal" ontology and instead proposed an approach that saw society not as prior to the individual, but rather as an expression of the agreements and conscious projects of its members. The ideas of thinkers such as Thomas Hobbes, John Locke, Bernard de Mandeville, and others therefore opened up a break with the classical and medieval Aristotelian paradigm that saw society as an ontological entity with its own properties and modes of existence.

In the late twentieth century, the analytic and pragmatist theories of social action have become dominant. What has come to be known as the "postmetaphysical" understanding of modernity has come to refer to the ways that modernity is a horizon of reason-exchange and pragmatic forms of communication and collective construction of meaning. The social therefore is rooted in individual capacities—say for speech, language, communication, cognition, moral reflection—but is only activated in an intersubjective (i.e., social) context where they can be exercised. This results, advocates of this thesis maintain, in a conception of modernity that is constantly in creation, subject to rational inquiry and critique, whose norms and institutions should always be inherently revisable. This is understood as "postmetaphysical" in the sense that our understanding of norms and of society more generally no longer relies on any foundational assumptions about what constitutes values, social reality, and so on. Rather, we begin from common practices and capacities (such as communication, discourse, etc.) and construct the rational community.

But all along, the classical problem still remains. What is society? Does it possess particular properties and modes of existence? And, if so, what are the implications for social critique and moral judgment, let alone its implications for how we conceive of society as a whole? Recently, there has been a renewed interest in these social–ontological questions that have been passed over by the bulk of modern social science and social philosophy. In many ways, this was initiated by the work of John Searle and his project of creating a social ontology out of his theory of collective intentionality and his previous work in the philosophy of mind, language, and speech-act theory. But whereas Searle relies on a theory of social facts rooted in language, other approaches are coming to the fore. All ask the basic question about *what constitutes the social*. The research program of contemporary social ontology is therefore not reducible to one approach or school, but must be seen as renewed interest in the question of how we can approach the very existence of society and the social itself. The present book offers a series of stimulating and original chapters that explores the social-ontological aspects of capitalist society. What it shows is that the project of a social ontology is deeply related to the questions of critical theory, or Marxism, to the project of understanding society as historically situated and therefore as an important area of research for those interested in moving beyond the sterility of the analytic and mainstream approaches to the social and human sciences. Once we begin to inquire into the very nature of what constitutes society, we may well be on our way to formulating a deeper, more compelling understanding of the social world and our potential to transform it.

New York City
Summer, 2016

Michael J. Thompson

# Acknowledgments

The editors wish to thank Michael Thompson, Series Editor of Political Philosophy and Public Purpose at Palgrave Macmillan, for his ongoing support and guidance while preparing this volume. We also wish to thank Chris Robinson, editor of U.S. Politics, Public Policy, and Political Theory, and Elaine Fan, editorial assistant, also at Palgrave Macmillan for their production assistance and marketing expertise. At Iowa State University (ISU), for their support of the 2015 Symposium for New Directions in Critical Social Theory, we thank Paul Lasley, Chair of the Department of Sociology; Arne Hallam, Associate Dean of the College of Liberal Arts and Sciences; Chad Gasta, Chair of World Languages and Cultures; and Heimir Giersson, Chair of Philosophy and Religious Studies. We also extend our gratitude to faculty, students, and staff in ISU's Department of Sociology who assisted with the 2015 Symposium or with the preparation of this manuscript, especially Darcy Besch, Chet Britt, Rachel Burlingame, Deb McKay, and Nick Van Berkum.

# Contents

1  The Social Ontology of Capitalism: An Introduction    1
   *Daniel Krier and Mark P. Worrell*

Part I  Abstract    13

2  Social Ontology and Social Critique: Toward a New
   Paradigm for Critical Theory    15
   *Michael J. Thompson*

3  Critical Theory in the Twenty-First Century: The Logic
   of Capital Between Classical Social Theory, the Early
   Frankfurt School Critique of Political Economy
   and the Prospect of Artifice    47
   *Harry F. Dahms*

4  The Sacred and the Profane in the General Formula
   for Capital: The Octagonal Structure of the Commodity
   and Saving Marx's Sociological Realism from Professional
   Marxology    75
   *Mark P. Worrell*

5 Social Form and the 'Purely Social': On the Kind
   of Sociality Involved in Value                                      121
   *Patrick Murray and Jeanne Schuler*

Part II   Concrete                                                     143

6 Debt in the Global Economy                                           145
   *Tony Smith*

7 Representing Capital? Mimesis, Realism,
   and Contemporary Photography                                        173
   *Christian Lotz*

8 Demand the Impossible: Greece, the Eurozone Crisis,
   and the Failure of the Utopian Imagination                          195
   *David N. Smith*

9 The Constellation of Social Ontology: Walter
   Benjamin, Eduard Fuchs, and the Body of History                     235
   *Kevin S. Amidon and Daniel Krier*

10 The Body Ontology of Capitalism                                     263
   *Daniel Krier and Kevin S. Amidon*

11 The Morality of Misery                                              277
   *Tony A. Feldmann*

Index                                                                  291

# LIST OF CONTRIBUTORS

*Kevin S. Amidon* (PhD, Princeton) is Associate Professor of World Languages and Cultures at Iowa State University. He has published articles on critical theory, gender history and theory, eugenics, race theory, evolutionary thought, the Frankfurt School, German and American history, opera, and theater. His current research projects include book-length studies of the cultures of investigation and persuasion in German life sciences during the early twentieth century, and the status of Hören (hearing, attention, obedience, and ownership) in the German opera of the 1920s

*Harry F. Dahms* (PhD, New School for Social Research) is Professor of Sociology, Co-Director of the Center for the Study of Social Justice, and Co-Chair of the Committee on Social Theory at the University of Tennessee-Knoxville. He is the editor of *Current Perspectives in Social Theory* and director of the International Social Theory Consortium. He is the author of *The Vitality of Critical Theory*, has edited and coedited other books, and has published in *Sociological Theory, Current Perspectives in Social Theory, Comparative Sociology, Critical Sociology, Basic Income Studies, Bulletin of Science, Technology and Society*, and other journals, along with chapters in encyclopedias and handbooks. Currently, he is finishing a book manuscript, *Modern Society as Artifice: Critical Theory and the Logic of Capital*

*Tony Feldmann* (MA, University of Kansas) is a doctoral candidate and graduate teaching assistant in the Department of Sociology at the University of Kansas. His areas of specialization include political psychology, critical theory, and political economy. His research focuses upon understanding aspects of authoritarianism, especially the reasons why some people hold self-defeating political attitudes while others do not and how social relationships impact political attitudes. He recently presented "The Anatomy of Authoritarianism: Unforgettable Theory and Uninterpreted Data" (with Shane Wilson) and coauthored a chapter with Daniel Krier, "Social Character in Western Premodernity: Lacanian Psychosis in Wladsyslaw Reymont's *The Peasants*," in *Capitalism's Future: Alienation, Emancipation and Critique* (Brill)

**Daniel Krier** (PhD, University of Kansas) is Associate Professor of Sociology at Iowa State University, where he has organized a series of symposia on critical social theory. His books include *Speculative Management: Stock Market Power and Corporate Change* (SUNY Press); *NASCAR, Sturgis and the New Economy of Spectacle* (with William Swart: Brill) and an edited volume (with Mark P. Worrell); and *Capitalism's Future: Alienation, Emancipation and Critique* (Brill). Krier has published articles or chapters in the *American Journal of Economics and Sociology, Current Perspectives in Social Theory, Critical Sociology*, and *Fast Capitalism*, and a number of edited volumes in critical theory

**Christian Lotz** (PhD, University of Marburg) is Professor of Philosophy at Michigan State University. His main research area is post-Kantian European philosophy. Recent book publications include *The Art of Gerhard Richter: Hermeneutics, Images, Meaning* (Bloomsbury Press, 2015); *The Capitalist Schema: Time, Money, and the Culture of Abstraction* (Lexington Books, 2014); *Christian Lotz zu Karl Marx: Das Maschinenfragment* (Laika Verlag, 2014); *Ding und Verdinglichung. Technik- und Sozialphilosophie nach Heidegger und der Kritischen Theorie* (ed., Fink Verlag, 2012); and *From Affectivity to Subjectivity: Revisiting Edmund Husserl's Phenomenology* (Palgrave, 2008). Lotz has published numerous articles in critical Marxist thought, aesthetics, and continental philosophy. His current research interests are in Marx and aesthetical realism, as well as in contemporary European political philosophy

**Patrick Murray** (PhD, St. Louis University) is Professor of Philosophy at Creighton University. He writes widely on political economy and Marxist thought. His books include *Marx's Theory of Scientific Knowledge* (Atlantic Highlands, NJ: Humanities Press International [1990])

and *Reflections on Commercial Life: An Anthology of Classic Texts from Plato to the Present* (1997). He has also edited a special issue of *Telos* on Religion and Politics

**Jeanne Schuler** (PhD, Washington University, St. Louis) is Associate Professor of Philosophy at Creighton University. She writes and teaches on nineteenth-century philosophy, political philosophy, modern philosophy, and Marxist philosophy

**David Norman Smith** (PhD, Wisconsin) is Professor and Chair of the Sociology Department at the University of Kansas. He is the author of *Marx's Capital Illustrated* (Haymarket, 2014) and the editor of *Marx's World: Asia, Africa, the Americas, and Global Accumulation in Marx's Late Manuscripts*, forthcoming from Yale University Press. He has published journal articles and book chapters across a variety of topics in critical and social theory, including charisma, authority, and genocide

**Tony Smith** (PhD, State University of New York, Stony Brook) is Professor of Philosophy at Iowa State University. He has published widely in Marxist philosophy and political economy. His books include *Beyond Liberal Egalitarianism: Marxism and Normative Social Theory in the Twenty-First Century* (Brill), *Globalisation: A Systematic Marxian Account* (Brill and Haymarket), *Technology and Capital in the Age of Lean Production: A Marxian Critique of the "New Economy"* (SUNY), *Dialectical Social Theory and Its Critics: From Hegel to Analytical Marxism and Postmodernism* (SUNY), and *The Logic of Marx's Capital: Replies to Hegelian Criticisms* (SUNY). He recently coedited with Fred Moseley, *Hegel's Logic and Marx's Capital: A Reexamination* (Brill). He publishes journal articles and book chapters on a variety of topics in Marxism, ethics, and political economy

**Michael J. Thompson** (PhD, City University of New York [CUNY]) is Associate Professor of Political Theory in the Department of Political Science at William Paterson University. His most recent book is *The Domestication of Critical Theory* (Rowman & Littlefield, 2016), and his next book, *The Republican Reinvention of Radicalism*, is forthcoming from Columbia University Press. He is also the Founding Editor of *Logos: A Journal of Modern Society & Culture*

**Mark P. Worrell** (PhD, University of Kansas) is Associate Professor of Sociology at State University of New York College at Cortland (SUNY

Cortland) and Associate Editor of the journal *Critical Sociology*. Worrell has published widely in the pages of *Telos, Fast Capitalism, Current Perspectives in Social Theory, Critical Sociology, Logos, Rethinking Marxism, Humanity and Society,* and elsewhere. Worrell's books include *Dialectic of Solidarity: Labor, Anti-semitism and the Frankfurt School* (Brill), *Why Nations Go to War* (Routledge), *Terror* (Routledge), and the coedited volume with Daniel Krier, *Capitalism's Future: Alienation, Emancipation and Critique* (Brill). He is currently working on a synthesis of the classical and critical traditions of sociological theory to be published by Ashgate

# List of Figures

Fig. 4.1 The new general formula 91
Fig. 8.1 Default, it's not in the cards 206

# LIST OF TABLE

Table 10.1   Body ontology of capitalism: Marx *avec* Lacan    273

CHAPTER 1

# The Social Ontology of Capitalism: An Introduction

*Daniel Krier and Mark P. Worrell*

This book emerged from the 2015 Symposium for New Directions in Critical Social Theory at Iowa State University, May 11–12. The original idea for the Symposium was proposed at an April 2007 meeting of the Midwest Sociological Society in Chicago and was put into motion the next year as a biennial gathering of a handful of sociologists, Germanists, and philosophers in Ames, Iowa, with the goal of surveying the state of critical social theory in hopes of establishing vectors for future interdisciplinary research. As of June 2016, the Symposium has grown into a larger and more formally structured workshop incorporating several days of sessions devoted to the reinvention of critical social theory and critical sociology. Revised and thematically integrated papers from the 2014 meeting were published in 2016 as *Capitalism's Future: Alienation, Emancipation and Critique*, edited by Daniel Krier and Mark P. Worrell, as Volume 85 of the Studies in Critical Social Sciences (Brill). The present volume is dedicated to an exploration of the ontology of capitalist society.

---

D. Krier (✉)
Department of Sociology, Iowa State University, Ames, IA, USA

M.P. Worrell
Department of Sociology, SUNY Cortland, Cortland, NY, USA

© The Author(s) 2017
D. Krier, M.P. Worrell (eds.), *The Social Ontology of Capitalism*,
DOI 10.1057/978-1-137-59952-0_1

Social ontology has reemerged once again as a hot topic in the social sciences and philosophy. One current attracting attention is the area of "speculative realism," where the search for a "substance X" is underway whereby the mind attempts to imagine what reality is in the absence of mind—this amounts to an elaborate set of "suicide notes" addressed to the Big Other (you'll miss me when I'm gone). On a more serious front, the current popularity of the rubric springs from John R. Searle's 1995 book, *The Construction of Social Reality*, an influential book (cited over 4000 times) that supplants crude materialism with a dumbed-down version of the social realism that defines the classical work of Marx and Durkheim. Crude materialism, treating objects in the social world as things or substances determined by their material essences, permeates contemporary academic discourse, even among sociologists and social theorists who should know better. Race, gender, sexuality, money—widely recognized and researched as historically contingent, socially constructed, structurally determined categories—are nevertheless treated in many studies (including those published in top journals) as crude, material essences. Searle gestures toward a basic sociological move into the relational realm: social things supposedly lose their crude materialist substance to emerge as socially constructed resultants of the "collective intentionality" of social actors. Searle's writings are the inspiration behind the influential Cambridge Social Ontology Group (CSOG, pronounced "*see*-sawg") organized in the 1990s around Tony Lawson's work. Lawson's most recent book, *The Nature and State of Modern Economics* (Routledge), is representative of the field. The group's book series and articles spring from monthly and semi-annual workshops that center upon the trend's self-consciously realist paradigmatic posture. Lawson's realism is bounded by an attempt to specify the conditions necessary for neoclassical economics to be valid: "atomistic ontology" that requires "constant conjunctions" of recurring phenomena in unchanging "closed systems." CSOG promotes what its members view as a more robust "open systems" approach to the study of economic phenomena, capable of acknowledging history, contingency, complexity, and change. At their best, the ideas discovered and debated within the CSOG circle are recycled concepts that were the common coin of 1970s organizational theory (see, e.g., Richard Scott's *Organizations: Natural, Rational and Open Systems*) or "economic sociology" as it developed in the 1980s. At their worst, these self-labeled heterodox theorists identify structuring principles in markets parallel to Adam Smith's "invisible hand" such that economic regulation and discipline become ontically reducible to the aggregate decisions of individual actors. Rather than an emergent, immanent order of social facts, we find a flattened ontology of individual choice.

In Lawson's and other CSOG writings, Veblen and Hayek are frequent inspirations, with occasional and shallow nods to Marx. Entirely absent from Lawson's publications are references to classical social philosophers and important contemporary theorists such as Hegel, Durkheim, Freud, Weber, Lacan, and Berger. Their works are devoid of the basic categories foundational to critical social theory, failing to incorporate and problematize capital, commodity, value, work, production, or even, as discussed by Krier and Amidon in Chap. 10 of this volume, the body. Their work reflects the same "atomistic" ontology that they purport to criticize, substituting a thin, depthless notion of social relations for a granular ontology of academic economists.

The secret of Searle's and CSOG's success appears to be their appearance of originality: Searle does not engage with foundational thinkers in the realm of social ontology claiming instead the position of the "first author" in the field. This intellectual travesty authorizes tenure and promotion-seeking academics in a variety of disciplines to forego lengthy engagement with complex readings: if one wishes to publish articles about social ontology, one now begins with Searle, Lawson, and others in the CSOG constellation.

> As a great wizard once put it, why, anybody can have a brain, it is a very mediocre commodity. Back where we come from we have universities, seats of great learning, where men go to become great thinkers, and when they come out, they think deep thoughts, and with no more brains than you have. But, they have one thing you haven't got: tenure.

Ignoring Marx and more than a century of critical political economy rooted in Marx, allows both Searle and Lawson to embarrassingly "discover" the social ontology of money: "money is not a crude material reality but something socially constructed, who knew?" Such claims of originality are, in our view, a result of "collective intentionality": these authors have agreed to ignore, avoid, and distantly disparage already-foundational works. Searle's *The Construction of Social Reality* completely ignores Berger and Luckmann's *Social Construction of Reality* (a book cited 40,000 times since publication). Carol Gould published *Marx's Social Ontology: Individuality and Community in Marx's Theory of Social*

*Reality* in 1978, a book far closer in spirit to the current volume, which was itself based upon Georg Lukács' multi-volume *Ontology of Social Being*. Tony Smith who addresses the "social ontology of capitalism" as early as his 1993 *Logic of Marx's Capital*.

A compelling social ontology must foreground deep structure, historically determined but frequently repressed, limiting "social constructionism" and "collective intentionality." Searle's notion of "background" simply does not cut it: social ontology must acknowledge myriad forces that consciously and *unconsciously* structure and determine social life, from embodied organic drives that generate imaginary projections, to ceremonially regulated moral energies, to highly charged distinctions between the sacred and profane, to the valorization imperative in capital itself. Social facts are incredibly complex and multi-layered things, fraught with antinomies and contradictions, and while they may appear to be the result of situational action and collective intentionality, a valid ontology must account for their determination from afar and below.

The "facticity" of things social may appear quaint and unbearably Durkheimian, however, when we examine its etymology, the term is more than interesting, it is essential for any sociologically relevant ontological program. "Fact" is derived from the Latin *factum* and the range of possible meanings includes "deed, action, event, occurrence, achievement, misdeed, real happening, result of doing, something done, in post-classical Latin [a] thing that has really occurred or is actually the case, thing known to be true ... use as noun of neuter past participle of *facere* to make." *Facere* is the shared root for both "fact" and "fetish." A *factum* denotes not just an action or thing done but also an "evil deed" by a *malefactor*. A fact is not only believed to be real but is actually real; it is a thing that may preexist our individual existence but it is nonetheless made (*manufactured*) through concerted effort, a fact is a *feat*, in other words, with definite *features*, but that normally leads across time and space to *stupefaction* on the part of makers and remakers, the eventual *petrifaction* (hardening, or reification) of our creations, and, ultimately, when the sun sets for any fact, the *putrefaction* or rotting of the thing, the degeneration into a putrid monstrosity. For sociology, the main point is that our creations are more than subjective or intersubjective realities, that they impose themselves upon us as authorities, and that to grasp their social nature we cannot reduce them down to smaller parts, nor, by contrast, project them behind the world, turning them into what appear to be metaphysical entities.

The sociological meaning of "use-value" has so far been underappreciated. Usefulness, proper, falls to the side of singularity, destruction, and the concrete while any "value" must fall to the opposite side, that of universality, "indestructibility," and the collective. Marx uncritically retained the preexisting terminology of political economy but, rather than throwing it out, we can see that the idea of a use-value, a weird combination of the abstract universal and the concrete singularity, belongs both to the sublime dimension of exchange relations (socially) and within the post-exchange dimension of *personal* psychology as a fetish. The world becomes populated not only by active people and their passive things but "actors" wielding their phallus-status objects as enchanted mirrors, signifiers pointing toward the invisible dimension where value and prestige are entangled. Normally, we would associate the phallus object with neurotics and misery, however, in the denouement of the *Wizard of Oz*, after being sociologically placed back in their feet, we find characters who have problems with neither their fantasies nor do they have problems with their realities, they simply enjoy mutual reciprocity within the social structure via their trophies of surplus enjoyment. However, the "value" that is imagined to adhere to the "use" in the ordinary world of commodity fetishism, is far from subversive. Outside the land of Oz, our things take on personalities and aura while our lives become more thing-like. We are things in our jobs, our worth is measured by our pay and the symbols we can secure to advertise our coordinates and humiliate our neighbors in the ceaseless war of images and moral vibrations.

If we look only with the material eye, there appears to be little in the way of a "social" ontology here: supply and demand of material goods, supply and demand of workers, supply and demand balanced in a transparent, efficient free market determines the rewards, profits, and the distribution of production to various branches of industry. This would appear to be nothing more than circuits and flows of matter. However, behind these circuits moves some "invisible hand," the market as big other, a self-propelling subject-substance that determines all. Hence, the social ontology of capitalism, from these perspectives, is a simplified "market ontology." Like the Calvinist who used wealth accumulation as an index of one's capacity to magnify the glory of god by toiling unceasingly within the prepared calling, accounting and capital accumulation indicate, if not salvation, at least the proper alignment of determinate being and the fountain of grace. The danger, here, though, is overshooting the social and flying off into the misty realm of hypostatized absolute subjectivity.

Dialectics (split reasoning) is the objective gaze that sublates the twin aspects of the concrete and the abstract, the singular and the universal through particular theoretical creativity that enables the theorist, through negative synthesis, to get "on top" of the social totality (not identical with the paranoid gaze of the imaginary absolute) much as his or her predecessor, the magician, could control their alienation and doubling, in effect, to become the self-conscious Thing itself, to become an effective power in a world of hostile powers. Since at least the time of Plato, thinkers have struggled to overcome the twin dead ends of materialist reduction and transcendentalism. Reductions do have the virtue, reflected in the etymology of the word, of bringing back or restoring the human to this world, rather than some hidden counterworld and transcendentalism was (or is) appealing because it reflects in a distorted manner the truth that we are more than our matter, that there is something excessive about human life that makes us the "freaks of nature" (Fromm). Neglecting a few key predecessors, we can probably credit the Jena circle of philosophers with laying the foundations for what would become modern sociological thought with the first "perfect" sociological analysis of any "social fact" taking the form of Marx's analysis of the commodity in *Capital*. Marx's so-called "historical materialism" (Marx never used this phrase himself) draws on Hegel's phenomenological method of constructing an articulated procession of ideal-typical models that revealed the objective social logic of the commodity's emergence from accidental and fluid exchange relations of simple barter between communities to the fully crystallized universal form where money and money as capital reign supreme over greater expanses of the earth. While Marx had aspirations beyond the critique of political economy, the "economics" project consumed most of his career and while the Hegel-to-Marx trajectory is the most famous and influential intellectual line to trace, another, connecting Hegel to the founding of modern academic sociology by Durkheim and his disciples, can also be mapped.

As Worrell argues in Chap. 4, contemporary Marxism has, for the most part, lost the thread, populated as it is with non-sociologists who routinely read Marx from either a materialist perspective and bring in, through the back door, an unconscious transcendentalism. The task of the future is to recover the genuinely sociological Marx and to synthesize Marxist sociology with the classical tradition as it was practiced by the Durkheimians; what is needed is a new paradigm of thought we call "Marxheimian" sociology (drawing, roughly, upon the insights of Hegel, Marx, Durkheim, Mauss, Freud, and Lacan). Not every chapter in the present volume will live up to the demands of this new, synthetic aspiration, not everyone here identifies as a "Marxheimian," but some do and these contributions function as a prolegomenon for future studies.

In "Social Ontology and Social Critique" (Chap. 2), Michael Thompson constructs a theory of critical social ontology as a means to diagnose the existence and nature of social pathologies in capitalist societies. He begins by outlining four branches of social ontology that are common in the literature and then demonstrates how each can be dialectically synthesized to construct a critical theory of social ontology. Thompson then proceeds to show how this theory of a critical social ontology can serve as a theoretical foundation for a richer, more satisfying and more radical form of social critique by reconstructing the way in which the descriptive knowledge of social facts can also serve as normative judgments about their existing, empirical state of society. He concludes by outlining how this critical social ontology can provide theorists with a more trenchant critique of capitalism and its social pathologies.

In Chap. 3, "Critical Theory in the Twenty-First Century," Harry Dahms maps the various theories that have illuminated the patterns of economic transformation shaping forms of political, social, and cultural life in modern society. Dahms argues that his underpinnings and consequences resulting from those apparently economic transformations are not simply and broadly economic in nature, but specifically *capitalist*. From the outset, critical theory has scrutinized how "the mighty cosmos of the modern economic order" (Max Weber) is fraught with compounded levels of alienation. If, according to Dahms, we situate the origins of dialectical theorizing in Hegel's and Marx's respective critiques of alienation, efforts to explicate the history of the modern age have been based on two categories. For Hegel, "spirit" as enlightened, self-reflexive intelligence was (and was to be understood as) the driver of historical change. By contrast, for Marx, as the nineteenth century wore on, *spirit* came to be supplanted by "capital" as the dominant driver, with *capital* denoting an *artificial*, non-human form of intelligence. The first generation of Frankfurt School theorists defined critical theory as the program of deconstructing how the spread of *capital* is mediated (and concealed) politically, socially, and cultural, albeit while abandoning the need to update Marx's critique of political economy for the twentieth century. Since the onset of globalization during the latter part of the twentieth century, efforts in critical theory to highlight the problematic nature of modern society *qua* capitalism, especially those that have been influenced and inspired by Habermas and

Honneth, *de facto* constitute efforts at *normalizing* the reign of capital and the realm of alienation. At the same time, it has become increasingly apparent that *capital* is no longer the driver of socio-historical change, and no longer serves as an adequate means to focus the kind of critique that is most needed and important, as human needs are interfering with the needs and operations of *capital* to an ever-increasing extent. Rather, similar to the historical period when *capital* began to replace *spirit*, we are currently undergoing a change in the trajectory of "human" civilization: as *capital* is being supplanted by *artifice*, the latter is being revealed as the true specter behind the former, and proliferating indications suggest that we are in the process of entering what promises/threatens to be a *post-human* civilization.

In "The Sacred and the Profane in the General Formula for Capital" (Chap. 4), Mark Worrell argues that residual materialism and ordinary realism of the kind that plagues children and "savages" has rendered Marxist critiques of the commodity and capitalism not only counterproductive but exposes a secret resentment and perverse will to power. Contemporary Marxism does not, generally, operate from a truly dialectical materialist foundation but fantasizes about revolutionary class struggle and one day placing all capital under new management. The methodological objectivity and "stereoscopic" conceptualism arrived at through a dialectical analysis, perhaps best comprehended in the chapters on the dual nature of the commodity in the first volume of *Capital*, is seldom used by common one-eyed Marxists. Rather, we find over and over and over, that ideological compressions and distortions, not unlike the kind found in dreamwork, are made to stand in for actual critical theory. What is required is a reexamination and reconstruction of the general formula for capital, as Marx developed it, such that the objective gaze that clearly distinguishes between the sacred and the profane, the *supraliminal* and the *infraliminal*, are maintained yet superseded. If we aim to march out of the swamp of value then we need a disenchanting grasp of the ontic depth of capitalism rather than redoubling confusion with imprecise ideology that does little more than help to solidify the hegemony of an elite class over the rest of humanity.

In Chap. 5, "Social Form and the 'Purely Social': Toward a better Understanding of Value and the Value-Form," Patrick Murray and Jeanne Schuler wonder what sort of sociality is involved in societies where wealth is produced on a capitalist basis, wealth takes the social form of the commodity. This question is explored with special reference to what Marx calls the value-form, that is, to his claim that value must be expressed in exchange-value, more particularly, in the (antagonistic) polarized relationship between commodity and money, the universal equivalent.

In the social ontology of capitalism, debt has become one of its most fundamental social forms, a constitutive though fictitious structure that subsumes and disrupts social life. Tony Smith, in Chap. 6, "The Political Economy of Debt and the Present Moment of World History," reveals the destabilizing consequences and precariousness of debt-based capital. Smith maps striking developments in the role of debt that distinguish our historical period. Smith presents seven "stylized facts" about our social world. From the standpoint of most mainstream economic theories they are all anomalies, caused by extraneous factors. As Thomas Kuhn taught long ago in *The Structure of Scientific Revolutions*, however, there is some point past which the accretion of anomalies and ad hoc explanations calls established paradigms into question. Smith argues that a Marxian framework extrapolated from the third volume of *Capital* offers a superior basis for comprehending these crucially important features of the contemporary world. From here, Chap. 6 proceeds by examining three dimensions of macro-monetary circuits: the *use-value dimension* of innovations that create dynamic new markets and expand established ones; *the social relations dimension* of labor markets and labor processes that enable surplus value to be produced, and *the monetary dimension*, that is, the difference between the aggregate of money accumulated at the conclusion of a circuit (M') relative to the aggregate invested at its beginning (M). An argument is given that the valorization process from M to M' requires the insertion of credit by the financial sector. Part Two constructs a historical narrative of the return to growth after the global slowdown of the 1970s, focusing on the three dimensions discussed in Part One. Part Three begins by noting a number of striking features of the monetary dimension today, including the astounding and absolutely unprecedented amount of debt that has been created; the fact that ever-greater amount of debt are required to obtain a given increment of growth; and the greater share of debt created within the financial sector that remains within that sector, generating self-sustaining financial bubbles. Smith argues that these features of credit in the contemporary economy are rooted in the proliferation of national innovation systems that are dynamic in use-value terms but hamper valorization. The final section explores the implications of the political economy of credit for social relations, concluding that the normative issues they raise could not be more profound.

In Chap. 7, "The (In)Visibility of Capital. Reflections on Film, Lukács, and Contemporary Critical Realism," Christian Lotz presents critical reflections on the possibility of a contemporary concept of aesthetic realism in connection with two photo-artists and filmmakers, Edward Burtynsky and Allan Sekula. Both artists are concerned with globalization, the exploitation of the earth, labor, and global capital in their work. The basic question connected with their work is whether it is possible to represent the real abstractions of capital and the effects of global capital in images, photography, and other works of art. Lotz argues that Burtynsky's work ultimately mystifies reality and falls back onto a subjective aesthetical position and discusses the possibility of renewing Lukács' concept of realism and mimesis for contemporary critical aesthetics.

In Chap. 8, "Demand the Impossible: Greece, the Eurozone, and the Anti-Utopian Complex," David Norman Smith writes that the "anti-utopian complex," according to Theodor Adorno, loomed large in traditional, "uncritical" theory and goes on to evaluate that thesis in the light of the unfolding events in the tense dialogue between Greece and the eurozone, in the context of the still-reverberating effects of the global economic crisis of 2008. In January, 2015, the radical anti-austerity party Syriza came to power in Greece—and yet the ensuing negotiations with the eurozone and the IMF continued to revolve mainly around severe proposed austerity measures. Syriza's role in the negotiations has come under intense scrutiny, and questions have arisen about the very meaning of anti-austerity politics. The purpose of this chapter is to explore those questions, by means of a careful analysis of the positions taken before and after January 2015 by the leading economists in Syriza, including Yanis Varoufakis, Costas Lapavitsas, and John Milios. It becomes clear that all of these key figures, each of whom professes a kind of Marxism, have from the start been consistently reluctant to depart significantly from the eurozone's conventional economic wisdom. Smith's intent is to explore that fact in the light of Adorno's critique of anti-utopianism.

"The Constellation of Social Ontology: Walter Benjamin, Eduard Fuchs, and the Body of History," our ninth chapter by Amidon and Krier, says that Walter Benjamin is best known among scholars for his work on "The Work of Art in the Age of its Technological Reproducibility," in which he argues that all visual art, including its modern emanations like film, has always been constituted through modes not just of production, but also of reproduction. Relatively unknown in the scholarly literature, however, is that these claims about art and reproduction took shape as part of a larger set of arguments about the nature of historical knowledge and the ways that knowledge emerges and derives from embodied, corporeal practices. Benjamin made these arguments in his essay on "Eduard Fuchs: Collector and Historian" (1937). This essay and its history further show that Benjamin's thought belongs at the center of the Frankfurt School's emergent critical theory in the mid-1930s, and reveals significant institutional and methodological links between Fuchs, Benjamin, and the major figures of the Frankfurt School like Max Horkheimer. More broadly, Benjamin's work on Fuchs can be seen as a methodological attempt to demonstrate how critical methods that do justice to the material of history by attending successfully to the forgotten remnants of social, political, and economic life can create the possibility of concrete social ontology in the present.

Critical social theory powerfully negates symbolic structures of political economy and imaginary projections of ideological culture but never quite knows what to do with corporeal bodies. In Chap. 10, "The Body Ontology of Capitalism," Daniel Krier and Kevin S. Amidon review Marx's account of body ontology in his post-1859 writings (especially *Capital, Vol. 1*), in which value (abstract labor) is absorbed as a sublime substance during the labor process. They analyze body ontology in Marx's work and in Lacan's psychoanalytic social theory, exploring the relationship between structurally wounded bodies and imaginary projections. Zizek's embodied account of wounded subjects of sublime ideological objects is used to interpret the body fantasies of late capitalism (undead, cyborg, armored subjects). Following Marx and psychoanalytic theorists, Krier and Amidon conclude that body ontology is necessary to adequately comprehend and critique symbolic and imaginary productions of capital.

Tony Feldmann's "Morality of Misery" (Chap. 11) says that it is not uncommon for social welfare programs and policies to come under harsh criticism and inspire moral indignation. Opposition to these programs and policies is often grounded in the belief that the "undeserving" are receiving certain benefits or "luxury" goods. Surprisingly, this moral indignation cuts across social class, and even those who stand to benefit from social welfare programs frequently oppose them. Feldmann explores the origins and nature of this moral sentiment, which he calls "the morality of misery." This peculiar conception of fairness uses suffering to justify suffering. The morality of misery is rooted in the experience of commodity exchange and wage labor, and it is a feedback loop leading people to support their own oppression. The theories of Lukács and Postone are, finally, examined to draw out further implications of misery for critical theory.

# PART I

# Abstract

CHAPTER 2

# Social Ontology and Social Critique: Toward a New Paradigm for Critical Theory

*Michael J. Thompson*

## INTRODUCTION

Late modernity confronts the Enlightenment project with a distinct problem, one that plagues modern practical philosophy as well as modern culture more broadly. This problem can be described as the absence of a grounding that can secure normative values that can in turn provide coherence for judgment. Contemporary philosophy and social theory have embraced an anti-foundational and postmetaphysical path in order to provide a means out of this dilemma. This view advocates a conception of practical reason that emphasizes the reflexive self-creation of norms and values that take as their criterion of legitimacy the intersubjective agreement of participants in discursive activity. Reason is taken to be embodied not only in the practice of reason-exchange, but also in the noumenal and epistemic powers of agents engaged in discursive practices oriented toward the mutual agreement of norms. This has been the hallmark of much of what now passes for a "critical theory" of society, and it is largely marked by a turn away from a more radical, more comprehensive and, I think, more satisfying (albeit more demanding) philosophical project that seeks to provide and to clarify value-concepts grounded in ontological

M.J. Thompson (✉)
Department of Political Science, William Paterson University, Wayne, NJ, USA

properties of human sociality. According to this view, we can elaborate a critical social ontology that is not simply *descriptive* of social reality as well as the basic features of human sociality, but also provides a *critical* or *evaluative* criterion constituting a critical–practical rationality.

The emergence of modernity was strongly associated with a project across the natural sciences and philosophy more generally to overcome the metaphysical baggage that plagued the traditions of thought that carried over from the medieval and early-modern periods. The strong influence of Scholasticism was premised on a religio-metaphysical system that grounded reason and nature in a transcendental rationality embodied in divine or eternal law which in turn shaped and influenced natural law. But as pressures from nominalist thought began to grow, an alternative understanding of ontology and epistemology began to take root. According to this view, what could be known were particular objects, not universals nor essences. Since they could not be observed, they were seen to be "metaphysical" in the sense that they were not properly objects of science or of rational cognition (cf. Groff, 2013). I can know that the round object in front of me is a ball, but there is no universal category of "ballness" that can be seen to exist in any valid sense of the word. Instead, we have names that serve to delineate particular objects, but no universal concepts exist. This philosophical impulse also led to empiricism, or the doctrine that valid knowledge about particulars—the only valid knowledge of the objective world—could only be validated by sensual experience itself.

In this sense, features of human social life that had previously been seen as axiomatic in understanding moral and political life from the classical period through the medieval age—such as the Aristotelian ideas about the naturalness of human community—were being undermined and displaced by an analytic, mechanistic and atomist philosophical view that would become central to the projects of liberal and market-based society. No longer could we speak of "social relations" that existed prior to individuals or of a common good let alone any universal features of social life since they were to be seen as constructed by us rather than inherent to us. For Hobbes, this became one of the most central aspects of his political theory: namely that the classical ideas about the social essence of human life, or the idea that social relations and relations of social dependency that Aristotle had placed at the core of his ontology of human life were now seen to be fictions. Man was isolated and individual, society atomistic and aggregated. Any social relations or institutions that existed were constructed by us through consent, not in any way natural to us as a species. Locke and later empiricists and utilitarianism as well as Kant's philosophical project all shared in this basic line of thinking when it came to any question of an ontology of sociality.

In this sense, the basic fact of a social ontology is not a search for some kind of material substrates for human life nor is it a search for rigid categories from which we can derive explanations of the social world. Rather, it is meant to highlight the notion that the categories of human freedom, self-determination and so on all have an irreducibly social basis (cf. Brown, 2014) and that this sociality itself has certain basic features that can be seen to be constitutive of our collective and individual lives. In this sense, as P.F. Strawson correctly notes, "each must see himself in some social relation to others whose purposes interact with his. If our subject is man in his world, it seems necessary to admit that this world is essentially a social world" (Strawson, 1992, pp. 80–81). To make such a claim therefore invites us to think about the nature of the social as a distinct object of inquiry, as something with ontological weight and that must be considered as a crucial element in any critical theory of society.

But this is precisely the idea that was under attack by empiricism, nominalism and utilitarianism at the birth of modern social and political theory. According to these movements, the individual was empirically cognizable, not "society" itself. Add to this that within the modern philosophical project more broadly there was a fevered attack on the notion of ontology and metaphysics. Ever since Kant, the mainstream tenets of the western philosophical tradition has labored under a bias against metaphysics and against ontology. This should be of little surprise since the critique of metaphysics that Kant provided was constructed in opposition to the early- and pre-modern concerns with the transcendental metaphysics and being. There are two important implications of this move in philosophy. First, it entails a separation between facts and values, between knowledge claims that are premised on what exists in any ontological sense on the one hand and knowledge claims that deal evaluative-normative claims on the others. Even more, he pointed to "regulative" versus "constitutive" reasons which further pushed the noumenal from the phenomenal realm. Regulative ideas were those that were capable of constituting objects *as objects of cognition* rather than as objects in and of themselves. Rational reasons were therefore those that were accountable to themselves, their own rational reasons rather than any kind of substance that inhered in or acted behind what was grasped by consciousness. As such, any ontological speculation was cast out of the realm of rational possibility since it violated the boundary set by Kant between noumena and phenomena. And besides, what we were now to be pursuing was a rationalist project that defended the capacity of the autonomous, reason-giving subject that Kant saw as essential to the Enlightenment project.

A second implication is that reality becomes a *construction of cognition*. Reality is now dependent on the epistemic subject in the sense that regulative ideas are what give shape to the chaos of experience. Constitutive reasons would be those that are internal to the object-domain itself, making things what they in essence are. But this is not possible given Kant's insistence on the separation of reason as a capacity of cognition on the one hand and the objective world as merely an object of that cognition on the other. The contemporary return to the Kantian doctrine and the nonmetaphysical interpretations of Hegel have therefore sought to construct a postmetaphysical intellectual framework where we are to see practical rationality constituted by reason-giving by concept users who rely upon reasons themselves rather than the rational structure of the object-domain itself to count as what is valid rationally. But this poses important problems, namely that we are barred from comprehending the actual, essential structure of objects, something that Hegel and Marx both saw as essential for a critical grasp of reality. Only once we can comprehend the rational structure of objects in the world can we reconstruct them in cognition and determine the Idea itself, or that unification of the conceptual structure of cognition and the rational structure of the object-domain. This allows us further to grasp the ways that descriptive and normative claims themselves dialectically sublate into a higher, more total knowledge of the world with mechanisms, relations and purposes that are *immanent to those objects*.[1]

But if modernity is defined by the exchange and justification of reasons by rational autonomous agents, then there must be a means by which we can know or *judge* the extent of the validity of these reasons and justifications? The project of pragmatic justification sees this as circumscribed by the practices themselves and the obtaining of mutual agreement by intersubjectively acting participants using only rational reasons as a criterion of objective validity. But the more we think about this, the more question begging it seems to be, for it appears increasingly unable to provide us with a convincing, let alone compelling, form of rational judgment, that is, one that can provide us with judgments about the objective social world and the kinds of goods and ends toward which social life ought to be organized. Clearly, there is an impasse of sorts. For on the one hand, we can plainly see that the critical rejection of the transcendental metaphysics and the religio-ontological projects of the pre-modern period was in order. But at the same time, it follows from this that the solution offered up by Kant—and absorbed into the basic fabric of modern social science and mainstream philosophy—opens us up to a kind of rationalism that is unable to defend against its own relativist implications. What the critical theory tradition, going back to its origins in Hegel and Marx, posits is that there is some sense in which the Kantian chasm between noumena and phenomena must be overcome in order for us to possess objectively valid knowledge that itself has ontology as its basic criterion of validity. Indeed, whereas the renewed Kantian-pragmatist project in critical theory is unable to keep in view is that only ontological claims or those normative claims that have ontological weight can be seen as adequately critical. Only once we are able to grasp the whole, the totality of social reality, and construct normative claims with that social reality in view can we begin to articulate a critical theory of judgment. Indeed, critical reason and critical judgment, facts and values, are dialectically sublated into a higher form of critical cognition.

In what follows, I want to explore just this thesis and suggest that a more compelling and more rational path for critical theory is one that seeks to place a critical social ontology at its center and to keep in view the notion that normative claims are critical only to the extent that they carry descriptive claims about the essential structures of sociality within them. According to this view, norms must be evaluated according to an objective criterion that is stronger than the epistemic reason-giving and linguistic-discursive theories can provide. This criterion is rooted in the social–ontological categories that serve as the desideratum for any valid social knowledge and therefore any diagnostic or critical account of the social world. This means that the advantage of a critical social ontology is that it can provide us with a means to sublate the division between facts and values, between our cognitive grasp of the social world and our normative-evaluative diagnosis of it. This is a powerful mode of critique because it can enable us to bring to critical awareness the perverted and distorted forms of sociation (alienation, reification, etc.) that plague modern forms of life. A critical social ontology therefore grants us a more stable ground from which objective ethical postulates can be articulated and defend against the dangers of ethical relativism on the one hand and epistemic abstraction on the other.

## The Limits of Contemporary Critical Theory

Contemporary critical theory has sought to deal with the problem I have outlined above by moving toward a paradigm that we can broadly describe as one of pragmatic justification. According to this basic view, communication and the justificatory structures inherent in the pragmatics of communication oriented toward mutual understanding will be able to maintain a rational structure as well as the open-ended inquiry and creativity that a truly democratic, non-coercive society demands. No ontology is needed here since we are concerned, as Habermas continually maintains, with the problem of discursive justification and the extent to which individuals are able to come to a rational, mutual understanding about the object-domain: "Fundamental to the paradigm of mutual understanding is, rather, the performative attitude of participants in interaction, who coordinate their plans for action by coming to an understanding about something in the world" (Habermas, 1987, p. 296). Hence, the project of pragmatic justification holds that the relation between subject and object, so central to Idealist philosophy, is overcome not by move of monological reason or through the paradigm of active labor, but rather through the act of argumentative discourse embedded in an intersubjective lifeworld premised on rational justification. Hence, Kant's problematic of the chasm between the noumenal and phenomenal worlds is overcome. As Habermas states the solution: "The unbridgeable gap Kant saw between the intelligible and the empirical becomes, in discourse ethics, a mere tension manifesting itself in everyday communication as the factual force of counterfactual presuppositions" (Habermas, 1990, p. 203).[2]

The project of pragmatic justification takes us back to Kant via the pragmatist theory of action to pose the thesis that epistemic claims can be understood not in transcendental form, as Kant had argued, but in terms immanent to the practice of linguistically mediated communication. Hence, the domain of justification constitutes a kind of realm of objectivity, moving emphasis away from the object-domain itself.[3] But where this project suffers is in the important problem that is brought to light by Hegel's immanent metaphysics on the one hand and Marx's objectivist ontology of sociality on the other. For both, any conception of critical rationality had to grasp the ways that thought and the objective world related to one another, not as a construct of a rational subject (as in Kant and Fichte) but more correctly that cognition should pierce into the rational structures of the objects of consciousness themselves. This is why

Hegel presciently rejects the approach outlined by contemporary Kantian-pragmatists when he maintains that any moral truth or conception of the good or right cannot be based on "the external positive authority of the state or of the mutual agreement (*Übereinstimmung*) among persons, or through the authority of inner feeling and the heart or the spirit which immediately concurs with this" (Hegel, 1970, p. 46). What reason discloses to us is rational structure of *what actually constitutes those objects*; construed this way, rational thought therefore has an ontological metric for measuring its own correctness or incorrectness.[4]

This is why the Kantian-pragmatist thesis elaborated by Habermas and others (Alexy, 1990; Böhler, 1990; Forst, 2011, 2015) is insufficient as a valid critical theory of society. Critical rationality must disclose for us the ontology of sociality insofar as the social–relational structures and processes that constitute any given aspect of social reality forms the context for the constitution of its members and therefore determines the extent to which those social forms are able to promote the kinds of relational, common goods requisite for a robust kind of social freedom. Even more, for Hegel and Marx, the concept of self-determination has to have the basic sociality of the agent in view since a person is only free and self-determined to the extent that they cognize themselves and act within interdependent social–relational contexts that promote their own welfare as well as the good of the social whole and that these are reciprocally constituted. But the problem with approaching objective moral truths through the process of justification and the exchange of reasons alone is that the "reasons" being exchanged no longer possess the requisite ontological ballast to grant them critical weight. Indeed, even more, the exchange of reasons and processes of justification that eschew ontological concerns are open to the socialization pressures of the existent reality and its norms and value-patterns, thereby distorting the noumenal capacities of agents (cf. Habermas, 1996, p. 368ff.). When reason is dissolved into the practice of discourse, there is little room left for the importance of speculative (*begreifende*) thought and the ways that certain truth-claims should be evaluated based on ontological considerations. The reason for this was that both saw—indeed Marx perhaps more strongly than Hegel—that the power of social–institutional forces was too strong for mere pragmatics to overcome. The main issue was that cognition was shaped in intricate ways by the power relations and structural-functional pressures of the existent reality—a reality that was itself seen to be a distorted form of sociality. Operating within that framework means that we would simply reproduce many of the basic assumptions and value-patterns that underwrite the basis of moral cognition as well as the semantic basis of communication. Epistemic reasons are not sufficient to defend rational agency against the pressures of reification.

Hence, what we can call a problem of *epistemic refraction* takes hold once we see that concrete forms of social power have the capacity to shape the presuppositional categories of thought that will serve as the formal foundation for communicative forms of reason. As such, discursive forms of justification are open to epistemic relativism insofar as it is unable to secure universalistic claims outside of mere mutual agreement, something that cannot be secured in any truly rational sense without some degree of appeal to the structure of the object of reference. An ontology of society can therefore help in securing claims about the valid, rational structure of social life in order to diagnose pathologies of that sociality as well as of the kinds of defective forms of cognition that accompany them. Second, it reproduces, rather than overcomes, Hegel's charge of the impotence of the mere ought. Since the nature of objectivity is moved from the object-domain, or the ontology of sociality to that of the "structure of justification" or the internal syntactic structures of language constituting communication, we become unable to address the ways in which power relations distort and affect the cognitive powers of subjects as well as the ways that norms and come to cement and infiltrate the conceptual powers of agents.

It is this basic, but important, philosophical problem that a return to ontology can help us to solve. Indeed, Habermas and his followers have long seen that the overcoming of the subject-object divide is an essential step for critical rationality. What then is the role of ontology in critical theory? My answer is that it provides us with the crucial element of a critical theory of judgment that is able to articulate a conception of an *objectively determinable interest*, one that is rooted in the kinds of social forms, norms and practices that might best promote the common interest of a society and its members. This common interest must be construed as promoting and cultivating a structure of interdependent reciprocal relations since that forms the essential ground and hence objective moment for the capacity of any kind of critical judgment of social reality. Kant's distinction between regulative and constitutive ideas therefore marks a real moment of departure between the epistemic-pragmatic turn in critical theory on the one hand and the critical–ontological view that I am putting forth here since the former should be able to ground a critical–practical rationality that has the potential for us to explode the defective forms of cognition that eventuate from and also perpetuate defective forms of sociality.

## The Concept of Social Ontology and its Dimensions

To speak of a social ontology is not to speak of something transcendent or transcendental; nor is it to speak of something externally foundational or *a priori* to our knowledge of the social world. Instead, it entails looking at sociality as something ontological in that it is *trans-individual* insofar as it is not contained within or circumscribed by an empirical agent or subject; it is also *objective* (i.e., they are not simply mental states or representational ideas), and that it has some kind of *causal power* in the sense that it produces effects in the world that are not simply the product of a single agent or individual actor. Ontology is not a reification of the social, nor is it a static concept. Rather, it has different levels of development and change, and can be seen to be shaped and reshaped in different ways. But these different forms and levels of development and change can be judged based on the kinds of ends that it achieves. In this sense, a social ontology has as its object *sociality itself* as a distinct and centrally defining characteristic of human phenomena. More specifically, it seeks to lay out conceptual categories that are determinate of social reality. This does not entail reifying the social against the creative, reason-giving capacities and practices of social agents but instead seeks to utilize the ontology of the social as a criterion of the validity of values, norms and practices. For giving us a ground for the judgment of what kinds of reasons, what kinds of practices, institutions, norms and so on should count as better than others. It is a kind of thinking that is aware that there exist rational structures in the world which can be reconstructed in and through cognition.

This means that philosophy's role is to be able to grasp the structures that constitute both the real world and conceptual thought and that this process is one that leads us toward a comprehension of reason itself. In this sense, Hegel and Marx saw—albeit in somewhat different ways—that a critical knowledge about the world would have to be accountable to the structures within the world or those structures and processes that constitute the objective world. We cannot simply hold reasons accountable to their own internal validity or to some social, intersubjective norm or agreement since this would bypass the object about which those reasons are accountable. The main reason for this was that it was an insufficient means to counter the problem of relativism and therefore such an approach would be open to the sub-rational conditions of contradiction and arbitrariness in our practical rationality.[5] In contrast, an ontological approach anchors our reasons and forms of justification within an objective realm and looks for universal reasons that inhere within that object-domain. A critical theory of society therefore must make an assessment of the objective structures of the social world on the one hand. But it must also seek to understand these structures, these relations and processes, institutions, norms and so on and grasp how they can be seen as either promoting or negating the kind of relational, common goods that are requisite for robust forms of sociality and individuality.

All of this implies that sociality is more than an *epistemic* concern—it must also be an *ontological* concern to the extent that we are able to understand the ways that different shapes of social forms and relational structures articulate different kinds of goods and ends. This means that a critical theory of judgment is not to characterized by the intersubjective exchange of reasons grounded in rational communication, but rather in the content of claims and the extent to which the institutional ends and purposes of society are able to satisfy the unique ontological needs of a collective, common social good. Critical judgment therefore is a kind of critical thinking that poses the ontological frame as an essential component of any kind of rational political discourse, thinking, or institutional logic. The central question a social–ontological investigation therefore seeks to keep in view is the extent to which an objective interest exists which any rational society should seek to track and any critical sense of judgment must place at the center of its self-critical awareness. The general object of a critical social ontology and its role as shaping a critical theory of judgment can now be seen to consist in the capacity to discern an objective interest that is immanent within the social–relational structure of social life and the extent that this can be used to shape and articulate a critical–practical reason.

### *Four Dimensions of a Social Ontology*

Social ontology does not look for the content of all forms of social life, but rather for the basic underlying categories that undergird different forms of social reality. What conceptual structures are essential for the explanation of social reality and, perhaps to go even further, what conceptual structures and mechanisms can we detect that will allow us not only to comprehend that reality but also to judge it according to critical–rational principles. We can see that the first forces our cognition to deal with *objective structures of reality* and the second with the dynamics of *potentiality and actuality of those objective structures*. From an analytic perspective, the ontology of social reality must be broken down into four distinct branches or dimensions. In much of the literature on social ontology, each of these dimensions is generally taken on its own and more often taken to be incompatible with the others (cf. Renault, 2016). However, it is clear that in order to construct a critical social ontology, we will need dialectically to unify these four branches of social ontology and the distinctive areas of reality that they seek to theorize. This is achieved once we see that each dimension dialectically leads us to the next and ultimately to a comprehensive theoretical structure that can be seen to be not only a conceptual scheme, but also immanent within the concept of society and therefore of social reality itself.

## *Substance*

Things instantiate properties that make them what they are, or which constitute them in some basic, essential sense (Lowe, 2006). An ontology of substance is concerned with this essential structure of being. It seeks an answer to the question of what exists, or what objects actually are in their essence rather than in their particular, accidental forms. In Aristotle, this is generally understood as resting with the "final cause" of any thing: the essential substance or essence of a vase is that it holds water, and so on. Aristotle contrasts the substance of any thing with the accidents that affect it (Loux, 1978). Hence, although not all tables and chairs look the same or take on the same form, they have a commonality as an object in that they possess the function of allowing people to sit in them. Spinoza's monistic ontology is also substantialist in that it takes the rational structure of the world to be reducible to god, or to a panlogicism that can explain the essence of all things in some basic, fundamental and mechanistic sense: all things ultimately are functions of this rational substance.

What is essential for my purposes here is that a substantialist ontology seeks to grasp the *essential structure of things*, an essential structure that is *immanent* to the object itself.[6] Hence, when applied to a social ontology, the substantialist dimension inquires into the *essential structure* that makes social life what it is. But once we begin to examine this question, the substantialist view requires us to go beyond it. For as Hegel and Marx knew, it was not possible to proceed as Aristotle and Spinoza had, with answering the question of first principle of what any thing is but rather we can only grasp the essence of any thing as a result of rational investigation. We begin to see that part of what makes human sociality what it is, an essential part of its basic structure, is that it is *relational*: individuals require others and the relations with others in order to exercise biological and cultural forms of life, and so on. The nature of these relations constitutes the essential structure of sociality and can be understood as a descriptive account of what it means to be social as well as a ground for normative claims about what shapes of sociality might provide for the development and freedom of its members. Hence, the substantialist view quickly forces us to the next dimension of social ontology, that of the existence of relations.

## *Relations*

Things can also be understood as a function of their relations with other things, they can be produced by *relatum* and they are themselves *relata*. The social relations that constitute the essential structure of human social life possesses its own distinctive ontological characteristics. According to this view, the relations between entities is more central that the entities themselves. This view is in dialectical tension with the substantialist view which would seek to understand society itself as an entity whereas the social–relational ontology seeks to make the structure of relations the essential substance of what society is. However, whereas the substantialist view does not ignore the existence of relations, it places them in a subordinate position to the entities that are nodes in the relations. A relational ontology, by contrast, sees that the modes themselves are predicated on the relational field within which they are ensconced. Hence, the relational view and substantialist view are at odds concerning what is primary: the entities being related or the relations linking the entities.

Relational ontologies therefore see that relations are predicates for the substantial entities that are related by them. Hence, a rook or a bishop in the game of chess only have substantive meaning in relation to each other, to their relation to the board on which chess is played, and to the rules that govern their motion during play. To change the relations between these things is to change what those objects in fact are. Similarly, a key only has substantive meaning in relation to a lock: the nature of one thing is dependent on another, hence the *relatum* are given primacy, on this view, to the *relata*. Of course, human beings, too, have relations: to each other, to the world as a whole, nature and to themselves as subjects. But in this case, human relations with others not only constitute an *arbitrary* feature, but a necessary feature of human life since it can be shown that relational structures between social members in fact give rise to the kinds of properties and powers that are themselves uniquely human (language, cognition, etc.). Subjects are therefore, on this view, conceived as "relational subjects" insofar as they give rise to relational goods and properties.[7] The nature of the division between the individual and society therefore is sublated. The question is whether these relations are constitutive of who they are or the other way around. For Marx, the question is settled dialectically in that he sees that human agents create social relations which then have reflexive powers over them. Social relations and social reality or being are therefore dialectically related and one is not subordinate to the other.[8]

It is important that we do not view these kinds of relations that I have just described as mechanical insofar as each element of their relation acts upon the other in some uni-directional, causal sense. The kinds of relations that serve as the substantive, structural essence of sociality must instead be comprehended as reciprocal in the sense that Hegel discusses it in his *Logic*. For Hegel, the nature of reciprocal relations are different from causal relations in that the "first cause, which first acts and receives its effect back into itself as reaction, thus reappears as cause, whereby the action, which in finite causality runs on into the spuriously infinite progress, is bent around and becomes an action that returns into itself, an infinite reciprocal action" (Hegel, 1969, p. 237). What this means is that reciprocal actions (*Wechselwirken*) are to be understood as a kind of *structure of relations* that also possess a dynamism or processual logic as a totality and unity.[9] Each *relata* within any given structure of *relatum* is therefore to be understood as having taken part in self-determination in the sense that the element is interdependently related to a reciprocal structure that constitutes a structure of necessity for the development of each *relata* and the whole that they collectively constitute. Therefore, relations may be the essential substance of social life, but these relations are themselves to be seen as dynamic, as working toward some purposes or ends. As such, they can also be seen as processes, as systems of reciprocal action that possess a *telos* and which actualize the members of that social–relational nexus. Individuals are therefore ensconced in a structure of intrinsically reciprocal relations that possess an ontological determinateness (cf. Donati, 2013). This relational structure is the framework of sociality, something that itself possesses causal powers or the capacity to shape ends and goals that members of any social act participate toward. At the same time, this relational structure also acts upon each individual member and aids in constituting that individual's individuality.[10] Therefore, we can see that any ontology of social relations that possesses causal powers also has the capacity to produce certain ends and can be considered a *process*.

## *Process*

Things are dynamic in that they exist in process which means that the reciprocal relations within any structure possess the power to generate outcomes and particular kinds of ends or goods. They are not static entities. Process ontology is the view that the nature of existence must be grasped as dynamic and in motion rather than static, analytically comprehensible entities. According to the processual dimension of ontology, we must see that being is something that unfolds along a time horizon and therefore possesses a developmental character. In this sense, what is important to point out is that different stages of the time-horizon posit distinct and qualitative changes in the structure of being.[11] Processes possess both mechanistic and organic features (see Ross, 2008, p. 62ff.) constituting a dynamic structure where particular moments of that structure constitute and are constituted by the reciprocal-relational activity of the entity as a whole. In social terms, processes are essential for understanding human agency and culture as an achieved status: as a kind space of collective, developmental change that can also be an object of rational reflection. In this way, Hegel sees that the process of history is teleological in the self-understanding of human freedom not because of a transcendent ontological plan, but because the development of social–ontological properties of human interdependence and the reflection of that reality in cognition through the process of recognition leads toward a self-understanding of freedom as social freedom. Indeed, even once we posit that process is an essential aspect of the human biological and psychological life, it is also true of the sphere of culture as well. Processes are shaped and affected by the kinds of structured relations within which they are enacted, and these processes in turn result in the *actualization* of ends. Process is therefore dialectically related to *substance* and to *relations* in that the structure of relations that exist are determinate of the shaping of the very substance of the object.

Hence, although Aristotle privileges a substantivist conception of ontology, he also sees as part of the substance of any thing that it exists in motion—i.e., that it is constituted by an organic process of development and change that reaches an end-state.[12] Process is an element of ontology once we grasp that things, objects, are never simply what they are as things in themselves (substantivist ontology) nor merely as the result of the relations with other things. Rather, things exist within a *dynamic context of reciprocal relations and processes* that constitute them and which they also in turn constitute through their particular actions. They can only be understood outside the function that it plays within a system. Hence, our understanding of hearts requires not only a substantivist view that they are made of muscles, electrical impulses, arteries and so on; we must also see that it is related to other organs to which it supplies blood; and hence we must grasp that it is not only a static object ensconced in relations to other things, but that it *works in process* through those relations, it has a function, a *telos*.[13] Its end, its purpose, is to perform a specific function which can only occur within a context of relations.

The nature of process also opens up for us the critical question of potentiality and actuality which I explore in more detail in the next section below. We now have the basic vocabulary for an evaluative language by which we can think about the difference between the proper achievement of any end-state and the defective end-state that may pervade the emiprical manifestation of an object.[14] If one seeks to make wine and it instead becomes vinegar, it has failed to become wine—perhaps because the structural conditions of the wine shaped the processes of the chemical reactions in such a way that they failed to become what, under different circumstances, could have become wine. As with hearts, we can diagnose hearts that are defective by noting the way that they fail to achieve an end-state. The distinction between potentiality, actuality and empirical existence is crucial here: the three are in dialectical tension and they are ontological categories insofar as they are categories about states of being. In this sense, Aristotle's distinction between the end (τέλος) and its non-realized or deficiently realized, "pathological" state (ἀτελής) as vinegar can be grasped from both an objective-factual as well as a normative-evaluative sense. This is because any given social reality can be scrutinized with respect to the question of how much the potentialities of its deeper purposes or ends have been brought forth and realized.

Once we inquire into the function of society, the end, its *telos*, so to speak, is such that it exists for the good of all of its members. But this can only be achieved via the rational unity of free individuals who in a self-determined fashion but toward collective ends. The reason for this is that a kind of social freedom that picks up on the ontological premise of sociality is also one that must reflect the notion that particulars and universals are related into a more unified relational whole. In social terms, it means that each member of society comes to grasp and to recognize that his own welfare is dependent on the *relational goods* that the community as a whole are able to achieve and that the *means* for these kinds of goods are irreducibly social in nature in that they require joint forms of action and interdependence without which they could either not be achieved or at least achieved deficiently.

This is the primary context, Hegel and Marx believed, that would be able to make clear for us the self-determining content of modern life insofar as true, modern forms of freedom were only possible within a context of social relations and processes that had as their proper ends the enhancement its members and, at the same time, the conscious awareness of those members as rational individuals, that they would need to endorse those practices, norms and institutions which had precisely those ends as their proper *telos*. Hence, there is a necessary cognitive dimension to this social–ontological reality insofar as these relations, processes and the essential substance that they produce as the essential structure of any community are reproduced by the intentional acts of those individuals. Hence, there is, in our final dimension of social ontology, a constructivist aspect to sociality since a crucial component of sociality concerns the norms of collective intentionality that organize and shape social facts.

### *Constructivism*

The last branch of social ontology I wish to consider I will call *constructivist* which broadly means that human intentional agency is the predicate for the objective significance and very existence of social facts. The constructivist thesis therefore holds that the ontological is a result of the efforts, practices and activities of human beings. Labor is one essential dimension of constructivism, and this plays a role in Marx's and Lukács' respective social ontologies. But there is another, more contemporary development in philosophy that has made a claim to a comprehensive, constructivist social ontology. This is concerned with the ways social facts are produced and generated by the collective intentionality and constitutive rules of the members that make up the society itself. According to this view, largely put forward by John Searle and his philosophical social ontology, individuals act cooperatively to assign status functions to objects, ideas and practices and act and think according to constitutive rules that allow us to assign certain functions to objects and practices thereby granting them social status insofar as they are collectively accepted by enough members of that social group. In this sense, social facts are seen as the product of a combination of rules that organize the cognitive and intentional activities of individuals toward certain common understandings about the world. The constructivist element of social ontology therefore is concerned with the ways that social facts are the products of the cognitive and linguistic practices of cooperative individuals.

Searle's social–ontological account of social reality can therefore be incorporated into a broader critical social ontology once we see that the kinds of constitutive rules and forms of collective intentionality that he describes are not only mechanisms for ascribing power relations and legitimating them, but that they are also in themselves shaped and formed by the prevailing structure of social relations that govern the various developmental and reproductive processes of the community (see Searle 1996; 2007). The power of this approach is that it shows how social phenomena are generated by social actors themselves, but the forms of collective intentionality that they utilize to create social facts. The weakness of this approach, however, is that it is essentially abstract: it does not integrate the material component of social reality—i.e., the ways that control over resources shapes norms, ideas, social relations and so on. It also does not consider the objective features of sociality that make up a more comprehensive social ontology. What is needed for a fuller, more critical account of sociality is to bring together the constructivist dimension of social ontology together with the other aspects of social ontology.

But the collective intentionality approach to social ontology opens up for us the critical capacity immanent within the ontological project. Since, there exists a collective-intentional element to social facts, the moment of critique opens up once the fabric of norms and constitutive rules that govern our collective intentionality are interrogated for the kinds of objective social relations, structures and processes that they promote and help to recreate. This brings us to what I believe is one if not the fundamental insight of the critical theory tradition: namely, its enquiry into the forms of consciousness within society that aid in the reconstitution of pathological and inhumane forms of social life. We can gain insight into the pathologies of social life via a social ontology because this enables us to examine the ways that shapes of sociality in terms of institutionalized social formations and consciousness promote ends that may not be in for the good and self-determined interests of all. Once we consider the problem from this angle, we can see that a critical social ontology can be understood as bringing together a critical theory of norms with the principles immanent within the objective features of sociality itself thereby granting us a kind of desideratum for a critical theory of judgment.

## THE ONTOLOGICAL GROUND OF CRITIQUE AND JUDGMENT

What these basic categories of a social ontology are meant to illustrate is the way that we can come to grasp the essential features of human sociality as an ontological reality, not simply an arbitrarily posited and self-created convention. Sociality now is not simply a feature of human life, it also possesses causal powers (Elder-Vass, 2015; Ruben, 1985) and can be seen to be associated with certain kinds of what we can call "relational goods," or those kinds of goods that are produced jointly (i.e., by means of our sociality) and that are needed for sociality to exist in any vibrant and useful sense. Goods or ends can be seen as relational goods to the extent that they (1) can be seen to be essentially social in terms of how they are produced insofar as they are dependent on cooperative, relational forms of action to be achieved; and (2) can be evaluated based on the extent to which those goods are able to provide the requisite self-development of the members of the community. In this respect, a critical social ontology still has in view the basic principle laid out by Aristotle that society is an organization of its members who associate for some end or good.

Through understanding the *concept* of sociality, we are therefore able to provide a ground for critical judgment. Hegel's position on this was that through our grasping of the conceptual dynamics of any thing, we will be able to engage in a critical engagement with the empirically existent forms that thing may take in the world. Objective-factual and normative-evaluative claims are therefore dialectically fused into a form of critical judgment once we see that we can contrast the existence of any thing with the extent to which it realizes of instantiates its immanent rational structures, processes and end-states.[15] We can distinguish this approach from the Kantian–pragmatist approach because the social–ontological method raises the issue of the essential forms of sociality that must underwrite any valid claims about the means by which we shape social norms and institutions. The locus of examination must be on the ways that pathological social formations can be understood to operate as the negation of a more positive, more emancipatory form of sociality. We do not post sociality as a fact that exists *external* or *a priori* to those social forms, but instead see them as the immanent substance of what all social life actually is. The moment of judgment therefore emerges once we are able to identify the ways that capitalist society (or for that matter, any other form of society that is able to possess rational self-awareness of its practices) promotes ends that negate the fuller forms of equal, interdependent sociality and the most developed forms of relational goods that can be articulated by that community.

Now we can see that mere mutual agreement and understanding is not enough. Since the lifeworld is an insufficient ground for the conceptual development and realization of the ontological domain of social reality and its possibility to secure freedom, it is only through certain kinds of social institutions and practices that the social–ontological can come to consciousness. For Hegel, this comes about through the process of *Bildung* that occurs through institutions that promote the common interest, that reveal to the subject the social–relational and interdependent structure immanent within our sociality. This means that the ontological reality of this social–relational interdependence is brought to rational awareness when we grasp that it is a universal characteristic of our being, it counts as what is in some basic sense and that our conceptions of the good can only be understood in those terms.[16] For Marx, it is only through the class consciousness of working people that this cognitive realization can be achieved since they come to see the contradictions of a system that is organized for the benefits of the few but which has the potential to deliver a common good. Both see that the relational structure of social reality is the true essence of human reality; that human action is essentially social and interdependent. This interdependence also is the essential basis for the kinds of goods and social forms that any community articulates. As such, we begin to see that the nature of freedom and the good can be construed as features immanent within an interdependent sociality. This is why Rousseau, and indeed Marx for that matter, posit the notion that there is an objective basis for judging the kinds of institutions and practices within the community. That objective basis can be understood as an *objective common interest* once we grasp that the good of each is dialectically fused to the good of all. The common good is therefore immanent to the kinds of norms and practices that maximize the relational goods that promote the interdependent relational processes that constitute our social reality. To understand which practices, which norms, which institutional formations are good in any critically useful sense of the word, we need to be able to endorse those practices not simply through some mutual agreement and justification, but we must also and, more importantly, *point to the ways that such practices, norms and so on are able to promote social–relational structures, processes and ends that can fulfill the concept of our sociality as a shared form of reciprocal interaction that promotes mutual development and common goods.*

## Capitalism as Pathological Sociality

The basic line of reasoning of the critical social ontology approach can now be stated in more concise form. Critical judgment utilizes social ontology as a ground for explaining and evaluating the social forms that comprise the existent reality. Since this social ontology is constituted by a structure of interdependent social relations which are dynamic in nature and which are oriented toward relational goods and ends which are in turn recreated through the collective-intentional rules of the community, we can see that any social forms that distort this structure can be seen as pathological. In this sense, a critical–practical rationality emerges as a *critical space of reasons* (Thompson, 2016) that is able to keep in view the social–ontological as a frame of reasoning about the rightness of norms and the evaluation of the ends and goods around which the purposes of the community are organized. If we reflect on Marx's critique of capitalism, not simply as political economy, but as a comprehensive social formation, we begin to get an idea about how a critical social ontology can lead us to think in a new, critical space of reasons by exploring the pathologies of capitalist life as negations of the proper, correct forms of sociality that have as their immanent rationality the self-determined freedom of the members of an interdependent community pursuing common goods.

Think of Marx's critique of capitalism in the *Economic and Philosophical Manuscripts* in this regard. The aim is to show that this essential sociality that circumscribes the basis of human life, this "social essence" that constitutes us as human beings (*Gattungswesen*), forms the basis for a critical conception of judgment which can illuminate the defective features of existing social forms. What we need to do is proceed negatively, that is, through an analysis of the pathologies and thwarted potentialities that any historically bound culture evinces. We cannot remain within a negative dialectic, as Adorno would have it, but instead must seek to understand that social pathologies are comprehensible as an inversion of some basic set of needs that and potentials that any social context produces. We must, then, comprehend the ontology of social reality phenomenologically at first, through the experience we have with the world. But we must then move beyond the phenomenological membrane in order to grasp the inner principle that constitutes the nature of our sociality (i.e., through the four dimensions of social ontology discussed above as basic categories of sociality as an objective unity and reality).[17] Our experience with the world must be tempered by mediated reflection, or the application of rational-critical categories that keep in view the social essence of human life. Hence, Marx, in the *Economic and Philosophical Manuscripts,* holds that:

> [T]he social character is the universal character of the whole movement; as society itself produces *man* as *man,* so it is *produced* by him. Activity and mind are social in their content as well as in their *origin*; they are *social* activity and *social* mind. The *human* significance of nature only exists for *social* man, because only in this case is nature a *bond* with other *men,* the basis of his existence for others and of their existence for him. Only then is nature the *basis* of his own *human* experience and a vital element of human reality. The *natural* existence of man has here become his *human* existence and nature itself has become human for him. Thus *society* is the accomplished union of man with nature, the veritable resurrection of nature, the realized naturalism of man and the realized humanism of nature (Marx, 1961, p. 129).

Marx's thesis here absorbs the ideas of *substantive, relational* and *processual* ontologies I explored above in order to construct a theory about the ways that human life—individual and collective—is essentially social. In this sense, thought, language, labor and so on, are all *social products* and therefore are expressions of a fundamental social reality that marks human life as distinctive, as essentially being what it is.

The substance of human social reality is therefore, on Marx's view, something objective in nature: it is something that we can understand as relational, processual and constructivist. It is, in the final analysis, man's interdependence with others that constitutes his *Gattungswesen* which we can see now as concept that is essentially ontological in the fourth sense laid out above (i.e., that the substance of man's true being, his *Gattungswesen,* is social–relational, processual–developmental and constructivist through the activity of labor). These need not be "directly communal," but rather need to be seen *as the ontological reality of socially relational, interdependent human actions and processes that underwrites the substance of what it means to be human in its fullest sense*:

> Even when I carry out *scientific* work, etc. an activity which I can seldom conduct in direct association with other men, I perform a *social*, because *human*, act. It is not only the material of my activity—such as the language itself which the thinker uses—which is given to me as a social product. *My own existence* is a social activity. For this reason, what I myself produce I produce for society, and with the consciousness of acting as a social being (Marx, 1961, p. 130).

Marx seeks to show that this basic social ontology must be the means by which we understand the pathology of alienation which has been made possible by the emergence of private property:

> Private property has made us so stupid and partial that an object is only *ours* when we have it, when it exists for us as capital or when it is directly eaten, drunk, worn, inhabited, etc., in short, *utilized* in some way; although private property itself only conceives these various forms of possession as *means of life*, and the life for which they serve as means is the *life* of *private property*—labor and creation of capital (Marx, 1961, p. 132).

The pathological effects of private property are here seen to be the product of the fact that it undermines the crucial social essence of human collective and individual life. Marx here argues that we can understand the negative effects of private property only by comprehending that it is an institutionalization of a false understanding of human *being*—one that rests on the liberal conception of human agency and independence that both Hegel and Marx saw as only partial in its conception of human essence. Once this independence is posited as the essence of man, relations become dependent rather than interdependent; the kinds of goods that this kind of community will pursue will not be common, relational goods, but particularistic goods; equality and interdependent forms of social relationality are displaced by power, alienation, reification and human degradation. This is a pathological sociality once we have the general social–ontological account of human relations and processes in view, for it is only by questioning the ends and purposes of the activities, the structural form that relations take, the end-states achieved by social institutions and collective actions, and so on, that grant us a moment of critical judgment.

What is central to Marx's critique of capitalism—and one which critical theorists should have at the base of their critical work as well—is that social pathologies are the negation of the essence of the kind of human life that modern forms of social organization can make possible: that the end, the proper *telos* of our labor, our social relations, our institutions, our forms of life and norms should be to enhance and enrich the common goods that allow for our social and individual development and perfective freedom. The problem with capitalism is therefore that it violates this basic tenet—a tenet that Marx derives from a basic social–ontological account of the potentialities of modern social life. Therefore, even in *Capital*, Marx retains this essential evaluative view when he asks us to imagine as an alternative to capitalist social relations and economic life:

> a community of free individuals, carrying on their work with the means of production in common, in which the labor power of all the different individuals is consciously applied as the combined labor power of the community. All the characteristics of Robinson's labor are here repeated, but with this difference: that they are social instead of individual … The total product of our community is a social product. (Marx, 1977, p. 78)

For Marx, as for Hegel, the common interest of the community serves as the evaluative mechanism by which the organization of social relations and the purposes or ends of social life are to be gauged. Since capitalism is a system of social extraction and inequality where this inequality of power of social resources grants particular members of the community to steer social practices and efforts toward their own projects and away from the projects that benefit the community as a whole, we can see that it constitutes a distinct example of a pathological form of sociality (see Ross, 2015; Thompson, 2015b). Add to this, the various pathological practices and forms of life to which it gives rise: to alienation, reification, to self-interest, conformism and so on.

## Conclusion

By seeing a critical social ontology as the ground for a critical theory of judgment, we can perhaps glimpse a new paradigm in critical theory. Indeed, as I have been suggesting here, Hegel and Marx shared in this structure of thought and it laid the basic foundations for their respective social theories. The idea that an objective conception of the good and an ontology of sociality exists means that the pragmatist turn in critical theory has short-changed the critical project. For one thing is certain: a thoroughly critical and thoroughly rational form of judgment will require us to do more than simply exchange reasons or engage in recognitive relations.

The norms that a rational, free agent endorses should be grounded in the ontological reality of human sociality. The reason for this is that the properties of this sociality are only truly actualized once they are able to promote the good its members who collectively make up society as a self-determined form of free association. We can therefore discern an objective expression of a common interest, one where each has the rational obligation to those social norms and institutions that cultivate the social–relational structures and processes that promote a common ground for free, developed individuality. In this way, critical theory can benefit from constructing a critical social ontology as the basis for a politically relevant form of practical reason and the capacity for a more compelling form of critical judgment and authentic subjectivity.

## Notes

1. This idea of an "immanent metaphysics" is an essential idea that Hegel initiates in order to save the metaphysical project within the context of a post-Kantian critical philosophy. According to this idea, the function of reason, of philosophy, is to be able to explain the world on its own terms, not according to the pre-critical metaphysics of theological or transcendent "reasons." As Robert Stern notes, "far from being a form of pre-Kantian metaphysics that tries to claim access to some extramundane absolute, Hegel's idealism is a form of absolute theory that can be treated as in line with the transcendental turn, of giving us a conception of the world that will show how the need for explanation can be satisfied without going *beyond* it" (Stern, 2009, p. 61).

2. Terry Pinkard's reconstruction of Hegel's philosophical project follows a similar line when he claims that: "the ends of modern life must (1) be reflectively justifiable yet have a non-reflective subjective hold on the agents, (2) be internal to the history of modern agency such that they cannot be established outside of the free-standing social practices of modern life and have their intelligibility depend on how they are understood to have successfully made up for the insufficiencies of what historically preceded them, and (3) be such that they can be justified by the 'absolute knowing,' which is the result of the *Phenomenology of Spirit*" (Pinkard, 1994, p. 274).

3. Pinkard takes this approach when reinterpreting Hegel by arguing that the ends of a modern form of life should "combine the *subjectivity of the agent*—his basic desires, wants and ideals—with the *objectivity of justification*—with what counts as a justification in the social practice defined by those ends—and that objectivity should be generated by 'absolute knowing.' That is, the motivations of the agent—what actually impels him to act—should mesh with the justification for what he is doing, with whatever particular ends he is pursuing, and that justification should be reflectively available to the agent" (Pinkard, 1994, p. 274). Also cf. Pippin (1989, p. 175ff.). Against this approach, Rolf-Peter Horstmann argues that it is "extremely difficult to see how this approach can avoid the sort of epistemic relativism that Hegel himself clearly repudiated: the view not only that our knowledge claims can only be justified contextually, but also that the states of affairs to which those knowledge claims refer, what Hegel calls the 'other' of the concept, can be dissolved entirely into certain epochally or culturally dependent conceptual constellations" (Horstmann, 2006, p. 70).

4. Stephen Houlgate remarks that "A fully self-critical philosophy must thus start from the twofold idea that (a) thought is the awareness of being and (b) being is itself simply what thought discloses. This means that the science of logic cannot be anything other than *ontology*: because the study of thought must be, at the same time, the study of *being*" (Houlgate, 2008, p. 121). Hegel's basic idea, one also shared by Marx, is that a critical conception of reason is one that has an explanatory function in understanding the object (Kreines, 2015), not a mere exchange of reasons toward agreement about that object (see Rosen, 2014). Hegel's move is to show that the analysis of the thought of being is sufficient grant us an ontology that is rational and critical whereas Marx reverses this and believes that we must see how *structures of being* shape and determine *structures of thought*. Nevertheless, despite this important difference, both see that there are ontological categories of the objective world and that they must be grasped as rational structures of both thought and being and not merely empirical phenomena distinct from noumena.

5. Rolf-Peter Horstmann has argued on this point in defense of an ontological approach to Hegel's philosophical project that: "He is

essentially concerned, in a radical departure from the entire philosophical tradition of the modern period at least, with establishing a new paradigm for the proper philosophical comprehension of reality. The attempt to establish this new paradigm depends entirely for Hegel on successfully communicating a basic insight: that we require an entirely new way of conceptualizing reality, one that is grounded not in the contingent epistemic apparatus of cognitive subjects but in the very constitution of reality itself" (Horstmann, 2006, p. 73).

6. Hegel therefore holds that "Substance is the *Absolute*, that which is actual in and for itself—*in itself* as the simple identity of possibility and actuality, an absolute essence that contains all actuality and possibility; *for itself* this identity is absolute *power* or simply as self-relating *negativity*" (Hegel, 1969, p. 246). In this sense, substance is the essential structure of any thing containing its immanent powers of change and development as inchoate properties of that thing. Unfolding the dynamics of substance means inquiring into the relations and processes that constitute the dynamism of that substance which in turn reveals itself as the concept.

7. As Donati and Archer insightfully note: "The term '*Relational Subject*' refers to individual and collective social subjects in that they are '*relationally constituted*,' that is, *in as much as they generate emergent properties and powers through their social relations.* These relational goods and evils have internal effects upon the subjects themselves and external effects upon their social environments" (Donati & Archer, 2015, p. 31). Also see the broader discussion by Benjamin (2015).

8. Carol Gould is therefore incorrect, in my view, when she argues that Marx privileges substance over relations. In her view, "for Marx, although such individuals do not exist apart from their relations, and in fact develop and change themselves through these relations, yet the existence and mode of activity of these individuals is the ontological presupposition of the relations into which they enter. These individuals, who are agents, according to Marx, may be regarded as constituting these relations by their activity and therefore cannot be seen as products of these relations. Thus, these individuals have fundamental ontological status and are not to be understood as mere nodes of relations or as wholly constituted by their relations" (Gould, 1978, p. 38).

The more correct view is to see that there is no privileging of one over the other, but a dialectical relation between the two as well as with the processual ontology I will describe below.

9. Dieter Henrich notes on this aspect of Hegel's logical system that: "This unity permits the independent existence of its determinations but still holds these independent moments within the unity of its own organized form, not merely with respect to the movements of these moments but in every aspect of their actual existence as well" (Henrich, 2004, p. 253).

10. Hence Richard Dien Winfield argues that "In ethical community, the good at which conduct aims contains the activity of its realization insofar as membership involves knowing and willing goals whose achievement reproduces the whole, thereby securing the unity of each member's volition with the performance of the rest" (Winfield, 1996, p. 318). Christopher Yeomans also argues that this structure of reciprocal relations can be considered a "structure of freedom." See Yeomans (2012, p. 216ff.) for a discussion of reciprocal relations and their implication for rational agency as well as Donati and Archer (2015, p. 33ff.) for a discussion of *reflexivity* from a sociological perspective.

11. Georg Lukács therefore points out that: "A careful and correct approach to ontological problems always requires one to keep constantly in mind that every leap signifies a qualitative and structural change in being, in the course of which, though the transition stage may contain certain preconditions and possibilities of the later, higher stages, the latter cannot be developed from the former in a simple straight-line continuity" (Lukács, 1980, p. 2).

12. Aryeh Kosman has recently commented on this idea in Aristotle that the "realization that he defines motion to be is in fact an activity—an *energeia*. It is the activity of a subject's being able to be something than it now is, prior to its having realized that ability by actually having become other than it now is. This activity is the thing's most fully exercising its *ability*, its most actively being *able to be* something qua being able to be it, while not actually *being* it. This is what Aristotle means by saying that a motion is the realization of what is able to be, as he puts it, *qua* able to be; it is the *activity* of being able to be" (Kosman, 2013, p. 68).

13. Hegel's metaphysics places this concept of process and change at its core. As Frederick Beiser has noted: "To state that a natural

object serves a purpose is not to hold that there is some intention behind its creation, still less that there is some concealed intention within the object itself. Rather, all that it means is that the object serves a function, that it plays an essential role in the structure of the organism" (Beiser, 2005, p. 101). Also cf. this discussion with Hahn (2007, pp. 9–53).

14. Hegel in particular, after Aristotle, saw that the nature of the given reality, of *Dasein*, needs to be contrasted with the fuller reality, *Wirklichkeit*, that any thing can achieve. As Charles Taylor rightly notes, "what exists is not to be seen as simply there, as merely contingent, but rather as the manifestation of a thoroughgoing systematic web of necessary relations" (Taylor, 1975, p. 258). This further emphasizes the necessary, dialectical relation between relational and processual dimensions of ontology.

15. Mark Tunick rightly claims on this aspect in Hegel's metaphysical project that "Hegel looks at a practice he sees around him and develops an account of its purpose or rationale, an interpretation of the meaning the practice has, of its 'concept,' which he then uses to criticize manifestations of the actual practice that diverge from this purpose" (Tunick, 1992, p. 14). Marx, too, utilizes this same logic in construction his critical theory of scientific judgment, see Thompson (2015a).

16. Stephen Houlgate therefore remarks that "This does not just mean that we sense that we ought to help others; it means that our practical activity must be habituated, by life in corporations and in the state, to being the actual pursuit of universal right and welfare" (Houlgate, 1995, p. 878).

17. This can be understood in Hegelian terms as Robert Stern notes: "Idealism for Hegel ... is a position that does not treat finite things as 'ultimate and absolute' in themselves, but relates them to an enduring and infinite 'ground' of some kind, of which these finite things are limited realizations; but what idealism in this sense requires, Hegel thinks, is that we move beyond 'empirical cognition.' This is because this infinite ground is not something that is apparent to us in experience, but can only be something we arrive at through reflection" (Stern, 2009, p. 68). I think this is one reason that the ontological approach is superior to the recognition paradigm promoted by Axel Honneth and his followers in contemporary critical theory in the sense

that recognition must be seen as a phenomenological framework through which we can move into a rational form of comprehension once it is mediated by reason. Hegel's theory of recognition is therefore a kind of path toward a rational comprehension of the ontological structure of human life as social and interdependent and this ontological framework is the foundation, the basis for human self-realization and self-determination (see Thompson, 2016).

## References

Alexy, R. (1990). A theory of practical discourse. In S. Benhabib & F. Dallmayr (Eds.), *The communicative ethics controversy* (pp. 151–192). Cambridge, MA: MIT Press.

Beiser, F. (2005). *Hegel*. New York: Routledge.

Benjamin, A. (2015). *Towards a relational ontology: Philosophy's other possibility*. Albany, NY: State University of New York Press.

Böhler, D. (1990). Transcendental pragmatics and critical morality: On the possibility and moral significance of a self-enlightenment of reason. In S. Benhabib & F. Dallmayr (Eds.), *The communicative ethics controversy* (pp. 111–150). Cambridge, MA: MIT Press.

Brown, M. E. (2014). *The concept of the social in uniting the humanities and social sciences*. Philadelphia: Temple University Press.

Donati, P. (2013). *Sociologia della relazione*. Bologna: Il Mulino.

Donati, P., & Archer, M. (2015). *The relational subject*. Cambridge: Cambridge University Press.

Elder-Vass, D. (2015). Collective intentionality and causal powers. *The Journal of Social Ontology, 1*(2), 251–269.

Forst, R. (2011). *The right to justification: Toward a constructivist theory of justice*. New York: Columbia University Press.

Forst, R. (2015). Noumenal power. *Journal of Political Philosophy, 23*(2), 111–127.

Gould, C. (1978). *Marx's social ontology: Individuality and community in Marx's theory of social reality*. Cambridge, MA: MIT Press.

Groff, R. (2013). *Ontology revisited: Metaphysics in social and political philosophy*. New York: Routledge.

Habermas, J. (1987). *The philosophical discourse of modernity: Twelve lectures*. Cambridge, MA: MIT Press.

Habermas, J. (1990). *Moral consciousness and communicative action*. Cambridge, MA: MIT Press.

Habermas, J. (1996). *Between facts and norms: Contributions to a discourse theory of law and democracy*. Cambridge, MA: MIT Press.

Hahn, S. S. (2007). *Contradiction in motion: Hegel's organic concept of life and value*. Ithaca, NY: Cornell University Press.

Hegel, G. W. F. (1969). *Wissenschaft der Logik* (Vol. 2). Frankfurt: Suhrkamp.

Hegel, G. W. F. (1970). *Grundlinien der Philosophie des Rechts*. Stuttgart: Reclam.

Henrich, D. (2004). Logical form and real totality: The authentic conceptual form of Hegel's concept of the state. In R. Pippin & O. Höffe (Eds.), *Hegel on ethics and politics* (pp. 241–267). Cambridge: Cambridge University Press.

Horstmann, R. P. (2006). Substance, subject and infinity: A case study of the role of logic in Hegel's system. In K. Deligiorgi (Ed.), *Hegel: New directions* (pp. 69–84). London: Acumen Press.

Houlgate, S. (1995). The Unity of theoretical and practical spirit in Hegel's concept of freedom. *The Review of Metaphysics*, 48(4), 859–881.

Houlgate, S. (2008). Hegel's logic. In F. Besier (Ed.), *The Cambridge companion to Hegel and nineteenth-century philosophy* (pp. 111–134). New York: Cambridge University Press.

Kosman, A. (2013). *The activity of being: An essay on Aristotle's ontology*. Cambridge, MA: Harvard University Press.

Kreines, J. (2015). *Reason in the world: Hegel's metaphysics and its philosophical appeal*. New York: Oxford University Press.

Loux, M. J. (1978). *Substance and attribute: A study in ontology*. Dordrecht: D. Reidel Publishing.

Lowe, E. J. (2006). *The four-fold ontology: A metaphysics for natural science*. New York: Oxford University Press.

Lukács, G. (1980). *The ontology of social being. Volume 3: Labor* (D. Fernbach, Trans.) London: Merlin Press.

Marx, K. (1961). *Economic and philosophical manuscripts in Erich Fromm, Marx's concept of man*. New York: Frederick Ungar.

Marx, K. (1977). *Capital* (Vol. 1). New York: Vintage.

Pinkard, T. (1994). *Hegel's phenomenology: The sociality of reason*. Cambridge: Cambridge University Press.

Pippin, R. (1989). *Hegel's idealism: The satisfactions of self-consciousness*. Cambridge: Cambridge University Press.

Renault, E. (2016). Critical theory and processual social ontology. *The Journal of Social Ontology* (forthcoming).

Rosen, S. (2014). *The idea of Hegel's science of logic*. Chicago: University of Chicago Press.

Ross, N. (2008). *On mechanism in Hegel's social and political philosophy*. New York: Routledge.

Ross, N. (2015). Hegel's logical critique of capitalism: The Paradox of dependence and the model of reciprocal mediation. In A. Buchwalter (Ed.), *Hegel and capitalism* (pp. 163–180). Albany, NY: State University of New York Press.

Ruben, D. H. (1985). *The metaphysics of the social world*. London: Routledge and Kegan Paul.

Searle, J. (1996). *The construction of social reality*. New York: The Free Press.

Searle, J. (2007). *Freedom and neurobiology: Reflections on free will, language, and political power*. New York: Columbia University Press.

Stern, R. (2009). *Hegelian metaphysics*. New York: Oxford University Press.

Strawson, P. F. (1992). *Analysis and metaphysics*. Oxford: Oxford University Press.

Taylor, C. (1975). *Hegel*. Cambridge: Cambridge University Press.

Thompson, M. J. (2015a). Philosophical foundations for a Marxian ethics. In M. Thompson (Ed.), *Constructing Marxist ethics: Critique, normativity, praxis*. Leiden: Brill.

Thompson, M. J. (2015b). Capitalism as deficient modernity: Hegel against the modern economy. In A. Buchwalter (Ed.), *Hegel and capitalism* (pp. 117–132). Albany, NY: State University of New York Press.

Thompson, M. J. (2016). *The domestication of critical theory*. London: Rowman and Littlefield.

Tunick, M. (1992). *Hegel's political philosophy: Interpreting the practice of legal punishment*. Princeton: Princeton University Press.

Winfield, R. D. (1996). Ethical community without communitarianism. *Philosophy Today, 40*(2), 310–320.

Yeomans, C. (2012). *Freedom and reflection: Hegel and the logic of agency*. New York: Oxford University Press.

CHAPTER 3

# Critical Theory in the Twenty-First Century: The Logic of Capital Between Classical Social Theory, the Early Frankfurt School Critique of Political Economy and the Prospect of Artifice*

*Harry F. Dahms*

## INTRODUCTION

There are many different versions of critical theory, both within the tradition of the Frankfurt School, which inaugurated the idea and the concept of 'critical theory', and beyond the latter, in the sense of feminist, poststructuralist, postmodernist, postcolonial and queer critical theories, to name the most prominent incarnations. Still, despite the variety of critical theories, at their core there is synchronicity with the type of critique the Frankfurt School theorists first developed and refined, as they drew on the works of Karl Marx, Sigmund Freud, Max Weber and other social theorists and philosophers. Yet, this core, as delineated in Max Horkheimer's programmatic essay, 'Traditional and Critical Theory' (1972 [1937]),

---

*I would like to thank Lawrence Hazelrigg, Alexander Stoner, and especially Lain Myers-Brown for reading the manuscript and pointing out typos and errors.

H.F. Dahms (✉)
Department of Sociology, Knoxville, TN, USA

© The Author(s) 2017
D. Krier, M.P. Worrell (eds.), *The Social Ontology of Capitalism*,
DOI 10.1057/978-1-137-59952-0_3

eight decades ago in terms of a radical philosophy of social science, ever is in danger of being pushed to the side. Though widely recognized in its importance, the core of critical theory frequently has been put second, or entirely ignored, in the interest of more immediate causes that are also consistent with the impetus of critical theory, such as agendas driven by concrete goals like emancipation, liberation, social justice, or the elimination of suffering, or by practical concerns, including forms of *praxis* directed at revolutionary (or, at the very least, qualitative) social transformation, or strategies that fall under the rubric of politics.[1]

Yet, did (and does) such a core exist? If critical theory in fact did—or was supposed to—have a discernible core that applies to the tradition and should define the latter, and which must be viewed as sacrosanct, as it were, it should be possible to demarcate it clearly. Despite countless attempts to construct, update or reconstruct critical theory, and to formulate related working definitions (e.g., Habermas, 1984, 1987 [1981]; Geuss, 1981; Honneth, 1991 [1985]), one key dimension of the programmatic core of critical theory, as promised during the early phase of the Frankfurt School, and put forth strongly by Horkheimer (1972 [1937]), has been unduly overlooked, or willfully ignored. In short, this neglected dimension concerns the rigorous (and no less radical) examination of *the gravity concrete and specific socio-historical conditions and circumstances exert on endeavors in the human sciences, to illuminate the vicissitudes of successive societal configurations in the modern age*. Once recognized and identified explicitly, implications result from this core concern, in no uncertain terms, for the tradition's approach to scrutinizing—*critically*, to be sure—the evolving logic of the dynamic capitalist economy at the national and global levels. How and in what way did the early Frankfurt School identify and deploy this program, if at all? Assuming that the tradition's programmatic core concern is indeed both unique and important, it is conceivable that it never again has been laid out as clearly, and that, as a result, subsequent proponents of critical theory have been laboring to explicate what may well be *most* important about the tradition and its contributions to illuminating the conditions of social life in the modern age, without being in the position to acknowledge the core explicitly, spell out its import rigorously, and advocate and apply it effectively. Concordantly, the potentially pernicious influence the economy exerts in and on human civilization, in recent decades and especially at the current historical juncture, is likely not to have received the necessary attention. How capitalism, and especially the *logic of capital* (Dahms, 2015a, 2015b) increasingly may be inversely related to the possibility of qualitative social progress, and detrimental to sustaining the idea of the pursuit of the common good, also likely would have been neglected.

Along the lines of a research institute designed to rely on and integrate all the human sciences—the humanities as well as the social sciences—Horkheimer (1993 [1931]) a few years earlier had initially suggested and then established an overall division of labor to be implemented and pursued at the Institute for Social Research in Frankfurt. The members of the Institute were engaged in the critique of capitalism on three levels. On the first level, they endeavored to revitalize Marx's critique of political economy, to be applied to the later stage of capitalist development reached during the first decades of the twentieth century. Acknowledging the persistent and intensifying division of labor in the social sciences, Horkheimer determined that—on the second level—the members and affiliates of the Institute would be responsible for specific dimensions of modern social reality, for example, for sociology, psychology, economics or law. Since each individual social science is concerned with a specific analytical and theoretical agenda and set of phenomena, critical theorists started out from the assumption of the relative autonomy ('inner logic') of the social sciences's respective tasks in relation to the diverse dimensions of social life ('social value spheres') that are the domain of these disciplines (see Dahms, 1997, 1999). The goal was to critically evaluate the relative importance of different inner logics, respectively, in light of prevailing patterns determining how exactly industrialized capitalist societies fulfill an array of functions. In this context, Friedrich Pollock was responsible for providing an updated diagnosis of political economy along Marxian lines, while it fell to the community of scholars at the Institute—on the third level—to generate a highly sophisticated, systematic critique of postliberal capitalism and its effects on political, social and cultural dimensions of life.

Since its inception in New York in the mid-1930s, Frankfurt School critical theory has gone through a number of permutations. Though the tradition's origins commonly and correctly have been situated in Germany in the late 1920s and early 1930s, the concept of critical theory was, strictly speaking, formulated in the United States.[2] It is doubtful that, absent the need to emigrate from Germany after Hitler's rise to power, the concept would have been formulated explicitly at all (Dahms, 2017). At the very least, there would have been much less of an incentive to develop as radically different a perspective on the social sciences as spelled out in Horkheimer's distinction between traditional and critical theory if the National Socialist take-over would not have occurred, since there would not have been an imminent need for the members of the Institute for Social Research in Frankfurt to leave Germany.

To be sure, the agenda of critical theory was at play even before the concept, 'critical theory', was formulated by Max Horkheimer, and seconded by Herbert Marcuse (2009 [1937]), in New York. In particular, Horkheimer from early on had been concerned with the implications resulting from social change in early twentieth-century modern capitalist societies, for the tools we develop and employ to grasp the nature and direction of change. As a philosopher with a strong interest in sociology, Horkheimer understood that the key concepts employed in the social sciences and the *Geisteswissenschaften* (the humanities) to meaningfully assess and interpret the human condition at the individual and the collective level under conditions of continuous industrialization were not merely means to reflect on the nature of social change in the modern age, but also reflections and expressions of social change (see Abromeit, 2011).

## CRITICAL THEORY IN THE TWENTIETH CENTURY: MODERN SOCIETY AND THE SOCIO-LOGIC OF CAPITAL

Despite the many different conceptualizations and definitions of critical theory that have been formulated and advocated over the course of the last half-century or so—since related debates and conflicts have accompanied efforts to advance rigorously critical analyses of modern society as a whole, or of specific dimensions of modern society—there has been a single overarching concern that has distinguished Frankfurt School critical theory from other types. This theme pertains to the manner in which the spread and deepening of economics in its capitalist form has been permeating non-economic modes of life in the modern world, with regard to politics, culture and society, with discernible consequences at the levels of individual psychology and collective social psychology. Indeed, critical theory may well be understood as an explicitly stated and determined response to ongoing transformations and modulations in and across modern societies producing both latent and manifest catastrophes that cannot be grasped, nor explained adequately, at the levels at which those catastrophes are discernible. Rather, especially the early critical theorists of the Frankfurt School observed and interpreted social, political and cultural catastrophes as symptoms of an underlying economic logic of which concrete social forms are expressions to such an extent that their illumination and analysis require an understanding of causality that was novel and unexpected at the time.

Especially in the mainstream social sciences and humanities, there was and continues to be a notable lack of recognition that such a causality is in force, even though it had been foreshadowed both by the classics of social theory, especially Marx, Durkheim, and Weber, and even by developments in theoretical physics, in terms of quantum mechanics and relativity theory—developments that coincided with the establishment of sociology as a social science during the 1890s and early twentieth century (see Dahms, in preparation).

Put simply, modern society is sustained by a nexus of interconnected social, economic, political and cultural processes which are mutually reinforcing and sustaining, as well as energized and maintained by the sum total of focused activities of a sufficiently large segment of the population whose members are willing or determined to accumulate ever more personal wealth. These processes mediate between different logics that are not as such compatible with each other but which, in modern society *qua* capitalism—and *only* in this socio-economic system—are being forced onto the same 'wavelength', as it were, in order to ensure the stability of social order as materialized in form of a particular system of social and economic structures. Yet, the actors that are driven by the impulse to expand their wealth are neither responsible for the peculiar causality that is sustaining modern society, nor are they in control of it. Instead, they endeavor, more or less successfully, to tune into what appears to be the economic logic without which modern society neither could have come into existence, nor be able to maintain itself or expand its mode of control, both qualitatively and quantitatively, to ever greater numbers of individuals, to more and more countries and regions of the world, and to the Earth's biosphere. This economic logic is the *logic of capital*. Yet, paradoxically, what appears as an economic logic in fact is a social logic, the *socio-logic of capital* that is being maintained and mediated through processes whose sway and workings with which we are amply familiar: alienation, anomie and the Protestant ethic (see Dahms, 2007, in preparation; Dux, 2008).

In order to appreciate the specific nature of this logic, and the specific kind of causality that it engendered, which it continues to promulgate as well as rely upon, and which is eminently incompatible with everyday-life assumptions and what frequently has been referred to as 'common sense', it is necessary to understand, first, the economic logic of capital. To illuminate the latter as it began to reconstruct the human species and, along with it, inevitably, the relationship between society and nature during the nineteenth century, was the achievement of Marx's critique of political economy (see Postone, 1993). However, it was neither by accident, nor as a distraction from focus on the economic logic of capital, that sociology as the social science of *modern* society began to take shape alongside Marx's efforts. As it was concerned with the social forms that enable individuals as members of modern society to construct meaningful life histories, regardless of how *rational* or *irrational* the larger social context in fact may be—and depending on which definitions of rationality and irrationality are being employed or deployed—sociology emerged in response to indications that modern society is a highly counterintuitive system of phenomena.

Importantly, the operation of modern society cannot be gleaned from what is observed directly at the surface of social processes, institutions and forms of organization, but requires a stance on the part of sociologists that recognizes the inevitability of more and more social forms being drawn into a kind of *maelstrom* which diminishes the number and strength of static social forms, and increases the number and strength of dynamic forms. As Marx put, 'all that is solid melts into air', although, sociologically speaking, it does not *melt* into air, but turn into matter that can be molded according to necessity, circumstance and context, is exceedingly adaptable, and creates the appearance of social, political and cultural forms remaining relatively stable, while the economic underground is in perpetual turmoil. Yet, the non-economic forms are undergoing rapid transformations as well, even though individuals who struggle to make sense of their world and who try to pursue sensible and minimally predictable lives *perceive* the social world as being much more stable than it is. This condition triggers rapidly proliferating experiences of dissonance that appear to increase individuals' determination to hold on to politics, culture and society as dimensions that provide a semblance of stability. Without this determination, which manifests and is expressed in myriad ways, modern society as capitalism presumably would not be able to prevail, and it is for this reason that it would not have been possible to explain the machinations of twentieth-century modern capitalist society solely, or even above all, with reference to Marx's critique of political economy.

The members of the Institute for Social Research, especially Max Horkheimer, recognized the importance of analyzing and explaining the inner workings of modern society adequately and accurately, beyond the scope of traditional theory and mainstream sociology. Transcending the limits of the latter is a necessary precondition for conceiving of strategies to bring about qualitative social change consistent with shared norms and values, which in turn must not be a function of the repressive regime of twentieth-century political economy, but they require a non-regressive foundation for laying the foundation for a more just society, a society in which the reconciliation of facts and norms would be conceivable in non-violent fashion.

Put differently, whereas diagnosing and scrutinizing modern capitalism as a system built around the promulgation of disembodied economic value is impossible without the analyses Marx provided, it is highly likely that without a thorough and refined understanding of how the logic of capital is *mediated* in modern society through social, political and cultural forms—how modern capitalism rests and is contingent on the socio-logic of capital—as addressed and studied especially by Emile Durkheim and Max Weber, desirable and practically conceivable strategies for advancing qualitative social transformations are likely to be unattainable.[3] Indeed, one of the many reasons why Marx's vision of a better world may well have been perverted, betrayed and abandoned is that Marx's diagnostic tools on their own might not be a suitable basis for developing effective strategies to prepare and execute qualitative social change, in the absence of insights generated by a kind of critical sociology inspired by, and capable of appreciating, the critical impetus of Durkheim's and Weber's respective conceptualizations of the responsibility of sociologists to acknowledge and illuminate that peculiar causality alluded to earlier.

As a consequence, meeting the challenge of illuminating change in modern society depends on three important insights. First, the meaning of guiding concepts is not static, but changes with shifting conditions in modern society which, considering its accelerating pace of change, produces an ever greater need to be cognizant of this fact. Secondly, to grasp modern society accurately, it is necessary to assess the gravity concrete socio-historical circumstances exert on the process of illuminating modern society. Thirdly, if both the changing meaning of concepts and the gravity of socio-historical conditions are recognized sufficiently in their specificity, then both the concepts and the specific socio-historical conditions can serve as means to identify the nature and track the direction of socio-historical change in specific contexts.

All three challenges must be met in order to circumscribe the constitutional logic of modern society. If successful, this process constitutes a form of radical basic research. Identifying the constitutional logic of modern society is a necessary precondition for developing research agendas in the social sciences and humanities that relate constructively to the nature of their challenges, respectively (Dahms, 2017). The goal is for the social science and humanities disciplines to contribute to illuminating the constitutional logic further, rather than getting caught up in the machinations of modern society, and ascribing significance and causality to factors and phenomena that are surface appearances, rather than in any way related to underlying forces. This approach is radical in the sense that it is committed to follow the logic of the challenge at hand, rather than framing the challenge itself in relation to the specificity of socio-historical conditions and their imperatives and preference with regard to how social-science challenges are to be postulated, e.g., by implicitly subscribing to ideologies, such as neoliberalism.

Since the beginning of critical theory, the significance of the three implications for how to position social research has been watered down further and further. In the first generation, it was most conspicuously present, partly due to the emigrés' experience during the 1930s and 1940s, though not consistently and equally for all the members of the Institute for Social Research. Today, we need a new focal point for criticizing the current condition—conceptually—radicalizing the tradition that began with the critique of alienation in the early Marx, continued with his later critique of commodity fetishism, morphed into Georg Lukács's critique of reification, to be followed by Horkheimer's critique of instrumental reason and Adorno's critique of identity thinking (Wellmer, 2012 [1984]). With Jürgen Habermas's *Theory of Communicative Action* (1984, 1987 [1981]) as a critique of functionalist reason, which implicitly presumed, and even codified, the purported achievements of the postwar/Cold War era (which, from today's perspective, evidently are turning out not be of a reliably lasting nature; see Allen, 2016; Bailey, 2013), the tradition began to take on a much more traditional (as opposed to rigorously critical) veneer, which to date has culminated in Axel Honneth's recognition paradigm (Honneth, 1996). My proposal for focusing critical theory's energies in our age, the twenty-first century, is the concept of *artifice*: to the extent that social scientists apply established concepts, methods and frameworks to the study of the modern condition that were consonant with earlier incarnations of the latter, they describe the artifice of modern society, rather than scrutinizing the proliferating discrepancies between the categories employed and the realities discerned. The paradox is that social scientists-including critical theorists-increasingly are running the risk, against their very intentions, and in large measure due to the counterintuitive constitutional logic of modern society (see Dahms, 2017), to perpetuate, legitimate, and even amplify the hollowing out of social forms, in terms of what is *social* as well as of what is *modern*: artifice as alienation transposed onto the totality of modern society, with anomie and the Protestant ethic as the ever less discernible corollaries of alienation.[4]

## CLASSICAL SOCIAL THEORY AND THE TRANSITION FROM *SPIRIT* TO *CAPITAL*

The classics of social theory—above all Marx, Durkheim and Weber—were concerned with identifying and making accessible in rigorous fashion processes that violated established notions of causality in natural science, philosophy and political economy (as the precursor of economics as a social science). A. R. Lacey has defined 'causal principle' as follows:

> Name for a variety of principles, such as that every event has a cause, that the same cause must have the same effect, or that the cause must have at least as much reality as the effect.
> This last principle (somewhat akin to the principle of sufficient reason) usually says that what causes something to be of a certain sort must itself be of that sort to at least the same degree; for example, what makes something hot must itself be hot. This goes back to Aristotle's principle that actuality is prior to potentiality; that is, what is potentially so-and-so can only be made actually so by something that is itself actually so. (Bothamley, 2002, p. 81)

What Marx, Durkheim and Weber discovered in different yet compatible and complementary ways, as a consequence of different guiding interests, and with different results, is that modern society relies on a set of processes that persistently mediate between a large-scale economic process (based on capital accumulation and industrialization) and social, political and cultural processes that range from the level of the individual to the level of the nation-state, from the minutest human experiences to the condition of humanity and global civilization. Undeniably, there is a link between how human beings economize and how society relates to nature. Today, this link is tangible in the most conspicuous ways, for example, in the fact that between 1970 and 2010, the global population of vertebrate animals has decreased by 52 %, whereas the global human population has doubled within the same time frame, from approximately 3.5 billion to approximately 7 billion people (see McLellan, Iyengar, Jeffries, & Oerlemans, 2014).

In broad strokes, and partly relying on the writings of Dieter Wolf, we may conceive of the formation of modern society as the transition during the seventeenth century, from *nature* to *spirit*, as traced and spelled out in Georg Wilhelm Friedrich Hegel's dialectical philosophy.[5] According to Hegel's rendering of German idealism, the human condition until the end of the Middle Ages was a function of nature as the force to be reckoned with. How human beings organized their lives, individually and collectively, was a response to the fact that nature was beyond control. Even though humans for eons had made efforts to contain nature's potentially destructive power, success was limited. As a consequence of the Age of Enlightenment, however, the prospect of humans understanding the world they inhabit sufficiently well for their mode of existence no longer to be, at least not at the same level of intensity, a function of nature, appeared on the horizon of the future. Relying on Immanuel Kant's critiques as a necessary mode for relating to the world in enlightened fashion, that is, for the first time somewhat *realistically*, as opposed to through religion, and in turn also critiquing the historically insensitive and limited purview of Kant's critiques, Hegel posited that human existence, if understood properly and deeply, should be a function of 'spirit' as the capacity to relate to reality at all levels, by means of the self-reflective intellect and the ability to reason.

However, as 'spirit' started asserting itself alongside the formation of a novel type of society with dimensions both *civil* and *bourgeois* (see Dahms, 2006), it did so with the proverbial wings of republican politics entwined with the establishment of market economies. Both facilitated the process of industrialization, and took the form of what Marx analyzed and criticized along different lines as a social structure centered on the bourgeoisie as the newly ruling class. Modern society as bourgeois society continued to evolve in a manner that *appeared* to be conducive to what Hegel had identified as the civil dimension of modern society, as the corollary of its bourgeois dimension, but the latter established itself at the expense of the former, and was conducive to transforming incipient market economies into economies based on the capitalist mode of production—*capitalism*.

Ergo, the promise for the future of human history that opened up with the shift in the human condition and its corresponding form of social organization—modern society—from society as a function of nature to a function of 'spirit', was warped when spirit took on the form of *capital*, as the first kind of 'artificial intelligence'—a contorted and severely delimited and limited form of spirit, as Max Horkheimer and Theodor W. Adorno (2002 [1947]) laid out in terms of the critique of instrumental reason. As has been pointed out elsewhere (Dahms, 2000), even though the critique of instrumental reason resulted from the early critical theorists' flawed critique of political economy, the impetus in the early Frankfurt School to illuminate the phenomenon I am referring to here as the 'logic of capital' (though not the corresponding terminology, as 'logic of capital' is a more recent concept) was strong enough to advance the cause of critical theory to the next level.

## THE PLIGHT OF THE EARLY FRANKFURT SCHOOL'S CRITICAL THEORY OF *POLITICAL* ECONOMY

As far as the analysis of economic conditions, forms of economic organization, and economic processes in modern capitalist societies is concerned, 'plight' characterizes the early Frankfurt School and the project of critical theory at least in three regards. Plight applies *generally* to the classical critical theorists' lack of success during the 1930s and 1940s in deepening further the mode of analysis Marx had developed in his critique of political economy, with regard to subsequent incarnations of capitalism, at a comparable level of rigor and precision.[6] Plight also applied, *in particular*, to the specific contribution made by the designated economist at the Institute for Social Research, Friedrich Pollock, who from the 1920s and the early 1940s focused to a greater extent on political rather than economic categories and dimensions of societal change. Finally, plight also applied in the sense of *pledge* or *promise*: even though the Frankfurt School never was entirely successful in explicating once and for all, and precisely, the pivotal purpose and distinguishing features of its diagnoses of the continuous reconfiguration of capitalism, among the human sciences, the tradition emerged as the determined effort (and concurrent commitment) to putting forth a mode of analyzing and scrutinizing the link between the economy, on the one hand, and politics, culture and society, on the other, to discern and highlight the problematic character of their relationship, whose importance for human existence has been increasing since the beginning of the modern age.

Yet, pointing out the Frankfurt School's plight with regard to economic analysis is not to suggest that the tradition's achievements—especially the particular mode of reflexivity its representatives have been pursuing and advocating, as indispensable to both social theory and the human sciences (see Geuss, 1981; Hazelrigg, 2009)—are any less remarkable and significant, particularly to the history of social and political thought. Nor does acknowledgment of plight, when viewed from today's vantage point, necessarily translate into the claim that the early Frankfurt School's analyses of capitalist economic issues, and especially its overall agenda, were without value. Rather, despite—and perhaps in part, *because*—of the nature of this plight, and the corresponding neglect of the critique of political economy, the main representatives of the first generation, above all Horkheimer, Herbert Marcuse and Adorno, were able to develop a specific mode of analyzing and scrutinizing modern capitalism whose pertinence and acuity has continued to grow in subsequent decades (see Dahms, 2000). The classical critical theorists' concerns are especially relevant with regard to vexing aspects of the dynamic relationship between politics, economics, society and culture that a more sophisticated critique of political economy may have neglected. Still, by the latter part of the twentieth century, evidence had begun to mount for the need for critical theory to engage in rigorous and systematically focused analysis of political economy, a need that has turned into imminent urgency in the early twenty-first century, not least because of the acceleration of social change and of life in society (see Rosa, 2013 [2005]).

Since Horkheimer envisioned the core of critical theory as an explicit and systematic engagement with the gravity concrete socio-historical conditions exert on the process of social research and the development of the theory of society, including especially critical theory itself, it is necessary to establish how exactly concrete socio-historical conditions facilitate and impede the formulation of research questions, and the pursuit of research and theory. Lack of concern with regard to this issue translates more or less directly into a process of normalizing that which is specific, unusual and especially problematic, in a manner that perpetuates and solidifies the defining features of particular societal circumstances in time and space. In modern capitalist societies, moreover, how precisely societies are modern *and* capitalist must be considered, recognized and explicated fully, in order to reduce as much as possible the likelihood that the formulation of questions, and the processes of research and theory formation themselves, reflect and are expressions of existing societal conditions. For instance, if modern capitalism is fraught with competition and the Protestant work ethic, it is inevitable that research and theory replicate, perpetuate, and deepen competition and work-ethic, paradoxically, in the attempt to illuminate how competition and work-ethic are integral to modern society.

Critical theory emerged as the explicit effort to track and trace the permutations of social life that resulted from the ongoing dynamics of capitalist market economies as they changed, as it were, under the feet, around the bodies, and above the heads of people living their lives, more or less successfully, in what they experienced as normalcy of everyday life. Yet, this experience was saturated by patterns endemic to corporate capitalism—without individuals being fully cognizant of this fact, and in the absence of categories and tools conducive to illuminating this condition, interpreting the latter as natural and inevitable characteristic of life in mass societies.

In the reception of Horkheimer's classical essay (1972 [1937]), this aspect has been overlooked or de-emphasized with an astonishing degree of consistency, to the detriment of the contributions critical theorists could and should have made since the 1930s. In classical critical theory, the aspiration to confront this issue persisted latently, in transposition of Marx's corresponding contentions as they preceded the philosophy of social science, and never fully materialized. In subsequent generations, the aspiration largely disappeared. There are two primary reasons for this initial latency and subsequent disappearance. First, critical theory constitutionally emerged as an explicitly comparative project, as it was grounded in the concrete life experiences of its proponents, who had reached adulthood in Germany, and who fully engaged in the process of social research only in exile in the United States (see Dahms, 2017). Even though the programmatic conceptualization of critical theory came about in New York in the 1930s, this fact has tended to be downplayed as only marginally relevant. Yet, contrary to most later critical theorists, the early members of the Institute for Social Research lived in, actively experienced, and reflected upon three different incarnations of modern society. Most of the members had reached adulthood in Weimar Germany—which at least nominally, was a democratic republic—and then lived through the transformation of an incomplete modern society, into National Socialism as a form of social organization that at the same time was in some regards rabidly anti-modernist (with regard to cultural modernity) and in others radically hyper-modernist (with regard to rationalizing modernization), depending on how we endow the meaning of *modern*. After having experienced three versions of modern society in Germany, if we include the warped modernity of the Imperial period that ended in military defeat and socialist revolution in 1918, the early critical theorists experienced and lived in a fourth version of modern society, upon their arrival in the United States. Horkheimer's contention of the need to scrutinize the bearing specific socio-historical circumstances have on the human sciences, including critical theory, indeed does reflect that his work is expressive of the fact that it is not possible to develop an adequate theory of modern society—and corresponding understanding of critical theory—solely on the basis of extensive primary experience with one single version of modern society. After all, in the absence of the opportunity to compare at least two incarnations of modern societies, it is difficult to conceive of a reliable safeguard against conflating unique features of one's own particular modern society, with features of the genus, modern society, in general.

In this context, Pollock's task was to accomplish for the 1930s what Rudolf Hilferding had achieved in 1910, namely to provide 'a study of the latest phase of capitalist development', as Hilferding had subtitled *Finance Capital* (1981 [1910]). However, while Hilferding did not claim to treat the later stage of capitalist development as a qualitatively different politico-economic and socio-economic arrangement, but merely as the continuation of the logic Marx had identified, Horkheimer and Pollock started out from the assumption that the political economy that emerged during the 1920s, and especially during the 1930s, called for a different type of critique.[7] As a result, the early Frankfurt School's critique of capitalism took the form, on the one hand and under the leadership of Horkheimer, of a social–philosophical critique of western civilization in the spirit of Marx's critiques of alienation and commodity fetishism that culminated in his and Adorno's *Dialectic of Enlightenment* (2002 [1947]). On the other hand, in the hands of Pollock, the critique manifested itself as a peculiar hybrid between traditional economic theory and a positivist reading of Marx in terms of 'state capitalism'—indeed, as a form of *traditional Marxism* (see Postone, 1993). In combination with Adorno's appropriation of Lukács's reconstruction of Marx's critique of alienation within the framework of Marx's later critique commodity fetishism, in terms of *reification*, the early critical theorists' critique of capitalism thus culminated as a critique of *instrumental reason*.

The agenda of the early Frankfurt School translated into the interpretation and experience of a 'socially' constructed world—really, a world constructed by capital that is being experienced and interpreted as social and socially constructed—as given, as if it were possible to presume the existence of life in modern society once and for all, whereas critical theory is a radical form of epistemology: patterns of social life exist not as persistent forms, but as expressions of the transmutations of the logic of capital. It is here that Pollock failed—critical theory as rendered here, in the spirit of Horkheimer, must have been alien to his thought—as he was not able to look through the facade of capitalism to the forms that result from it and that reveal its logic.[8]

In his most controversial contribution, published in 1941 and entitled 'State Capitalism: Its Possibilities and Limitations' (1941a), Pollock identified as the key to analyzing capitalism the ideal-typical concept of 'state capitalism', contending that the latter had constituted the vanishing point for analyzing advanced capitalism, and reached its height in National Socialism (esp. Pollock, 1941b), though this general trend could be observed elsewhere also. The central feature of state capitalism was the suspension of the market mechanism in economies dominated by large corporations: in state capitalist societies, the primacy of the economy characteristic of liberal capitalism had been replaced by the primacy of the state. Pollock introduced a set of crucial distinctions. First, four aspects of the new economy are better explained in terms of 'state capitalism' than in terms of the primacy and relative autonomy of the economic sphere, such as '[s]tate organized private property monopoly capitalism', 'managerial society', 'administrative capitalism', 'bureaucratic collectivism' and others. The four aspects are '[1] state capitalism is the successor of private capitalism … [2] the state assumes important functions of the private capitalist … [3] profit interests still play a significant role, and … [4] it is not socialism' (Pollock, 1941a, p. 201). Private capitalism had been succeeded by a non-private, 'public' form of capitalism. Medium-sized businesses that had dominated the industrial economies of the later nineteenth century had been replaced by 'monopolistic' enterprises during the early decades of the twentieth century, and nineteenth-century categories of political economy, as well as its Marxian critique, had been superseded by early twentieth-century political economy. Indeed, the utility of core categories and distinctions of economic theory, such as market vs. planning, private vs. public, had become doubtful. Instead of providing a compelling economic argument as to why the larger size of businesses mattered, independently of related implications for the market/planning and private/public distinctions, he asserted that with the rise of 'monopolistic' economic organizations, the administrative state had turned into a central *economic* player.

Pollock distinguished two forms of state capitalism—totalitarian and democratic—whose respective nature can vary greatly, depending on the specific form of government and the social groups that control it (p. 201). With the economic process now being fully manageable, three related concerns arise: what are the ends of economic production, what is the purpose of it being administered, and who are the administrators and distributors of economic output?

With reference to the 'new set of rules', Pollock (1941a, pp. 204–207) distinguished between market capitalism as an economy where 'men meet … as agents of the exchange process, as buyers or sellers', as opposed to state capitalism as a system where 'men meet … as commander or commanded' (p. 207), especially with regard to the working population. Yet, Pollock skirted the issue of the inner logic of both economic production and distribution, and asserted that in state capitalism, the profit motive is replaced by the power motive. Though Pollock might have considered necessary conditions for levels of productivity reached during the early twentieth century in the most advanced industrial societies to be maintained, once large corporations were subject to state supervision and regulation in state capitalism, he did not do so. Instead, he assumed that once high levels of industrial production had been reached, a shift of society's economic planning function from monopolistic corporations to the state would not be detrimental to productivity. In state capitalism, there no longer is a need to heed the inner logic of the economic process, as the entrepreneurial and capitalist functions are being 'interfered with or taken over' by management and the government (p. 210). Private ownership of production and distribution facilities will continue, but control of monopolistic industries and their enterprises will be in the hands of government. Pollock also presented arguments for why there can be an adequate incentive structure for a state capitalist system; why the separation of price and production will not hurt the latter; why the state capitalist system does not need to suffer from the kind of wastefulness and inefficiency characteristic of market capitalism and why economics as a social science will lose its object (pp. 203, 210, 215, 217)?

A new ruling class of 'key bureaucrats in the business, state and party that are allied with the remaining vested interests' (p. 221) will control the economy, and 'capitalists' of old lose any necessary social function, though free professions and owners of small- and medium-sized businesses will play a role. The majority—salaried employees—'are subject to the leader principle of command and obedience' (p. 222). Appearance and essence of the new state will be the one: embodiment of power and instrument of the ruling class.

Yet, can a non-totalitarian, democratic form of state capitalism function? 'If our thesis proves to be correct', Pollock wrote, 'society on its present level can overcome the handicaps of the market system by economic planning. Some of the best brains [of the United States] are studying the problem [of] how such planning can be done in a democratic way, but a great amount of theoretical work will have to be performed before answers to every question will be forthcoming' (p. 225). Economics as a social science will become superfluous. Since state capitalism was capable of covering up and domesticating class conflict and social inequality by means of full employment, this non-progressive form of social, political and economic organization even would be able to manage successfully the danger of social and political unrest resulting from remaining underlying economic contradictions. For this reason, as well as due to its economic superiority, Pollock regarded state capitalism as a social formation that, once in place, could continue to exist for a long period of time.

In Pollock's view, the logic of capital accumulation followed closely the patterns characteristic of liberal capitalism, and thus did not call for a thorough revision of the mode of analysis in Marx's critique of political economy—nor whether and to what degree the categories of classical economic theory Marx had criticized still were viable. As a consequence, Pollock's analysis was not a critique of political economy in the Marxian sense.

Given the relative lack of an infrastructure conducive for focused economic analysis at the Institute, Pollock was in a poor position to take on the challenge of updating Marx's critique of political economy for postliberal capitalism on his own. By contrast, in his major work, *Behemoth*, the first comprehensive study of National Socialism, Franz Neumann rejected Pollock's analysis—'The very term "state capitalism" is a *contradictio in adjecto*' (Neumann, 1942, p. 224)—and proposed instead the concept of 'totalitarian monopoly capitalism' (p. 261).[9] Neumann insisted that the market process had not been suspended in National Socialism, but rather exposed the Nazi government to tremendous economic and financial pressure: the capitalist mode of production continued unabated, albeit in a highly organized, integrated and state-coordinated fashion (Neumann, 1942, pp. 227–228).

The difference between 'state capitalism' and 'totalitarian monopoly capitalism' is more than nomenclature. Pollock's term places greater emphasis on the state than Neumann, as far as the inner logic of the economy is concerned. To Pollock, state capitalism signifies a qualitative transformation expressing the shift of society's economic planning function from the economy to the state. To Neumann, by contrast, in Nazi Germany, the economic planning function continues to be held by large corporations, many of which actively supported the Nazi regime, for example, using politics to curry favorable business conditions. Neumann also cautioned that Pollock's vision amounted to the proclamation of the end of history and the demise of any possibility for future qualitative societal transformations.

Both *state capitalism* and *totalitarian monopoly capitalism* imply more manifestly cooperative forms of business–government relations. The difference is mainly one of emphasis, especially in light of the fact that Pollock presented state capitalism as an ideal-typical model; state capitalism stressed the amplified role of the state, whereas totalitarian monopoly capitalism ceded more importance to the economy. More importantly, however, this difference signals distinct modes of theorizing the inner logic of the economic process. According to Pollock, compared to the challenge of understanding the politics of state capitalism, the inner logic of capitalist production is secondary. According to Neumann, the inner logic of capitalist production and its understanding remain central: it is not possible to discern the nature of totalitarian monopoly capitalism without sophisticated grasp on the inner logic of the economic process under changing conditions, and its relative independence from the state.

Horkheimer initially had considered this new development in the relationship between economy and the state a temporary return to an authoritarian form of government. By 1940, however, Horkheimer agreed that the rise of authoritarian regimes like National Socialism was not an aberration in the logic of capitalist development, but a necessary consequence under conditions where capitalist production had created its own potential undoing, the Great Depression. Accordingly, the rise of authoritarian regimes had to be theorized in terms of capitalist categories, but not, paradoxically, in terms of the logic of capital. As Wiggershaus (Wiggershaus, 1994 [1986], p. 280) put it, 'Horkheimer held that the epoch of liberal capitalism must be conceived as a process which made a spiral of lasting despotism possible by atomizing human beings and producing large-scale companies and gigantic organizations'.

The problem with Pollock is that he was a traditional, mainstream economist with positivist leanings, working with a Marxist agenda, and disinterested in the nature of modern economics, including its socially constructed and mediated character (see Dahms, 2011). He was a traditional Marxist economist for whom the concept of state capitalism served as a means to evade adherence to and amplification of Marx's critique of political economy. His interest in examining and scrutinizing the inner logic of the capitalist economic process, and especially the logic of capital, was limited, to whatever degree it may have been present. It is ironic, in retrospect, that *Dialectic of Enlightenment* (2002 [1947]) was dedicated to Pollock, as there is no tangible evidence that he appreciated the theoretical and intellectual contribution it represented, as far as his own work and agenda was concerned. There is no related indication of the latter in any of his later writings, and the mode of theorizing Horkheimer and Adorno developed and applied in *Dialectic of Enlightenment* is exceedingly incompatible with Pollock's mode of thinking. This is at least as true of Horkheimer's concern, as laid out in his 1937 essay, 'Traditional and Critical Theory', with the impact specific socio-historical conditions have on efforts in philosophy and social science, including economics, to illuminate the vicissitudes and destructive dimensions of modern societies.

Though Pollock and Neumann came closest to a theory of economic process and organization in advanced capitalism, and their perspectives negotiated the gap between traditional and critical Marxism differently, with regard to critical theory's ability to confront the 'socio-logic' of capital, at successive stages in the expansion and spread of capitalism, their writings were as much contribution and impediment.[10] In retrospect, the work of Neumann was far more sensitive to the specificities of the role and intricacies of economic processes and organization in National Socialism, and consequently, would have provided a more constructive foundation for the kind of work that was most needed *after* World War II, in Germany, in the United States and elsewhere.

In terms of his conceptualization of *critical theory*, Horkheimer (1972 [1937]) was explicitly concerned with how the logic of capital both manifests itself in, and how it shapes, social life, in ways that must be scrutinized both systematically and radically. By contrast, Pollock's concept of 'state capitalism' is indicative of a perspective that lacked appreciation of a phenomenon such as the logic of capital as an object of study for critical theory. Neumann's concept of 'totalitarian monopoly capitalism', on the other hand, comprised observations consistent with the need to examine the logic of capital, even though he did not do so himself, instead focusing on political and economic processes and organization fundamental to National Socialism as an incarnation of postliberal capitalism, at the institutional level.

However, at the same time, the members of the Institute for Social Research during the 1930s paid far less attention to the underlying logic of capital on its own terms, instead delegating related responsibilities to the member who may well have been least well-suited to take on the challenge, despite his related academic credentials. As a result, the early Frankfurt School neglected to examine precisely the types of impact the *socially mediating and constitutive nature* of capital had on forms of social, political and cultural life (see Postone, 1993; also Brentel, 1989). Rather than paying as close attention as possible to the minutiae of economic processes and their increasing power to influence and shape individual and social dimensions of human existence, as Horkheimer had promised it in his programmatic essay on critical theory, the influence of capitalist economics on politics, culture and society—as well as academia—was implicitly presumed at a general level. Yet, this generalized attitude was not conducive to grasping the specificity of the processes of social meditation the logic of capital inculcates, such as alienation, commodity fetishism and reification, thus making it *both practically and theoretically* difficult, if not impossible, to distinguish clearly between 'human' nature and the nature of the 'social', on the one hand, and how their forms of appearance are expressive of the logic of economic processes rather than characteristics of human and social existence. As a consequence, the critique of modern society became separate—indeed, independent—from the critique of political economy.

Pollock's theory and critique of 'postliberal' capitalism as 'state capitalism' provided an easy, and probably welcome excuse not to hone in on the intricacies of the logic of capital, arduous and tedious as such an effort inevitably would have appeared to the members of the Institute for Social Research, given their individual interests, talents and proclivities. Pollock's influence on the Institute's program and related efforts to conceive of, develop and apply a qualitatively superior form of social research might best be described as comparable to a *virus* that in some regards prevented the programmatic core concern from taking hold and critical theory from 'running properly'.

In retrospect, the bulk of such efforts, in danger of succumbing to the lure of professional success to begin with, were ever in danger to fall prey to the temptation to assimilate to facets of traditional theory—for example, to work toward a general theory of society, of the economy, of the state—to confront evidence that the latter most definitely would not assimilate to—or seriously consider the importance of—critical theory. As a consequence, as is especially the case in the desire to frame later versions of critical theory in terms of particular *paradigms*—an approach that is not compatible with Horkheimer's design for critical theory—there is at least a degree of obliviousness regarding the need to examine with exactitude the gravity concrete socio-historical conditions have been exerting on the process of engaging in, and of advancing especially critically and theoretically oriented forms of, social research. As a result, recent incarnations of 'critical theory' may exemplify, to a far larger extent than they should, the workings of twenty-first century capitalism, rather than applying critical self-reflexivity to the possibility and danger that what is put forth as 'critical theory' could be, to a larger degree than it should, a form of traditional theory, appearing in the garb of critique.

## CRITICAL THEORY IN THE TWENTY-FIRST CENTURY: FROM THE LOGIC OF *CAPITAL* TO THE LOGIC OF *ARTIFICE*

Critical theory frequently is assumed to be concerned above all with emancipation, liberation and the critique of ideology, in order to prepare a kind of political praxis that will foster qualitative social transformations in modern society, which ought to engender ever greater correspondence between facts and norms. Undoubtedly, the successful reconciliation of the latter—in terms of explicitly stated values shared by the majority of a given population—has constituted the vanishing point of critical theory from the start, even if not spelled out in those terms across all three generations. Yet, critical theorists did not envision such reconciliation as taking the form either of superimposition of 'norms' onto 'facts' (assimilation of the material conditions prevailing in a particular society to prevailing norms and values—however the latter may be identified, and by whom—regardless of the myriad social, political and economic costs that might or would result), or of superimposition of 'facts' onto the normative structure of society (with norms and values turning into a function of the existing distribution of wealth, political and social structure, and so on, whatever the corresponding social, political and cultural costs). Neither of these two options, to be sure, would deserve the designation, 'reconciliation', as both presumably would involve an application of force according to the logic of power, rather than heed the nature of more or less incremental, dialectical back-and-forth approximations of discernible improvement. Indeed, the constitutional logic of modern society is such that 'reconciliation' is conceivable to most actors exclusively in terms of one option or the other.

The legitimacy of modern society to a large extent rests on its ability to provide individuals as members of more or less diverse social groups, within the overall system of social structure, with opportunities to direct their efforts, in everyday life as well as public life, at working toward the establishment of a social universe that is consistent with the values that guide their lives, regardless of where exactly those values originate, as long as they are consonant with conditions experienced as authentic. At the same time, however, modern society frustrates those efforts for most of its members most of the time, and for many of its members all of the time. It is in this context that the importance of knowledge of differences and similarities between and across societies of the same type, especially with regard to modern societies, is difficult to overestimate. Although modern societies share many features, they also are characterized by differences which could and should serve as the basis for learning processes enabling those societies that tackle a specific set of challenges—for example, a certain type of social problem—more effectively than others, to provide the latter with the know-how needed to handle those problems more effectively also, potentially along a spectrum of indicators. Yet, to date, this potential for 'learning from other worlds' (see Jalata & Dahms, 2015; Parrinder, 2001) while theoretically easily conceivable, hardly has had any practical impact, except when imposed by force by imperial powers. Rather, in most cases, modern societies appear to maintain order and function precisely by shielding themselves against knowledge of how similar societies confront challenges that all societies must meet, in more successful fashion. This shielding appears to be symptomatic of one aspect of the underlying logic of modern societies—their constitutional logic. In the absence of comparative historical analysis that is informed especially by the work and perspective of the first generation of critical theorists, the most problematic aspects of the constitutional logic of modern society are likely to remain concealed, and to continue to fester.

Critical theory must break with the desire to frame the process of critically analyzing modern society on the basis of 'optimistic' assumptions about the direction of social change upon whose prevalence the operations of modern society are contingent. Put differently, critical theorists must develop and deploy a set of categories that pertain to the disturbing actuality of modern society, with special attention being paid to the consequences that result from its operations for humans, animals, the biosphere, forms of solidarity and the horizon of the future. Critical theorists also and especially must scrutinize how modern society rests on and expands a system of capitalist economic production that comes at the price of intensifying social and environmental destruction. Given the limitations of resources on planet Earth, which are being depleted rapidly, and the apparent imminence of further population growth, in the context of a global socio-economic structure characterized by proliferating and deepening inequality, it is necessary to evaluate modern society not in terms of what we would prefer to think it represents or to infer it has the positive potential of becoming, if conditions were right to facilitate the realization of the potential modern society represents. Instead, to the extent that critical theory is a normative project, it is necessary to identify and apply standards in the process of social research that pertain to the myriad costs which go hand in hand with maintaining modern society as is. The latter constitutes a social system which, in light of its history to date, does not appear to have the capacity, or the impetus, to undergo the kind of qualitative transformations that would enable actors to work to comprehend, diminish, limit and overcome the price human beings, animals and the planet pay in order to sustain it. Willingness to comply with this 'price' is related to the desirability of maintaining economic growth in its present form as the seeming precondition for keeping modern society stable.

Yet, from individuals concerned with the condition of the environment or the planet, to collective actors in charge of navigating the tension between purportedly democratic politics—from the local to the global level—and a global economic system that is inversely related to the possibility of democracy, the price to be paid and the costs to be shouldered in order to maintain the existing system exact a kind of emotional, psychological, social and cultural destruction that presumably is impossible to sustain. Furthermore, this destruction is bound to erode the motivational structure without which neither modern society can function, nor most individuals. Indeed, more or less clearly, a growing number of individuals appear to sense that modern society, absent its capacity to undergo qualitative transformations that would lead—or at least would be conducive—to greater correspondence between facts and norms, represents a 'structural lie' of sorts, a promise that is becoming discernible as unrealizable:

> [I]n the early decades of the 2000s, as both the culture of Western modernity and the institutional salience of *the* State begin to retreat as the exclusive, even essential, resources of collective life, there is good reason to repeal resistance at least enough to think of the global realities of these new times as revealing, perhaps aggravating, social antimatter of global proportions. States, for one, have as chief among their interests supporting those elements of their culture that encourage the idea that all is well, at least on the national interior. Though they seldom can get away with the deception, sooner or later the legitimation crisis tears at the veil of secrecy and the national public sees the true seamy side of their society. (Lemert, 2011, p. 230)

There are mounting indications that the present is *not* a time when legitimation crises necessarily or at all lead to revelations about the 'seamy side of society' (see also Wolfe, 1978), but rather, may amplify the determination for many not to confront or acknowledge this seamy side—to pretend that it does not exist, thus presenting a concrete form of 'social antimatter' that may well have a tendency to proliferate, as it is highly synchronous with modern society as artifice, and indicative of the concept of *capital* no longer having the explanatory power it use to represent. Indeed, we may have been undergoing a process of transition from modern society being a function of capital to it turning into a function of artifice, as the human motivation force behind facilitating and supporting capital that gave it some sense of direction and purpose is disappearing, and all that is left is capital's hollow shell—a black hole that is sucking in everything, despite, against, and possibly due to proliferating resistance.

## Notes

1. Two recent collections are informative in this regard, though not necessarily illustrative of too great an emphasis on more practical or praxis-oriented agendas: Wilkerson and Paris (2001) and Ludovisi (2015).
2. Horkheimer (1972 [1937]). See Claussen, Negt, and Werz (1999), esp. Claussen (1999) and Werz (1999).
3. As the last eight years have taught us, one could argue that even with the help of sociology, desirable long- or medium-term qualitative social change has been hard to come by, although, as will become apparent in the next section of this chapter, to date, sociology has not lived up to its potential as far as scrutinizing the mediating forces facilitating the socio-logic of capital is concerned.
4. As the corresponding concept that highlights the process quality of artifice, I propose "abligurition": "To spend in luxurious indulgence" that is highly wasteful and not conducive to sustainability at any level. It shines light on how modern society in fact works, as opposed to how we are supposed to presume it works. The shift in biomass represented by populations of vertebrate animals mentioned earlier, from animals (and plants) to humans, is symptomatic for how societies as well as individuals operate and "maintain" themselves today, at the expense, potentially, of all others, in a manner that continuously extracts resources from the planet and from other humans. It this process is allowed to continue unabated, it inevitably will spell doom. See Dahms (in preparation).
5. Especially Wolf (1979). Wolf is one of a number of sophisticated and prominent scholars who have dedicated their time and energy to providing reinterpretations of Marx's writings that highlight their intensifying relevance today, even though their interpretations are not without conflicts and disagreements, such as Moishe Postone (1993), Helmut Reichelt (2001, 2008) and Hans Georg Backhaus (2011); see also Larsen, Nilges, and Robinson (2014).

6. Plight in this general sense has continued to plague the tradition of critical theory to this day. Ronge and Ronge (1979) and Fay et al. (1980) were noteworthy attempts to integrate economic analysis into critical theory since the 1930s. More than a decade before discussions about globalization, Ronge and Ronge (1979) cautioned that "late capitalism" was not necessarily characterized by increasing politicization (p. 205)—an issue that will be addressed below—and that the "self-organization" of capital (p. 206) could serve as an anchor for promoting the common good. Perhaps the boldest, most rigorous and pertinent attempt to date to delineate a critical theory of the underlying logic of modern century capitalism that is situated explicitly within this tradition, is Postone (1993).
7. For a detailed examination of the evolution of Pollock's role at the Institute and his concept of "state capitalism," see Dahms (2000), especially pp. 332–352.
8. For recent depictions of this logic, see Chibber (2013) and Vogl (2015 [2010]). Regarding the notion of "*socio*"-*logic*, see Postone (1993, chap. 3).
9. For his critique of "state capitalism," see pp. 221–234.
10. While Postone (1993) has provided the most promising foundation for theoretically sophisticated critiques of the global economy, it must be supplemented with a social theory of the deepening artificiality of contemporary societies–for critical theory to embrace what should be its defining challenge today.

## References

Abromeit, J. (2011). *Max Horkheimer and the foundations of the Frankfurt School.* Cambridge: Cambridge University Press.

Allen, A. (2016). *The end of progress: Decolonizing the normative foundations of critical theory.* New York: Columbia University Press.

Backhaus, H. G. (2011). *Dialektik der Wertform. Untersuchungen zur marxschen Ökonomiekritik* (2nd ed.). Freiburg: Ça ira.

Bailey, T. (Ed.). (2013). *Deprovincializing Habermas: Global perspectives.* London: Routledge.

Bothamley, J. (Ed.). (2002). *Dictionary of theories.* Detroit: Visible Ink.

Brentel, H. (1989). *Soziale form und ökonomisches Objekt: Studien zum Gegenstands- und Methodenverständnis der Kritik der politischen Ökonomie.* Wiesbaden: VS Verlag für Sozialwissenschaften.

Chibber, V. (2013). *Postcolonial theory and the specter of capital.* London: Verso.
Claussen, D. (1999). Die amerikanische Erfahrung der Kritischen Theoretiker. In Claussen, Negt and Werz (1999), pp. 27–45.
Claussen, D., Negt, O., & Werz, M. (Eds.) (1999). *Keine Kritische Theorie ohne Amerika* (Hannoversche Schriften 1). Frankfurt: Verlag Neue Kritik.
Dahms, H. F. (1997). Theory in Weberian Marxism: Patterns of critical social theory in Lukács and Habermas. *Sociological Theory 15*(3): 181–214. See also Dahms (2011), pp. 45–92.
Dahms, H. F. (1999). Postliberal capitalism and the early Frankfurt School: Toward a critical theory of the inner logic of social value spheres. *Current Perspectives in Social Theory, 19*, 55–88.
Dahms, H. F. (2000). The early Frankfurt School critique of capitalism: Critical theory between Pollock's 'state capitalism' and the critique of instrumental reason. In P. Koslowski (Ed.), *The theory of capitalism in the German economic tradition: Historism, ordo-liberalism, critical theory, solidarism* (pp. 309–366). Berlin: Springer. See also Dahms (2011), pp. 3–44.
Dahms, H. F. (2006). Does alienation have a future? Recapturing the core of critical theory. In L. Langman & D. K. Fishman (Eds.), *The evolution of alienation: Trauma, promise, and the millennium* (pp. 23–46). Lanham, MD: Rowman and Littlefield. See also Dahms (2011), pp. 223–248.
Dahms, H. F. (2007). Confronting the dynamic nature of modern social life. *Soundings. An Interdisciplinary Journal, 90*(3–4), 191–205.
Dahms, H. F. (2011). *The vitality of critical theory (Current Perspectives in Social Theory, 28).* Bingley, UK: Emerald.
Dahms, H. F. (2015a). Toward a critical theory of Capital in the 21st Century: Thomas Piketty between Adam Smith and the prospect of apocalypse. *Critical Sociology, 41*(2), 359–374.
Dahms, H. F. (2015b). Which capital, which Marx? Basic income between mainstream economics, critical theory, and the logic of capital. *Basic Income Studies, 10*(1), 115–140.
Dahms, H. F. (2017). Critical theory as radical comparative-historical research. In M. Thompson (Ed.), *The Palgrave handbook of critical theory.* New York: Palgrave Macmillan.
Dahms, H. F. (in preparation). *Modern society as artifice: Critical theory and the logic of capital.* London: Routledge.
Dux, G. (2008). *Warum denn Gerechtigkeit: Die Logik des Kapitals. Die Politik im Widerstreit mit der Ökonomie.* Göttingen: Velbrück.
Fay, M., et al. (1980). *Starnberger Studien 4: Strukturveränderungen in der kapitalistischen Weltwirtschaft.* Frankfurt/M.: Suhrkamp.
Geuss, R. (1981). *The idea of a critical theory: Habermas and the Frankfurt School.* Cambridge: Cambridge University Press.
Habermas, J. (1984 1987 [1981]). *The theory of communicative action* (Vol. 2) (T. McCarthy, Trans.). Boston: Beacon Press.

Hazelrigg, L. (2009). Forty years of *knowledge and human interests*: A brief appreciation. In H. F. Dahms (Ed.), *Nature, knowledge and negation* (Current Perspectives in Social Theory, 26) (pp. 189–206). Bingley, UK: Emerald.
Hilferding, R. (1981 [1910]). *Finance capital. A study of the latest phase of capitalist development* (M. Watnick, S. Gordon, Trans.; T. Bottomore, Ed.). London: Routledge & Kegan Paul.
Honneth, A. (1991 [1985]). *The critique of power* (K. Barnes, Trans.). Cambridge, MA: MIT Press.
Honneth, A. (1996). *The struggle for recognition: The moral grammar of social conflicts* (J. Anderson, Trans.). Cambridge, Mass.: The MIT Press).
Horkheimer, M. (1972 [1937]). Traditional and critical theory (M. J. O'Connell, Trans.). In *Critical theory: Selected writings*. New York: The Seabury Press, pp. 188–243.
Horkheimer, M. (1993 [1931]). The present situation of social philosophy and the tasks of an Institute for Social Research. In *Between philosophy and social science: Selected early writings* (G. F. Hunter, M. S. Kramer, and J. Torpey, Trans.). Cambridge, Mass.: The MIT Press.
Horkheimer, M., & Adorno, T. W. (2002 [1947]). *Dialectic of enlightenment: Philosophical fragments* (E. Jephcott, Trans.). Stanford, CA: Stanford University Press.
Jalata, A., & Dahms, H. F. (2015). Theorizing modern society as an inverted reality: How critical theory and indigenous critiques of globalization must learn from each other. In H. F. Dahms (Ed.), *Globalization, critique and social theory: Diagnoses and challenges* (Current Perspectives in Social Theory 33). Bingley, UK: Emerald, pp. 75–133.
Larsen, N., Nilges, M., & Robinson, J. (Eds.). (2014). *Marxism and the critique of value*. Chicago: MCM Publishing.
Lemert, C. (2011). *The structural lie. Small clues to global things*. Boulder, CO: Paradigm.
Ludovisi, S. G. (Ed.). (2015). *Critical theory and the challenge of praxis: Beyond reification*. Burlington, VT: Ashgate.
Marcuse, H. (2009 [1937]). Philosophy and critical theory. In *Negations: Essays in critical rheory* (J. J. Shapiro, Trans.). London: MayFlyBooks.
McLellan, R., Iyengar, L., Jeffries, B., & Oerlemans, N. (Eds.). (2014). *Living planet report 2014: Species and spaces, people and places*. Gland, Switzerland: WWF.
Neumann, F. (1942). *Behemoth. The structure and practice of National Socialism*. New York: Oxford University Press.
Parrinder, P. (Ed.). (2001). *Learning from other worlds: Estrangement, cognition, and the politics of science fiction and utopia*. Durham, NC: Duke University Press.
Pollock, F. (1941a). State capitalism: Its possibilities and limitations. *Studies in Philosophy and Social Science, 9*, 200–225.

Pollock, F. (1941b). Is National Socialism a new order? *Studies in Philosophy and Social Science, 9*, 440–455.

Postone, M. (1993). *Time, labor and social domination: A reinterpretation of Marx's critical theory*. Cambridge: Cambridge University Press.

Reichelt, H. (2001). *Zur logischen Struktur des Kapitalbegriffs bei Karl Marx*. Freiburg: Ça ira.

Reichelt, H. (2008). *Neue Marx-Lektüre: Zur Kritik sozialwissenschaftlicher Logik*. Hamburg: VSA-Verlag.

Ronge, V., & Ronge, P. J. (1979). *Starnberger Studien 3: Bankpolitik im Spätkapitalismus. Politische Selbstverwaltung des Kapitals?* Frankfurt/M.: Suhrkamp.

Rosa, H. (2013 [2005]). *Social acceleration: A new theory of modernity*. New York: Columbia University Press.

Vogl, J. (2015 [2010]). *The specter of capital* (J. Redner & R. Savage, Trans.). Stanford, CA: Stanford University Press.

Wellmer, A. (2012 [1984]). Adorno, advocate of the non-identical, Soltau, N. (tr.). Erlenbusch, V. and Dahms, H. F. In H. F. Dahms & L. Hazelrigg (Eds.), *Theorizing modern society as a dynamic process* (Current Perspectives in Social Theory, 30), pp. 35–60.

Werz, M. (1999). Kritische Theorie im Exil. In Claussen, Negt and Werz (pp. 102–121).

Wiggershaus, R. (1994 [1986]). *The Frankfurt School. Its history, theories, and political significance* (M. Robertson, Trans.). Cambridge, MA: MIT Press.

Wilkerson, W. S., & Paris, J. (Eds.). (2001). *New critical theory: Essays on liberation*. Lanham, MD: Rowman & Littlefield.

Wolf, D. (1979). *Hegel und Marx: Zur Bewegungsstruktur des absoluten Geistes und des Kapitals*. Hamburg: VSA-Verlag.

Wolfe, A. (1978). *The seamy side of democracy: Repression in America*. Harlow, UK: Longman.

CHAPTER 4

# The Sacred and the Profane in the General Formula for Capital: The Octagonal Structure of the Commodity and Saving Marx's Sociological Realism from Professional Marxology

*Mark P. Worrell*

In *Capital* Marx sought to drain the swamp of value and demystify the phantom-like objectivity of commodities but, with some exceptions, his followers, far from wishing to drain the swamp, would prefer to wrestle alligators (for one version of this argument see Postone, 1993, p. 124, 360 ff.). The problem with the desire to struggle over surplus is that Marxism contains *no disenchanting, infraliminal moment within its analysis of the commodity* and, without that infraliminal dimension, it is doomed to irrelevance as a theoretical constellation capable of moving beyond the commodity form because, while they renounce valorization and commodities, they do not necessarily renounce value and, while demonizing the *capitalist class*, have a romance for capital itself. It matters not if we ask a communist or a recovering communist, the only difference is timbre, not substance:

M.P. Worrell (✉)
Department of Sociology, SUNY Cortland, Cortland, NY, USA

© The Author(s) 2017
D. Krier, M.P. Worrell (eds.), *The Social Ontology of Capitalism*,
DOI 10.1057/978-1-137-59952-0_4

Capitalism is something of a goose from the standpoint of abstract reason and the ideal of perfection. It's easy to make game of that goose, and it's a lot of fun when you stay up in the sky. But she's the only creature on this earth that ever laid golden eggs, and in my humble but mature opinion she's the only one that ever will. My advice to organized labor is: Grab all the eggs you can get your hands on—of course—but watch out. Don't kill the goose!" (Eastman, 1955, pp. 113–115)

The reason for this critical failure to negate capital itself is that the default, if unconscious, paradigmatic ground of Marxism (if not the mature Marx) is an empirical realism masking a background transcendentalism—while most Marxists believe that their materialism "excludes transcendence" (Gramsci, 1971, p. 454) many "Marxists" are, at heart, actually Kantians operating from a positive ontic stance that is alien to critical social theory (Marx, 1976[1867], pp. 493–494; 677; 683. All further references to volume one of Capital will be abbreviated to an uppercase C). Materialism of the Marxist variety, "is in most cases not a consistent monism; in one or other guise a second principle is surreptitiously introduced along with matter in order to explain spiritual phenomena more easily" (Adler, in Horkheimer, 1972, p. 16). Marx worked for nearly 30 years to reach a *sociological* comprehension of the commodity and while Comte made "sociology" popular a generation earlier, Marx's dialectical analysis of the commodity and the capitalist mode of production found in the first volume of *Capital* was, I would argue, the first sociologically 'perfect' analysis of what we, following Durkheim, call a "social fact" (see Worrell 2009). It is also worth pointing out that the most well-known exponents of contemporary Marxist theory are not sociologists but economists, philosophers, and geographers which might go a long way in explaining why, from the sociological perspective, they tend to wind up in the cul-de-sac of materialism (value is a thing) or wildly overshoot the social into hyper-realist mysticism (after World War III, the only thing left will be cockroaches, radioactive Twinkies, and value). Agger says that "no matter how neutered, Marxism always threatens to break out of its disciplinary prison" (Agger, 1989, p. 194). I think Marx is "always threatening" but as far as Marxism goes, it may spill out across disciplines but is usually neutered by its own contradictions and seems, oddly enough, to want to break *into* prison more than it wants to break out.

What the mature Marx (and Durkheim) share is a *sociological* realism inherited from the Hegelian tradition (see Beiser, 2005, pp. 212–213, 294 on Hegel's realism) that, in Marx's case, grasps the commodity as a carrier of value and a thing that is external, coercive, and irreducible. In other words, as a form of authority, a commodity's social foundations are irreducible. Yet, if we wish to *de-authorize* a thing, disenchant it, and withdraw recognition from a social fact, then the ordinary and one-sided realism of Marxism leads nowhere but back to value here, there, and everywhere: "Even the animal has gone beyond this realist philosophy, for it consumes things and thereby proves that they are not absolutely self-sufficient" (Hegel, 1991[1821], p. 76). Marxism cannot free society from the hegemony of the commodity if it shares the same perverted gaze as the capitalist class. To talk about commodity production and the labor theory of value and so on is to accurately assess the facticity and reality of capitalism but it fails to move consciousness beyond the facticity of the capitalist regime of accumulation and merely transposes consciousness to new coordinates within the geometry of alienation. Indeed, there is nothing more *bourgeois* than to think in terms of 'commodity production' (Marx, 1970[1859], p. 54). The ontic irreducibility of a fact does not preclude a disenchanting, critical methodological objectification of the commodity to, not the dumb singularization of base materialism, nor methodological individualism, but, rather, to expose the direct social relations hidden from sight beneath a reflective shell. The ontic drift away from Marx's hard-won sociological insight on the part of Marxism is not surprising because Marxists, like capitalists, dream day and night of commodities and capital.

Collective consciousness usually has what it takes to bend the wills of individuals to its wishes and inverts and twists the mind such that subjects fall into mystifications, for example, finding value in nature or confusing signifiers (prices, for example) with the things signified. Critics often break through the ideological defenses thrown up by society but they are nonetheless subject to, and possessed by, the same forces as the common lot (Durkheim, 1951[1897], p. 319) and are often defeated by an inability to control the confluence of incompatible intellectual currents creeping in from the sides to disintegrate analysis—how often do we hear a good Marxist conjure a whirlwind of signs emanating from the far corners of the ontic universe, from ordinary materialism, nominalism, realism, vitalism, and so on? Marx has his problems; there is no point trying to defend his half-baked theory of communist association (Worrell & Krier, Forthcoming) but one thing he did grasp perfectly is the ontic status of the commodity and the social nature of value, however, one would never know that by reading contemporary critics who project fetish interpretations in every direction and flail about uncontrollably like understudies at the Smirnoff Ice Capades.

When Marxists cannot even figure out the relationship between price and value or cannot get through their heads that "exchange-value" is the necessary mode of expression of "value"—as if there are two values, one social and another value *somewhere else* then the entire project seems futile. One more attempt at clarification is worthwhile but if critical theory cannot extricate itself from the pits of reductionism or the befuddling clouds of transcendentalism then Marxism will fail to be more than a secular religion for pale male academics. What I will do in the remainder of this chapter is point to a few of the most common Marxist fetishes, uncoil the general formula for capital to the point where we unveil the organic composition of capital, analytically introduce the twin dimensions of, on the one hand, the supraliminal or the "subjective-substantial" (sacred) and, on the other, the "infraliminal" (profane) and locate exactly where value is and where it is not, map the octagonal structure of the commodity, and reveal the precise relationship between prices and values with an eye toward the various points of vulnerability vis-à-vis devaluation and derealization.

## Capitalists and Anti-capitalists: The Twin Poles of the Cult of Value

The problem with Marxist anti-capitalism is that, as others have pointed out, it often shares presuppositions with capitalists. Sociologically, if anti-gods are still nonetheless gods, anti-capitalists can be, unbeknownst to themselves, capitalists at heart because, to both the capitalist and the Marxist, value is sacred and, in its spectacle form (Debord, 1983), it appears to saturate the entirety of the material world. In other words, from the spectaclized gaze, the value of the commodity is not merely socially real but *really* real (*ontos on*). It is ironic that some of these same critics can turn right around and confuse a price (a mere signifier) with the social substance of value. The way out of the morass is not through pitting one fetish against another but theoretical decompression and stereoscopic objectivity.

A decisive move that will be made in this chapter is a conceptual separation of the sacred and the devalued profane with regard to the social ground of the capitalist mode of production and accumulation. Here I am doing nothing that Marx does not do himself in *Capital*. Anytime we split or divide things we should be wary of fetishism, however, we are not creating a new, doubled, mystified interpretation of the commodity but analytically separating and decompressing what has become a distorted and *one-sided* Marxist mythology regarding value and commodity production (the negation of the negation). Berman completely loses the thread when he claimed for Marx the astonishing ability to melt together the sacred and the profane, the material and the spiritual (1988, p. 132) when his method does the exact opposite: separating the material from the spiritual, reintroducing a "duality" (not really) where there is realist "interfusion" and confusion. Pseudo-critical mystifications can assume several other varieties:

- splitting value into value and exchange-value;
- conflating price and value and neglecting the concept of fictional or fictitious value;
- splitting capital into different species, for example, industrial and finance (capital fetishism);
- regressing to a pre-sociological materialist paradigm or flying off behind the world (inherent value, ultra-realism where we find ideas such as commodities as "storing" value and conflating concrete production with 'value creation' via fetishistic retrogressions and retrojections);
- failing to grasp the quality–quantity dialectic in the relationship between the labor process and valorization;
- neglecting the decisive aspect of devaluation and derealization and, therefore, seeing value everywhere (spectacle);
- myriad conceptual compressions, distorting shorthands, and so on.

Marxology is rife with compressions such as "commodity production" and "labor theory of value," and so on, as if the whole club exists for, as Steinbeck put it, the "temporarily embarrassed capitalist" (2002, p. 27). Ideological compressions like these are akin to the mechanisms that Freud discloses in his work on dream interpretation (1965[1900]). Dreams, as it turns out, like myth and ideology, represent breaks from reality and, perhaps, this is the reason the fascination with Marx, in the United States at least, is limited to bored, middle-class dreamers who could not even threaten "a Sunday-school picnic" (Steinbeck, 2002, p. 27). Dreamers have a tendency to project their fantasies and confusions into the mirror of nature and interpersonal operations.

Marx makes perfectly clear that, first, exchange-value is identical with the concept of value. In "Value, Price, and Profit," for example, Marx says that when he speaks of value he always has in mind exchange-value (Marx,

1935, p. 28). We can certainly discuss value separately from the exchange relation. The substance of value is labor in the abstract; however, Marx has a name for the analysis of value apart from the exchange relation as realization: "abstract value" (C, p. 141). How many Marxists have ever noticed this or, if they have, would know what it means or what to do with it?

In all of Marx's works the precise phrase "abstract value" appears only a few times (Engels used it once as far as I know, in a non-economic context; Marx used it in a footnote in the *Critique*; and in *Capital* it appears once). Marx says, "If we say that, as values, commodities are simply congealed quantities of human labour, our analysis *reduces* them, it is true, to the level of *abstract value*, but does not give them a form of value distinct from their *natural* forms. It is otherwise in the value-relation of one commodity to another" (C, p. 141, emphasis added). His point here is that, yes, we (those who alienate the living) can reduce a thing down to an abstraction (value is abstract labor or "labor pure and simple" without regard for particularity) but, paradoxically, the abstraction, divorced from any *relation*, *appears* (and can only *appear*) to befuddled consciousness in its concrete or natural form (hence, the illusion of inherent or intrinsic value endorsed by vampires and other econo-monsters). The secondary alienation following the first alienation ('compound alienation') brings the abstract thing back around to the concrete domain but in a mystified form. We are supposed to know that, as far as value goes, its "objective character" is "purely social" and "can only appear in the social *relation* between commodity and commodity" (C, p. 139, emphasis added) and that value "differs from its stiff and starchy existence as a body" (C, p. 144). Value, as a moral subject-substance, "is realized *only* in exchange," that it "emerges" in the *relation* between two commodities (C, p. 142, emphasis added), that matter has *nothing* to do with value itself and is, indeed, the total disregard of matter (C, p. 138), and that value is, beneath its obfuscating but expressive material shell, the *relation* between people (C, p. 149, 167) and "only within the limits of this relation" (C, p. 148). Now, try getting any of this across to Marxists who point to some isolated physical object outside any exchange relation whatsoever when asked to show you value or who wonder, after 30 or more years of pondering Marx, what he meant by the phrase "purely social." To quote a modern classic: "Doesn't anyone notice this! I feel like I'm taking crazy pills!"

Value is already an abstraction (concrete labor rendered generic, labor without regard for particularity) but disconnecting value from the social relations of exchange renders it doubly abstract (abstract here means one-sided and removed from its social ground). This is why "exchange-value" is the *necessary* mode of expression of "value." Again, if we mistakenly regard value as a *double* concept then there is one that is social and one external to the moral domain. This is not social science in any form, rather, we are in the presence of Marxist theology or evil sharks on bad nature television. If Marx had been this type of realist by the time he published *Capital*, the famous footnote on Peter and Paul (C, p. 144) and the footnote on royalty would have been completely different:

Marx: Peter (singularity) knows himself as a human being (universal) in the use-value form of Paul (the particular equivalent) who recognizes his claim to be a human—"Peter only relates to himself as a man through his relation to another man, Paul, in whom he recognizes his likeness" (C, p. 144). In other words, no Paul, no universality. But, of course, for the deluded Peter, he thinks he has an immediate relationship to the universal (because he loves Christ and reads Badiou). Likewise with royalty. "For instance, one man is king only because other men stand in the relation of subjects to him. They, on the other hand, imagine that they are subjects because he is king" (C, p. 149).

Contrast this position with another where Peter, capitalists, vampires, Marxologists, children, savages, and so on, imagine that Peter is not a human being because he is recognized by Paul, but, on the contrary, Paul treats and regards Peter the way he does because he is obviously *already* a human being. Here, the status conferred is reversed from "he is king because we treat him as such" to the opposite, where "we treat him like a king because he is king." The same reversal applies to things like commodities or gold or any other object invested with authority. For the *social* realist gold has value because we expend time and energy to extract it from the earth and then use it as a medium of exchange whereas, for the ordinary realist, we dig up gold because it is value. Of course, in the bourgeois necroverse, gold really does already have value and we will all kill one another to obtain more than our fair share, so, we can go on killing one another for it, or, we can break the spell that it holds over people. The usefulness (material body) of gold, for example, contains no value, it is not in its materiality that value is located. Here, Marx and Durkheim merge with the insight that non-material and even imaginary things can be nonetheless objectively real in the eyes of whole classes and even have physical effects (Durkheim, 1995[1912], p. 369). The existence of a god, for example, would not constitute a literal truth but would be socially and practically true for millions of people. We do not punish children who give up on the tooth fairy but people die everyday for their failure to recognize the prevailing god (collective representation) of their society. Any dumb little use-value can, in some contexts, be imagined to wield awesome powers and some Marxists, like any Average Joe, do confuse use-values with value.

Marx's clumsy adoption of an older terminology ("use-value") from the preexisting terminology he found in political economy exacerbates the problem. What is meant by "use-value" is simple but not obvious: use and consumption falls on the side of the concrete and the specific, in other words, I may value a thing for whatever reason and say "this is a value to me." At the level of *personal psychology*, then, it is true that a commodity, once sold, can fall out of the exchange relation and, for the owner and user, nonetheless *retain* some sense of being a "value" (not merely utility or usefulness) and used as some kind of "phallus" by which to impress others and signify social status. Even here, though, it is usually the "logos" of the thing, rather than its physical qualities, that matters most: this thing is my BMW. The signifier functions as a vague but prestigious image that bends the mind back to the fantasized exchange moment, when the owner presumably sacrificed $60,000 for the BMW thing. For the working person we should excuse this swerve in thought: "If you must sweat like a mule to earn your beer," says Bageant, "you might as well call it a value" (Bageant, 2010, p. 200). For professional Marxologists, however, we should expect more.

While many Marxists make the error of duplicating and fetishizing value (value fetishism is the splitting of the value concept into two species, just as capital fetishism is the splitting of capital into two species)—see the third volume of *Capital* for more on this problem of capital fetishism—a few compound their problems by then misconstruing price for value. I was once asked how there can be value without a price. Are not profits priceless? Where there are prices there are always values we are told. However, Marx indicates that price and value are separate concepts and that we can affix a price to some object that has no value whatsoever—here we are in the domain of imaginary or *fictional* (purely "fictitious") value (C, p. 203, passim). From another angle, though, where we find prices in the absence of value we might use our anthropological eye to locate alternate modes of impersonal and authoritative social energies underlying the price/signifier. "Price" is not limited to the domain of the economic. Before "price" had anything to do with the estimation of commercial values it was related to honor, esteem, and reputation, and was related to the words "praise" and "prize." Of course, we might find that, yes, the mere act of exchange has been constructed in which dupes pay for worthlessness; *value is not merely the result of exchange in itself as hardcore constructionists would have us believe*, otherwise we go no further than notions such as the worth of a thing being whatever a person is willing to pay for it (e.g., C, p. 126) but it might also be the case that what looks like junk is actually a bearer of *another modality of authority* exchangeable for money or convertible into a money form.

The poststructuralist tendency is to see things like "empty signifiers" when, in reality, signifiers are merely borne aloft by forces that have escaped the one-sided analytic eye. If one cannot see anything but people *laboring*, one discounts other modes of *human assemblage and alienated ebullience*. In fact, many of the instruments circulating in the financial and finance–gambling sphere (not to mention religion) are in fact worthless from the standpoint of labor theory which leads to another erroneous interpretation on the part of Marxists, and that is the notion of "hot air"—that some circulating paper is backed or grounded by *nothing*. Something, beyond the sun, has to make that air *hot*. This points to the one-sided, labor fetish of Marxism and and the labor theory of value—Marx does not have a labor theory of value but an *abstract* labor theory of value (Marx, 1970[1859], pp. 56–57, 61, 64); where we think we see "worthless" scraps of paper floating around what we are sometimes missing is that a mere piece of paper can also be a piece of institutional *authority* in paper form backed up (grounded) by some *other* kind of social power (e.g., C, p. 226). In the case of quantitative easing, for example, it was not technically correct to see it as a case of simply injecting "hot air" currency into the market. The Chinese response to QE1 and QE2 suggests that their capital investments were being degraded, and they were, but when a carrier battle group appears on on the doorstep of debt-buyers around the globe to conduct training (intimidation) it sends the message that US bonds and currency are backed by *force* and as long as Uncle Sam can force feed debt to nations while engaged in target practice just over their heads, US currency and bonds are "worth" something, are exchanged for money, and stay in circulation. It is better to pay *imperial tribute* than it is to have your nation turned into a parking lot. Marxism needs to incorporate *fear value, tribute cost,* and *survival price*, and a few more ideas, into its lexicon. Marxism must go beyond itself, as Marx himself did with the concept of the fetish imported from ethnology, and start to integrate perspectives from other disciplines.

It is an interesting fact that mathematicians, when trying to solve big problems, routinely shift perspectives by indirectly solving corollaries. For example, when Fermat's "last theorem" was solved by Andrew Wiles, it was accomplished not by discovering Fermat's actual proof, but through another route altogether: modularity and elliptical curves. Analogously, by grasping, for example, Durkheim's theory of the totem or Weber's theory of charisma (the kind of work pioneered by David Norman Smith) we can gain a better apprehension of Marx's theory of the commodity. And the ordinary realism that plagues most Marxism results in mystifying Marx's works such that he emerged fully formed by the time he was a young adult. Lefebvre (2009[1968]) was correct when he located the birth of a different Marx with the publication of the *Critique* in 1859—in contrast to, say, Althusser, who places a decisive shift in Marx's thinking at 1857 and the emergence, here, of the "mature Marx" (Althusser, 1969, p. 35). An ordinary realist perspective is capable of unifying all of Marx's writings but at the cost of hypostatizing value and forcing the critical spirit to adopt for itself the enchanted, monist belief of its opposition. Realism, in the case of Marxism, leads to a kind of intellectual Stockholm Syndrome where anti-capitalists see with capitalized eyes. Before we launch into uncoiling the general formula for capital we should start with its opposite, the circulation of commodities: C–M–C.

## COMMODITY CIRCULATION AND THE GENERAL FORMULA FOR CAPITAL

The "critical theory of society begins with the idea of the simple exchange of commodities..." (Horkheimer, 1972, p. 226). The world of commodity circulation (C-M-C) is one where people sell in order to buy (C, p. 247). I sell my widgets for money that I then use to purchase food. For wage-workers, the sale of labor power enables the acquisition of necessities. Wage workers experience capitalism in a unique way. The worker sells labor power in exchange for wages that are used to purchase goods to satisfy their needs and wants. It is not that workers are necessarily underpaid, labor power is bought at its value, but that workers are overworked; the workday is prolonged beyond what is necessary for the reproduction of labor power. Capital is, then, the command over unpaid labor and not the exploitation of consumers with prices that are inflated over and beyond values (C, pp. 264, 266, 682). In reality, however, workers tend to be both negatively and positively (relatively and absolutely) exploited by being simultaneously underpaid and overworked and prices routinely run above actual values. In some times and places, workers can be worked to death and priced out of existence (C, p. 343). The theological fear of sinful waste (C, p. 303) results in the creation of a surplus and once we enter the kingdom of money as capital we have entered the domain of the absolute idea (C, pp. 205, 241) where the spirit of limitlessness (anomie) and the pursuit of infinity reigns supreme (C, p. 617; cf. Durkheim's analysis of "infinity disease" in *Suicide*).

Marx's theory of surplus value hinges on surplus labor (C, p. 353) but, as a reminder, labor is not labor power (C, p. 277) and labor is not itself value and value, an abstraction, a product of alienation, a non-physical effect (C, p. 725) of the capital relation, does not flow from the veins of concrete workers or machines. This is decisive. *If we wish to view the labor process as a value-creation process* we must shift from a concrete and qualitative register of production to an abstract and quantitative one (C, p. 302) that is external to production per se, that is, apply to it a "measuring rod" that is alien and external to its nature as utilities (see Marx, 1973[1857], p. 412 for the inverse expression). Even though value is embodied in carriers or bearers it is, itself, purely and collectively ideal (C, p. 190) and only *realized* or made socially *real* in the exchange relation (C, p. 177). On top of this layer of alienation, weirdly, the shift from labor to surplus labor, work to valorization, the transition from useable things to value and surplus value which, paradoxically, is merely the quantitative extension of the labor process, is obviously not simply a matter of "more of the same" even though, to the materialist eye, it can only appear to be "more of the same." The extension is one of quantity not quality yet the effect is itself qualitatively irreducible. In the chapter on the labor process and valorization we find the following distinction:

> Labor process—concrete/qualitative—useful products—prolongation yields surplus goods, worker exploitation and *brutalization* (reduction to subhuman, deformed brutes);

However, when we now look at this concrete process through the alien gaze of the "would-be capitalist" (C, p. 291) we find something altogether different:

> Valorization—abstract/quantitative—commodities—prolongation yields surplus goods bearing surplus value and the transformation of humans

(capitalists and workers) into *monstrosities* (capitalist society populated by vampires, werewolves, the living dead, and so on).

The labor process (concrete) may be viewed abstractly or rendered a one-sided abstraction and it is here that, suddenly, the labor process is viewed as a "value-creating process" (C, p. 302) but only through quantification and reduction from the concrete (real) to the abstract (symbolic and imaginary).

With Durkheim, we could say, surplus value is greater than and different than the sum of its parts (*sui generis*). Externally, of course, value and surplus value are indistinguishable but, internally, god-like value distinguishes between the two (C, p. 256) and this distinction, later absorbed within itself and made whole and indecipherable, is only possible from the critical and *objective* gaze if we take note of the *quantity–quality dialectic* at the center of Marx's sociological grasp of the commodity as a bearer of value: in the first breath of *Capital*, Marx says that things "may be looked at from the two points of view of quality and quantity" (C, p. 126). This is literally dialectics as "split reasoning." In a letter from 1870 to Kugelmann, Marx said, "… Lange is naïve enough to say that I 'move with rare freedom' in empirical matter. He has not the slightest idea that this 'free movement in matter' is nothing but a paraphrase for the *method* of dealing with matter—that is, the *dialectical method*" (Marx & Engels, 1988, p. 528). This image of moving through matter is really better grasped as moving freely between the material and the ideal and unraveling the fetish, separating out the abstract from the concrete, the ideal from the material, and demystifying the enigma of the commodity. While disenchanting the commodity, Marx relocates it from the domain of the alien *thing* to that of comprehensible *object* and, in so doing, places the commodity on the proper social ontological plane.

So-called historical or dialectical materialism—Marx himself never used either phrase—opens up the ground for *objective* sociological explanation that would otherwise fall back into simple materialism or fetishism where the world appears possessed by a transcendental powers (C, p. 302). For a tiny version of this dialectical method see Weber's "Science as a Vocation" (1946) where the quantity–quality polarity is explored, pointing a way toward something like vocational enjoyment and creative freedom within a bureaucratic and undemocratic setting.

True, with Durkheim, Marx would say that capital is a social fact (C, p. 381) in that the "laws" of capitalism are "coercive and external" to the individual (Weber says the same thing in his essay on the Protestant ethic) but positive human freedom cannot be achieved until consciousness is animated by the spirit of objective sociological insight where the invisible becomes visible (C, pp. 346, 147) and the commodity is disenchanted such that it is no longer a commodity at all but a free concrete satisfier of needs: it was always just us in our external, transfigured (alienated) form; we went too far, lost sight of things, fell in love with money, and became imprisoned in an enchanted cell of our own making (C, p. 187)—in Weberian–Marxist terms, the *iron cage of commodity fetishism*. Value as a substance is a *subject-substance* (C, pp. 255–256) and contingent upon a way of *treating and regarding* labor, products, and human exploitation (see Smith, 2016).

Recall that labor power is the special commodity that possesses the capacity, as it is consumed, to "produce" more "value" than it is worth (C, pp. 342, 679) because the limits of exploitability of labor power are not determined analytically or by nature (fixed) but normatively, variably, in terms of class struggle (C, p. 344). Workers can feel or intuit that they are being "screwed" by their employers but the labor contract and the fact they are paid not for labor performed but after the fact, renders the feelings incapable of rational expression. Another important aspect is that the mediator or middle term that vanishes (C, p. 187) in commodity circulation is not human life but the crystallized remains of abstract human life, money, rendering the shorthand expression C-C. Workers seek money and want as much as possible and what they fail to grasp is that, from the standpoint of the regime of accumulation, their concrete lives are the mediators that vanish. What Marx has, then, is really a theory of human sacrifice (C, pp. 354, 271) and contractual slavery (C, p. 416). We might represent the circulation of commodities, *from the standpoint of the lived experience of the worker*, in a slightly different manner. As a seller of labor power, I stand, with regard to my share of goods, in a relationship of moral deficiency (C'–C). Or, to say the same thing, as a seller of labor power, I stand in a relation of deficiency with regard to my share of purchased goods. But this representational innovation can be explored more fully at some later date. What is important now is that the fate of the mediator is different in the pursuit of surplus value through production for exchange.

We will now uncoil the general formula for capital (C, p. 247) until we arrive at the revelation of the organic composition of capital. In the "second volume" of *Capital*, Marx rolls this out from its most condensed and fetishized form (M–M') through a series of more elaborate representations:

$$M-C-M'$$
$$M-C \ldots C'-M'$$
$$M-C\ L/mp \ldots P \ldots C'-M'$$

We can bump the formula out a bit more until we arrive at the following:

$$M-C\ [MP + LP] \ldots P \ldots C'(C + \Delta C)-M'(M + \Delta M)$$

The terms take on a new meaning in the general formula in relation to commodity circulation (C, pp. 320 ff.): here, capital (M) purchases labor power (L) and means of production (mp) and puts them into motion in production, that is, the labor process (P) where a different mass of commodities (C' or, what is the same thing, C' = (c + v) + s) are sold and a surplus of value (M') is realized, out of which, after sundry expenses, a residue of profit will accrue to the capitalist. In this formulation, finally the dynamic relationship between living labor power and the means of production, the technical composition, comes into focus (C, p. 762). Here is the rub: the mediating moment, C, includes human life as a means to some alien end, surplus value—human life is sacrificed for the enjoyment of a class of elites. A voice from Weber's essay on the Protestant ethic regarding tallow out of cattle and money out of men rises in the background (2002[1905], p. 11). For theory, on the other hand, the problem is the moment of *devaluation* that should differentiate clearly and distinctly between twin ontic dimensions within the production and value realization processes is absent (at this point we cannot make a distinction between the technical and the value or organic composition of capital because they are intertwined). Marx saw clearly and early on that the eventual valuation of things came at the expense of the initial *devaluation* of human beings (1964[1844], p. 107). "When Marx says that other values are 'resolved into' exchange value, his point is that bourgeois society does not efface old structures of value but subsumes them" (Berman, 1988, p. 111). Once capitalism is "in the saddle" to use one of Weber's well-known sayings, all other values persist only as "as residual temptations, which ... prove unsatisfying and frustrating" (Jameson, 1991, p. 144). But as things stand in the above expression from volume two of *Capital*, we cannot move beyond, for example, a distinction between, say, the totemic ritual creation of mana and modern commodity production—we could construct a perfectly adequate representation of totemic ritual that follows closely the contours of Marx's diagram because, at this level, we are dealing with completely generic forms of human practice linked by the concept of consubstantiality. Totems and commodities are clearly anthropological and sociological analogs of one another, from the standpoint of mystified consciousness, but without the breaching and decompression offered by the *devaluation* moment we fall into a closed loop where value is hypostatized as a material substance flowing from the veins of laborers and machines. Nothing is dumber than the view that finds commodities making more commodities. What is required is not a fetish *splitting* of the general formula but a dialectical *objectification* of the general formula such that an infraliminal moment, the profane and concrete (technical) ground of *non-value*, is separated and differentiated from the spectral and spiritual domain of value as it eventually takes possession of material transformed into creators and carriers of value. The "access to truth is by way of the profane" (Kracauer, 1995, p. 201). There is a fear that critical negation can be carried so far that it dissolves everything to the point of nothingness (Goldmann, 1976, p. 138), but, fear not intrepid theorists, one can criticize the commodity and capitalism until pigs fly and there will still be plenty of "facticity" leftover. We are only following Marx when, for example, in his chapter on the labor process and valorization, the commodity, and in mapping the general law of accumulation, and so on, by continuously dividing (*diairesis*) the problem, shifting his gaze back and forth from the analytic singular to the synthetic universal, from the concrete to the abstract, from reality to the fetish-inverted *reflection*, from the "Teutonic" to the "Romantic"; here is what is really going on and, now, with a weird gaze, here is what the capitalist (and some—a lot—of Marxists) imagine to be going on. As Lenin says, "If Marx did not leave behind a '*Logic*'... he did leave the *logic of Capital*..." (in Althusser, 1969, p. 175). If no infraliminal dimension can be analytically carved out within the capitalist system of "commodity production" via the dialectical gaze (that keeps both the dimensions of the singular and the universal rigorously separated, opening up the possibility of an objective third, particular gaze within the conceptual and theoretical constellation that we construct), we would capitulate to the full totalization and infinitizing of the capitalist absolute and we would be powerless to negate the infinite. The "dialectical method" represents the capacity to transform the social fact from thing into object, in other words, grasp its constructed nature within the sociogony. Correct intellectual grasp is only a first precondition for change, but it is necessary if insufficient. It is true that we as individuals cannot simply wish away capitalism by thinking about it differently, this was the take-away from the 2015 New Directions in Critical Social Theory symposium at Iowa State University, yet all social facts can be dissolved (and eventually will) through changes in not only material conditions but also collective consciousness, the way we regard and treat things, and the way we act and feel on those changes. Recall that marijuana, not too many decades ago, possessed the occult capacity to transform America's youth into homosexual communists and, within no more than a couple of generations, the plant has emerged from its previous status as a dark commodity carrying impure value into the sphere of low-class bourgeois markets. Notice the opposite trajectory for ivory: once legally traded, Kenya has taken the radical step to destroy its 105 tons of confiscated ivory stock (in contrast to Botswana which turns illegal ivory into public art) as a bid to symbolically demonstrate that ivory *no longer has value*. Botswana transposes the romance of ivory into the sphere of public aesthetics whereas Kenya disenchants it entirely.

## REMAPPING THE GENERAL FORMULA FOR CAPITALISM

Having already reviewed the progression of simplest expression (M-M') to the most complex form presented by Marx we can proceed to work out a more sociologically elaborate and precise model of the general formula to specify the exact coordinates of value as a real social substance and better articulate the function and coordinates of alienation in its various modalities (Fig 4.1).

The initial moment, here, is the devaluation (d) of commodities as they are purchased and enter the production process as a mass of utilities to be consumed in the production process (up) or simply a devalued mass of people, materials, and machines (Marx, 1973[1857], p. 403). Marx does have a category of *not-value* for a reason (1973[1857], p. 403). Devaluation, at this point, will mean that things bought and put to use (means of production or labor power) are no longer values but merely utilities (do not take this term too far!) to be consumed in the labor process. Once bought, a thing falls into the infraliminal dimension of the Real of use and transformation. Anyone who believes that a thing retains value after the exchange moment is guilty of (a) mystified value reification of the kind we find in ordinary realism or (b) psychological fetishism of the kind we find in infantile-savage magical thinking.

If the commodity is exchanged via money for another commodity [C-M-C], then its value-character disappears in the moment in which it

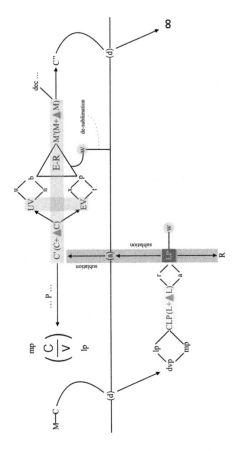

**Fig 4.1** The new general formula

realizes itself, and it steps outside the relation, becomes irrelevant to it, merely the direct object of a need. If money is exchanged for a commodity [M-C], then even the disappearance of the form of exchange is posited; the form is posited as a merely formal mediation for the purpose of gaining possession of the natural material of the commodity. "If a commodity is exchanged for money [C-M], then the form of exchange value, exchange value posited as exchange value, money, persists only as long as it stays outside exchange, withdraws from it, is hence a purely illusory realization, purely ideal in this form, in which the independence of exchange value leads a tangible existence" (Marx, 1973[1857], p. 260). To conceive of something *persisting* as a value once it falls out of the exchange relation (and denying that its little "soul" went to "heaven" leaving behind only its husk) is to fall prey to a superstitious form of thought that sees value where it is not—this is the presupposed and *posited* "value-in-process" (Marx, 1973[1857], p. 536) illusion that Marxist realism shares with the capitalist class for whom moral substances transcend society itself (they are all transcendentalists). It must be remembered that, as Marx puts it, the self-valorization process is only an *appearance* (1981[1894], p. 358) in that it appears to be an autonomous, self-moving system. In Hegelian terms, here, both the capitalist and the Marxist share an unethical will to perversion for the enjoyment of being-for-self. The flip side of this paradigmatic form is transcendental idealism that much, if not most, of Marxology shares with Kant and Christian theology. In the era of transcendentalism, the sublime was that which could bring the soul to the threshold of the inaccessible but, after Hegel, who brought heaven down to earth, the sublime was identical with refined, multi-modal expressions of moral surplus. Today, in the era of consumer capital, every human being (or, really, everyone being human) has formal access to the sublime, just as Christianity extended souls to those who lacked bodies (Mauss, 1979, p. 81). The infraliminal, in contrast to the supraliminal, is mere profanity, the real of "worthless" sweat and toil that culminates in useful objects. Things in the production process are imagined by ordinary consciousness as values, and they certainly are value-able, that is, able *to be* values *again* (why else purchase labor power and means of production?) if and when it were to reenter an *exchange relation*, but, sociologically, once a thing *falls out* (Marx's expression) of the exchange relation and into the infernal domain of use it is *merely profane*. A former commodity that finds itself in the labor process has to continuously ask the question: to be a value (the commodity of the future) or not to be (waste) but it never is a value *after* the moment of devaluation and *before* alienation that *retroactively posits* the thing as a sublimity. Again, this does not prevent *ordinary* consciousness, capitalists, accountants, priests, and Marxologists, from valuing and evaluating things *as if* they were *always already* values. It should not be difficult to see that the capitalist viewpoint is an expansion upon this logic whereby everything that comes in and goes out of the labor process was always and already conceived ideally as being value for the sake of value. This is nothing less than magical thinking where the ideal connections and operations are confused for the real connections and operations (Freud, 1950[1913], p. 104). "The *lie* of the ideal has so far been the curse on reality; on account of it, mankind itself has become mendacious and false down to its most fundamental instincts—to the point of worshiping the *opposite* values of those which alone would guarantee its health, its future, the lofty *right* to its future" (Nietzsche, 1967a, p. 218). Again and again, if we wish to free consciousness from the alien gaze imposed upon us by capital, the eye that sees value everywhere, then we have to puncture that delusion with the objective gaze—that negative, synthesizing theoretical *particularity* that can grasp the singularity of use and the universality of value in whatever form it assumes. Here is the crux of the problem: Marxism claims to approach the commodity from a dialectical perspective, however, what we find, time and time again, is the kind of realism that we should find from the standpoint of the particular equivalent, the alter ego of the singular relative: the value is identical with the physical existence of the thing (Hegel, 1991[1821], p. 79), but Marx's actual dialectical method is radically different because, while approaching the commodity from the coordinates of particularity it divides the commodity into its dual aspects and does not conflate value with its material expression. Capitalists "treat their products as commodities" (C, p. 172) but critical theory should not, otherwise, we will never arrive at the necessary unveiling of the irrational forms associated with commodification (C, p. 173). The royalists treat the king as royalty but the anti-royalist should treat the king like trash. But when the the commodity comes down the street, Marxists knee-benders genuflect like everybody else. Christianity and capitalism already form a fully developed "cult of man in the abstract" (C, p. 172); the goal is not more abstraction but a new 'cult of man' in the *concrete* (Durkheim) but we cannot arrive at this cult of the concrete if we replicate the presuppositions of vulgar economics or pseudo-critical economism. From this point in the model, from utilities for production or useful products (up) to the emergence of the labor product (LP), everything runs according to convention until we arrive at the octagonal structure of the commodity (the negative heaven of the commodity world).

Means of production (mp) and labor power (lp) are fused in the concrete labor process (CLP) yielding labor products (LP). Here is where we find "value creation" if and only if we shift perspective from the concrete to the abstract. Recall, value is a form of collective thought, a way of treating and regarding things, not an atom of matter enters into this "supra-natural" (C, p. 149) stuff as value (C, p. 138), so it is a fetish form of consciousness that imagines things like value *transference* from machines and people to concrete goods. The value of a commodity is not *in* the material commodity; the *bearer*, as we will come to see, functions as an *activated mirror* that masks a social relationship between people (C, pp. 148–150).

When "value creation" (from the standpoint of the pervert's gaze) is extended beyond what is necessary for the reproduction of labor power, we find ourselves pushed along the continuum from abstraction and impersonality into another register where, and this is important, alienation is pushed so far (compounded) that the impersonal and abstract is transformed into the monstrous and chimerical. It is little wonder that Marx reveled in the monstrous deformities of the proletariat (1964[1844], p. 121; Worrell, 2008, pp. 1–4) because exploitation pushed to the maximum resulted in the creation of the personified Revolution capable of overthrowing the prevailing regime of capital accumulation (Marx & Engels, 1972, p. 344). Collective repression, in other words, resulted in a "return of the repressed" in the form, not of workers, but a revolutionary and unstoppable Thing. This *monsterization process* is empirically verifiable except for the fact that the corresponding "revolutionary" *product*, The Worker of Marxist orthodoxy was a myth, as the Frankfurt School discovered repeatedly and to its dismay (Worrell, 2008). The emergent Thing was the ground upon which Nazism, fascism, antisemitism, totalitarianism, and various and sundry forms of authoritarianism drip from the meat grinder of capitalism.

"Valorization" is, as we saw earlier, a tricky concept because, of course, unless we adopt a "savage" gaze, any surplus value "created" here in the *intensification* or *prolongation* of the workday, relatively and absolutely (r + a), beyond what is necessary for the rejuvenation of labor power, is imaginary and anticipatory. Let us recall that workers engage in concrete labor only. Concrete labor is real whereas we can never find "abstract" labor in reality. Marx makes this plain: *abstract labor is not real* (1981[1894],

p. 954) but a "perverted" and mystified way of *regarding* labor in thought (Marx, 1970[1859], p. 49) and the transformation of the real through calculations and abstractions; abstract labor, the substance of value, is an imaginary form of real, concrete labor (Marx, 1970[1859], pp. 69–70). The attempt to maintain an ordinary realist perspective (in contrast to the sociological realist form of Marx) has led thinkers off into the most twisted and comic formulations, completely estranged, by the way, from Marx's text, such as, and this is my favorite: the socially totalized and interdependent and self-mediating categorically instrumental and generally compulsive and historically determinate theory of abstract labor. Abstract labor must be some kind of *thing* that we can get our hands on, we are told, because thoughts and ways of thinking exist only in the minds of *individuals*. The attempt to avoid psychological reductionism (and, no doubt, we must avoid that) leads off into these absurd notions because what all but a few Marxists have realized is that collective consciousness (social) is not reducible to consciousness (individual)—Marxists generally do not have a sociological grasp of collective consciousness, therefore, if value is, as Marx says, purely ideal, they conclude that because consciousness is only in the brains of individuals, there must be some non-ideal supplement that accompanies the form of thought. This problem of collective consciousness is one that completely eluded Durkheim's critics and also the breaking point that separates the mature, sociological Marx from his regressive followers; the problem revolves around the concept of the *externality* of something like value (C, p. 381; Marx, 1964[1844], pp. 168–169; Marx, 1981[1894], p. 953).

The externality (C, p. 381) of social facts means, among other things, that they are experienced by individuals as preexisting, objective realities as opposed to merely subjective realities.

> There is no principle for which we have received more criticism; but none is more fundamental. Indubitably for sociology to be possible, it must above all have an object all its own. It must take cognizance of a reality which is not in the domain of other sciences. But if no reality exists outside of individual consciousness, it wholly lacks any material of its own. In that case, the only possible subject of observation is the mental states of the individual, since nothing else exists (Durkheim, 1951[1897], pp. 37–38).

Note well the language deployed by Durkheim: "individual consciousness" in contrast to consciousness per se. The reality "outside" of *individual* consciousness is located in *collective* consciousness, which is a separate but connected system of consciousness within the mind of the individual (we have one brain and at least two minds generally in conflict with one another). Hegel holds the same basic assumptions; with regards to, in this case, deities (collective representations in contrast to the representations peculiar to a given individual) he said:

> I may have ideas of objects which are wholly fictitious and fanciful; what constitutes the idea here is in such a case my own, but only my own; it exists merely as an idea; I am at the same time aware that the content here has no existence. In dreams, too, I exist as consciousness, I have objects in my mind, but they have no existence. But we so conceive of the consciousness of God that the content is our idea, and at the same time exists; that is, the content is not merely mine, is not merely in the subject, in myself, in my idea and knowledge, but has an absolute existence of its own, exists in and for itself. This is essentially involved in the content itself in this case. God is this Universality which has an absolute [i.e., moral or social] existence of its own, and does not exist merely for me; it is outside of me, independent of me. There are thus two points bound up together here. This content is at once independent and at the same time inseparable from me; that is, it is mine, and yet it is just as much not mine (1974[1840], p. 116).

The standard and erroneous criticism against this notion of externality is that a thing cannot be known while simultaneously being outside the mind. Again, being outside "individual consciousness" is not identical with being outside consciousness or the mind of the individual. Some representation being "external" to the mind of the individual has to be grasped with the etymology of the term; external comes from the Latin *exterus* which means that a thing is *foreign*. It is a mistake to think of things as being merely external when, in fact, what people do is externalize thoughts and representations such that their own thoughts return in the form of alien commands and powers. The vulgar materialist view is responsible for mistaking objective and external for exterior, over and against a receptor of sensations (Durkheim, 1951[1897], pp. 313, 315). Externality is better thought of as "consecrated" (p. 314) and, as such, a force that is difficult to evade, though, some do in fact evade it as nonbinding (pp. 316–317). Jones indicates that, for Durkheim, externality refers to a "logical point, and does not mean" that a fact is "literally outside of as external in the sense of the material world" though it does not exclude external materialization (Jones, 2001, p. 138; Durkheim,

1951[1897], pp. 314–315; Boutroux, 1914, pp. 198 ff.). This has less to do, I think, with a "logical" point per se, and more to do with plain old psychology and morality (Durkheim, 1982, p. 41). Social categories "do not present themselves to the individual consciousness so much as logical necessities but as moral necessities" (Degré, 1985, p. 88).

In simple terms we have conflicts between the currents of thought and we are disturbed by the experience of a thing or some Other bearing down on us "as if" it were an autonomous reality existing somewhere outside of our minds. "We say for instance that 'the group says,' 'the group feels,' 'the group thinks.' But these are all psychological activities that actually pertain only to individual human beings ... [T]he group has no brain" (Harding, 1947, pp. 47–48). No doubt, there is no such thing as a group brain, however, for a thing to be in *consciousness* is less a personal experience and more collective:

> My idea is ... that consciousness does not really belong to man's individual existence but rather to his social or herd nature ... Our thoughts themselves are continually governed by the character of consciousness—by the 'genius of the species' that commands it—and translated back into the perspective of the herd. Fundamentally, all our actions are altogether incomparably personal, unique, and infinitely individual; there is no doubt of that. But as soon as we translate them into consciousness *they no longer seem to be* (Nietzsche, 1974[1887], p. 299).

Of course, as Kant and others suspected, there is a real out there, over and against us, but we do not have access to something as an experience outside of thought (good luck, speculative realism). The words on this page appear to be physical marks out in front of the reader but the *experience* is based on a constructed image in the mind. Likewise with music. "We say of course that music 'addresses itself to the ear'; but it does so only in a qualified way, only in so far, namely, as the hearing, like the other senses, is the deputy, the instrument, and the receiver of the mind" (Mann, 1948, p. 61). The metaphors are, admittedly, crude but still get the point across. This insight does not lead to idealism nor to psychology but to the weirder domain of sociology (what Durkheim called *collective* psychology) where matter is imagined to be intertwined with spirit and where minds are multiple.

In terms of basic psychology, the formulations by Kant and Freud sharpen our understanding of how something that is constructed in the mind can *appear* to be going on *outside* of the mind (Durkheim,

1995[1912], p. 369), hovering over us, to use Kant's imagery. Two aspects should to be delineated here: one, love is the condition whereby the ego blends with the external world; the biophilic character (Fromm, 1973) or Sartre's "starfish world" (Sartre, 1948, p. 56) is one of omnierotic, Whitmanesque love for the totality of existence; a non–diseased society populated by well-adjusted individuals would not be experienced as a system of alien and dominating entities on the part of its members. Secondly, we need to avoid the notion of some transcendental ego or centralized group mind, which is made all the more difficult when Durkheim says, following Post, that "it is not we who think, but the world which thinks in us" (1982, p. 201). This is simply a way of presenting the idea that the self is, in addition to a "me" also a "we" (Durkheim, 1973, p. 13) submerged in the "organic" totality of life. "It was not *he* who was thinking of the insurrection, it was the insurrection, living in so many brains like sleep in so many others, which weighed upon him to such a point that there was nothing left in him but anxiety and expectation" (Malraux, 1961, p. 41).

If we wish to adhere closely to Marx's actual text we find that abstract labor is neither material nor transcendental but concrete labor without regard for particularity, reduced through calculation, to an abstraction. The abstraction process is not a mystery and Marx is consistent in his portrayal of abstract labor as a form of thought: disregarding, reduction, positing, representation, abstraction, quantification, identification, "purely ideal," etc. (C, pp. 134–150, 190). My qualitative work is reduced, in thought and in practice, to a quantum of time and that is not a way of thinking peculiar to this or that capitalist but to everybody trapped in the capitalist system, it is collective consciousness, a fact of life. A concept like valorization falls on the side of abstraction; valorization is, quantitatively, not really "surplus labor" per se (in the sense of excess concrete labor) but surplus *abstracted* labor from a retrospective or anticipatory vantage point. Imagine widgets going to waste within the production process—if they fail to materialize later within the exchange moment (the realization of value) they never had any value, they were never crystals of value. But, again, the important thing here is that value is not, and never really was, located within the infraliminal dimension of production. Marx makes this plain: production is not the realization of value (C, p. 137); the technical composition of production is not identical with the reflected value composition (C, p. 762). Production is the derealization of the worker and the emergence of the labor product (1964[1844], p. 108). I may valorize my product but it is not, yet, value in the same way that I may Simoniz my automobile, yet, it is not yet Simon. Or maybe it is not just like that. Anyways, Marxism has (or should have) no interest whatsoever in sharing the presuppositions and prejudices of the capitalist class—unless, of course, it *secretly desires to itself become a capitalist class*: "under new management." The propensity to see value here is due to the alienation (a) of the labor product (LP) that *retroactively* alters the way consciousness perceives the labor product. Alienation, the dispossession, displacement, conceptual abstraction, calculations, and quantifications transform a labor product in consciousness into a commodity. This is why this precise aspect of alienation (a) is conceptually located on the boundary between the sacred and the profane. Alienation is the entry point into the moral sphere where people and things enjoy a pseudo-transcendental existence as things greater than and different than the sum of their parts, in short, sublimity arrived at through sublation. Alienation, then, is the multi-faceted "mechanism" of negation where *the entire infraliminal domain is canceled upward into its weirdly distorted reflection and enchantment*. It is crucial for us to keep in mind that the process of *aufheben* is actually different than what we usually hear from Marxists.

Following Zizek, *aufheben* or "sublation" does not leave anything behind (the repressed always returns, to follow Freud on this point). The aspects that are negated or canceled are preserved in the subsequent moment of transcendence, in weird and uncanny forms. It is not the case that just the desired aspects are preserved but that all the negations are also preserved in the ocular shift from the infraliminal to the supraliminal; hence, once we arrive at C' (c + v) + s, we find both forward motion into the exchange relation and a *retroactive reconstruction* of the dynamic relation between labor power and means of production into the *organic* or *value* composition of capital expressed (in an *inverted* form) as C over V whereby C stands for constant capital and V signifies variable capital. The whole thing can be summed up in the phrase "production for exchange" and the bourgeois drive to realize surplus value. Simply put, labor power and means of production (the technical composition) are sublated into their new perverted social forms as values. They have returned in new, twisted, and uncanny forms. According to the marketing perverts at General Electric, for example, the firm's commitment to their employees is expressed in its investments in "human capital." People are forced to sell all they have remaining, their time, physical energy, and ability to labor, and reappear in the labor process as flexible blobs of variably exploitable capital. Human life as a unique form of being (lacking instincts) dooms them to an historically unique transition into non-being—human death in the capitalist regime of accumulation means the slow motion murder of life into commodities. Because they live in *this* odd manner, they are doomed (cf. Foucault, 1970, p. 278). Now we can clearly grasp why both capitalists and anti-capitalists see value where it is not: both gazes (capital and anti-capital) suffer from anamorphotic distortion created by the "gravitational" effect of the commodity (see Zizek on the anamorphotic blot). Capitalists and anti-capitalists both suffer from a surplus of desire, in other words. The anti-capitalist is the return of the capitalist repressed, the undead counterpart of the capitalist monster. Where critique should aim for the comprehension that "this is just us" and we do not have to treat and regard these things as values, Marxism and capitalism both express a desire for *acquisition*. If they were anthropologists, the run of the mill Marxists would confuse alienated collective effervescence for mana: "Yes, these ritualists really have conjured up an angry proto-god! Put a bag over its head and make haste for the boat." If nothing else, at least the racist European anthropologists of the past could see plainly that the totem was nothing more than a coconut. The neoliberals (and anti-neoliberals) of today, in contrast, valorize the cultural heritage of the sacred coconut and, not only for what it means to the few leftover coconut worshipers hawking souvenirs, but what it means to us as former racist enslavers who denigrated the sacred coconut as nothing more than a nut. There is the contradiction of the pseudo-sanctity of neoliberal capitalism: in celebrating the value of cultural products, the alienated surplus, the producers themselves, past and present, are rendered worthless. *Where there is valuation there is devaluation, its precondition.* The subversion of capital will be possible not when we are capable of treating people like worthless trash, we already do that, but when we are willing to treat our products as valueless. Ironically, every Marxist I know has a mania for recycling—the return of the living dead, nothing is permitted to simply go to waste. Celebration of production, the product, productivity, and so on amounts to the veneration of the alien and the obscene, the abominable, that which takes us away from the human being. Capitalism and the capitalized psyche confuses production for creation and genesis.

Once the whole infraliminal apparatus is "thrown up" into the sublime dimension, all the material and concrete aspects are intertwined and infused with the moral and abstract. We are now in the domain of entanglement and "possessed" matter: machines and people are imagined to be and treated as if they were forms of capital, products are treated like gods, and value is made real in the exchange relation where the thing meets its maker, money, and its personification. The commodity, as we know, has a dual aspect: (a) the concrete and qualitative use-value or utility and (b) the exchange-value or value that the thing represents. Concrete labor produces the utility and the value of the thing results from the abstraction of labor and its presence in the exchange relation. What I want to do now is explode further this double aspect to reveal the eight-sided structure of the commodity.

On the side of "use-value" or utility (UV) we can divide its utility into use (u) and non-use (n) or use and uselessness—if we want, use-value and uselessness-value: obviously, as a consumer with needs, the thing has a use but as a producer of the thing I am prohibited from using, say, my widget if I would like to ultimately exchange it for money. The moment of bearer (b) represents the unification of the built-in contradiction of (u) and (n). A bearer (or carrier, prop, envelope, raft, etc.) is simultaneously a use and non-use of the thing or a transformation of the body into a possessed bearer or carrier function. When we talk about the commodity as a "bearer," we have to keep both paradoxically opposed functions in mind. On the side of pure abstraction, exchange-value (EV) we simply demarcate the twin moments of abstract labor (x) or the *subject-substance* and the socially necessary quantity of labor time (t) or *magnitude* the thing represents in the mind of the alienator. Price (p) unifies both (x) and (t) but is identical with neither. Prices fluctuate around values and, in extraordinary circumstances or in generalized bamboozling, there may be prices with no underlying values, or the pricing of other forms of authority.

The realization of the value of the commodity, and, yes, here we have actual commodities and value, is found only in the *realizing* exchange relation, the necessary mode of expression of value. All the weird contradictions of the commodity, being a use and useless, being physical and nominal, wearing a price, and so on are overcome in circulation via duplication and polar opposition (Marx, 1970[1859], pp. 89–90). Yet the price attached to the bearer is only a claim (Marx, 1970[1859], p. 69) being made and a casting of "wooing glances" on the part of the "narcissistic" commodity. What is important is that the commodity has to be *recognized* by a buyer and thereby retroactively esteemed as a real value. The realization moment is a flash: before the actual sale the value is only a might be, it is not yet redeemed and, as soon as the thing is bought, it undergoes a *social* devaluation and falls back into the profane dimension of use and *personal* psychological fantasies (the imaginary prolongation of value beyond the exchange relation). Where was the value, really, in all this? The value of a thing is a flash in the pan, the duration of the transaction—not because the exchange relation per se makes things into values, no, but the exchange relation is the only coordinate within the entire process in which the value is *realized*. Of course, for the capitalist, the poor devils who sell their labor power to the capitalist, the consumer, and, unfortunately, the few remaining Marxological critics of the system, value was *always, already present* from the beginning and enduring, like the Revolution, into the furthest temporal horizon. As Weber would say, as far as individuals go, it is an immense cosmos and unalterable order. And that insight, the facticity of the commodity and the omnipresence of value, is *true*, from the standpoint of capitalist abstractions and bourgeois ideology and law—it is common sense. Yet, that truth, the facticity of the commodity and the *practical* transcendental reality of value, leaves no way out except waiting around for the imaginary revolutionary proletariat that will never arrive or hope that a catastrophe brings capitalism to its knees, as if capitalism does not engineer its own catastrophes for its own purposes. The other Marxist myth is that the contradictions of capitalism leads automatically and inexorably toward self-destruction when, in fact, capitalism creates, lives off of, and even thrives on crises. Capitalism does not just eat crises for breakfast it is itself an unfolding crisis just as Marxism is constantly in a state of crisis (see, e.g., Korsch, 1970, pp. 53ff.) where it undergoes reclamations and deeper or closer readings that lead in circles of realist misapprehension. Global warming and climate change do not spell the end of capitalism; there are trillions of dollars to be made off of climate change. Every disaster or setback is like an energetic bounce to ever-higher levels of accumulation. And, the notion that the spontaneous and radical *event* can be staged at decisive moments, before capital can react, bringing capital to its knees, is completely negated by capital's social media and big data capacity to know, keystroke by keystroke, what the event is doing before the event knows what it is doing. Trust me, as soon as you hear of an Event there will a T-shirt available for $19.99 to commemorate your participation. How does one resist? If one does not want to read Marx, then read Nietzsche and Whitman. Stop cooperating with your masters (Nietzsche) and form a new concrete and biophilic brotherhood (Whitman) rather than dreaming of class struggle and social cataclysm. And if you cannot read, just do what most people do and steal the stuff (material and time) you need to live.

Where to attack: the entire process can be short-circuited at various points. In our diagram, if the repressed remainders (R) can be prevented from returning (the Freudian uncanny) defetishization would be automatic. The emergence of a moral surplus in the sublime depends, from the beginning, upon excessive labor, appropriation, and quantification. The first moment of alienation after the creation of the labor product is decisive; appropriation is the separation of the producer from the product, the setting of a thing apart and, consequently, the transformation of a thing into a Thing of alien proportions and capacities (1964[1844], p. 108) that is not unlike the taboo quality of anything that is *set aside* as forbidden in the realm of religion and magic. At all the moments of waste (w) the theft and losses inflicted upon workers can be reclaimed. In other words, if alienation involves appropriation and dispossession, *repossession* short-circuits commodification and would-be values remain at the infra-liminal level of use and free distribution. This goes on all day long but in a primarily non-systematic and unorganized manner.

## Material Repossession

Reich once said that what had to be accounted for was "not the fact that the man who is hungry steals or the fact that the man who is exploited strikes, but why the majority of those who are hungry *don't* steal and why the majority of those who are exploited *don't* strike" (1970, p. 19). However, the amount of disorganized stealing and striking taking place is impressive. Roughly 75 percent of employees "steal" (take back what was theirs already) from their employers and that is not an insignificant fact (CrimethInc, 2001, p. 275). Obviously, millions of employees have an intuition that what they produced was actually theirs, a product of their efforts, and that even if it is illegal they should repossess it for themselves. And millions engage in "time theft," wasting as many hours as they can get away with. Leftist professors might recoil from the image of the criminal but "'Even the criminal thought of a villain is greater and more sublime than all the wonders of heaven'" (Hegel, handed down by Marx via Lafargue, in Lukács, 1978a, p. 33). "The artist is the brother of the criminal..." (Mann, 1948, p. 236). Indeed, the criminal participates in the sublime by virtue of violating taboo (the criminal is invested with a quantum of the impure or negative sacred). "In the darkest region of the political field the condemned man [the criminal] represents the symmetrical, inverted figure of the king" (Foucault, 1977, p. 29; on the analogous refuse-saint identity, see Badiou, 2003, p. 56). Crime, then, should not be dismissed as irrelevant to liberation, after all, the good (and the legal) is, as the old saying goes, just the evil we choose to ignore. Durkheim was at pains to make this point: we do not throw people into prison because they are criminals per se, but, rather, they are "criminals" because we throw them into prison (1984[1893], p. 40). Law is molded like clay by the servants of the bourgeois class for the benefits of the elite (London, 2006[1908], pp. 37–47, 59). While few criminals are revolutionaries, *all revolutionaries are criminals*. Who was Jesus but a criminal on the cross (Nietzsche, 1967b p. 99). "Socrates and Christ broke with their times. They did not simply formulate necessary developments of world history; they were considered criminals in the eyes of their society" (Strong, 1988, p. 109).

> Of course, stealing hardly levels the playing field. The higher your social position, the better your opportunities are to steal and the less danger you're in if you get caught. Steal five bucks, go to jail—steal five million, go to Congress. Yet the worse off you are, the harder it is to make ends meet without stealing … If you don't steal from your boss you're stealing from your family (CrimethInc, 2001, pp. 276–277).

Obviously, millions of people are not only wishing for free things but acting upon those desires and while stealing does not come close to equilibrating inequality the redistribution of billions of dollars worth of goods every year is nonetheless significant. If the purchase of a single commodity is a reaffirmation of the whole commodity system than the theft of even a single product or hour is a rejection of the entire system (CrimethInc, 2001; see also CrimethInc, 2011). When a state hysterically subjects petty thieves to decades of incarceration for the loss of no more than a few dollars worth of goods (three strikes and you're out) we should interpret this as a prime weakness in the system. The whole capitalist system of class exploitation actually leaks like a sieve. The World Health Organization recently estimated that anxiety and depression result in one trillion dollars worth of lost annual global productivity; billions are lost annually in the United States to theft and workers routinely deprive their employers of time and energy, means of production, and finished goods.

More than 20 years ago, one of my coworkers was fired for stealing a couple of ounces of dehydrated cheese powder from a Kraft plant in Springfield, Missouri where macaroni and cheese was made. Firing a worker for the theft of two ounces of powder (from a 2200-pound-per-hour flow) is ridiculous until you realize that, from the standpoint of management, any problem can be dealt with (food poisoning, broken machines, waste, etc.), but the one thing that keeps managers up at night is the worry that sellable product is leaving the facility through the back door. I saw workers accidentally ruin tens of thousands of dollars worth of product yet were not fired. It happens. I personally drove a forklift right through a wall and accidentally ruined all kinds of tools, machinery, and product and was not fired or even reprimanded. At worst, I received "the look." I was caught sunbathing while on the clock yet nothing was said even though my supervisor did not like me because, as he put it, I was a "talker" and a "trouble maker." Yet, the theft of two ounces of product was the line that could not be crossed for employees. Ironically, some operators (including myself most nights) would go home with so much cheese embedded in their uniforms they looked like walking cheese puffs but that was different than putting a much smaller quantity of cheese powder in a bag for consumption later. While I worked at the Kraft industrial plant, the third shift supervisor was fired after stealing a lawn mower and assorted other items for use on his farm (cheese for hogs, as a reminder this was Missouri). This was the same person who previously chased one of his employees around the plant with a *handgun* but was not dismissed (or arrested). But steal anything and a line has been crossed.

Basically, anything that is, was, or could again one day ascend to the commodity realm is of greater moral significance than the human being—which ought to tell us a great deal about the value of unskilled or easily trained labor power. If our cheese thief had been one of the two people on our shift with the knowledge to operate either the cook room or the drying machinery he would not have been fired or even reprimanded. One of my coworkers was a man named Jim who, though he did not know it, was one of only a few people in the United States with the skill to run the drying room at Kraft. Basically, it would have taken the solidarity of less than a half dozen men to shut down half the cheese powder production in North America—they could have demanded the moon and Kraft would have been forced to pay them. The machinery was dilapidated and the instrumentation in the control room was little more than a quasi derelict enigma; the entire process boiled down to the intuition, feel, and the experience of the operator. When job engineers from the main plant inspected our facility and asked Jim questions about moisture content and, instead, received a demonstration on what good cheese "feels like" a look of horror spread across their faces. The happiness of America's kids and Kraft profits depended on Jim and just a few other men—they could have had all the lawnmowers and cheese they wanted and Kraft would have not only been powerless to stop them but would have probably loaded their trucks for them. Here, knowledge really was power because, like myself, people *without* years of training and experience with the drying machinery would last, perhaps, 15 or 20 minutes at best before the whole thing turned into mayhem with showers of orange sauce raining down from above; one wrong move would necessitate at least a four-hour shutdown of the entire operation and a full cleaning of the system which also meant, in all likelihood, shutdown of the cook room as well when they ran out of chilled storage tanks. But Jim was a redneck Presbyterian which meant that he liked to work hard and, due to his conscientiousness and skills, Jim, though he did not know it, could look forward to a long career of high-wage, full-time employment with benefits because he was simply irreplaceable. Unfortunately, most workers are not in possession of irreplaceable skills so demanding the moon is less likely than stealing an ounce or two of cheese.

Who knows if theft and reappropriation is the road to freedom but somewhere between the 75 percent of employees and consumers taking back some portion of their product to the limit of 100 percent of employees and consumers repossessing all of their product and the means of producing it lies the breaking point where capitalism can no longer function. The life of petty crime, however, is not for everyone.

> A mind sufficiently refined as to be moved more by the form than the matter of things and, without any reference to possession, to experience disinterested pleasure in sheer reflection upon the mode of their appearance—such a mind contains within itself an inner irrepressible fullness of life, and since it does not need to appropriate to itself those objects in which it lives, neither is it in danger of being despoiled by them. (Schiller, 1966, p. 196)

Here we find a connection between the criminal and the refined product of the moral sciences in concept of resignation: for the criminal, lack is necessity and the pilfering of goods is the repossession of not only lost calories and so on, but also the reclamation of "value" lost to the world of employment, underemployment, and unemployment. If a person is to have values he or she will have to work for them, steal them, or beg for them (the capitalist system offers few options: work, suck, or die). For the type that wear fancy pants, on the other hand, the destruction of hostile forces is achieved through voluntary reconciliation with reality (Schiller, 1966, p. 195). However, the vast majority of reconcilers are just well-compensated and docile tools of the system (professionals) while a few have an actual *profession* and spiritual task that, unlike the ordinary professional and "privileged hirelings of the state" (Weber, 1946, p. 153), entails, at least potentially, a transvaluation of values completely out of harmony with the values created within the capitalist system.

## The "Calling"

Since the beginning of modernity a central problem has been how to reconcile service, sympathetic association, and individuality. Devotion to one's particular calling unifies the necessity to serve and "sway" with others (Shakespeare, 1973, p. 41) while developing actual individuality with its own particular and singular values. Here the person with the calling and the criminal renegade may overlap. Unlike ordinary criminals who want things because they are valuable, true revolutionaries are criminals who fail to *recognize* the value of things. Again, it is worth returning to Marx's early insight that the precondition for the valorization of things on their way to becoming commodities is the devaluation of human life.

Surplus value (M') is, in essence, not merely excessive human labor in the abstract but the manifestation of human degradation, the lack of dignity for men and women who sell their time and energies, the lack of justice and solidarity, egoistic indifference, and so on. In short, the creation of relative and absolute quantities of surplus value are simultaneously objectifications of anomie (deregulation or bourgeois anarchy) and the corresponding hyper-regulation of the mode of production (fatalism), including the negation of alternative modes of subsistence that force individuals to reduce themselves to being exclusively sellers of labor power. It is true that "labor is *an* activity of self-creation" but labor, by itself, is not *the* "activity in which individuals ... come to be what they are" (Gould, 1978, p. 40, emphasis added; see also Postone, 1993, for a criticism of Lukács). Labor is where you become what you are not. The narrow materialist designates labor as the "genuine humanization of man" (Lukács, 1978b, p. 42) but the standard Marxist fetishism of labor fails to recognize that the working up of any material *surplus* (not merely those realized within the capitalist mode of production) always involves the dehumanization (here we mean going beyond mere exploitation and the reduction of the human to a particular expression of being into the realm of brutalization or beyond). No matter who owns and controls the means of production, labor is, unless you are a religious fanatic, to be avoided as much as possible, and, where surpluses are involved, either capitalist or communist, labor devolves into human exploitation (Dahrendorf, 1959, p. 82):

> In terms of the speculative coincidence of the opposites, or of the "infinite judgement" in which the highest coincides with the lowest, consider the fact that Soviet workers were awakened early in the morning by the music from the loudspeakers playing the first chords of the *International*. Its text, "Arise, you chained in slavery!" obtains a deeper ironic meaning: the ultimate "truth" of the pathetic original meaning ("Resist, break the chains that constrain you and reach for freedom!") turns out to be the its literal meaning, the call to the tired workers "Get up, slaves, and start working for us, the Party nomenklatura!" (Zizek, 2000, p. 115)

It is actually those with the fewest needs to satisfy ("primitive man") and the least accumulated surpluses that were the wealthiest of humans (Sahlins, 1972) who prefered napping and rites to hunting and gathering. For Marxism it is always labor that makes the horizon of nature and necessity recede into the distance and thereby increasing the sphere of freedom and culture; hence, the necessity to liberate the means of production and put it under control of the proletariat. And it should be noted that the labor ontology spelled out by Lukács (and echoed by Gould and many others) is exactly the formulation we should expect from a person clawing their way back into the Party. However, if we follow orthodoxy and traditionalism out to its fullest conclusions, we find that anyone working for the production of any kind of material surplus (and all societies above the level of hand-to-mouth existence require surpluses otherwise no circulation of any form would be possible)—the superfluousness of objects makes possible the superfluidity of social life—would be permanently trapped within a world of alienation and morality reduced to a one-sided value form. "Robot Marxists," those that wish to fully automate production thereby saving people *from* the drudgery of work, do not realize that they have literally pinned their hopes for life on the ascendency of the dead (see Postone, 1993, p. 357), and some do realize, at least unconsciously, the limits of labor as the fundamental manifestation of human development because automation does not necessarily open the way for an expansion of *positive* human freedom, but this is a problem that is dealt with elsewhere (see Worrell & Krier, Forthcoming). Before we conclude, however, we need to say something about the division of labor.

Marxist labor ontology makes the error of rendering all forms of praxis down to nothing more than *derivatives* of labor but this overlooks nearly 50,000 years of moral history where, until relatively recently, work was avoided like the plague and everybody who could push work onto others did so. "Man all too easily grows lax and mellow/He soon elects repose at any price" (Goethe, 1976, p. 9). The only people who ever desired work and sought an excess of it were ascetics, hermits, and monks who deprived themselves of the good (food and sleep, for example) and lavished themselves with the bad, such as torture and work. Labor desired was part of a larger religious project. It was not until the Reformation that labor within a *calling* (and only within the circumscribed limits of the calling) was an approved form of conduct that put, potentially, whole societies on the plane of the sacred. Prior to this moment, labor was either purely profane, a form of spiritual punishment among fanatics and the insane, or, in the case of secret knowledge, a taboo thing (e.g., blacksmithing magic). The freely chosen calling (since cooled off into the profession, and a calling is as distinct from a profession as is an intellectual from an academic) forms the basis for the dignity and security of the specialized and vocational expert who is no longer absolutely interchangeable with another person who is merely able-bodied. The calling, if there can be said to be callings today, as opposed to mere professions, transforms the homogenous member into a "restricted" (i.e., circumscribed) heterogeneous individual (Bataille, 1979, p. 68) with clearly demarcated boundaries that, in the geometric sense, may be touched but not broken. The calling or vocation "is the inescapable condition of our historical situation. We cannot evade it so long as we remain true to ourselves" (Weber, 1946, p. 152).

Of course, the social division of labor, if it is a virtue, can be pushed to its vicious extremes in the forms of the forced or detailed division of labor where people are reduced, at best, to stupidity (Smith, 1937[1776], p. 734) and, at worst, to little more than members of the "living dead" (Hegel, 1979[1802–1804], p. 249)—at the threshold of death, variable capital practically vanishes and only capital per se would exist, since there would no longer be a differentiation between tools and people (talking tools). The Marxist response is to reject the division of labor in all forms rooted in a mystical conception of "Man," the microcosmic mirror of the universe (completely in line with Leibnizian monadology as far as this goes) that results not in *forms* of humanity but humanity or the human *per se*. This is another problem of Marxism and neo-Marxism: the formlessness of the imagined communist association of lounging and ruthless politics (if the fully liberated person is restored to its state of perfection by virtue of being free from labor exploitation—where once I was man, I am, finally, Man—then why associate at all in any manner that resembles a durable form?) But we do not always-already have everything it takes to be human within us. If this *were* true, capitalism (and all other forms of society that produce any kind of surplus whatsoever) has rendered finite what is, in truth, our infinite nature. Here again we find the recurring longing for a counterworld always on the horizon of the future and a sacrifice of the world we live in for a future utopia. But we live in *this* world (Hegel) and the infinity of the universe is not within you (otherwise, we would be *complete as individuals* if not for some particular form of society or mode of production that has crippled each of us). Quite the opposite is true, anyways, and that means that only with cooperation within this particular society and within the social division of labor, is the multidimensionality of human life possible. Of course, the capitalist division of labor is horrible for most and it is also true that in eradicating all divisions of labor we rid ourselves of the vicious, but the vicious is only the perversion of the virtuous and, consequently, the negation of all divisions of labor throws us back into a formless world of idiocy beyond merely vicious—it would be tantamount to hell on earth.

It was not the division of *labor* that was the essential thing anyways but, inversely, the *division* of labor, or, really, the *division* of anything. A calling or a chosen profession sets parameters and limits and, in so doing, differentiates the individual from others. Even when two or more individuals are doing the same thing "it is no longer the same thing" (Borkenau, 1981, p. 340). Each profession, then, has its own knowledge, dignity and honor as well as an ethical system that is unique to it and that distinguishes it from other professions. Regulating entry, participation, and expulsion affords members a moral status, solidarity, organization, and a quantum of the sacred. Marxism, tragically, gets it *backwards* and wants to negate the division while keeping the labor, or in some versions eliminate both the division and the labor (Robot Communists), thereby delivering humanity back to (a) the world of the purely profane, animal existence in other words, a world of interchangeability and expendability (Marxist regimes are famous for mass purges after all and one key to survival in totalitarian regimes is to possess skills and knowledge that render a person indispensable) or (b) evacuating everyone from the field of work and transporting all individuals, decked out with basic incomes—it remains to be seen if this will work out in some European nations—fueled by the subterranean world of dead production, to the non-stop world of politics and symbolic warfare of a kind hitherto unimaginable. "What would be left of [mad dog] socialism when socialism itself had unfastened their collars and had filled their pans with food? The socialist must, first of all, be a human being" (Man, 1985, p. 76). Devaluation and the reduction of life to nothing more than labor power and "variable capital" is obviously ensconced within the overarching problem of dehumanization. To reverse Freire's expression, we are concerned with the dead and dehumanized because our aim is for the restoration of the human. Not only is humanization "the people's vocation" (Freire, 1993, p. 23) but the real vocation is also one route back toward revaluation beyond the reduction of life to nothing more than, at the end of the day, exchange-value. If an individual has an "ontological vocation" (Freire), it cannot be enacted by a substitute or a vanguard element leading the way—revolutions are carried out by those with a calling but those lacking it cannot be dragged by the nose toward freedom when they will gladly settle for less.

The profession, the vocation, and so on are routes to labor that resist devaluation because it is not mere labor. Under the capitalist regime people pay to work but, in the best case scenario, the professional (sometimes formally but not actually subsumed) is bribed to not cause trouble and can carve out a life of minimal toil. It is true that most professionals voluntarily work too hard but only because they have not adopted disobedience as their personal philosophy and because they often care too much for their products (they have, in other words, not made the successful transformation of their particularity into a twofold particularity).

Marxists line themselves up, unconsciously, to be the champions of devalued labor power when they reject the division of labor. Marxism is not the solution to capitalism, it is a symptom of capitalism and unwittingly works against the revolution it prophesizes; it is not unheard of for Marxists to align with conservative business types when it comes to low wages and slashing government spending (Galbraith, 1969, pp. 77–78) and when it came to beating fascists, the Communists set out to prove to capital that a Red could not be worked to death (Worrell, 2008). The reduction of labor to the level of brutes does not, as Marx thought, make revolution inevitable. Quite the opposite, the creation of a class of dehumanized dregs makes it that much easier to accumulate even greater quantities of wealth (Hegel, 1991[1821], p. 266). Oddly enough, during the second world war, the Frankfurt School set out to find radical workers in the most advanced industrial capitalist nation on earth, the kind of workers that could defeat fascism and who might love communism and, try as they might, they not only did not find *any* radical workers at all (literally zero) but, additionally, they found that the workers who would make the best communists (with respect to the rejection of antisemitism and fascist propaganda) have no interesting in things like communism. Even today, with millennials, socialism sounds good on paper until they get a few use-values to their name and then they want more capitalism, better jobs, and more stuff.

Luther's revolution was decisive because it raised labor, through the concept of the calling, out of the profane and the morally impure and placed it on the level of the positive sacred. Of course, this can be seen as a great boon for capitalists who need lots of enthusiastic, self-negating workers but raising the moral status of labor "in the eyes of the lord" also raised the value of labor power for some. Marx himself would dismiss all of this as nothing more than the creation of a "golden chain" that can be "loosened somewhat" (C, p. 769) and that is undeniably true. However, this points to a much larger problem and one that we will have to pursue elsewhere (partly in Worrell & Krier, forthcoming) whereby Marx fails to see that his model of social freedom, communist association, leads nowhere beyond a formless assemblage of dumbed-down rebels. It seems clear that capitalism, despite all the ideology of individualism, wants nothing more than *bodies* that can be worked to death if only deregulation (anomie) could be absolutized. Marx, by contrast, wanted to save the individual, that is, the autonomous and non-alienated person, the social atom that cannot be divided, but it terminates in barbarous pragmatism and hyperfluid relations of contingency. Marxism, apart from Marx, demanded the "soul of man" in the great cause but, like capital, ended up with millions of corpses. Starting out from opposite positions, capitalist egoists and Marxist altruists both thrive on the immiseration of humanity while promising Paradise in the future. And Marxists are perennially dismayed over the fact that workers are more than happy to pass up a soviet utopia for beer and bass boats.

Weber was correct to criticize Marxists who reduced religion down to nothing more than an opiate and Protestantism as merely self-serving ideology cooked up by the entrepreneurial class. This is not a defense of capitalism or Protestantism, far from it, but it is also undeniably true that nowhere else have workers en masse received a greater share of their wealth than in nations where Protestantism flourished and where other ideological strands adopted the so-called Protestant work ethic, for example, modern, middle-class Catholics in the United States who "got with the program" (the entrepreneurial types) as compared with traditional (bureaucratic) Catholics who lagged behind (McClelland, 1961, p. 359). Protestantism raised the standard for what it means to be a "good worker" for all workers (see Man, 1985, p. 77 on the German manifestation) turning many people into "virtual Calvinists" with no other connection to that strain other than working in a community of individualists, being forced to keep up, and where those that succeed form a model for responsible decision-making (McClelland, 1961, p. 369) in the face of an inscrutable and terrifying higher authority. But more importantly, if perversely, it gave people a form of ethical (as distinguished from moral or legal) conduct in the world of everyday, collective life outside of the cave, hut, or monastery.

But to return to our main point, the presence of robust and vibrant *non-economic values* within the world of work impedes the accumulation of a positive surplus and the corresponding negative excesses; it is the *evacuation of morals from the world of labor* (the carving out of an infraliminal dimension of pure material extraction and brutalization or, even further, the monsterization of life that enables the emergence of a one-sided form of value in the world of commodity exchange). Surplus value = the lack of morals; more wealth = less morality; where wealth and property flourish we find more murder and suicide because wealth is, at bottom, legal murder and obligatory suicide. When brutalization continues unabated and brutes are pushed further into the domain of the inhuman we can expect a rise in monstrous crimes (the rampage shooter and the suicide bomber) and demagoguery like Coughlinism during the Great Depression, Buchananism, or the Trumpism of today (see Worrell, 1999, 2008, 2013, 2014, 2015).

One might be tempted to believe that, like Eastman, I am imploring people to not kill the goose that lays golden eggs but Eastman was wrong: it is not capitalism per se that lays golden eggs but *labor power* that is the magic goose, to stick with the metaphor. Well, then, this seems to lead nowhere but to a drive for something like reunionization and solidarity-building and who would deny that bigger and stronger unions would not benefit the average wage earner? Benefit, however, is not the same as providing a positively free existence and we all know that unions were, in their own ways, a source of irrationality and corruption. Organizing to raise the value of labor power and regulate work is not pointless but has to be imagined in a larger program for the regulation of ethical life in the widest possible sense, not merely in narrow economic and labor terms. The calling, the social division of labor and specialization, criminality, reflective dignity, and critical theory, all lie on the same plane of *sociological particularity* (in contrast to the infinite unity of the highest and lowest, universal and singular, capital and laborer). "All the interconnections of man to man such as love and friendship are limited, particular, finite, in nature ..." (Feuerbach, in Wartofsky, 1977, p. 45). Everything, including the infinite unity of the universal and the singular, hinges on mediating particularity, on limitation and internally self-divided into the abstract and the concrete—the function of the particular is not located in its infinite wealth in its relation to its singular other but the opposite: the development of deep, specialized wealth of content within the limited sphere of action and the resulting web of mutual reciprocity and interdependence, and not in some infantile dream of being an independent "individual" or a "personality."

The way forward, for some, is not to wait for something to happen from outside the system, or for something to happen at the top or bottom of the system, and less still does it involve the *sacrifice of intellect* for the sake of contradictory association, but from that obscure and enigmatic dimension within the system where the ego's positive enjoyment of the eros of life is arrived at through *ecstatic resignation* (Schiller, 1966, p. 195) that we locate in the concept of a calling or the "higher mission" free from the fanatical (e.g., Calvinist) pursuit of indices of salvation in the imagined eyes of the Big Other. This resignation is not identical with false hope and patient, obedient waiting and neither is the ecstatic merely anomic excitement and adventurism (Fromm, 1968, pp. 6–7). For anyone *possessed* with sufficient drive and discipline to pursue a coherent mission (as opposed to the inspired expansiveness and play) the lack of a calling would result in restlessness, ennui (Mann, 1955[1927], p. 12) and contingency; "we know of no great artist who has ever done anything but serve his work and only his work" (Weber, 1946, p. 137). "Am I concerned with *happiness*? I am concerned with my *work*" (Nietzsche, 1982, p. 439). Marxism dreams of a world without possession (in the broadest sense possible) but merely living in a human society means to be possessed, that is, to be under some external control (Hegel, 1991[1821], p. 76) and to deny this would be the equivalent of collapsing the psyche down into pure subjective isolation.

A calling or, now, the vocation marks a differentiation between work and *the* work, the individual's quest. Weber's little dialectic in "Science in a Vocation" points to a way out: the person with a "calling" is capable, within their specialization, to *control their own doubled aspect*, the quantitative and qualitative, by formally and adequately conforming to the quantitative expectations of the prevailing norms, where there is counting, while, on the level of the qualitative, where it really counts, retaining mastery and even turning abstraction back upon itself—bending the perverted gaze back upon itself. In the vocation the process of creation (*praxis*) and its objectification (*poiesis*) is unified in our *particular* social function (*energia*). "The individual attains actuality only by ... *determinate particularity*" and must limit his or herself to "one of the moments of civil society through his activity, diligence, and skill ... and only through this mediation with the universal does he simultaneously provide for himself and gain *recognition* in his own eyes and in the eyes of others" (Hegel, 1991[1821], p. 238). We must do or die, that is our choice, and no mode of production, event, or party will ever liberate all of humanity from production, moral surplus, and the return of the repressed. There was a time when social scientists dreamed out loud about steering society along a rational course (Lynd, 1939, pp. 180–201) but the mere suggestion, today, seems laughable. We have the Leviathan by the tail and even if anyone manages to make critical theory great again it will be of little use prior to the moment of derealization and the full-on collapse of the global system. Popular culture seems to have this premonition regarding an imminent night of monsters.

Liberal morality demands that we love what we would otherwise be forced to do (autonomy!) but we may also choose not to love what we do but simply do what we love, to follow it to the end; the lover of life, says Zarathustra, "loves beyond reward and retribution" (Nietzsche, 1982, p. 373). Yes, without regard for reward and retribution but for some other, big and small. In a depressed letter to his nephew (Mauss) Durkheim revealed that "In order to work joyfully, I must see that my work serves someone and something" (in Besnard, 2000, p. 98). We may protest that a concept like the calling is mired in irrationality, and it is, yet, there is no rationality without its opposite and, crucially, without the irrational there is no art (see Adorno, 1997, p. 43), beauty, and nothing sublime: "Without the tensions motivated by the irrationality of melody, no modern music could exist ... chordal rationalization lives only in continuous tension with melodicism which it can never completely devour" (Weber, 1958, p. 10). Nearly 100 years ago, Weber concluded his "Science as a Vocation" with lines that still resonate: "We shall set to work and meet the 'demands of the day,' in human relations as well as in our vocation. This, however, is plain and simple, if each finds and obeys the demon who holds the fibers of his very life" (1946, p. 156).

## References

In-line citations to the first volume of Marx's *Capital* have been shortened to "C."
Adorno, T. (1997). *Aesthetic theory*. Minneapolis, MN: University of Minnesota Press.
Agger, B. (1989). *Socio(onto)logy*. Urbana, IL: University of Illinois Press.
Althusser, L. (1969). *For Marx*. New York, NY: Vintage.
Badiou, A. (2003). *Saint Paul*. Stanford, CA: Stanford University Press.
Bageant, J. (2010). *Rainbow pie*. Melbourne: Scribe.
Bataille, G. (1979). The psychological structure of fascism. *New German Critique, 16*, 64–87.
Beiser, F. (2005). *Hegel*. New York, NY: Routledge.
Berman, M. (1988). *All that is solid melts into air*. New York, NY: Penguin.
Besnard, P. (2000). The fortunes of Durkheim's *Suicide*. In W. Pickering & G. Walford (Eds.), *Durkheim's suicide* (pp. 97125–97162). London: Routledge.
Borkenau, F. (1981). *End and beginning*. New York, NY: Columbia University Press.
Boutroux, E. (1914). *Natural law in science and philosophy*. New York, NY: The Macmillan Co..
CrimethInc. (2001). *Days of war, nights of love*. Salem, OR: CrimethInc.
CrimethInc. (2011). *Work*. Salem, OR: CrimethInc.
Dahrendorf, R. (1959). *Class and class conflict in industrial society*. Stanford, CA: Stanford University Press.
Debord, G. (1983). *Society of the spectacle*. Detroit, MI: Black & Red.
Degré, G. (1985). *The social compulsions of ideas*. New Brunswick, NJ: Transaction.
Durkheim, E. (1984[1893]). *The division of labor in society*. New York, NY: The Free Press.
Durkheim, E. (1951[1897]). *Suicide*. New York, NY: Free Press.
Durkheim, E. (1995[1912]). *Elementary forms of religious life* (K. Fields, Trans.). New York, NY: Free Press.
Durkheim, E. (1973). *On morality and society*. Chicago, IL: The University of Chicago Press.
Durkheim, E. (1982). *The rules of sociological method*. New York, NY: Free Press.
Eastman, M. (1955). *Reflections on the failure of socialism*. New York, NY: Grosset.
Foucault, M. (1970). *The order of things*. New York, NY: Vintage.
Foucault, M. (1977). *Discipline and punish*. New York, NY: Vintage.
Freire, P. (1993). *Pedagogy of the oppressed* (Rev. ed.). New York, NY: Continuum.
Freud, S. (1965[1900]). *The interpretation of dreams*. New York: Avon.

Freud, S. (1950[1913]). *Totem and taboo.* New York, NY: Norton.
Fromm, E. (1968). *The revolution of hope.* New York, NY: Harper.
Fromm, E. (1973). *The anatomy of human destructiveness.* New York, NY: Holt, Rinehart and Winston.
Galbraith, J. (1969). *The affluent society.* New York, NY: New American Library.
Goethe, J. (1976). *Faust.* New York, NY: Norton.
Goldmann, L. (1976). *Cultural creation.* Saint Louis, MO: Telos Press.
Gould, C. (1978). *Marx's social ontology.* Cambridge, MA: MIT Press.
Gramsci, A. (1971). *Selections from the prison notebooks.* New York, NY: International Publishers.
Harding, E. (1947). *Psychic energy.* Princeton, NJ: Princeton University Press.
Hegel, G. W. F. (1979). *System of ethical life and first philosophy of spirit.* Albany, NY: SUNY Press.
Hegel, G. W. F. (1991[1821]). *Elements of the philosophy of right.* Cambridge: Cambridge University Press.
Hegel, G W. F. (1974[1840]). *Lectures on the philosophy of religion* (Vol. 1) (E. B. Speirs & J. B. Sanderson, Trans.) (Reprint). New York, NY: The Humanities Press.
Horkheimer, M. (1972). *Critical theory.* New York, NY: Continuum.
Jameson, F. (1991). *Postmodernism.* Durham, NC: Duke University Press.
Jones, S. (2001). *Durkheim reconsidered.* Cambridge: Polity.
Korsch, K. (1970). *Marxism and philosophy.* New York, NY: Monthly Review Press.
Kracauer, S. (1995). *The mass ornament.* Cambridge, MA: Harvard University Press.
Lefebvre, H. (2009[1968]). *Dialectical materialism.* Minneapolis, MN: University of Minnesota Press.
London, J. (2006[1908]). *Iron heel.* New York, NY: Penguin.
Lukács, G. (1978a). *The ontology of social being, 1, Hegel.* London: Merlin.
Lukács, G. (1978b). *The ontology of social being, 3, labour.* London: Merlin.
Lynd, R. (1939). *Knowledge for what?* Princeton, NJ: Princeton University Press.
Malraux, A. (1961). *Man's fate* (H. M. Chevalier, Trans.). New York, NY: Random House.
Man, H. (1985). *The psychology of marxian socialism.* New Brunswick, NJ: Transaction.
Mann, T. (1955[1927]). *Magic mountain.* New York, NY: Heritage Press.
Mann, T. (1948). *Doctor Faustus.* New York, NY: Knopf.
Marx, K. (1964[1844]). *The economic and philosophic manuscripts of 1844.* New York, NY: International Publishers.
Marx, K. (1973[1857]). *Grundrisse.* New York, NY: Penguin.
Marx, K. (1970[1859]). *A contribution to the critique of political economy.* New York, NY: International Publishers.

Marx, K. (1976[1867]). *Capital* (Vol. 1). New York, NY: Penguin.
Marx, K. (1981[1894]). *Capital* (Vol. 3). New York, NY: Penguin.
Marx, K. (1935). *Value, price, and profit*. New York, NY: International Publishers.
Marx, K., & Engels, F. (1972). *The Marx–Engels reader*. New York, NY: Norton.
Marx, K., & Engels, F. (1988). *Collected works* (Vol. 43). London: Lawrence and Wishart.
Mauss, M. (1979). *Sociology and psychology*. London: Routledge and Kegan Paul.
McClelland, D. (1961). *The achieving society*. New York, NY: Free Press.
Nietzsche, F. (1974[1887]). *The gay science*. New York, NY: Vintage.
Nietzsche, F. (1982). *The portable Nietzsche*. New York, NY: Penguin.
Nietzsche, F. (1967a). *Ecce homo*. New York, NY: Vintage.
Nietzsche, F. (1967b). *Will to power*. New York, NY: Vintage.
Postone, M. (1993). *Time, labor, and social domination*. Cambridge: Cambridge University Press.
Reich, W. (1970). *The mass psychology of fascism*. New York, NY: Noonday.
Sahlins, M. (1972). *Stone age economics*. New York, NY: Aldine de Gruyter.
Sartre, J. (1948). *The wall*. New York, NY: New Directions.
Schiller, F. (1966). *On the sublime*. New York, NY: Frederick Ungar.
Shakespeare, W. (1973). *Coriolanus*. New York, NY: Penguin.
Smith, A. (1937[1776]). *The wealth of nations*. New York, NY: New Modern Library.
Smith, D. N. (2016). Capitalism's future: Self-alienation, self-emancipation and the remaking of critical theory. In D. Krier & M. Worrell (Eds.), *Capitalism's future: Alienation, emancipation and critique* (pp. 11–62). Leiden: Brill.
Steinbeck, J. (2002). *America and Americans and selected nonfiction*. New York, NY: Penguin.
Strong, T. (1988). *Friedrich Nietzsche and the politics of transfiguration* (Expanded ed.). Berkeley, CA: University of California Press.
Wartofsky, M. (1977). *Feuerbach*. London: Cambridge University Press.
Weber, M. (2002[1905]). *The protestant ethic and the spirit of capitalism*. New York, NY: Penguin.
Weber, M. (1946). *From Max Weber: Essays in sociology*. New York, NY: Oxford University Press.
Weber, M. (1958). *The rational and social foundations of music*. Carbondale, IL: Southern Illinois University Press.
Worrell, M. (2008). *Dialectic of solidarity*. Chicago, IL: Haymarket.
Worrell, M. (2009). A faint rattling: A research note on Marx's theory of value. *Critical Sociology*, 35(6), 887–892.
Worrell, M. (2013). *Terror: Social, political, and economic perspectives*. London: Routledge.

Worrell, M. (2015). Imperial homunculi: The speculative singularities of American hegemony (drones, suicide bombers, and rampage killers, or, excursions into Durkheimian geometry). *Current Perspectives in Social Theory, 33*, 217–241.

Worrell, M. (2014). The commodity as the ultimate sociological monstrosity: Capitalism and the four horsemen of the Apocalypse, or reading Marx's *Capital* through Durkheim's *suicide*. *Fast Capitalism,* 11. Retrieved from www.fastcapitalism.org

Worrell, M. (1999). The veil of piacular subjectivity: Buchananism and the new world order. *Electronic Journal of Sociology, 4*(3). Retrieved from www.sociology.org

Worrell, M., & Krier, D. (Forthcoming). Atopia awaits! *Critical Sociology*.

Zizek, S. (2000). From *history and class consciousness* to *the dialectic of enlightenment* ... and back. *New German Critique, 81*(Winter), 107–123.

CHAPTER 5

# Social Form and the 'Purely Social': On the Kind of Sociality Involved in Value

*Patrick Murray and Jeanne Schuler*

The basic error of the majority of Marx's critics consists of … their complete failure to grasp the qualitative sociological side of Marx's theory of value. (Rubin, 1972, p. 73)

> Money thereby directly and simultaneously becomes the *real community* [*Gemeinwesen*], since it is the general substance of survival for all, and at the same time the social product of all. But as we have seen, in money the community [*Gemeinwesen*] is at the same time a mere abstraction, a mere external, accidental thing for the individual, and at the same time merely a means for his satisfaction as an isolated individual. (Marx, 1973, pp. 225–226)

There are striking passages in social science, philosophy, and literature that depict emptiness as a pervasive condition in the modern world. From Dickens and Weber to Camus and Walker Percy come descriptions of lost or lonely persons unhinged from traditions, drifting through this world. Another pervasive theme echoes the traditional condemnation of greed in a modern form: the consumer. Consumers are portrayed as grasping and obsessed; they exit the Thanksgiving feast to wait for stores to open and bargains to flow. In the Gilded Age, tycoons built extravagant summer

P. Murray (✉) • J. Schuler
Department of Philosophy, Creighton University, Omaha, NE, USA

© The Author(s) 2017
D. Krier, M.P. Worrell (eds.), *The Social Ontology of Capitalism*,
DOI 10.1057/978-1-137-59952-0_5

mansions that were shuttered most of the year. Some critics point out the links between a restless emptiness and greed. One way to fill a vacuum is to go shopping, chasing a phantom of fullness. Ads promise the fulfillment that life fails to deliver. The "festival" mall evokes the excitement and connections missing from the daily grind. Consuming offers solace for life's disappointments; new phones, films, and restaurants are a quick fix for the soul. For these critics, modernity clearly engenders emptiness, anomie, greed, cynicism, and materialism. The focus is on the culture and the individuals damaged in these ways. The sources of this driven emptiness are less apparent.

Marx has usually been thought of as investigating capitalism as an "economic system," a mode of production. Less often has Marx been consulted to understand the sociological features of capitalist societies. The customary divisions into economy, social relations, and culture—forces of production, relations of production, and superstructure—lie in the background. But treating economy, society, and culture as separable—even if interacting—misconceives Marx's basic concepts. The concept of the commodity is key to understanding the experience of the consumer: what kind of category is it? Does the commodity form bear cultural content, content with far-reaching social consequences? The barren sociality engendered by capitalism is felt in multiple ways. The emptiness intrinsic to the value character of commodities reverberates in the emptiness that characterizes forms of modern subjectivity. Greed in its modern guise emerges from a drive that goes beyond the marketplace to the processes that sustain it, namely, the production of commodities laden with surplus value.

The assumptions at play in overlooking the sociological depth of Marx's theory betray a theoretical emptiness that Marx calls "the bourgeois horizon." Marx identifies "the bourgeois horizon" as the philosophical orientation that structures political economy, much of modern philosophy, and many forms of socialism. It trades in bifurcations, separating what belongs together: mind versus world, subjective versus objective, form versus content, and concept versus object. The sterility of "the bourgeois horizon" in separating wealth and labor from their constitutive social forms and purposes—where the qualitative sociological content lies—explains what I.I. Rubin calls "the basic error of the majority of Marx's critics," namely, "their complete failure to grasp the qualitative sociological side of Marx's theory of value" (Rubin, 1972, p. 73). The phenomenologically attuned concepts that Marx arrived at in order to grasp the emptiness of modern life are far from empty.

Sociological studies of modernity may not think to probe the social content of the specific "economic" forms that constitute capitalist societies. In *Marx, Marginalism and Modern Sociology*, Simon Clarke argues that Marx's profound critique of economics was passed over, while neoclassical economics rose to dominance:

> There was a scientific revolution in nineteenth-century social thought ... It was inaugurated by Marx's critique of the ideological foundations of classical political economy, which he located in the political economists' neglect of the social form of capitalist production. (Clarke, 1982, p. 240)

Economists, both classical and neoclassical, attempt to construct a social science based on categories applicable to every society, such as needs (or preferences), wealth, labor, instruments of production, and land. But no such science is possible: no particular society can be understood solely through general categories. Certainly, no qualitative sociological insights can be derived from such categories. Clarke argues that consequences of the missed opportunity provided by Marx's scientific revolution spread. Modern sociology uncritically adopted the horizon of neoclassical economics and ceded to it the "economic" realm in a disastrous disciplinary division of labor.[1] *Capital*, by contrast, does not begin with the generality "the wealth of nations." It begins with the sociologically potent observation that, in societies where wealth is produced on a capitalist basis, wealth takes the social form of the commodity. *What sort of sociality is involved in this form of wealth?* This is the question that we want to explore, with special reference to Marx's claim that value must be expressed in exchange-value, more particularly, in the (antagonistic) polarized relationship between commodity and the universal equivalent, money.

A commodity is a useful thing that *has* an exchange-value, by which Marx means a price, but, as Marx puts it, a commodity *is* a value. Wealth, throughout history, has had a specific social form: value is the specific, and peculiarly abstract, social form of wealth in the commodity form. Marx describes value as "purely social" [*rein gesellschaftlich*], as well as "supra-sensible" [*übersinnlich*], which means that the value character of a commodity cannot be detected anywhere on or in the body of the commodity (Later, we will turn up reasons to qualify this statement). Gender is a sort of sociality; it is expressed on, in, and by gendered bodies in countless ways. It must be quite a peculiar sort of sociality that cannot be represented on or in the thing that has that social form. This strange sociality involved in the commodity led Karl Polanyi (1968) to characterize capitalism as the "disembedded economy," as if it were divested of social form. *What is the sociality of value such that it cannot be manifested by the body of the commodity?* To answer this question requires us to develop the basic concepts of social form, value, abstract labor, and the purely social.

## Social Forms and General Traits

What is social form? The concept has its roots in human sociality, which is a trait characterizing humans wherever they exist. Humans are not self-sufficient; from birth onward, our lives are bound together. We exist with others and thanks to others. Being social is a species trait. In modern life, we sometimes posit individuals over against society and its institutions, but this apartness or independence is its own mode of sociality, just as indifference is a mood, not the absence of mood. At the beginning of the *Grundrisse*, Marx traces the notion that sociality is a thing apart from individuals back to the peculiar sociality of bourgeois society:

> Only in the eighteenth century, in 'civil society', do the various forms of social connectedness confront the individual as a mere means towards his private purposes, as external necessity. But the epoch which produces this standpoint, that of the isolated individual, is also precisely that of the hitherto most developed social (from this standpoint, general) relations. (Marx, 1973, p. 84)

The asocial sociality of commercial life may make it seem that they do, but individuals do not constitute themselves apart from society and its institutions.

Every society is constituted by particular ways in which humans exist together. There is no one species-wide sociality. A society is a system of resources, tools, beliefs, actions, and needs. It is a way of living and opens a horizon onto what is real and what matters. How a society is organized involves ends or goals. Thus, each society serves specific ends that shape its practices and institutions. These ends might concern the salvation of souls, service to the gods, allegiance to rulers, military conquest, or the glory of battle. There is no reason to insist on only one such goal. Society's ends and its social forms are linked: because society has particular ends, it is formed in relation to them. Social forms penetrate society to varying degrees. In history, social forms may develop from singular events, rudimentary institutions, or social movements. Social forms involve power because forms matter. These ends and social forms are what Aristotle calls final and formal causes: the power of the telos or purposive character inherent in social structures. Social forms always have moral implications; that is why a purely descriptive social science fails to grasp the reality of social life. For example, modern wage labor, a specific social form of labor, requires the mutual consent of employer and employee, which, formally at least, recognizes both parties as equally free persons.

Are not some human traits universal or natural? By attending to social form we do not deny general or shared features of human existence, such as wealth, needs, kinship structure, psychological dispositions, custom, or even universal human rights. Reflection on a common human nature is often indispensable to inquiry. Being social is a general trait of humans. While humans possess universal traits, such as language, the universal features shared by all societies do not have the constituting power of a form. Heidegger's (2010) analysis of *Dasein* in *Being and Time* is compelling, but establishing the equiprimordiality of the work world, discourse, mood, and understanding describes how humans exist in every setting. These identifiable general ways of being human fall short of being forms. Universal traits are static and unsaturated; they are not situated in history and lack the dynamism of forms. They lack qualitative sociological content.

The particularity of history shapes human existence in essential ways. All social forms exist as particulars *of* something more universal. There is no form of a society in general. What can be called Use-value Romanticism holds that what is useful can exist without specific social form. It claims that general traits, such as being useful, are sufficient designations. Useful things, or wealth pure and simple, presumably could be made and used by persons anywhere at any time. Every society involves tools, but every tool tells the story of its society. The general definition of a tool does not explain how instruments produce value (and surplus value) in capitalist societies: Marx calls instruments of production constant capital to disclose their specific social form and purpose. When social form is overlooked, denied, or disguised, Use-value Romanticism, with its penchant for general traits, will pop up.

Throughout history, social forms are readily apparent. Harvest festivals and the ruins of pyramids, roads, and temples testify to the social forms of ancient peoples. What are the social forms that constitute modern capitalist societies? We could start by saying that capitalist society involves money and making ever more money. A few people possess much money while most scrape along. The median household in the United States has about half the wealth it would need to own outright a median house and car—and nothing else. It is not the goal of the family to make money, but household consumption of commodities is mostly how families today meet needs. And that takes money. Money and its power in, and often over, our lives are visible. Money is found in societies widely in history, where its scope and roles vary. We have to dig deeper for the ends that capitalist society serves. Money is a visible marker of what is not easily grasped because of the kind of social form that it is, that is, money that functions as capital. But to dig deeper requires intellectual strengths in short supply in the modern world. Living in capitalist society encourages forms of skepticism that make understanding it difficult.

## Skepticism About Purposes and Forms

What sets capitalist societies apart is how they engender skepticism about forms in general and purposiveness in particular. Modern science is proudly said to put an end to teleology. Ends and forms carry a sour, scholastic taste for many. Wariness about final causes and common purposes leads liberals to urge that no society should have set goals: we should fight for the liberty to pursue our own ends and resist paternalism. Adults do not need nannies. The domination of peoples throughout history may have allowed for collective purposes, but that domination has largely been eclipsed by modern democracy. Citizens freely abide by minimal social contracts to protect liberty and secure property and basic welfare. Market exchanges are further expressions of personal choice. Individually chosen ends are OK. Involuntary social ends are not. For this liberal mind-set, a society that has no goal, no common good, is one of history's greatest achievements. This modern readiness to dismiss final causality hinders our understanding of capitalism.

Skepticism about ends adds to the difficulty of recognizing the specific social purpose of capitalism and the social forms that constitute it. A related skepticism is directed at forms and essences. This skepticism arises from crude empiricism (things are collections of sensible properties) and nominalism (only particulars exist; kinds, or universals, are useful fictions invented, like filing cabinets, as tools). John Locke called nominal essences "the workmanship of the understanding," that is, they are constructs of the mind. Empiricism, nominalism (anti-essentialism), and constructivism are default intellectual positions for many today. In this view, essence talk amounts to intellectual domination where a priori and fixed forms flatten actual existing differences. This skepticism is inspired less by science than by poor phenomenology and a view of freedom as unconstrained and self-defining from the bottom up. All limits on freedom must be repudiated. But we find that capitalism simultaneously establishes a self-centered sort of individual liberty and systematic coercion. Capitalist freedom and oppression must both be addressed. But that first requires recognition of capital's end and forms.

Skepticism about essences and ends blocks the recognition of social forms and purposes. Since social forms are actual, this skepticism leaves us strangers to our world. The skeptic is stymied when universal human traits are separated from specific social forms. This kind of skeptic views society as the aggregation of individuals and their actions. Capitalism becomes the label for the current—uncomprehended—stage of history. It is not constituted in any inherent ways. Without social forms in our intellectual repertoire, we turn to human nature and the usual suspects such as greed or self-interest to explain the world. The skeptic cannot answer the fundamental social question: what is capital? As a predisposition, this skepticism infects ordinary experience and is entrenched in academic life. It impedes every effort to grasp capitalism as a distinctive mode of production, helping capital to cover its tracks.

## Social Forms: From Commodities to Value

The social form of modern society includes the telos or end of capitalism. What does capitalism strive for? As we have seen, we cannot get to particular social forms with universal categories that hold everywhere, such as needs, tools, natural resources, or human productive activity. In every society, products are made that require human labor. This universal trait cannot comprehend actual societies; it cannot capture the animating power of capitalist forms. Classical economists make this mistake when they identify the value of commodities with the labor embodied in them, regardless of the social form and purpose of the labor. Since value is specific to capitalist society, such a claim is a category mistake. As Moishe Postone (1993) points out, Traditional Marxism, too, commits this error of thinking about labor rather than the specific social form of labor in capitalist societies.

Marx begins *Capital* by discarding the economist's project of explaining actual social phenomenon with only general categories: *Capital* is not a study of "the wealth of nations." Marx deliberately limits his inquiry to societies where wealth generally takes the form of a commodity, that is, a useful thing with a price, and he quickly raises the crucial question: what do all commodities share that allows for valid prices? Marx assumes that, generally, prices are not arbitrary; a thousand dollars per gallon of gas is a price, but thankfully not a valid one. Marx addresses a social world in which market forces work to establish prices that, for the most part, are valid, though not fixed. If prices are valid, they must measure something; otherwise, any price would be per se valid. What they measure must be shared by all commodities, since valid prices allow each commodity to be compared quantitatively with every other one. Since each different commodity has its price, so many barrels of oil must equal so many bushels of corn. The name for what all commodities share is value.[2]

The concept of value is often misunderstood. Value typically refers to a subjective reaction that is thought to be projected on to things; here, value is purely subjective. This skeptical—and transhistorical—view of value cannot explain the historically specific value that is the "third thing" shared by commodities that makes them commensurable. As common to all commodities, value is not an individual's projection, and it "cannot be a geometrical, physical, chemical or other natural property" (Marx, 1976, p. 127). What can it be?

Commodities have prices and exist as values. The value embodied in commodities is expressed—necessarily so, Marx argues—in prices. A wool coat embodies more value than a cotton sock. Marx contrasts the usefulness of the coat with its value as the sensible to the supra-sensible. What makes the coat useful is tangible, such as the warmth provided by its woolen fabric. What determines the coat's value is not perceived. But it would be a mistake to draw the line between the sensible and supra-sensible sharply, as if value were not felt throughout our lives. As with gravity, we recognize its effects even when we do not understand its unseen source. The source is mysterious, but a thing's value as compared to that of others is felt and often matters more than its usefulness. What is more valuable brings the pleasures of prestige: "Veblen effects," if you will. Value appears in prices, name brands, and in our awareness of what something is worth—its value. What something is worth is usually conveyed by price. The thing's worth overlaps but is not the same as its quality. Quality is also comparative but this comparison reflects tangible useful properties, not mere quantities. The sensible and the supra-sensible dimensions that are separated in theory are inseparable in experience.

Growing up in capitalist societies we learn ways in which value shows in—even structures—the world around us (Lotz, 2012). We judge a thing's value without needing to check its price tag. The perennial TV game show "The Price is Right" presupposes this sort of perceptiveness. We know when something is a good deal or is priced wrong. With our internalized price scanners we size up the best buy. While value is apparent in what something is worth, still, money is the only visible measure of value. Social forms permeate our experience of the commercial world. Value appears to those who live in commercial societies. We experience a quart of Ben and Jerry's as being of greater value than a Popsicle, much as we know that a boulder is heavier than a pebble. Value is sometimes treated as a placeholder for deeper realities, such as capital. But value belongs to our society like sacredness belongs to the Koran or to the waters of the Ganges. In each case, you can go deeper. Commodities are experienced as values, and value is experienced as more or less—of what is not so clear. If value were not manifested at all, analysis would slide back toward Use-value Romanticism, that is, toward use values imagined to be without any social form.

## The Commodity Spectrum: Simple Commodities, Commodities That are Commodity Capital, Ex-commodities, Potential Commodities, Quasi-commodities

For the most part, wealth functions as a commodity temporarily. Purchases that fill our home or surround us at work are being enjoyed or used productively. Not all participants in commodity circulation are individuals searching out consumer goods. Many are firms, some not-for-profit, most for-profit; commodities produced by not-for-profits differ from those produced by for-profits in that their sale does not yield surplus value. How much difference that makes is a subject for further thought. Marx must have chuckled to himself when he observed that commodities in the making within a capitalist firm are not handled as commodities: the next worker on the assembly line neither pays for nor sells what she is working on. The firm itself can be organized in more or less authoritarian, competitive, or cooperative ways, none of which is dictated by the capital form.

The ongoing circulation of capital that currently makes our lives possible is not continuously confronted: most commodities, once purchased, drop out of the market. If humans did exist like capital, caring only for value (more particularly, surplus value), capitalism would crash land (Marx, 1976, p. 179). Having a life, which goes under the commercial label of consumption, is a condition for capitalism. What we purchase generally becomes an ex-commodity. We take products home to use and enjoy. Yet even wealth no longer in circulation is not separable from social form. We recognize the value of products in the private sphere of consumption or while working in a firm or factory. This recognition is made explicit when we draw up and price a list of our valuables for a homeowner's insurance policy or when inventory is taken in the warehouse. Sometimes we buy commodities for domestic use, say a home, jewelry, or fine art, with the explicit recognition that such wealth doubles as a store of value or even with the speculative hope that its value will increase. In either case, the ex-commodity stores value as a potential commodity. Compared to other social forms of wealth, value is strange, but we do not need a theory to perceive its presence around us. Like gravity before Newton, value surrounds us, as familiar as it is mysterious.

Quasi-commodities of various sorts go beyond being willing and able to pay the price. Being willing to pay tuition at Princeton is not enough; one must first be admitted. Paying college tuition gets you a seat in a class but does not guarantee any credit hours: you have to pass the course. We talk loosely about how much a college degree costs, but there is more to getting one than plunking down the money. Nonetheless, in his recent book *What Money Can't Buy*, Michael Sandel (2012) ponders whether philanthropists can, in effect, buy an honorary degree.

## From Value to Abstract Labor and Time

As Marx's inquiry unfolds, it moves beyond recognizable experience to underlying abstractions. Value is the rabbit hole to access the stranger forms. A church steeple does not reveal Christian theology in detail. Value, however, gives even less of a clue as to what lies beneath it. We know that value is measured by prices, so value must represent a quantity of some kind. But of what kind? We do not find a unit of value the way we do in adding eggs up to a dozen. What is the substance of value that allows it to be quantified? What do all commodities share?

As diverse physical entities, commodities do not all share any particular useful properties; neither do they meet any common need—there is no need in general. We do not find any particular concrete trait that could be the substance of value. Social form must be particular, but it does not have to be physical any more than is the sacredness of Good Friday. When we look at the production of commodities, it involves tools, raw materials, labor power—and the money to buy all these. What products share is not any particular kind of concrete labor; likewise, what defines social form cannot be the universal trait of productive activity. Social form is particular. But the particular social form of the capitalist mode of production has its roots in the aspect of human labor that Marx calls abstract.

No labor exists as abstract—all labor is concrete—but every kind of labor, whether slave, serf, tribal, or free, can be considered in its aspect of being human labor in abstraction from its concrete character. Abstract labor is a universal trait of human labor inasmuch as any concrete human labor can be viewed abstractly as the exertion of human muscles and brains: "however varied the useful kinds of labour, or productive activities, it is a physiological fact that they are functions of the human organism, and that each such function, whatever may be its nature or its form, is essentially the expenditure of human brain, nerves, muscles and sense organs" (Marx, 1976, p. 164). Likewise, all human products can be viewed as embodied labor. When you ask, what do all capitalist commodities share that gives them value, the answer *begins with* the abstract labor congealed in them. As a universal human trait, however, it is not yet a social form. As a universal trait it can only be a partial answer to the questions: what is value? and what social sort of labor is value-producing?

As abstract, this substance is not visible. To grasp it we strip away the concrete features that distinguish cooking from mining to arrive at the physiological process that is involved in all labor. Human beings, like other creatures, expend energy in working. Concrete labor, from which abstract labor—undifferentiated human endeavor—is abstracted, takes time and is always oriented to specific purposes, such as drilling a well for water. Length of time is the only measure of the homogenous substance of congealed abstract labor. But abstract labor and the congealed abstract labor in products are tricky concepts. They express rudimentary features of labor and products. Duration is always a dimension of human activity. Abstract labor links the duration of human labor with products as values. Unlike actual things and activities, it is abstract. You cannot point to a quantity of abstract labor the way that you can pick up a single commodity. The term abstract labor can mislead us into thinking of abstract labor as an actual kind of labor. Concrete labors exist, but abstract labor as such does not exist. Abstract labor as the substance of value is not a kind of labor. Understood as concrete labor stripped of particular traits, the concept of abstract labor can be applied across history. Temporal duration and homogeneity are underlying features of any particular human labor taken as abstract.

## From Abstract Labor and Time to Money and Capital

Value is the social form of commodities that allows commodities to have valid prices. The substance of value is the homogeneous stuff of congealed abstract labor that all commodities share. But abstract labor is universal and not socially specific. To describe the social form or purpose of abstract labor in capitalist society goes beyond homogeneity and temporal duration to money. Making money is the usual purpose of producing commodities. Congealed abstract labor that cannot be converted into money has no value. Crops will be plowed under if the price sinks far enough. The abstract labor congealed in commodities must be realized in the market to validate its claim to value. Unable to be sold, a product of human labor lacks value (Marx, 1976, pp. 179–180).

A commodity without a buyer still contains congealed abstract labor in its general sense, but it is valueless. Such a commodity lacks the particular social form of labor that defines capitalist society: what we can call *practically abstract* labor. Practically abstract labor involves a process linking production, exchange, and consumption in which the commodity's value must be realized as money by being sold. Abstract labor in the general sense is not socially determinate; it does not have the power of a social form. Practically abstract labor is value-producing labor; the value of its products must be realized as money through sale. Practically abstract labor is a specific social form of labor with the power to drive the accumulation process and shape a capitalist way of life. In this socially specific form of labor, the congealed abstract labor must undergo a process of social validation in which labor counts precisely *as* abstract labor.

Value is a familiar feature of commodities. Commodities appear as values that make sense out of prices. Marx argues that the substance of value is congealed abstract labor. But unpacking this conclusion opens up further specificities of abstraction. The abstract labor constituting the substance of the value of a commodity is not measured by individual labor time but by the average time required to make that sort of thing. The socially necessary labor time sets the norm of value. Only socially necessary labor is value producing (Marx, 1976, p. 120).

But the refinement of the social form continues. What makes the concept of abstract labor yet more confounding is that, fully grasped, it is not tallied as individual sums of abstract labor, much less sums of average labor time, but it is produced initially as an aggregate result of all capitalist production that is distributed to individual commodities through competition in markets. In Marx's terminology, commodities sell at their prices of production—cost price plus profit, as determined by the average rate of profit—not their individual values (Marx, 1981, parts 1, 2). Practically abstract labor occurs when social production is undertaken privately. Value exists first as a social aggregate and not an individual or average quantity. Individual values are a heuristic fiction. The price of production of an individual commodity is arrived at through competition with other commodities to establish their respective claims to profit. What any individual commodity is priced at results from this competitive struggle over the aggregate.

Sometimes abstract means distant from reality. But in science, abstractions that are true reveal what is real—as only they can. We may not experience subatomic forces in nature. But, ultimately, properly formed abstractions have implications for our experience of the world. Value is that kind of abstraction. Once it is established through inquiry into the world, other consequences follow directly and indirectly. For example, value is necessarily expressed as money. Money in capitalist societies plays a unique role. It is necessary both as means and end. The goal in capitalism is to increase the profits that result from production and to repeat that process endlessly. The accumulation of capital is not the only goal in modern society, but it drives capitalist societies like no other purpose, and when it begins to break down—in a recession or depression—the consequences are all too palpable. Capital accumulation is a commanding collective social purpose. As a specific social form, capital powerfully shapes and subsumes many aspects of our lives.

## Two Meanings of Marx's Description of Value as "Purely Social"

What are the sociological consequences of the social forms that define capitalist societies, such as commodity, value, money, wage labor, and capital? How is the social form of value unique in comparison with other ways of structuring societies? We propose that there are two meanings to the phrase "purely social" [*rein gesellschaftlich*] in Marx's repeated statement that value is "purely social." The first meaning is that value is "purely social" in that value is, as we have seen, *strictly* a consequence of a specific social form of labor: value is strictly social. Value is not a consequence of labor regardless of its particular social form, as in the classical (Ricardian) labor-embodied theory, as well as in what Postone calls Traditional Marxism. The second meaning does not contrast specifically social to general conceptions of value, as the first does; it has to do with *the kind of sociality* involved with value and value-producing labor, which might be called sheer sociality, barren sociality, or even asocial sociality. Thus, Marx writes of the exchange process, "Men are henceforth related to each other in their social process of production in a purely atomistic way" (Marx, 1976, p. 187). The sociality of value is a purist sort of sociality, and this purity—or emptiness—belongs to the nature of value as congealed abstract labor that has proven itself socially necessary.

When Marx reaches the end of the rapid two-part argumentation that moves from a world of commodities with valid prices first to the underlying "third thing" that he calls "value" and then to congealed abstract labor as the substance of value, he describes value as "this social substance," this "ghostly objectivity" [*gespenstige Gegenständlichkeit*] (Marx, 1976, p. 128). He comes back to that point at the beginning of his exposition of the form of value in Section 3 of Chap. 1. After a bawdy reference to Shakespeare's character Dame Quickly, Marx writes, "Not an atom of matter enters into the objectivity of commodities as values; in this it is the direct opposite of the coarsely sensuous objectivity of commodities as physical objects. We may twist and turn a single commodity as we wish; it remains impossible to grasp as a thing possessing value" (Marx, 1976, p. 138). *Since the commodity's value nature is its specific social form, this means that its social form cannot show itself in any of the commodity's perceptible features.*

As a consequence, the commodity appears to be a useful thing "pure and simple" (Marx, 1976, p. 153, 227), that is, commodities appear to have no specific social form. That contributes to "the illusion of the economic," that is, the notion that there is an economy in general, which is usually identified with the capitalist mode of production. "This fiction arises entirely from the inability to grasp the specific form of bourgeois production and this inability in turn arises from the obsession that bourgeois production is production as such" (Marx, 1968, p. 529). The "fiction" is the notion of an economy-in-general, or "production as such," to which the capitalist mode of production is reduced by extracting all of its constitutive social forms and purposes. Martha Campbell puts the point this way: capitalism "claims to create wealth pure and simple and [to be] organized by this purpose" (Campbell, 2004, p. 86).

This illusion lays the basis for the pseudo-science of economics, which purports to be, as it were, the science of the economy-in-general. Since there is no such thing—rather, there are only socially specific modes of production—economics is missing its object of inquiry. Marx reminds us that value is "an identical social substance" and that the "objective character [of commodities] as values is therefore purely social" [*ihre Wertgegenständlichkeit also rein gesellschaftlich ist*"] (Marx, 1976, pp. 138–139).³ From this observation, he immediately draws the conclusion that is the key to his account of the expression of value: "From this it follows self-evidently that it [value] can only appear in the social relation between commodity and commodity" (Marx, 1976, p. 139). Since value cannot appear in the body of the commodity, yet it must appear, it must appear in relation to another commodity, more particularly, to the universal equivalent, money. *Our question is: does this follow simply because the objectivity of value is something social or because the sociality of value is of a particular kind, namely, the "purely social"?* Sociality, after all, comes in countless varieties and likewise is expressed in countless ways. Put another way, does Marx's argument in Section 3. The Value-Form, or Exchange-Value depend upon the peculiar, *pure* sort of sociality that is involved with value? We believe so. First, more on the sociality of value.

The description of value as "purely social" offers a clue as to the *kind* of sociality that value involves. Its sociality is of a blank, empty sort. To begin, it is the sociality of simple commodity circulation, the marketplace, which Marx describes as "atomistic." In this sphere of simple commodity circulation reign *liberty, equality, property, and Bentham* (meaning *narrow self-interest*) (Marx, 1976, p. 280). The basic social roles in this sphere are those of buyer and seller (to which we may add borrower and lender). These roles presuppose private property and the mutual, but indifferent, recognition of participants in the market as free and equal persons. Bitzer, the repellant student in Thomas Gradgrind's school in Charles Dickens's *Hard Times*, explains how markets arrange human relations:

> It was a fundamental principle of the Gradgrind philosophy that everything was to be paid for. Nobody was ever on any account to give anybody anything, or render anybody help without purchase. Gratitude was to be abolished, and the virtues springing from it were not to be. Every inch of the existence of mankind, from birth to death, was to be a bargain across

a counter. And if we didn't get to heaven that way, it was not a politico-economical place, and we had no business there. (Dickens, 1990, p. 219)

As we will see, these hard-shell commercial sensibilities are not the whole story.

Simple commodity circulation—the free market—appears to have no organizing goal, no common purpose to ground and orient its form of sociality. There seems to be nothing mediating the narrow self-interest of participants in the market. Consequently, this narrow self-interestedness appears to be natural, the default drive of human beings. In other words, the economists' "homo economicus," or "economic man," is an ideological offspring of value's sort of sociality at the level of simple commodity circulation. This appearance of the market leads liberals, especially libertarian ones like Friedrich Hayek, to endorse this form of sociality, precisely because it lacks—or appears to lack—any compulsory collective good. Instead, the market presents itself as an arena where property owners freely pursue their self-interested aims. As such, the sociality of this sphere of simple commodity exchange appears peculiarly *asocial*. Though participants are expected to respect one another's dignity as persons by exchanging property on a voluntary basis, there is no expectation of anything resembling Aristotelian *philia*, no sense of belonging to a purposeful polis—the attitude that Hayek derides as a "tribal mentality."

One necessary, and troubling, unintended cost of this "sheer" sociality is the transfer of human social powers to human products that Marx calls the *fetishism of the commodity*. Marx writes: "Men are henceforth related to each other in their social process of production in a purely atomistic way. Their own relations of production therefore assume a material shape which is independent of their control and their conscious individual action" (Marx, 1976, p. 187). The young Hegel's formulation of this reversal surpasses Marx's language in its vehemence:

> Need and labor, elevated into this universality, then form on their own account a monstrous system of community and mutual interdependence in a great people; a life of the dead body, that moves itself within itself, one which ebbs and flows in its motion blindly, like the elements, and which requires continual strict dominance and taming like a wild beast. (Hegel, 1979, p. 249)

This pure, asocial form of sociality boomerangs on participants in a market and subjects them to the constant "discipline" of prices that periodically lurches out of control.

We believe that Marx's argument in Section 3, The Value-Form or Exchange-Value, of Chap. 1 of *Capital* I, turns on this second meaning of value's being "purely social." It is because the sociality of value is pure that—unlike other forms of sociality, such as gender, religious affiliation, or ethnicity—it must be expressed through the polarized value-form; that is, the value of one commodity must be expressed in an exchange relationship with another commodity; more particularly, with money. Marx calls attention to the strange, driven sociality of value by contrasting it with other forms of sociality, such as military rank, when he writes: "This proves only that, within its value-relation to the linen, the coat signifies more than it does outside it, just as some men count for more when inside a gold-braided uniform than they do otherwise" (Marx, 1976, p. 143). The social character of the commodity—which is what value is—cannot be expressed by any of its physical features. On the contrary, the effect of the social character of the commodity's being expressed in a thing separate from itself, a sum of money, is that the commodity appears to be "use-value pure and simple" (Marx, 1976, p. 227), that is, the commodity has the illusory appearance of lacking specific social form altogether. Marx explains:

> The internal opposition between use-value and value, hidden within the commodity, is therefore represented on the surface by an external opposition, i.e., by a relation between two commodities such that the one commodity, whose own value is supposed to be expressed, counts directly only as a use-value, whereas the other commodity, in which that value is to be expressed, counts directly only as exchange-value. (Marx, 1976, p. 153)

Money is pure sociality *an sich*, in itself. As a fetish, money, a thing you can carry in your pocket like a rabbit's foot, packs social power of a peculiar, purist kind, namely, purchasing power, which is indifferent to the purchaser, the seller, and the useful character of what is purchased.

## More to the Story: Some Qualifications to the "Purely Social" Sociality of Value

Marx's claim that value is "purely social" must be qualified first by his own observations that there is no value where there is no use-value and that labor does not produce use-values on its own but rather only by working on, with, and through nature and within and through a specific social form: "All production is appropriation of nature on the part of an individual within and through a specific form of society" (Marx, 1973, p. 87). The fact that the expression of value in the value form is necessarily polarized brings home this inseparability of value from use-value. Value may be supra-sensible, but its necessary form of appearance, money, is material. Failure to recognize the implications of this leads to Use-value Romanticism. Any suggestion of a radical split between the social and the natural goes against the grain of Marx's historical materialist philosophy: describing value as "purely social" and "supra-sensible" already suggests that there is something perverse about it.

Marx argues that sheer sociality is far from the whole story about the type of sociality involved with value. For Marx argues that simple commodity circulation presupposes the circulation—and, ultimately, the boundless accumulation—of capital. *Value presupposes surplus value*—the aim of the circulation of capital. In the *Urtext*, Marx describes simple commodity circulation, the market, as "an abstract sphere of the bourgeois process of production as a whole, which through its own determinations shows itself to be a moment, a mere form of appearance of some deeper process lying behind it, even resulting from it and producing it" (Marx, 1987, p. 482). Capital, which is value that drives endlessly toward increase and accumulation, is the truth of value. The barren sociality of commodity circulation derives from the frightful emptiness of capital: Chris Arthur's essay "The Spectre of Capital" is an alarming meditation on the void at the heart of capital (Arthur, 2002, pp. 153–174). To account for the circulation of capital, which necessarily takes place both within and beyond commodity circulation, Marx introduces considerations that reveal a very different kind of sociality than that of the market. Whereas social class and the material character of the commodities being exchanged did not matter in the formally egalitarian space of the market, they do enter into the circulation of capital. At this more concrete level, we must distinguish between the class of owners of the means of production and subsistence, the capitalist class, and the class of "doubly free" wage earners, who support themselves through the constantly renewed sale of their own labor power. In the form of sociality that characterizes production on a capitalist basis, capitalists, by virtue of being owners of the means of production, are in charge of the production process. Capitalists direct production for the specific social purpose of acquiring—and accumulating—surplus value, that is, an increment of value above their original investment. Marx portrays this shift from the marketplace to the production site with reference to Dante's *Divine Comedy*: with the sale of labor power the wage worker goes from the relatively benign Plain of Acheron, simple commodity circulation, the "noisy sphere" where the purchase and sale of labor power take place, into the inferno of capitalist production, where the worker can expect to be skinned (Marx, 1976, pp. 279–280).

Realizing that simple commodity circulation is the necessary form of appearance of the circulation of capital dispels the liberal illusion that the free market has no compulsory collective purpose. The market does have one, in which the barren sociality of commodity circulation is embedded. This compulsory collective purpose, the endless accumulation of capital, is no one's choice for the common good. Further investigation of the capitalist mode of production reveals more features of this peculiar form of sociality, including inescapable class conflicts over the wage, the length and intensity of the workday, and the humaneness of working conditions—not to mention tendencies to throw the whole system into crisis.

What Marx calls the real subsumption of labor under capital involves the technical or material transformation of labor processes for the purpose of squeezing out more surplus value. In *Capital* Marx treats these transformations, which include cooperation, manufacture, and large-scale industry, under the heading of relative surplus value (Marx, 1976, part 4). Phenomena such as "efficiency, calculability, predictability, and control," popularly referred to as "McDonaldization" (Ritzer, 2000, p. 12) may be better conceived of as real subsumption under capital. The concept of real subsumption may be extended to commodities when they are materially altered to extract more surplus value. The two may go hand in hand; for example, changes in agriculture, processing, or transportation often alter the food delivered to consumers. Perhaps the best recognized examples of the real subsumption of commodities under capital involve "planned obsolescence," that is, speeding-up repurchases either by deliberately decreasing the durability of commodities or by styling them so as to go out of fashion quickly. "Junk food," often engineered to be quasi-addictive, is a costly manifestation of real subsumption (Albritton, 2009). Today's gigantic entertainment industry affords countless examples. Consider popular music coined "corporate rock" and scripts rewritten to satisfy bean counters and their test audiences. Does the emptiness of moneymaking leach into Hollywood blockbuster sequels and television sitcoms? Peter Weir's film *The Truman Show* offers an answer: when a reality sitcom abruptly goes off the air after 30 years of continuous transmission, two parking attendants watching the show pause momentarily, then ask, "What else is on?"

When we extend our inquiry conceptually beyond the marketplace to the production of commodities on a capitalist basis, we have to reconsider the starting point of the analysis, the assumption—which was appropriate at that level of abstraction—that the value nature of the commodity leaves no traces on the body of the commodity. With the real subsumption of commodities under capital, their value character, more particularly their surplus-value character in all its emptiness, marks them materially.

## Notes

1. In *From Political Economy to Economics*, Ben Fine and Dimitris Milonakis explore "the process by which political economy became economics, through the desocialisation and dehistoricisation of the dismal science, and how this heralded the separation of economics from the other social sciences at the beginning of the twentieth century" (2009, p. 1).
2. In fact, not every commodity is a value. As Marx points out, due to the independence of the price-form, "a thing can, formally speaking, have a price without having a value" (Marx, 1976, p. 197). Undeveloped land is a case in point. For more on this point, see Murray, 2005.
3. Marx describes value as a "supra-natural property" [*übernatürliche Eigenschaft*] that is "something purely social" [*etwas rein gesellschaftliches*] (Marx, 1976, p. 149). At the beginning of Section 4, *The Fetishism of the Commodity and Its Secret*, Marx describes the commodity as "a thing which transcends sensuousness" [*ein sinnlich übersinnliches Ding*] (Marx, 1976, p. 163).

## References

Albritton, R. (2009). *Let them eat junk: How capitalism creates hunger and obesity*. London/New York: Pluto Press.

Arthur, C. J. (2002). *The new dialectic and Marx's 'Capital'*. Leiden, NL: Brill.

Campbell, M. (2004). The objectivity of value versus the idea of habitual action. In R. Bellofiore & N. Taylor (Eds.), *The constitution of capital: Essays on volume I of Marx's 'Capital'*. Basingstoke: Palgrave Macmillan.

Clarke, S. N. (1982). *Marx, marginalism and modern sociology*. London: Macmillan.

Dickens, C. (1990). *Hard times* (2nd ed.) (Eds. G. Ford & S. Monod). New York and London: W.W. Norton & Company.

Fine, B., & Milonakis, D. (2009). *From political economy to economics: Method, the social and the historical in the evolution of economic theory*. London and New York: Routledge.

Hegel, G. W. F. (1979). *System of ethical life (1802/3) and first philosophy of spirit (Part III of the system of speculative philosophy 1803/4)* (H. S. Harris & T. M. Knox, Eds. and Trans.). Albany: State University of New York Press.

Heidegger, M. (2010). *Being and time* (J. Stambaugh, Trans.; Revised by D. J. Schmidt). Albany: State University of New York Press.

Lotz, C. (2012). *The capitalist schema: Time, money, and the culture of abstraction*. Lanham, MD: Lexington Books.

Marx, K. (1968). *Theories of surplus-value, Part II* (R. Simpson, Trans.; S. W. Ryazanskaya, Ed.). London: Lawrence & Wishart.

Marx, K. (1973). *Grundrisse* (M. Nicolaus, Trans.). Harmondsworth, England: Penguin Books.

Marx, K. (1976). *Capital: Volume one* (B. Fowkes, Trans.). Harmondsworth: Penguin Books.

Marx, K. (1981). *Capital: Volume three* (D. Fernbach, Trans.). London: Penguin.

Marx, K. (1987). *Economic manuscripts of 1857–1858* (V. Schnittke & Y. Sdobnikov, Trans.; L. Miskievich, Ed.). In K. Marx & F. Engels (Eds.), *Collected works* (Vol. 29). London: Lawrence and Wishart.

Murray, P. (2005). The new giant's staircase. *Historical Materialism, 13*(2), 61–83.

Polanyi, K. (1968). Aristotle discovers the economy. In G. Dalton (Ed.), *Primitive, archaic, and modern economics: Essays of Karl Polanyi*. Garden City: Doubleday.

Postone, M. (1993). *Time, labour, and social domination: A reinterpretation of Marx's critical theory*. Cambridge: Cambridge University Press.

Ritzer, G. (2000). *The McDonaldization of society*. Thousand Oaks: Pine Forge Press.

Rubin, I. I. (1972). *Essays on Marx's theory of value* (M. Samardzija & F. Perlman, Trans.). Detroit: Black & Red.

Sandel, M. J. (2012). *What money can't buy: The moral limits of markets*. New York: Farrar, Straus and Giroux.

# PART II

# Concrete

CHAPTER 6

# Debt in the Global Economy

*Tony Smith*

A number of striking developments in the role of debt distinguish our historical period. In the first section of the chapter, I shall present seven "stylized facts" about our social world. From the standpoint of most mainstream economic theories, they are all anomalies, caused by extraneous factors. As Thomas Kuhn taught long ago in *The Structure of Scientific Revolutions*, however, there is some point past which the accretion of anomalies and ad hoc explanations calls established paradigms into question. I shall argue that a Marxian framework extrapolated from Volume 3 of *Capital* offers a superior basis for comprehending these crucially important features of the contemporary world.

## Seven "Anomalies" Of Debt In Contemporary Capitalism

### The Scale of the Increase in Debt

In 1945, after years of government deficits to fund the costs of World War II, total debt in the US economy was $355 billion. By 1964, total

---

T. Smith (✉)
Department of Philosophy and Religious Studies, Iowa State University, Ames, IA, USA

© The Author(s) 2017
D. Krier, M.P. Worrell (eds.), *The Social Ontology of Capitalism*,
DOI 10.1057/978-1-137-59952-0_6

credit in the USA just exceeded $1 trillion. By 2007, the figure had skyrocketed to an astounding $50 trillion (Duncan, 2012, p. 2). The USA, enjoying the privilege of having a national currency that serves as the dominant form of world money, has been able to extend the credit creation process far beyond most other regions. Nonetheless, the explosion of debt has been a truly global phenomenon. Total debt in China, for example, more than tripled from $2.1 trillion in 2000 to $7.4 trillion in 2007. It then increased 400 % to $28.2 trillion by 2014. Comparable increases have occurred in Japan, South Korea, Australia, Germany and elsewhere (Dobbs, Lund, Woetzel, & Mutafchieva, 2015).

Debt has been at the heart of modern capitalism since it first emerged. Credit enabled merchants to continue operating before the return of their ships, industrial firms to continue producing before final sales to customers, and farmers to continue planting and harvesting prior to bringing crops to markets. Debt has allowed new merchants, new industrialists and new farmers to enter economic life and challenge incumbents. Debt has enabled states to prepare for and wage wars, which Marx and Weber both agreed provided a crucial spur to capitalist development. Debt furthered market demand for consumer goods, at first mostly luxury goods consumed by aristocrats, later mass-produced goods for mass consumption. All of these familiar considerations remain important in capitalist market societies today. But precisely because they have been so constant in the history of capitalism they are not sufficient to explain the astounding and unprecedented explosion of debt in recent decades.

### *The Combination of Increasing Debt and Declining Rates of Investment in the World Economy as a Whole*

In mainstream social theory, the primary role of the financial sector is to allocate investment funds efficiently, whether through mobilizing the "loanable funds" of savers (as assumed in neoclassical economics) or through the creation of credit ex nihilo (the superior Keynesian and Post Keynesian view). Of course credit is not extended solely for investment; consumer credit, for example, is obviously also important. Nonetheless, it seems natural to assume that credit and investment will increase roughly in sync, even if not in a direct one-to-one ratio. This has not happened. Despite the widespread availability of relatively inexpensive credit in the last decades, rates of investment in the capitalist world market as a whole have tended to *decline* in recent decades (This decline of rates of investment in the world market as a whole is even more perplexing when we consider that it has coincided with the greatest *increase* in investment in world history in China and other parts of East Asia).

### *The Increasing Ratio of Debt to Gross Domestic Product*

If capitalism in general and financial markets in particular worked the way economics textbooks say they work, an increase in the extension of credit would generally be correlated with an increase in the rate of growth in the world market. It would therefore seem reasonable to expect that the greatest explosion of credit in world history would be correlated with a higher rate of growth at the very least, and perhaps one unprecedentedly high. But rates of growth in the world market had been *declining* relative to debt levels even prior to the "Great Recession" of 2007–09. Debt has been giving "less bang for the buck," so to speak; ever-greater amounts of debt have been required in order to generate a given increment of economic growth: "In 1968 credit exceeded GDP by 1.5 times. In 2007, the amount of credit in the economy had grown to 3.4 times total economic output" (Duncan, 2012, pp. 2, 49).

### *The Rise of Financialization*

In mainstream paradigms, the proper role of the financial sector is to serve as a means for the efficient allocation of resources to firms in the "real" economy promising to contribute efficiently to the fulfillment of human wants and needs. According to Adam Smith's "invisible hand" thesis, updated in an immensely more mathematically sophisticated form in models asserting the rational efficiency of financial markets, these will be the most profitable firms. It follows that we should expect that the share of credit money remaining within the financial sector to be relatively small and relatively constant. But the portion of the credit created in the global economy since 1980 that circulates within the financial sector has been increasingly large. In the USA, the debt of the private sector as a whole jumped from 123 % of GDP in 1981 to 290 % by the end of 2008. While corporate debt increased from 53 % of GDP to 76 %, and household debt went from 48 % to 100 %, it was the financial sector's transformation that was most astounding, soaring from 22 % of GDP to 117 % (Roubini & Mihm, 2010, p. 83).

## The Frequency and Scale of Financial Crises

What has happened to the credit money created within the financial sector and then remaining within it? It is beyond dispute that much of this credit has fueled self-sustaining bubbles in financial assets in recent decades. There were only 38 financial crises between 1945 and 1971. The tally then jumped to 139 between 1973 and 1997, with the dot.com bubble, the housing bubble and numerous others yet to come (Wolf, 2008, p. 31). As I write, the stock markets of China, the USA and just about all "emerging markets" are in turmoil, strongly suggesting that the intensified rhythm of speculative boom and collapse continues to characterize our era. It is unclear, to say the least, how helpful established paradigms appealing to the "invisible hand" or the "rational efficiency" of financial markets are for comprehending this feature of the contemporary global market.

## Extensive and Persisting Global Imbalances

According to mainstream paradigms, massive imbalances in the *current account* (focused largely on cross-border trade) and the *capital account* (predominantly measuring cross-border flows of investment) are not supposed to persist in the global economy. In theory, any trade imbalances that do arise are supposed to be corrected reasonably quickly and efficiently by the workings of markets. Suppose, for example, a surplus nation's exporters have accumulated a considerable amount of foreign revenues through sales to a region suffering a trade deficit. At some point, those exporters will exchange the revenues they have accumulated in the currencies of the deficit region for their home currency (They may, for example, need the home currency to distribute dividends to home investors). This increases both the demand in currency markets for the home currency and the supply of the deficit region's currency, leading the former to appreciate while the latter depreciates. The exports of the surplus region will then be constrained, since they are now more expensive when measured in the currency of the deficit region. Imports from the deficit region are correspondingly spurred, having become cheaper when measured in the surplus nation's own currency. Rebalancing results, or so the story goes.

Things have not been working this way. Significant imbalances between surplus regions and deficit regions have persisted in the global economy (Pettis, 2013). The hope that matters would change in the aftermath of the Great Recession has proven vain. The US trade balance did improve somewhat in the immediate aftermath, only to deteriorate again. China's trade surpluses were once again at record heights in 2015 (Turner, 2015: 181). The Eurozone is obviously far more concerned with managing the consequences of significant and lasting imbalances between surplus and deficit regions than with overcoming them.

### *The Lack of "Deleveraging" in the Years Following the "Great Recession"*

The "Great Recession" was a "balance sheet recession"; high levels of debt on the liabilities side of balance sheets were no longer "balanced" by financial assets whose past value had proven wildly overinflated. A 2010 report of the McKinsey Global Institute examined previous episodes of "balance sheet recessions," and discovered that repairing the books of governments, corporations and households—that is, lowering debts to balance liabilities with the significantly lowered assets ("deleveraging")—has typically taken five to seven years. It is now seven years since the official end of the Great Recession, and debt has *increased* since 2009: "since 2007, global debt has grown by $57 trillion, raising the ratio of debt to GDP by 17 percentage points" (Dobbs et al., 2015, p. vi). This too is an anomaly from the standpoint of mainstream paradigms.

## Two Familiar Accounts

These features of our social world just sketched are striking and obviously important. Some account of their emergence and persistence is clearly needed. Most familiar attempts to account for them fit under one of two headings.

### *Moral Failures*

Right-wing moralists have a ready explanation for high debt levels: irresponsible borrowers indulged in consumption sprees beyond what their income allowed. Others, less inclined to blame victims of predatory lending, point to the greed of mortgage lenders, credit card companies, the payday loan companies that are no more than fronts for big banks and so on, who take advantage of the disadvantaged, imposing interest rates that would make Tony Soprano blush. Whether this is ultimately due to the failure of business schools to provide their students with adequate training in business ethics, or to their graduates' willful failure to heed the moral lessons they were taught, is left unclear.

A parallel moralism afflicts many discussions of global imbalances. Some wag their fingers at deficit regions living beyond their means. The world's premier deficit nation, the USA, is often accused of abusing its "exorbitant privilege"; having a national currency serving as the main form of world money, it is able to absorb a wildly disproportionate share of the world's material output in return for pieces of paper (Prasad, 2014). Other commentators shift the moral blame to surplus regions like China and Germany, which supposedly use their "savings glut" to engage in currency manipulation. By preventing an appreciation of their currency that would make their exports more expensive, they are able to artificially keep their exports high, while discouraging the growth of imports from deficit regions that could lessen global imbalances. The dumping of their savings glut in deficit regions also forces low savings rates and speculative bubbles there, with predictably harmful social consequences (Bernanke, 2005).

Far be it from me to deny that countless people have acted in countless morally problematic ways in recent decades. Lenders have exhibited high levels of greed and dishonesty; entire sectors have been dominated by Ponzi schemes; not all borrowers have been altogether honest when asked to disclose their financial status; agents in deficit regions have embraced hyperconsumerist lifestyles; the manipulation of currencies has undoubtedly occurred. However, it would be very difficult to argue that human nature suddenly became more corrupt in recent decades. If we want a more plausible explanation of the recent explosion of debt in the global economy, we must look elsewhere.

## *Political Failures*

Here again, we have a choice. For those convinced that state officials are incompetent at best and evil all too often, any social order that does not minimize the role of the state will invariably be plagued with serious difficulties. State officials, after all, love to hand out gifts they do not have, and make promises they cannot keep. The roots of the housing crisis, according to some, can be traced back to misguided legislation mandating that mortgages be extended to disadvantaged citizens, thereby forcing lenders to lower their lending standards beyond what prudence dictated. Theorists of the right also complain that governments have attempted to win momentary popularity by interfering with the market corrections necessary for medium-to-long-term stable economic growth. Any short-term gains have come at the cost of immense problems of moral hazard. Can we really be surprised if financiers take crazy risks once it has become clear they will be bailed out with public monies? From this perspective, Alan Greenspan's decision to keep interest rates at historic lows for six years caused the housing bubble as directly as the fire thrown on the gasoline tank caused the subsequent explosion.

Left liberals are astonished that anyone could think that programs addressing banks' redlining of poor communities should be blamed for predatory lending in those communities. The fault lies instead with the failure of the political system to regulate the financial sector effectively. Some regulators succumbed to political lobbying by the financial sector, including various subtle and not all that subtle forms of bribery. Others were sincerely seduced by the ideological power of the myth of rationally efficient financial markets. All were guilty of "forgetting" Keynes's message that the financial system will only fulfill its proper role in support of the satisfaction of wants and needs if it is subjected to effective political regulation (Davidson, 2009). As a result, the behavior or borrowers, lenders and ratings agencies became thoroughly distorted by perverted incentives and conflicts of interest.

Explanations that appeal to a failure of political will to account for the social pathologies associated with debt today are as ad hoc as appeals to the immorality of contemporary social agents. They too appeal to an extraneous factor, rather than the intrinsic workings of the global economy. This in itself does not make them wrong; they may still have at least part of the story at least partly right. But we should hesitate before accepting appeals to contingent and external factors as the whole story. At the very least, we should investigate whether an account can be developed that is more immanent to the phenomena we are attempting to explain.

In the following sections, I shall sketch an alternative Marxian explanatory framework that meets this criterion. A general pattern of capitalist development that Marx extrapolated from his studies and developed in the rough drafts making up Volume 3 of *Capital* will first be presented. This general pattern will then be modified in light of major developments in the world market since World War II. With this framework in place, we will be in a position to see that the supposed anomalies regarding debt in the contemporary global economy are not so anomalous after all.

## A General Pattern in Capitalist Development

Engels molded a number of unpublished manuscripts in widely varying states of completeness into Volume 3 of *Capital* (Moseley, 2015). In Part 5, Marx extrapolated from his historical studies a large-scale cyclical pattern in the world market unfolding over the course of many decades. In this section, I shall sketch the main phases of this pattern, supplementing the narrative in Marx's drafts when appropriate. I believe the pattern Marx discerned provides a helpful starting point for understanding the changing role of credit and accumulation in the different phases of what may be termed "systematic cycles of accumulation" (Arrighi, 1994).

Commodities, Marx tells us, do not have *value* unless they have *use-value* for those with purchasing power. So we may take as our *starting point* a set of firms investing in the commercialization of a cluster of radical innovations with use-values for either final consumers or other producers. To make the starting point as pure as possible, we can abstract from retained earnings and assume that these investments are made with newly created credit money, borrowed from banks or other financial institutions (Bellofiore, 2005). If profits are later won from sales, the initial investment is *valorized*. In more Marxian jargon, the commodities are shown to have the special "supersensuous" social property of "value," measured in money, the form in which value appears when the concrete labor producing the commodities in question proves to be abstract (value producing) socially necessary labor. The initial loans can now be repaid out of profits from sale. This encourages further loans to make further investments in the next generation of innovations. As more and more firms hope to share in the rewards from developing the innovations further, the *acceleration* phase of a systematic cycle of accumulation commences. Credit continues to fund new firms in the period before they are able to bring the innovations to market. Credit also prevents production and distribution from coming to an abrupt halt when payments come due before revenues have been received. Expanded accumulation can also be furthered by extending loans to those purchasing the new innovations.

Some of the additional credit money created in the course of a given circuit of investment and return enables the valorization of investments and loans in that particular circuit. Other infusions of credit are in effect a "prevalidation" of a valorization that will not occur until sales are made in some subsequent circuit. As long as non-financial sectors and financial sectors expand more or less in sync, capital accumulation can continue for an extended period.

This happy phase, however, necessarily tends to end for a variety of reasons. We may consider the use-value dimension first. Technological change generally tends to follow a specific pattern, a *technology trajectory* that can be mapped as an elongated S curve (Perez, 2002). The initial points on the trajectory form a curve with a small positive slope, representing a slow rate of advance as various designs and uses for the cluster of radical innovations are tried out. Most prove to be dead ends. This period of experimentation concludes when a *technology paradigm* is adopted, a shared social consensus among designers and consumers regarding the general form and function of the innovation. Once the paradigm has been adopted by a critical mass of technologists and end users, a period of rapid advances can commence, shifting the slope of the technology trajectory sharply upwards. As long as large portions of the opportunity space for further innovation remain unexplored, the slope remains steep. Eventually, however, the opportunity space of innovation begins to be exhausted, and the curve representing technological change levels off. Further incremental improvements to products, and further incremental productivity advances, bring relatively minor advantages. These use-value considerations provide one important part of the explanation why rapid growth in markets eventually slows down: the markets most closely associated with the established technology paradigm no longer grow rapidly as the opportunity space for innovations opened by the paradigm becomes exhausted.

Use-value considerations are, of course, only one dimension of capitalist development. Class relations matter as well. Growth in capitalism over time can continue only if class relations are successfully reproduced through macro-monetary circuits of commodities and money. Workers must receive wages sufficient to allow them to purchase the goods and services they and their dependents require to maintain historically specific living standards in the given period, but not so generous that continued capital accumulation is threatened. Their living labor must continue to produce commodity outputs with a greater value than the commodity inputs; in other words, surplus value must be produced. And the owners of investment capital (and/or their agents) must be able to maintain control over how the produced surplus value is allocated.

As Kalecki argued in his classical article, "The Political Consequences of Full Employment," maintaining capitalist class relations generally demands the threat of unemployment (Kalecki, 1971). The longer a period of expansion lasts, however, the more likely it is that labor shortages will emerge in crucial sectors and regions, leading to wage gains and a significant shift in the balance of power in labor's favor. The coercive pressure to sell labor power doesn't entirely disappear, but the pressure to accept terms dictated by capital weakens. Representatives of capital also tend to have weaker control over the labor process, making the production and appropriation of surplus value more precarious. Successful capitalist growth over an extended period, then, requires disciplinary mechanisms effectively ensuring the reproduction of the social relations of capitalism. When these mechanisms become less effective, the rate of investment tends to slow.

A third possible factor contributing to the tendency for a period of expansion to eventually slow is captured in Minsky's financial instability thesis, anticipated by Marx in Volume 3 (Marx, 1981, chap. 30; Minsky, 2008). In the course of an extended upswing, loans prevalidated in one circuit are in fact validated in the next as interest payments and principal are repaid. Over time, banks complacently begin to assume this will always be the case, leading to a lowering of lending standards. At some point, however, banks begin to worry that they have become overextended. The rate of growth in credit will then begin to slacken.

In my view, however, the single most important consideration in comprehending why the rate of accumulation slows down is the systematic tendency to an "overaccumulation" of capital investment (Brenner, 2006; Reuten, 1991). When more efficient producers enter a sector, this typically forces the least productive units of capital out of business. But other established units of production have strong incentives to remain operating if they can. They have already invested in fixed capital (machinery, buildings, etc.). If production is shut down now, there will be nothing to show for their past investments; if they continue in operation, they may be able to win at least the average rate of profit on their circulating capital (i.e., their investments in raw materials, wages, transportation costs, labor power, etc.). It is also the case that the management and work force of these firms have sector-specific skills that would be difficult to duplicate in any reasonable time period were they to shift operations to a different sector. Further, these units of capital likely have established relationships with suppliers and distributors, relationships that would again likely be difficult and costly to establish in other sectors within a reasonable time frame. And local governments and universities may be providing them with important support (infrastructure, research, etc.) that would be withdrawn were they to cease operating in the sector. There is, finally, always the hope that if they can hold on long enough, they may be able to introduce innovations allowing them to leapfrog over their competitors at some future point.

These considerations are all rational from the perspective of individual producers. But when they are acted upon, the result is irrational from the collective point of view: the sector as a whole tends to be afflicted with excessive productive capacity relative to what markets can absorb. As long as markets grow in sync with increases in productive capacity, this tendency is held in check. Sooner or later, however, markets cease growing rapidly enough, and excess productive capacity accumulates in the sector.

The outbreak of excess capacity in major sectors is not the outbreak of an overaccumulation crisis. That is because further lending doesn't automatically halt when rapid expansion ceases. Loans will continue to be made on the assumption that any slowdown is temporary, due to contingencies sure to change. At a later point, loans will still continue to be made because lenders do not want to write off their previous loans. Their liabilities will not be reduced if their assets decline, and so they are threatened with insolvency if their most important category of assets, the loans they have made, disappear from the books. Fear of insolvency motivates them to continue lending to troubled firms in the hope they can stay functioning until market conditions improve. If some firms must perish in the meantime, the hope is that those tied to other lenders will be the ones to fall. One last consideration to keep in mind here is that at this phase in the systematic cycle, when previous paths of accumulation are becoming exhausted, the promise of new paths is especially alluring. As increasingly desperate investors begin to borrow increasing amounts to chase the "next big thing," speculative frenzy begins to play a bigger and bigger role pushing the economy forward.[1] Amid the resulting inflation of financial assets, fraud thrives like bacteria in a kiddy pool.

Marx termed this period the "overexertion" phase of systematic cycles (Marx, 1981, p. 619).[2] Credit, still easily available (although perhaps at higher interest rates), enables capital accumulation to continue, despite fewer profitable innovations, shifts in the balance of power in labor markets and labor processes, a dawning awareness that lending standards have been too lax, and growing excess capacity in the major sectors of the world market. During this period, the connection between value and money is broken. Money can no longer simply be seen as the form of value, the objective validation of socially necessary production. Nor does money take the form of loans that prevalidate a valorization process occurring in a subsequent circuit of capital. The loans that are used to inflate the prices of capital assets are forms of money that have been decoupled from the value process, with no real hope of being recoupled in some later circuit.

In Marx's framework, the end of the overexertion phase is preordained, even if the precise timing of its end is indeterminate. The repayment of loans by some financial agents generally depends upon other financial agents rolling over loans and expanding their lending in the future. When the faith that lenders in the future will continue to lend at the required rates is called into question (often by some event trivial in itself), lending ceases to expand, loans cease being automatically rolled over, debts begin to be called in. A sharp rise in demand from borrowers, now needing cash to meet pressing debt obligations, pushes interest rates sharply higher, making it yet more difficult for others to roll their debts over. A panicked rush to hard cash to meet payments as they come due leads to a selloff of financial assets and a corresponding a sharp decline in their prices. The balance sheets of those still holding those assets rapidly erode, condemning many to insolvency. In brief, a generalized credit crunch sets off a cyclical downswing, revealing the fictitiousness of the fictitious capital.

In Part 5 of Volume 3 of *Capital,* Marx severely criticized the so-called "banking school" for advocating central bank operations to protect gold reserves by raising interest rates during a credit crunch. This policy greatly exacerbated the social costs of a downswing. But Marx did not believe that the more accommodating policies of the "currency school" could prevent severe downswings from occurring; they could only lessen somewhat their negative consequences. Sooner rather than later, overaccumulation in the "real" economy would have to be addressed by devaluation or the outright destruction of past capital investment. This process restores the connection between value and money that was broken when the prices of financial assets were decoupled from the process of the valorization of social labor.

There are no final crises for capitalism. Unless it is overthrown by collective political action, at some point a new cluster of radical innovations becomes available for commercialization. At some point, the labor force has been suitably disciplined by unemployment.[3] At some point, a critical mass of the bad loans of the financial sector is off the books. And at some point, so much productive capacity will have been devalued or dismantled that extended investment in expanding capacity again makes sense.

## A Marxian Overview of Contemporary Global Capitalism

It must suffice here to sketch the "deep structure" of the present historical moment in broad strokes. The global rebuilding after the devastation of World War II was fueled by the explosion of investment, credit money and (military spending) flowing into the world market from the USA. An extended period of global expansion commenced, based on innovations in the technologies of mass production. By the 1970s, however, Japanese and European capitals had caught up. Many were in fact more efficient producers of higher quality products than established US firms in economically crucial sectors of the world market (consumer electronics, autos, motorcycles, chemicals, business machines, steel, etc.). US producers, however, did not withdraw from these sectors in the face of more efficient competitors. This refusal was rational from their individual point of view, for reasons discussed in the previous section. But it generated a collectively irrational result: there was now excess productive capacity in every major sector of the world market, due to an *overaccumulation* of capital investment in those sectors. Lower rates of investment and profit followed (Brenner, 2006; Desai, 2013).

One way of overcoming an overaccumulation crisis is through the physical destruction of excess capacity. Another world war would have eliminated excess capacity very effectively. Thankfully, that was not on the agenda. A severe recession or depression could have done the job by bankrupting a critical mass of firms and devaluing previous investment in productive capacity. Given the level of excess capacity in place by the 1970s, however, the scale of the dismantling and devaluation required would have been truly enormous. Members of the ruling circles in the USA had an extremely strong incentive to avoid that outcome. Devaluing capital on the scale required would have inflicted massive harm on US capitals in particular, due to their now weaker competitive positions in key sectors of the world economy. The ability of the US economy to remain at the center of the world market would have been profoundly called into question. The dollar's rule as the dominant form of world money, and the hegemonic geopolitical power of the US state, would also have been threatened.

Following the general pattern of capitalist development Marx sketched in Volume 3, credit increased with the outbreak of overaccumulation problems in the USA. Nixon's unilateral decision to cut the tie between the main form of world money (the dollar) and gold allowed credit creation to jump far more sharply than would otherwise have been the case. As the creation of credit money expanded, however, inflation began to erupt.

Inflation is never a purely monetary phenomenon; it always reflects social relations. In the case at hand, inflation reflected the balance of power between capital and labor after the long post–World War II boom. While workers had the power to win wage increases, units of capital had the power to maintain profits by raising prices. Realizing that higher prices for wage goods counteracted the increase in their nominal wages, workers then demanded further wage hikes. Capital responded with yet higher prices. Central banks, fearing that inflation would become uncontrolled, periodically engineered credit crunches. However, the resulting economic damage quickly led them to lower interest rates again, beginning another round of inflation. Far from leading to balanced growth, the expansion of credit in the 1970s led to a toxic combination of inflation and stagnation ("stagflation").

If inflation reflects the social relations in society, then any "solution" must transform those relations. Unsurprisingly, the option selected by US elites was to destroy the power of labor to maintain its traditional share of the total social product. The "Volcker shock" engineered by the Federal Reserve in 1979 lifted interest rates to the stratosphere and kept them there until they had the foreseeable (and foreseen) effect of creating levels of unemployment previously considered politically unacceptable. Aggressive attacks commenced against state workers, beginning with Reagan's firing of striking airline controllers. Labor relations boards were stacked with rabidly pro-business members. With a green light from the state, the private sector initiated its own attacks on labor, using the weapons of technologically induced unemployment, technologically induced deskilling, an increasing use of part-time and temporary workers, and extensive capital flight, first to regions in the USA with low rates of unionization, and then across borders to regions where wage rates were a fraction of those in the USA (Smith, 2000, 2005).[4] As the rate of exploitation jumped, profit rates were restored (Mohun, 2009).

With this historical background in mind, we can now return to the "anomalies" presented in the first section of this paper. Once we realize how capital has mutated in our moment of world history, and how Marx's pattern of systematic cycles of accumulation needs to be modified in response, they do not appear so anomalous at all.

## The Non-anomalous "Anomalies"

### *The Explosion of Credit Money*

Once capital won the war on labor, a truly massive expansion of credit could commence without inflation in wage or consumer markets. Commentators praised central banks for having engineered a "Great Moderation," willfully blind to the underlying shift in social relations. In a rare moment of lucidity, Alan Greenspan, Volcker's replacement as head of the US Federal Reserve, did confess that the moderation of inflation rested on "the traumatized worker," incapable of winning wage increases due to the threat of downsizing and capital flight (Woodward, 2000, p. 168).

The explosion of credit money enabled productive capacity in non-financial sectors to be absorbed that would otherwise have been devalued or destroyed.[5] Together with the rise of the rate of exploitation, this contributed greatly to the recovery of profits from the global slowdown of the 1970s.[6]

The pattern of capitalist development sketched by Marx in Volume 3 remains a useful starting point for comprehending the contemporary economy. But it must be modified in one profound respect: *the unprecedented explosion of debt enabled what Marx termed the "overexertion" phase in the pattern to be extended to an unprecedented degree.* As a result, the social pathologies of this phase have been extended indefinitely as well.

### *The Declining Rate of Investment*

Profits recovered from the global slowdown of the 1970s, thanks in good measure to the explosion of credit. The explosion of credit allowed productive capacity to be absorbed that would otherwise have gone unused, thereby valorizing investments that otherwise would have gone unvalorized. It justified replacing productive capacity as it became worn out or outdated. It also justified the commercialization of promising paths of innovation. It even justified some regions (like China) increasing investment at a rate never seen before in world history. Nonetheless, the major sectors of the world market have continued to be beset by express productive capacity. If anything, these difficulties have tended to intensify with the rapid industrialization of China and other regions in East Asia. And so the recovery of profits did *not* motivate the sort of increased rate of investment in the world market as a whole that in the past has spurred "golden ages" of capitalist development.

It might be thought that the overaccumulation problems of the 1970s should no longer be relevant now. Countless new paths of accumulation have been created since then, associated with an extensive stream of innovations. Why have these paths not attracted high levels of investment for extended periods of time? To account for this, we must introduce a new difficulty for capital accumulation in the world market, one that sets the present period of world history apart from all previous eras: *there are more effective national innovation systems in place today than ever before.*[7] This is a recipe for continued technological dynamism. In capitalism, however, the most relevant matter is not the rate of innovation per se, but the time units of capital are able to appropriate high profits from innovations. When a cluster of innovations with significant commercial potential emerges today, every region with an effective innovation system will begin to allocate substantial funds to the relevant fields of research and development. As a result, innovating sectors in the world market tend to face overcapacity problems more quickly than ever before, making the period when high profits can be won from technological advantages ever more compressed.[8] When a new path of innovation and capital accumulation emerges, it now tends to stimulate a high rate of investment for a briefer period of time. This helps explain why astoundingly massive increases in credit have taken place for decades without any jump in the rate of investment in the world market as a whole. The fact that this rate has tended to decline is a paradox only if use-value considerations are confused with valorization.

### *Declining Credit/GDP Ratios*

There are unrelenting deflationary pressures on real wages from technologies and organizational changes that increase the rate of exploitation, the capital flight (and threated capital flight) from high-wage regions that is an essential element of capitalist globalization and so on. The constraints on new investments due to persisting overcapacity in all the major sectors of the world market and the resulting compression of the time high profits can be won from investment, provide another powerful deflationary force in the global economy. Given the intensity of these deflationary pressures, it should come as little surprise that it takes greater and greater amounts of debt to generate the same increment of growth. Rather than being an anomaly, this is precisely what we should expect.

## Financialization

As argued above, in a world of excess productive capacity in non-financial sectors, there is no reason to expect levels of investment in those sectors to increase, no matter how much new credit is created in the global economy. But the expanded credit that is not used to absorb otherwise unused productive capacity has to go somewhere. Under these circumstances, *financial speculation offers more favorable prospects for valorization of the newly created credit money than expanding productive capacity.*

Marx's own analysis of the mechanisms of financial capital has been surpassed in many respects by subsequent theorists of speculative capital like Keynes and Minsky. But one of his core theses remains crucially important: the financial sector is not inherently a means to further the material preconditions for human flourishing. The ultimate end in capitalist society is valorization ("M must become M'!"). When as a result of persisting overcapacity in non-financial sectors financial speculation offers the best hope for high profits, we should expect funds to become increasingly devoted to financial machinations. This is not a perverse inversion of how capitalism should function. It is exactly how it does function in such circumstances (Krier, 2005).

## Burst Bubbles

Given recurrent speculative bubbles, no special explanation for recurrent financial crises in recent decades is required; all bubbles invariably burst. What requires explanation is why the collapse of one bubble has been followed so rapidly by the rise of another. In the past, massive losses inflicted by financial crises would make investors wary of engaging in similar behavior for a long time. Typically, an entire generation would have to be replaced by another too young to have a collective memory of the collapse. In our historical period, however, new bubbles follow the collapse of old ones in a matter of months (weeks, days, hours). This is especially astounding if we recall the immense scale of the savings and loan debacle of the late 1980s, the collapse of the real estate bubble in Japan in the early 1990s, the tequila crisis of Mexico in the mid-1990s, the massive East Asian crisis at the end of that turbulent decade, the utter collapse of equities in the dot.com bubble, all of which proved merely a warm-up for the housing bubble and Great Recession of the first decade of this century. Each time, staggering amounts of money simply evaporated. One would have thought investors would have learned their lesson. But even the collapse of the massive housing bubble in 2008 was quickly followed by bubbles in commodities and the equities of so-called emerging markets, while the price–earnings ratios in US stock market once again soared to historic heights.

We know the answer to this mystery. Once the war on labor produced the "traumatized worker," an unprecedentedly loose monetary policy could be pursued with next to no inflationary consequences in labor and wage goods markets. State policy makers took the lack of inflation in those markets as a green light to rejuvenate the valorization of speculative capital after every burst bubble. The Federal Reserve Board and other central banks discovered that if they quickly pumped massive amounts of liquidity into financial markets, the damage to the financial system from the collapse of a speculative bubble could be contained. The injected liquidity could then enable a new round of financial asset inflation to commence.

Both critics of the right, who complain of easy money offered by irresponsible governments, and left liberals, who complain about the state's failure to regulate the financial sector adequately, are correct. Financial markets could not operate the way they do without state support. But both miss the key point: states *must* act in this manner if the moment of "overexertion" in the present systematic cycle of accumulation is to continue, that is, if the massive destruction and devaluation of excess productive capacity that would otherwise occur is to continue to be deferred. Recurrent irrational frenzy in finance is a "rational" response to this state of affairs, at least from the perverse standpoint of capitalist rationality. Frequently recurring crises are therefore not an anomaly in the contemporary global economy. They are another essential element of its workings in our historical moment, as is state monetary policy to protect the financial sector from the consequences of its excesses.

## *Global Imbalances*

In a historical period characterized by persistent and significant overcapacity in the major segments of the world market, there will be no significant and persisting increase in the rate of investment to spur economic growth. Some other source of growth must be found. Debt-fueled consumption is one possible option. It was taken. Profits from financial speculation provide another, and it was taken too. The two are intertwined by what economists term "the wealth effect." Wealthy households in the USA have indulged in perhaps the greatest explosion of hyperconsumerism enjoyed by any elite stratum in history. As the main beneficiaries of the incredible inflation of financial assets in past decades, and the sharp rise in the rate of exploitation, they have felt little reason to restrain their spending. Financial asset inflation also provided a basis for unlimited access to cheap credit; banks were happy to lend to households whose precipitous increase in (paper) wealth made the risks of lending to them appear to fall no less precipitously. Many working families also experienced a "wealth effect" from the inflation in house prices, a special category of capital asset. Households that saw the values of their homes appreciate were able to refinance mortgages at lower interest rates and then devote their savings to consumption. Or they could use their homes as ATM machines through so-called "home improvement" loans whose amount could be increased in line with the appreciation of the houses used as collateral. Or they could simply take out consumer loans for cars or other big consumer purchases, or credit card debt for more everyday transactions, for much higher amounts than they would have prior to the appreciation of the value of their homes. With house prices exhibiting a long-term upward trend, and with much of the long-term lending risks passed from the institutions granting mortgages to investors in mortgage securities foolishly trusting the triple A ratings awarded to mortgage-backed securities by ratings agencies, credit was happily extended to "subprime" borrowers, allowing the dance to continue until the music stopped (Blinder, 2013).

Debt-fueled hyperconsumerism did not just absorb excess productive capacity in the regions where the consumption took place. Other parts of the global economy could grow by exporting to them. Significant and growing trade surpluses accumulated in some regions, the mirror image of significant and growing trade deficits elsewhere.

By accounting identity, the current account (whose most important component is the balance of trade) and the capital account (primarily representing cross-border flows of capital investment) must net to zero. In other words, regions in the global economy with a net trade surplus must be characterized by corresponding net outflows of capital. In the most prominent case, China's increased trade surplus with the USA was conjoined with increasing purchases of US government bonds. The symbiotic nature of this relationship provoked the witty term Chimerica; as long as China was willing to keep purchasing US Treasury bonds, US consumers could continue to purchase high level of imports from China—which then provided China with the dollars to purchase the Treasury bonds and keep the game going.⁹ The cheap credit provided to the US economy by China and other surplus nations amplified both debt-fueled speculative bubbles and debt-fueled consumption in the USA.

Accounting identities can be maintained through a variety of paths, and the complex causal chains can be difficult to unpack in particular cases. We do not need to decide whether the expansion of consumption in trade deficit regions played the major causal role, forcing adjustments in surplus regions, as opposed to the accumulation of excess savings in surplus regions forcing capital inflows and trade deficits elsewhere. While US policies seem to have been designed to stimulate growth through increased consumption and the inflation of financial assets, with increasing trade deficits as the foreseeable result, there is little doubt that other regions of the global economy contributed to global imbalances by making expanded exports and trade surpluses the center of their growth strategy, at the cost of amplifying debt and speculative bubbles elsewhere. China and other surplus nations, for example, have regularly taken steps to prevent a significant appreciation of their currencies, since that reduce their surpluses by increasing the costs of their exports, measured in the (depreciated) currencies of importing countries.¹⁰

Whatever complicated forms of reciprocal causality can be discerned operating in the global flows of trade and investment, the key point to stress here is that some "engine of global growth" is required in the world market for the "overextertion" phase to continue. The US debt-fueled paroxysm of hyperconsumerism and financial excess provided it, stoked by capital inflows from surplus regions, provided it. As a result, China and the USA were responsible for 45–60 % of all global growth in the period immediately prior to the "Great Recession," with the USA absorbing an astounding 70 % of the net capital flow in the world economy (Westra, 2012, pp. 19–20).

### *The Lack of Deleveraging in the Global Economy*

A note inserted by Engels in Volume 3 pointed out that soon after Marx's day, states began to attempt to alleviate panics by infusing liquidity during credit crunches (Marx, 1981, p. 620). Central banks today are pushing that project to the limit, with the consequence that in regions where central banks have control over their regional currency *the moment of "overexertion" in the present systematic cycle of accumulation has been extended to an unprecedented degree.* The extraordinary policies of quantitative easing instituted by so many key central banks across the planet in response to the Great Recession are but the latest and most extreme illustrations of this point.

Anyone aware of the horrific human suffering inflicted by the extensive liquidations and devaluations of capital that occur when periods of overexertion conclude would be greatly tempted to regard extending the present period of overexertion indefinitely as a good thing. But without a sufficiently significant devaluation and destruction of previous capital investments, the major sectors of the world economy remain afflicted by excess productive capacity on a vast scale. Today, a greater and greater number of "zombie" firms walk among us, incapable of operating as proper units of capital (i.e., as vampires, not zombies), kept alive only through greater and greater transfusions of credit (Harmon, 2010). The fear of zombies is not just played out in the collective imagination of mass culture. It is internalized in the consciousness of every banker and CEO as well. To deleverage significantly now would be to admit that the game is over, and to condemn zombie capitals to death in massive numbers.

From this perspective, a high-stakes game of chicken is being played on the stage of the global economy. Today, after the mutation of the 'Great Recession' to an ongoing contained depression, it has become more and more doubtful whether yet another explosion of credit money, yet another massive inflation of financial assets, yet another intensification of global imbalances, can be engineered to ward off the devaluation of zombie capitals.[11] The unspoken and often unacknowledged fear is that despite the best effort of central banks, excess productive capacity must eventually be destroyed, if not sooner rather than later, then surely sooner or later (Albert, 2013). Some zombie firms must be killed outright, and not allowed to persist in their state of living death. But it is uncertain which units of capital from which regions must suffer this fate. Despite the rhetoric (and real complications) of globalization, it remains the case that capitalist states still attempt to protect capitals of importance to their national economies, selecting policies designed to shift the devaluation and destruction of value elsewhere (the European Central Bank acts analogously). State officials do not believe that exceptional and extreme policies like quantitative easing can be pursued until the end of time. But they may well hope that if they can just hold on long enough, "their" capitals will remain alive, and zombie capitals headquartered elsewhere will be the ones destroyed.

From this perspective, there is no mystery why deleveraging has not gone further—or, rather, anywhere at all. Due to the unprecedented amount of credit that has been created in the global economy, there is now an unprecedented amount of capital embodied in zombie banks and corporations. Borrowings can be shifted from one region to another, from one sector to another, from corporations to households or the reverse, or from the so-called "private" sector to the state. But if they were to be significantly reduced, it would lead to an economy littered with decaying zombie corpses. The present contained depression would not be so contained. The critically important central banks in the global economy will do everything possible to defer that day as long as possible, hoping that somehow enough devaluation and destruction of value will occur over time in regions of peripheral importance to global capitalism.

## Conclusion

The break from gold and the political war on labor enabled an unprecedented explosion of debt in the period after the global slowdown of the 1970s. Far more productive capacity has been absorbed by markets than would otherwise have been the case. Profits were restored. An unprecedented inflation in the value of financial assets commenced as well, itself contributing to the absorption of productive capacity through an orgy of hyperconsumerism undertaken by owners of those financial assets. Certain national economies accumulated vast surpluses through exports, others extensive deficits.

Financial crises are not exceptional occurrences in this arrangement. They are part of its everyday operations. In principle, at least, this arrangement can continue indefinitely. All it requires are states that can protect financial capitals from the consequences of their own actions. More specifically, after the Great Recession, central banks had to be willing to increase their balance sheets by buying up at something close to face value financial assets that would have bankrupted financial capitals if they had been valued at their market worth. Containing the ongoing contained depression has required a tremendous expansion of central banks' balance sheets.[12] That in turn confirms what should not be news to anyone: the supposedly fundamental distinction in modern socio-political thought between a "political" realm concerned with matters of general interest, and a "private" (non-political) economy where individuals and associations pursue particular concerns, is an illusion necessarily generated by the social relations of capitalism.

The valorization imperative of capital is the general organizing principle of the life of the community, shaping social relations. As such, it is inherently a political matter. The reproduction of a capitalist society requires a capitalist state that systematically conflates the "general interest" with "the general interest of capital."[13] This is a very old story. What is new today is the extent to which at the very heart of the so-called "private" sector we find central banks and treasury departments, serving as the collective lender (and sometimes purchaser of financial assets) of last (and sometimes first) resort, rescuing capital from itself at moments when it threatens to implode.[14] Marx observed that "(T)he credit and banking system ... abolishes the private character of capital and this inherently bears within it, through only inherently, the abolition of capital itself" (Marx, 1981, p. 742). The massive and likely permanent extension of the balance sheet of central banks will make it much more difficult to prevent this "inherent" dimension of the credit and banking system from being explicitly recognized throughout society. The economics editor of *The Financial Times* puts the point sharply: "the financial system is a ward of the state" (Wolf, 2014, p. 9).

Marx continued, "(T)here can be no doubt that the credit system will serve as a powerful lever in the course of transition from the capitalist mode of production to the mode of production of associated labour; however, only as one element in connection with other large-scale organic revolutions in the mode of production itself" (Marx, 1981, p. 743). As it becomes ever clearer that the untold trillions of public funds devoted to propping up the financial sector were not limited to one moment of emergency, but are a quasi-permanent public obligation of the state, the groundwork may be being set for a future legitimation crisis that abolishes the illusion of capital's non-political nature once and for all.

Due to the role of credit at this moment of world history, it may prove more and more difficult to explain why public funds cannot be devoted to pressing public priorities, from basic income guarantees in the face of massive precarious employment and involuntary unemployment to a rapid shift to less environmentally destructive forms of life. Imagine, for example, a world where the trillions of dollars of public funds that have propped up another stock market boom and enabled a return to billion dollar bonuses on Wall Street had been used to fund public banks charged with supporting worker-run enterprises responding directly to democratically articulated priorities in their communities (Smith, 2000, chap. 7; Smith, 2005, chap. 8).

The most important feature of our moment of world history may be the utter disintegration of capitalism's ideological façade, opening up a space of possibilities beyond it. Which of those possibilities will be seized remains to be seen.

## Notes

1. The mechanisms at work in speculative frenzies are fairly straightforward. Suppose a critical mass of investors believe (or, more accurately, believe that a critical mass of other investors believe) that a set of firms will likely introduce innovations in the future enabling them to expand at the cost of their competitors. The price of purchasing equity in them will then tend to rise. As it does, initial investors win significant gains. They are now able to increase their borrowings, since they appear to be extremely good credit risks. If a critical mass of the new borrowings is used for further investments in financial assets, capital asset inflation is ratcheted up again. With increased wealth, the borrowers' status as good credit risks is reinforced. They can be recipients of even more credit, and use it to inflate the prices of financial assets yet more. At some point, the value of these assets become completely decoupled from any reasonable assessment of the likely future prospects of the firms whose equity is being purchased. The ability of borrowers and lenders participating in self-sustaining financial bubbles to convince themselves that "this time it's different" should never be underestimated. Once a narrative explaining why the future prospects are so rosy has become dominant, financial agents issuing warnings will be ignored. They, after all, are not making money, while so many others are. Regulators who warn of bubbles will suffer the same fate (Admati & Hellwig, 2014; Blinder, 2013; Davidson, 2009).
2. "The maximum of credit is the same thing here as the fullest employment of industrial capital, i.e., the utmost taxing of its reproductive power irrespective of the limits of consumption. These limits to consumption are extended by the stretching of the reproduction process itself; on the one hand, this increases the consumption of revenues by workers and capitalists, while on the other it is itself identical with the stretching of productive consumption" (Marx, 1981, pp. 613–614).

3. Depending on circumstances, disciplining can take the form of "divide and conquer" strategies allowing capital to take advantage of racial, gender, ethnic, religious, regional or other divisions within the workforce. Or it may involve technological changes that erode the power of workers with specific skills in labor processes. In general, the most important weapon in capital's arsenal is probably the power to engage in a capital strike or capital flight that leaves working households without the monetary resources required to purchase the commodities necessary to meet their members' needs. (In exceptional circumstances, the mobilization of violence by legal [national guards] or extra-legal [death squads] forces may jump in importance.)
4. Wages were 20 % of US levels in Mexico, a mere 5 % in China (McNally, 2010, p. 53).
5. I do not want to downplay the devaluation of capital that did occur in response to the global slowdown of the 1970s. But there was no "'slaughter of capital values' on a scale sufficient to end [overcapacity and overproduction]" (Desai, 2013, pp. 24–25).
6. The easy availability of relatively cheap credit also allowed working households to maintain their standard of living, even as their wages were under increasing pressure. (The greater participation of women in waged labor contributed to this as well, as did cheap imports from China—the so-called "Walmart effect.") This weakened political resistance to the war on labor.
7. Today, four countries spend over 3 % of their GDP on research and development (R&D), and another six devote over 2 % of their annual economic output on R&D (The Economist, 2011, p. 97). (On the other hand, it is still the case that only a relatively small minority of countries have been able to establish effective national innovation systems, giving units of capital from those regions an immense competitive advantage in the world economy. Product and process innovations are competitive weapons in global markets, and a steady stream of significant innovations requires a national innovation system that only wealthy regions can afford.)
8. The intellectual property rights system complicates this picture, but does not negate it. See Smith, 2015, pp. 89–90.
9. "From 2000 to 2007, the US ran a cumulative current-account deficit of roughly $5.5 trillion, with nearly symmetrical offsetting increases in reserves in China and Japan" (Volcker, 2012; see Duncan, 2012, and especially Westra, 2012).

10. Regions enjoying trade surpluses had other reasons to accumulate dollar reserves. Dollars continued to be necessary for the purchase of oil and weapons in international markets. Dollars have provided a fairly secure store of value in an increasingly turbulent global economy. And the greater the reserves of world money held by a nation's central bank, the more protected its national economy is from sudden stampedes of capital outflows—and from the need to turn to the International Monetary Fund and its onerous structural adjustment programs to recover from such stampedes (Prasad, 2014).
11. Since 2008, growth in Chinese non-financial debt has risen from about 100 % of GDP to around 250 %. For a period, this served as an "engine of global growth." Now, however, some analysts estimate that over $5 trillion—half the size of the country's annual economic output—should be considered "troubled." Bad loans in Europe are estimated at over $1 trillion (Evis, 2016, A1). Corporate debt in emerging markets has generated less profit from each dollar or borrowed cash invested, leading to massive capital outflows in 2015 (Kynge, 2016). These examples of reasons for unease could easily be multiplied.
12. The balance sheet of the Federal Reserve rose three-and-a-half times between 2007 and mid-2012. The European Central Bank's tripled, while the Bank of England's increased fourfold (Wolf, 2014, p. 29). Japan provides an especially most extreme case. Public debt in the USA rose from 64 % of GDP to 104 % between 2008 and 2015; in Japan, it jumped from 176 % to 237 % (The Economist, 2015, p. 16).
13. Competition in the capitalist world market operates as a selection mechanism such that states that fail to accommodate the general interests of capital sufficiently tend to be systematically disadvantaged in geopolitical competition.
14. Similarly, at the heart of the innovation process in capitalism, we find the socialization of the costs of research. And at the heart of the capital/wage labor relation, we find the power of the state to discipline social labor to ensure that labor markets and labor processes allow the production and appropriation of surplus value. Capitalism is built upon profound category confusions. The supposedly public is private, and the supposedly private is public.

# References

Admati, A., & Hellwig, M. (2014). *The bankers' new clothes: What's wrong with banking and what to do about it*. Princeton: Princeton University Press.

Albert, D. (2013). *The age of oversupply*. New York: Penguin.

Arrighi, G. (1994). *The long twentieth century*. New York: Verso.

Bellofiore, R. (2005). The monetary aspects of the capitalist process in the Marxian system. In F. Moseley (Ed.), *Marx's theory of money*. New York: Palgrave Macmillan.

Bernanke, B. (2005). The global savings glut and the U.S. current account deficit. *Federal Reserve Board*. Retrieved January 5, 2016, from http://www.federalreserve.gov/boarddocs/speeches/2005/200503102/

Blinder, A. (2013). *After the music stopped*. New York: Penguin.

Brenner, R. (2006). *The economics of global turbulence*. New York: Verso.

Davidson, P. (2009). *The Keynes solution: The path to global economic prosperity*. New York: Palgrave Macmillan.

Desai, R. (2013). *Geopolitical economy: After US hegemony, globalization and empire*. London: Pluto.

Dobbs, R., Lund, S., Woetzel, J., & Mutafchieva, M. (2015). *Debt and (not much) deleveraging*. London: McKinsey Global Institute.

Duncan, R. (2012). *The new depression*. Hoboken: Wiley.

*The Economist*. (2011, October 1). R&D spending. p. 97.

*The Economist*. (2015, February 20). Fighting the next recession: Unfamiliar ways forward. pp. 16–20.

Evis, P. (2016, February 3). Toxic loans around the world weigh on global growth. *New York Times*, p. A1.

Harmon, C. (2010). *Zombie capitalism*. Chicago: Haymarket Press.

Kalecki, M. (1971). *Political aspects of full employment. Selected essays on the dynamics of the capitalist economy*. Cambridge: Cambridge University Press.

Krier, D. (2005). *Speculative management: Stock market power and corporate change*. Albany: State University of New York.

Kynge, J. (2016, February 10). The two moons pulling the tides of gloom for emerging markets. *Financial Times*. Retrieved January 5, 2016, from http://www.ft.com/intl/cms/s/0/40a00a08-cfe7-11e5-831d-09f7778e7377.html#axzz40pyAKNqx

Marx, K. (1981). *Capital*. New York: Penguin.

McNally, D. (2010). *Global slump*. Oakland: PM Press.

Minsky, H. P. (2008). *Stabilizing an unstable economy*. New York: McGraw-Hill.

Mohun, S. (2009). Aggregate capital productivity in the US economy, 1964–2001. *Cambridge Journal of Economics, 33*(5), 1023–1046.

Moseley, F. (2015). Introduction. In F. Moseley (Ed.), *Marx's economic manuscript of 1864–1865*. Leiden: Brill.

Perez, C. (2002). *Technological revolutions and financial capital*. Northhampton, MA: Edward Elgar.

Pettis, P. (2013). *The great rebalancing*. Princeton: Princeton University Press.

Prasad, E. (2014). *The dollar trap: How the U.S. dollar tightened its grip on global finance*. Princeton: Princeton University Press.

Reuten, G. (1991). Accumulation of capital and the foundation of the tendency of the rate of profit to fall. *Cambridge Journal of Economics, 15*(1), 79–93.

Roubini, N., & Mihm, S. (2010). *Crisis economics: A crash course in the future of finance*. New York: Penguin.

Smith, T. (2000). *Technology and capital in the age of lean production: A Marxian critique of the 'new economy'*. Albany: State University of New York Press.

Smith, T. (2005). *Globalisation: A systematic Marxian account*. Leiden: Brill Press.

Smith, T. (2015). The end of one American century … and the beginning of another? In R. Westra, D. Badeen, & R. Albritton (Eds.), *The future of capitalism after the financial crisis: The varieties of capitalism debate in the age of austerity*. New York: Routledge.

Turner, A. (2015). *Between debt and the devil: Money, credit, and fixing global finance*. Princeton: Princeton University Press.

Volcker. (2012). Is global financial reform possible? *Project Syndicate*. Retrieved January 5, 2016, from http://www.project-syndicate.org/commentary/is-global-financial-reform-possible

Westra, R. (2012). *The evil axis of finance*. Atlanta: Clarity Press.

Wolf, M. (2010). *Fixing global finance*. Baltimore: JHU Press.

Wolf, M. (2014). *The shifts and the shocks*. New York: Penguin Press.

Woodward, B. (2000). *Maestro: Greenspan's fed and the American boom*. New York: Simon and Schuster.

CHAPTER 7

# Representing Capital: Mimesis, Realism, and Contemporary Photography

*Christian Lotz*

### Introduction: Representing Capital

Since the crises of 2008, we can observe a heightened interest in Marxist theory, social-critical thought, and reflections on capitalism, though reactions in mainstream analytic philosophy are very limited. Economic and social crises are not only of interest for economic explanations and social-political thought, but also important for what one might call a phenomenology of capital, insofar as economic crises are changing the mode in and through which a society becomes visible to itself. As Marx demonstrates in many parts of his work, capitalist social relations disappear in their own results and the "thing-like" quality of the commodified relations no longer allow us to see the genesis of their becoming. Put differently, what is fluid, relational, becoming and not fixed appears as something stable, unrelated, being, and fixed. Capital becomes a thing instead of a *process*, labor relations disappear behind the surface of market relations and production "costs," and the social genesis of money disappears in everyone's pocket. Economic crises, however, make the invisible synthesis of labor and capital visible, as they let the economic, social, and political agents appear on one level. Imagine that 2008 would have turned into a

C. Lotz (✉)
Department of Philosophy, Michigan State University, East Lansing, MI, USA

major crisis, which would have meant that most of us would no longer have had access to ATM machines, bank accounts, payment options, and so on. However we imagine such a situation, one thing is clear: it would render the class relations and the underlying wealth production visible, as they could no longer be as easily fetishized behind the veil of money and capital. It is safe to assume though that the official rhetoric would have turned such a crisis into "systemic risk."

The problem of the relation between experience and the imperceptible and invisible is important for critical theory at least in three regards: [1] we find the problem of the visible and the invisible in Marx's genetic theory of social categories and the constitution of social totality, insofar as the genesis of those categories disappears, as he puts it, in their results and behind the surface of commodity exchange; [2] we find the problem of the visible and the invisible in the concept of fetishism, insofar as commodified relations no longer appear as what they are; and [3] we find the problem of the visible and the invisible in the organization and structure of critical theory itself, given that the need and necessity of theory is derived from the inaccessibility of social totality and social categories for immediate grasp. Theory, as Adorno puts is, is necessary because social totality and the essence of social reality is *not* accessible neither in experience nor in empirical approaches to this experience. The transparency of society to itself, that is, what the early Habermas called "reflection," has been approached differently in critical theory: whereas for Marx and the early Lukács, society becomes transparent to itself in and through class struggle, Adorno no longer believed in the possibility that capitalist society reflects itself in class struggle; instead, as he argued, theory has to take the empty place of social transparency.

Independent from these methodological, epistemological, and theoretical problems, however, we find the problematic relation between the socially visible and the socially invisible reflected in (critical) art and aesthetics; in particular, in the critical tradition of art and aesthetics in the twentieth and twenty-first centuries, which includes Brecht, Eisenstein, Kluge, Benjamin, Adorno, and, more recently, Rossler, Farocki, Sekula, and Pagen. We would do well to acknowledge Eisenstein's fascinating idea to make a film about capital (for which we only have a few pages of notes), Brecht's *Kriegsfibel*, which was supposed to make the effects of war visible, Kluge's major nine-hour poetic video puzzle project on Marx and capitalism entitled *Nachrichten aus der ideologischen Antike*, Farocki's film essay reflections on labor, and Sekula's lifelong attempts to reveal and reflect critically on the disappearing maritime world. All of these projects, and perhaps art as such, is confronted with the problem of visibility and invisibility because art works cannot remain within the conceptual and theoretical realm alone, insofar as they are in need of the sensual presence of meaning. The problem becomes more difficult, however, when artists either explicitly work from a critical and Marxist standpoint (such as Farocki and Sekula do) or implicitly want to address capital, capitalism, globalization, economic issues, and so on in their work. The question, then, is very simple: how can something that is as such socially and really abstract, such as money, capital, exchange, global structures, trade flows, banks, financial speculations, and so on be made perceptible? Put plainly, how can that which is invisible be rendered visible? Even more: how can capital, which as such, is unpresentable, be taken on in the arts? How would a musician deal with the issue of capital? Can painting be related to it? How can one deal with expansion triggered by capital, which is often invisible in its globalized dimension? Put in the words of Alan Sekula who has worked extensively on artistic issues related to photography, maritime life, and globalization, "in the past, harbor residents were deluded by their senses into thinking that a global economy could be seen and heard and smelled" (Sekula, 1995, p. 4). In a globalized economy, however, as Sekula has shown, maritime economic life disappears behind new phenomena such as containerization. To put his question differently, how can something that does not smell and cannot be touched, such as underlying capital flow, be reflected in a work of art that undeniably needs to exist in sensual form? Again, as Alan Sekula puts it in regard to the globalization of harbors, transportation, shipping, and containerization,

> What one sees in a harbor is the concrete movement of goods. This movement can be explained in its totality only through recourse to abstraction. Marx tells us this, even if no one is listening anymore. If the stock market is the site in which the abstract character of money rules, the harbor is the site in which material goods appear in bulk, in the very flux of exchange. Use values slide by in the channel; the Ark is no longer a bestiary but an encyclopedia of trade and industry. This is the reason for the antique mercantilism charm of harbors. But the more regularized, literally containerized, the movement of goods in harbors, that is, the more rationalized and automated, the more the harbor comes to resemble the stock market. A crucial phenomenological point here is the suppression of smell. Goods that once recked—guano, gypsum, steamed tuna, hemp, molasses- now flow or are boxed. (Sekula, 1995, p. 4)

Of course, the development of new media and their art forms during the twenty-first century has enriched the possibilities of dealing with these issues, since photography, film, radio, tv, and digital production can combine the traditional genres such as the fine arts, poetry, prose, music, and theater, in a never-seen-before complexity. It comes of no surprise, then, that some of the most critical artists of our time, such as Sekula, have opted for a "mixed media" approach that includes texts, photography, and film. Accordingly, as I submit, the new development in the arts, in particular in photography and film, are better equipped to take on the all-encompassing nature of capital, its invisibility, and its (possible) representation.

If we look back to Lukács, we should note that even for Lukács, it is impossible to represent capitalism *as such*. He writes:

> The practical damage resulting from this confusion can be seen in the great loss of unity and cohesiveness in proletarian praxis when compared to the unity of the objective economic tendencies. The superior strength of true, practical class consciousness lies in the ability to look beyond the divisive symptoms of the economic process to the unity of the total social system underlying it. In the age of capitalism, it is not possible for the total system to become directly visible in external phenomena. For instance, the economic basis of a world crisis is undoubtedly unified and its coherence can be understood. But its actual appearance in time and space will take the form of a disparate succession of events in different countries at different times and even in different branches of industry in a number of countries (Lukács, 1967, p. 74).

What Lukács has in mind is that the totality of capitalist social relations can only be grasped in philosophy, insofar as philosophy, in a classically Hegelian manner, oversteps the representational boundaries of the arts and can grasp the core of everything conceptually. One wonders, though, whether Lukács would have revised his position if faced with the enormous power and sophistication of contemporary media artists and the possibilities that (especially) film as an all-encompassing medium possesses, which can include dialogue, analysis and even conceptual reflection. Be that as it may, for Lukács, the central question of a critical aesthetics focused on the question not only of how to represent the capitalist world (which he saw best treated in Thomas Mann's novels [*Romane*]), but also of whether the underlying *tendency* and political position can be connected to a *future* overcoming of the present. As he has it,

> If literature is to render an image of life that is adequate, formally convincing and consistent, the sequence must be reversed. Whereas in life 'whither?' is a consequence of 'whence?', in literature 'whither?' determines the content, selection and proportion of the various elements. The finished work may resemble life in observing a causal sequence; but it would be no more than an arbitrary chronicle if there were not this reversal of direction. It is the perspective, the *terminus ad* quem, that determines the significance of each element in a work of art. (Lukács, 1963, p. 55; 1971, p. 510)

As I will try to demonstrate in what follows, this teleological rendering of the internal consistency of the art work can be well discussed, in regard to contemporary artistic photography and film, after introducing the problem of how to represent capital(ism) and after renewing the concept of mimesis and representation for critical purposes, I will only deal with two contemporary artists, Alan Sekula and Edward Burtynsky. As I will indicate, a critical concept of mimesis and a new realism is needed to further develop critical aesthetics in a Lukácsian spirit; for however one approaches the overall problem that I have introduced so far, the following is clear: without a strong concept of contemporary realism, which is opposed to post-structuralist relativisms, the problem of how to *represent* capital in the arts cannot be tackled.

## MIMESIS, REALISM, LUKÁCS

We should not forget that the modern concept of mimesis in the arts is only remotely connected to simple imitation, copying, or reproducing reality. A mimetic image, as I have extensively argued elsewhere (Lotz, 2015), differs from such simplified versions of the concept of mimesis. I will here offer a short version of this argument, as the concept of mimesis is central for a critical concept of aesthetics and realism.

## REALISM

The concept of representation has a long history, that is difficult to untangle, not only because epistemological considerations go hand in hand with aesthetical considerations, but also because the different languages handle the term in very different fashions. The conception that I would like to present here is closely connected to the German word for representation. There are two German terms for "representation" in this context: on the one hand, it can mean "Vorstellung," which refers to a mental representation, and on the other hand, it can mean "Darstellung," which means to present something to someone. Neither has to do with being a copy or imitation nor does it involve mental representations. The confusion is even deeper if we take into account that the German word for mental representations (*Vorstellung*) is also used, for example, for theater presentations. The word "Vorstellung" here means "show" or "presentation." Accordingly, even the term used for mental representations in German has a non-mental aspect, insofar as it has the sense of "to present" and "to show." Moreover, "vorstellen" as a verb can be used to introduce a person to another person. Finally, in the Latin context, the word "representare" did not mean that *something stands in for something else*; rather, the term was used in a legal context and meant that a person herself *shows up as* in the courtroom (accordingly, it comes closer to the German word "vorstellen"). Whereas we often think of representations as a relationship between something and something that it is not, here we can see that representation has the sense of an *internal* relation: something shows *itself as itself*. The problem of mimesis is not primarily whether the image imitates something prior to the image; rather, the problem is that that of which the image is an image *of* or that which the work is *about* always constitutes itself *as* something independent from the active construction—but not, and this is important, as *externally* independent. For example, when a child pretends to be a horse rider, then he/she does not simply imitate something outside his/her play. But how should this be the case, as there is no horse rider present who could be imitated in this moment? For, the pretended horse rider imitates something of its own kind, as the horse riding is not present as long as the child is not really riding a horse. It is not sufficient to point to the imitated as if it would be a sign. Accordingly, the horse rider imitation is a *coming about* of not only the horse rider, but also what a horse rider is (= image). Mimesis, accordingly, is an internal relation, namely, the relation between the performance and what comes into presence throughout the performance. As Adorno points out, we need to think of mimesis as the attempt to *become* the object: "although art is imitation, it is not imitation of an object; rather, through its gesture and its whole attitude, it is the attempt to reconstitute a situation in which the difference between subject and object did not exist" (Adorno, 1997, p. 70). Consequently, mimesis should not be conceived as something static; rather, mimesis is always a process or, as Gadamer has it, a *play(ing)*. That which the representation is about should *become* clearer, become more transparent, and should become *itself* during the mimetic process. Accordingly, the mimetic process is related to truth, since that which the representation is supposed to imitate should become more familiar and better known. In fact, mimesis, as Gadamer has argued, is "not merely a repetition, a copy, but knowledge of the essence" (Gadamer, 2003, p. 114). As a consequence, we should come to the conclusion that in a mimetic process, the relation between representation and the represented is not a copy or reproduction; rather, what presents itself in the representation is not something static that could be immediately identified; given that it comes into being and remains "fluid" throughout. Thereby, mimesis is a form of insight and *knowledge*.

We can now easily apply the foregoing insights about the concept of mimesis to the concept of realism. Realism, we might say, is not an arbitrary art form; instead, it is a specific way in which a work of art is related to the content that it projects (image). This internal relation can be constructed and put to work in a work of art as a relation of *presenting* that which the work of art is about. Accordingly, a work of art is realistic if it gives us a clear opening toward seeing that to which it is related and its content *better*. Something *shows* up in a realist work of art and should not be obfuscated.

In his critique of modern art, Lukács is primarily arguing that many works are limiting their own access to what they are about by artificially retreating to a position of unclarity, abstractness, and flight from reality. However, this does not touch the concept of realism as a *target* of an artistic practice that is *interested* in presenting something to the audience; instead, it simply formalistically plays with elements or retreats to some supposedly neutral position of art for the sake of art. Realism, we might say with Thomas Metscher, can be understood as the "lively presentation of reality" (Metscher, 2012, p. 91). As such, a realist work of art is always based on interpretation, that is, it is itself presenting that which it is about from a specific perspective and within a temporal horizon. I will come back to this point shortly; for, seen from a *critical* point of view, the specificity of the artwork's perspective should also be laid out as a *political* position.

Once, however, we leave behind the confusion of taking realism to mean naturalism or some form of naïve imitation, we can understand that it is the very goal of realism to work out and present an "essential image" (*Wesensbild*), which, in literature, can be seen in the task of presenting a sensual-intellectual totality of an individual life or a social situation. In a realistic work, character and structure go hand in hand. Accordingly, the goal of realism is *truth*, and seen from the standpoint of a critical aesthetics, truth can only be reached if the work reflects its own viewpoint *within* social reality, as according to critical theory, truth does not exist independent from its standpoint in society and praxis. We should be careful, though, to take Jameson's warning into account:

> Realism [...] is a hybrid concept, in which an epistemological claim (for knowledge or truth) masquerades as an aesthetic ideal, with fatal consequences for both of these incommensurable dimensions. If it is social truth or knowledge we want from realism, we will soon find that what we get is ideology; if it is beauty or aesthetic satisfaction we are looking for, we will quickly find that we have to do with outdated styles or mere decoration (if not distraction). (Jameson, 2013, p. 6)

According to Lukács and the concept if mimesis introduced so far, we need to see that realism is the base of *every* form of literature (Lukács, 1971, p. 501) and, in my view, of other genres, too. In this vein, the entire debate about the concept of realism between Bloch, Brecht, Lukács, and Adorno is not really about realism or anti-realism, insofar as both camps argue with the same idea, namely, that either artists such as Mann (Lukács' position) or artists such as Kafka (Bloch's position) deal *more* realistically with modern society and the position of the individual within it. Be that as it may, in a truly realist work of art, that is, one that can also be abstract, a model of world emerges that *as a whole* contains the essential and objective properties of the interpreted life through interpretation and the artistic image (Metscher, 2012, p. 101). As Lukács has it, "art is the selection of the essential and subtraction of the inessential" (Lukács, 1963, p. 53; 1971, p. 507). As Lukács further argues, the following principles apply to a transparent relation in a work with its own content: [1] it should display a unity of appearance and essence that is coherent (1971, p. 616); [2] it should be a "closed immediacy" (1971, p. 617), that is, the most perfect works attempt to present what they are about within their own artistic means and levels of sensual materiality. What Lukács means is that the process of understanding the work and of participating in the work does not need abstractions and comparisons on the side of the reader or audience (1971, p. 620); [3] in regard to literature, the unity of individual and typical becomes available to the recipient in the portrayal of human situations that make life as a whole in its process accessible; [4] every work of art produces its *own* world, that is, refers to an identifiable horizon of meaning through which all elements become accessible (Lukács, 1971, p. 617). All principles follow organically from the concept of mimesis as I outlined it at the beginning of this section.

## The Political Aspect of Critical Realism

Now, the concepts of mimesis and realism would remain uncritical if they would not be based on specific political positions that are reflected in the work itself. Lukács' assumption of a necessary transparence in regard to the political aspect is of course the true reason why his conception of realism did not find many supporters. The basic "hinge" of Lukács' critical attitude and historical judgment, which philosophers such as Adorno rejected as dogmatism, lies in his thesis (which he believes he shares with every Marxist) that the historical development will necessarily lead to a socialist society:

> For the Marxist, the road to socialism is identical with the movement of history itself. There is no phenomenon, objective or subjective, that has not its function in furthering, obstructing or deviating this development. A right understanding of such things is vital to the thinking socialist. Thus, *any* accurate account of reality is a contribution – whatever the author's subjective intention – to the Marxist critique of capitalism, and is a blow in the cause of socialism. In this sense, the alliance of socialism with realism may be said to have its roots in the revolutionary movement of the proletariat. (Lukács, 1963, p. 101; 1971, p. 561)

Seen from this point of view, it becomes clear that, according to Lukács, every intentional or unintentional attitude that does not speak from a socialist point of view falls behind historically achieved insights. For Lukács, then, the artist must *always* place herself within the horizon of a permanent revolution and the possibility of *new* developments, which, for Lukács, are either reactionary developments or openings toward a non-capitalist future:

> I have raised this more general sociological point in order to show the essential contradictions inherent in any historical development. A writer's negative reaction to a historical phenomenon may have many motives. His reaction may, of course, spring from inability to understand the new phase of social development. But it may also be the justified rejection of a reactionary phenomenon. The two things should not be confused. Admittedly, this kind of rejection and an inability to understand new developments may go together. (Lukács, 1963, p. 111; 1971, p. 572)

In addition, Lukács must interpret every position that remains based on an abstract negation of capitalism as a reactionary step back behind what he thinks is historically necessary. As a consequence, every artistic position that does not take on a *revolutionary* position, in the eyes of Lukács, remains fetishistic, insofar as the artist and her work takes on a supposedly "neutral" position that does not exist in reality. Even abstract negative attitudes are rejected by Lukács. For example, his critique of Expressionism is based on the thesis that expressionist art or artists only abstractly, that is, unpolitically, negate the existing reality (for more on this, see Lotz, 2016). Supposedly neutral or abstract positions, then, are themselves specific political positions, namely, in the eyes of Lukács, ultimately reactionary positions. As a consequence, Lukács *must* posit the conflict between capitalism and socialism as *the* historical conflict of our times: "In a larger perspective, the struggle between capitalism and socialism may be the formative principle of our age." In line with official East European socialist propaganda, Lukács interprets the world–historical struggle between capitalism and socialism also as a struggle between war and peace (1971, p. 465) and between antifascism and fascism:

> What determines the style of a given work of art? How does the intention determine the form? (We are concerned here, of course, with the intention realized in the work; it need not coincide with the writer's conscious intention). The distinctions that concern us are not those between stylistic "techniques" in the formalistic sense. It is the view of the world, the ideology or *Weltanschauung* underlying a writer's work, that counts. And it is the writer's attempt to reproduce this view of the world which constitutes his "intention" and is the formative principle underlying the style of a given piece of writing. Looked at in this way, style ceases to be a formalistic category. Rather, it is rooted in content; it is the specific form of a specific content. Content determines form. But there is no content of which Man himself is not the focal point. However various the *donnees* of literature (a particular experience, a didactic purpose), the basic question is, and will remain: what is Man? (Lukács, 1963, p. 19; 1971, p. 468)

What Lukács has in mind here is that the political position of the work of art can be translated in how concretely, that is, how materialistically, the artist deals with the human world as a *social* world, and since he assumes that we are living in a reality that should be rejected and historically negated, Lukács, coherently rejects art works that project an image of human beings that are "neutral," idealistic, apolitical, or asocial. As Michael P. Thompson points out:

This means that the key issue here is the cognitive stance to the object where the object is society itself. When Lukács says that non-realist art is the expression of decadence, he means that it is no longer able to communicate the totality to the reader; it no longer has the power to shatter the reification of the social world, and the work of art is left only with the ability to communicate alternative modes of feeling, but no sense of a grasp of the social dynamics that should awaken a sense of critique of the society. Instead, it leads one into the interior, into a world divorced from social and public concerns. (Thompson, 2014, p. 189)

Independent from Adorno's and Bloch's point that it could be *precisely* the retreat to the interior that more realistically displays the overall situation of modern societies, one would need to argue that for Lukács there is only *one* real social concern, namely, the overcoming of capitalism, which leads him to his dualistic and at times very reductive position a la "who is not with us is against us."

Seen from this revolutionary angle, which seemed to be too idealistic and abstract for philosophers working in the critical tradition after World War II, we can at least argue that Lukács is not incoherent, as the retreat to the interior immediately makes sense if we imagine a socially and politically unstable situation. However, even if we can no longer make much sense of Lukács' attacks on modern art, given what I have said about realism, we can at least acknowledge that his position is not totally incoherent. For when Lukács criticizes modernism as being based on the dissolution of the personality, on a projection of a dream-like reality, on creating intransparent images of reality, on loosely associated characteristics, on purely psychological associations, on meaningless destructions of rules for the sake of being destructive, on subjective turns, on escaping into the pathological and the anti-social, on affirming the feeling of arbitrariness, and on falling back onto anxiety as a reaction to reification (1971, p. 506), he criticizes not only the backward-looking political attitude, but also primarily the obfuscation of reality.

## Forgetting

What Lukács does not reflect in his considerations of realism is the fact that the problems of realist art are somehow "echoed" in Marxist theory itself, in the form of the relation between transparency and intransparency, as well as in the form of the relation between visibility and invisibility, both of which are deeply reflected in Marx's theory. The problem of visibility and invisibility, one could argue, is not only *the* problem of the entire fetishism chapter, but also reappears on every methodological level of Marx's mature theory. For example, think of the problem of commodity circulation and market relations. Marx's entire theory deals with the problem that all social relations, that is, relations contained in production, consumption, and distribution, disappear at the surface of commodity circulation. Put in modern terms, at the surface of the market exchanges and the processes of selling and buying, the *entire* content of political economy and the central functioning of capital and surplus value disappear and are no longer visible. It is as if the act of buying and selling is in itself an active act of *forgetting*, which is a very Nietzschean view of forgetting. It comes as no surprise, then, that the problem of memory and forgetting can be traced throughout all levels of Marx's *Capital*. For example, in the fetishism chapter, Marx states the following:

> We have already seen, from the most elementary expression of value, x commodity A = y commodity B, that the object in which the magnitude of the value of another object is represented, appears to have the equivalent form independently of this relation, as a social property given to it by nature. We followed up this false appearance to its final establishment, which is complete as soon as the universal equivalent form becomes identified with the bodily form of a particular commodity, and thus crystallized into the money-form. What appears to happen is not that gold becomes money, in consequence of all other commodities expressing their values in it, but, on the contrary, that all other commodities universally express their values in gold, because it is money. The intermediate steps of the process vanish in the result and leave no trace behind. Commodities find their own value already completely represented, without any initiative on their part, in another commodity existing in company with them. These objects, gold and silver, just as they come out of the bowels of the earth, are forthwith the direct incarnation of all human labor. Hence the magic of money. (Marx, 1990, p. 187)

What Marx points out here is the process through which the value-form, as he discusses it in the first chapter of *Capital*, becomes invisible in the result of its constitution, that is, in the real existing form of value, which is money. The steps, however, that lead to money as the universal mediator of social reality *vanish* in their result. As Marx puts it in the above quote, *the intermediate steps of the process vanish in the result and leave no trace behind*. When we find commodities on the market, they *already* come with a price tag and the fact that commodities are constituted by their *specific social form* disappears behind their appearance. Put differently, money stands for a complex relationship between the visible and the invisible, and it is as if the surface in capitalism is like a *symptom*, insofar as that which the symptom is a symptom of is forgotten *in* the symptom.

Similarly, Marx argues that this basic process of forgetting and displacement occurs at every level of money and capital. For example, in regard to commodity circulation, that is, *market* relations, he writes the following—with explicit reference to the process of forgetting:

> In present bourgeois society as a whole, this positing of prices and their circulation etc. appears as the surface process, beneath which, however, in the depths, entirely different processes go on, in which this apparent individual equality and liberty disappear. It is forgotten, on one side, that the presupposition of exchange value, as the objective basis of the whole of the system of production, already in itself implies compulsion over the individual, since his immediate product is not a product for him, but only becomes such in the social process, and since it must take on this general but nevertheless external form; and that the individual has an existence only as a producer of exchange value, hence that the whole negation of his natural existence is already implied; that he is therefore entirely determined by society; that this further presupposes a division of labor etc., in which the individual is already posited in relations other than that of mere exchanger, etc. (Marx, 1993, p. 247)

What Marx argues here is well known: at the surface of commodity circulation and everyday market relations, such as buying and selling as well as supply and demand, equal individuals seem to encounter each other as formally free individuals. In fact, market relations are only apparently made of individual transactions between individuals that are socially constituted through their exchange relations. In truth, however, these individuals are constituted by the relations that underlie market relations, but are forgotten and displaced underneath the market. Individuals are already determined as specific individuals and are constituted by the relations of production and consumption as well as by conditions of the relations of production and consumption.

Finally, let us briefly consider how Marx's overall problem of visibility and invisibility makes its way into recent Critical Theory. In his famous essay and lecture *Late Capitalism or Industrial Society*, Adorno treats the problem of abstraction and unification of capitalist social relations in the following way:

> previously separated moments of the social process, which living human beings incarnate, are being brought into a kind of overall equivalence. [...] Everything is one. The totality of the process of mediation, in truth that of the exchange-principle, produces a second and deceptive immediacy. It makes it possible for that which is separate and antagonistic to be, against its own appearance, forgotten or to be repressed from consciousness. This consciousness of society is however an illusion, because it represents the consequences of technological and organizational homogenization, but nonetheless fails to see that this homogenization is not truly rational, but remains itself subordinated itself to a blind, irrational nomotheism [*Gesetzmässigkeit*: lawfulness, juridicality]. No truly total subject of society yet exists. The mere appearance ought to be formulated as follows, that everything socially existent today is so thoroughly mediated, that even the moment of mediation is itself distorted by the totality. (Adorno, 1968, n.p.)

What Adorno has in mind is simply the totalization of Marx's thesis that the process of social constitution gets lost in the (seemingly) fixed results of these processes, given that in capitalist societies, according to Adorno, the *entirety* of capitalist social organization disappears behind the act of forgetting (for more on this, see Lotz, 2014). It is as if capitalist society forgets itself in its reality and becomes totally blind to itself. Consequently, Adorno combines his Freudianism here with basic insights of Marx's social theory. The thesis, however, is very similar: capitalist social relations disappear within or behind themselves.

This conclusion can now bring us back to the task of critical aesthetics and the task of realism. If it is true that we are living in a system that "forgets itself," how could artistic practice, the goal of which is (sensual) visibility, tackle this fact (if we assume that the artists have understood the problem)? As we will see further below, many contemporary artists are aware of this problem and they encounter the problem *in their own praxis*, especially if they are dealing explicitly with social issues. Two of these artists, Edward Burtynsky and Allen Sekula, reflect deeply on the problem of the invisibility of capital and the invisibility of its proper reflection in their works. This is nicely visible in this statement by art critique Buchloh on Sekula:

> This apparent "illegibility" of Sekula's work within current artistic practices (which in fact is more the result of cultural elisions) points to several parameters of exclusion. They concern first of all the question regarding the contemporary (im)possibility of an Iconography of labor in a self-declared post-industrial and post-working class society, where large segments of labor

and production are in fact concealed from common view since they are exported to the geo-political "margins." Accordingly, the experience of *production* and the conditions of industrial labor have been banned by a massive representational prohibition from modernist visual culture. (Buchloh in Sekula, 1995, p. 191)

What Buchloh points to in this statement is the relative unpopularity of Sekula within the contemporary art scene. Not only does Sekula deal with the invisibility of capital and production in our social reality; in addition, his praxis of making these issues visible are themselves repressed and forgotten, as the commodified and capitalist art world is unable to deal with what (invisibly) constitutes itself. What we encounter in Sekula's case, so to speak, is a "double bind" problem. In what follows, I will analyze a few selected aspects of Burtynsky's and Sekula's work that are of importance for the questions raised in this essay.

## Burtynsky

Edward Burtynsky's work has by now achieved a high standing in the art world. Primarily working in photography, over the years, Burtynsky developed several projects related to globalization, environmental destruction, extraction sites, commodity chains, as well as what he properly calls "manufactured landscapes." His recent projects on industrial landscapes and on water have been documented and accompanied by fascinating documentary films that show more closely how Burtynsky works, how carefully he develops his projects, and how sophisticated and professional his entire artistic praxis is. It is important to note that the films make visible important social contexts of his photographs that become invisible in the art gallery or museum. The latter point is important, as this ambivalence leads to an ultimately dissatisfactory way of "representing capital," despite the grandeur of his work.

Burtynsky's works are characterized by their large size, which, often from distance, show landscapes that have been deformed, manipulated, changed, or destroyed by economic processes (check http://www.edwardburtynsky.com/). Many of his images linger somewhere between abstraction and concretion. This "in between" status of many of his works is due to the invisibility of the context that underlie the pictures. The viewer encounters Burtynsky's images often without much information about the images, and because his works are primarily shown in art galleries and museums, they tend to compete with paintings. Most of his photographs are either of stunning beauty or of awe-inspiring sublimity. Burtynsky removes his pictures from their social and historical backgrounds and this strategy of "decontextualisation and desocialisation" (Toscano & Kinkle, 2014, p. 209) leads the interpreter to go back and forth between the extremely beautiful properties of the images that stem from the formal structures of his photographs, and the often devastating content of the pictures that are related to ecological catastrophes (such as the BP oil spill), ship disassembling in Bangladesh with inhuman labor conditions, or massive industrial projects and landscape changes in China. As other commentators have noted, Burtynsky "presents us with beautiful moments [...] without any inquiry into the process of their production" (Toscano & Kinkle, 2014, p. 206). Photographs are taken out of their context and serve then for the pleasure of the disinterested spectator, although with some inquiry the viewer can learn and get to know what these pictures are about. This process of reflection, however, cannot be found *in* the artworks and, hence, Burtynsky's works try to distance themselves from any interpretatory view of its content. Expressed in terms that I introduced above, Burtynsky's images are mimetic, but they are presented in such an extremely formal manner that they internally try to reject the mimetic moment. For the viewer, "the tension between aesthetics and conscience" (Liu, 2014, p. 470) becomes the central moment of the viewing process. On the one hand, the topics of his work invite the viewer to reflect more on what the pictures depict. On the other hand, however, the stunning formal properties and beauty of his work make it almost impossible to build up a reflective position on the side of the viewer. This tendency can be seen most prominently in his recent series entitled *Water*, which consists of many references to romantic depictions of sublime landscape configurations and to the distinction between the mathematical and dynamical sublime. As one commentator has it, "his 30-by-40 inch and 50-by-60 inch prints are almost hypnotic in their hyper reality, providing the viewer with a heightened sense of observation unattainable in the act of viewing the scene itself" (Pauli, 2006, p. 13). In addition, many of his works are characterized by the loss of the moving body and the loss of a fixed body position. Due to their massive proportions and odd framing, it is not clear for the viewer from which angle or position the picture was taken. The spatial dimension tends to disappear in some of his recent pictures taken from the air. There is no perspectival grip, which pushes these photographs toward the realm of abstract paintings.

Moreover, Burtynsky flattens out three-dimensional aspects, heightens the intensity and depth of colors, or reduces the color tones to an almost monochrome effect.

Given all of these aesthetic factors, it is safe to say that Burtynsky's images are not "overtly political" (Pauli, 2006, p. 22). Accordingly, most of his works remain neutral toward any judgment and establish a distance toward the devastating content. This neutrality is supported by the removal of human beings or human traces in most images, that is, although we see sites that are deeply connected to industries and to capitalism, one rarely sees laboring individuals or other economic factors, such as machines. As a consequence, the images become extremely "aesthetical" and extremely asocial at the same time. Burtynsky himself is of course aware of his strategy, but his political position is one of reformism. In an interview he states:

> The only thing we can do tomorrow that is different from today is to manage what we are doing in a better way. We happen to be very successful, and that may eventually be our undoing, because we are also very destructive. We must learn to be more conscientious custodians of the resources that we have been given. (Burtynsky in Pauli, 2006, p. 31)

Further critique of the driving force behind the historical dynamism that he reveals in his images can nowhere be found. Burtynsky remains also very close to the current stage of capitalism by using the most sophisticated technologies. For example, for the *Water* series, he uses drones and helicopters for achieving an extraordinarily high level of sophistication and professionality.

Finally, the aesthetic qualities of his work have a "romantic" touch, insofar as they capture particularly in industrial and landscape ruins moments of loss that are the consequence of the destructive dynamism of our times. As the artist himself underlines, "I think that a lot of what I photograph are the ruins of our society, the ruins in the landscapes, the things that are left behind" (Pauli, 2006, p. 48). However, this loss is not reflected in political or social terms; instead, Burtynsky shifts the critical aspect of his realism to an internal mental space and to memory. Overall, then, we should conclude that Burtynsky would be a primary object of Lukács' critique, insofar as his attitude toward the social totality that constitutes the topics and issues of his work is highly ambivalent. On the one hand, his entire work is based on a deep understanding (and empathy) with the destructions that Burtynsky observes all over the globe; on the other hand, however, his aesthetic strategy functions only by covering up the social reality behind the veil of purely aesthetical properties. As a consequence, the aesthetic principle that lies behind Burtynsky's work is a principle of forgetting.

## Sekula

It is safe to say that we should locate Allen Sekula's work on the other side of the artistic spectrum with which I am operating in this essay. Sekula's work is often overlooked by the official art world because his work explicitly rejects the "aestheticization" of art and because he often tries to bring in theoretical and reflexive moments that slow down the reception of his images. In contrast to Burtynsky, Sekula works in a multi-media fashion, that is, his images are often accompanied by texts, books, and, in regard to our topic, by a theoretical outlook that posits the task of representing capital always in connection with labor. In contrast to Burtynsky, Sekula reflects on his own profession, that is, photography, critically and in relation to economic issues (Sekula in Wells, 2002, p. 443). Sekula's projects often circle around the developments of globalization, containerization, the changes to the maritime world and global changes to harbors, labor conditions at sea, and so on. Water, capital, and transportation are deeply intertwined topics in his work, and Sekula is interested in making the disappearance of an entire world, which is related to the sea, visible in his work:

> The key technical innovation here is the containerization of cargo movement: an innovation pioneered initially by United States shipping companies in the latter half of the 1950s, evolving into the world standard for general cargo by the end of the 1960s. By reducing loading and unloading time and greatly increasing the volume of cargo in global movement, containerization links peripheries to centers in a novel fashion, making it possible for industries formerly rooted to the center to become restless and nomadic in their search for cheaper labor. Sixteen factories become mobile, ship-like, as ships become increasingly indistinguishable from trucks and trains, and seaways lose their difference with highways. Thus the new fluidity of terrestrial production is based on the routinization and even entrenchment of maritime movement. Nothing is predictable beyond the ceaseless regularity of the shuttle between variable end-points. This historical change reverses the "classical" relationship between the fixity of the land and the fluidity of

the sea. The transition to regularized and predictable maritime flows initiated by steam propulsion was completed a century later by containerization. If steam was the victory of the straight line over the zigzags demanded by the wind, containerization was the victory of the rectangular solid over the messy contingency of the Ark. As we will see. containerization obscures more than the physical heterogeneity of cargoes. but also serves to make ports less visible and more remote from metropolitan consciousness, thus radically altering the relationship between ports and cities. (Sekula, 1995, p. 49)

As we can see, Sekula explicitly works with the visibility/invisibility disjunction, as well as with the problem of how to make the traces of capital movements visible. The disappearance of the harbor in containerization is only one example of how one can address the problem of how to represent capital. Almost all of his careful work has affinities to the question that I discussed earlier in this essay. For example, Sekula writes:

I propose a more provisional funeral. If anything, the appropriate metaphor is found in Marx's notion of the 'dead labor' embedded in commodities. If there is a single object that can be said to embody the disavowal implicit in the transnational bourgeoisie's fantasy of a world of wealth without workers, a world of uninhibited flows, it is this: the container, the very coffin of remote labor-power. And like the table in Marx's explanation of commodity fetishism, the coffin has learned to dance. (Sekula, 1995, p. 137)

Given his interest in a disappearing world that once was the center of transportation and labor related to the sea, we also find in Sekula an aspect of mourning and loss; but in contrast to Burtynsky, this loss is rarely romanticized and, instead, the social causes of these losses are rendered explicitly visible. Accordingly, one could read Sekula's projects as projects of *aesthetic resistance* to the *real* process of forgetting. As Sekula has it,

the metropolitan gaze no longer falls upon the waterfront, and a cognitive blankness follows. Thus despite increasing international mercantile dependence on ocean transport, and despite advances in oceanography and marine biology, the sea is in many respects less comprehensible to today's elites than it was before 1945, in the nineteenth-century, or *even* during the Enlightenment. This incomprehension is the product of forgetting and disavowal. In this sense elites become incapable of recognizing their own, outside of narrow specialist circles. (Sekula, 1995, p. 54)

It comes as no surprise, then, that Sekula speaks of his own artistic practice as one of critical realism, the consequence of which is that his work operates critically in a field that is dominated by overtly aestheticized work, such as the work of Burtynsky. What Sekula says about the work of Andreas Gursky could equally be said about Burtynsky:

> Is Andreas Gursky a realist or is he idealizing late capitalist architecture and making a beautiful spectacle of it ... Gursky's overall project is a variation on Albert Renger Patzsch's *Die Welt ist schön*, tempered perhaps, with a kind of fatalistic cynicism. No doubt there are those for whom Gursky's globetrotting is an attempt to grasp Lukács' totality, but I'm not convinced. (Sekula in Baetens & van Gelder, 2010, p. 123)

## Conclusion

We can conclude that the categories of a critical aesthetics and its underlying concept of mimesis, as well as the attempt to develop artistic art practices that are based on realist assumptions, are still alive today, and given our ongoing crisis related to capital, globalization, and the fetishisms that constitute our social reality, recent artistic works show that artists today can be deeply concerned in their work with what constitutes the world within which we live. Realism is on the rise and formalisms are becoming less important. Artistic practice today begins to understand that the task of representing capital critically is as urgent as it has been since the inception of the capitalist world.

## References

Adorno, T. W. (1968). *Late capitalism or industrial society*. Retrieved February 27, 2016, from https://www.marxists.org/reference/archive/adorno/1968/late-capitalism.html

Adorno, T. W. (1997). *Aesthetical theory*. Minneapolis: University of Minnesota Press.

Baetens, J., & van Gelder, H. (2010). *Critical realism in contemporary art around Allan Sekula's photography*. Leuven: University Press of Leuven.

Gadamer, H. G. (2003). *Truth and method*. New York: Continuum.

Jameson, F. (2013). *Antinomies of realism*. London: Verso.

Liu, X. (2014). Ethical dilemma in "Documenting" manufactured landscapes in China. *Forum for World Literature Studies, 6*(3), 468–485.

Lotz, C. (2014). *The capitalist schema. Time, money, and the culture of abstraction*. Lanham: Lexington Books.

Lotz, C. (2015). *The art of Gerhard Richter: Hermeneutics, images, meaning.* London: Bloomsbury Press.
Lotz, C. (2016). Husserl, expressionism, and the eidetic impulse in Brücke's woodcut. In P. Costello & L. Carlson (Eds.), *Phenomenology and the arts.* Lanham: Lexington Books, 91–118.
Lukács, G. (1963). *The meaning of contemporary realism.* London: Merlin.
Lukács, G. (1967). *History and class consciousness. Studies in Marxist dialectics.* Livingston/Cambridge: MIT Press.
Lukács, G. (1971). *Essays über Realismus. Werke, band 4.* Darmstadt: Luchterhand.
Marx, K. (1990). *Capital* (Vol. 1). London: Penguin.
Marx, K. (1993). *Grundrisse.* London: Penguin.
Metscher, T. (2012). *Kunst—ein geschichtlicher Entwurf.* Berlin: Kulturmaschinen Verlag.
Pauli, L. (2006). *Manufactured landscapes. The photography of Edward Burtynsky.* Yale: Yale University Press.
Sekula, A. (1995). *Fish story.* Cologne: Richter Verlag.
Thompson, M. J. (2014). Realism as anti-reification. A defense of Lukács' aesthetic theory. *Jahrbuch der Internationalen Georg Lukacs Gesellschaft,* 14, 177–196.
Toscano, A., & Kinkle, J. (2014). *Cartographies of the absolute.* London: Zero Books.
Wells, L. (2002). *The photography reader.* London: Routledge.

CHAPTER 8

# Demand the Impossible: Greece, the Eurozone Crisis, and the Failure of the Utopian Imagination

*David Norman Smith*

### Preface

In January 2015, voters in Greece—the eurozone nation hit hardest by austerity and the site of an extraordinarily militant anti-austerity movement—elected a government led by Syriza, the newly influential, decade-old party of the radical left. Hopes ran high. Syriza pledged to roll back austerity and restore Greek pride. The telegenic new prime minister, Alexis Tsipras, and his irrepressible finance minister, Yanis Varoufakis, negotiated with Greece's stern, German-led creditors in an entirely new spirit—unapologetically, with more than a hint of defiance.

When, in late June, negotiations stalled, Tsipras called a referendum to vote on the creditors' uncompromising terms. The vote on July 5 was decisively *No, Όχι*—No to austerity, No to surrender. Just eight days later, Tsipras surrendered, accepting the harshest terms yet imposed on Greece. The elation of the post-referendum moment turned to indignation and doubt. Many Greeks felt betrayed; others were disconcerted. Yet when a

D.N. Smith (✉)
Department of Sociology, University of Kansas, Lawrence, KS, USA

snap election was held in September as a kind of referendum on Syriza's U-turn, Tsipras was re-elected handily. Not quite eight months after his initial election, Alexis Tsipras won nearly the same percentage of the vote for bowing to austerity as he had won earlier for vowing to end it.

How could this have happened? Pundits across the spectrum found this turn of events to be opaque and inexplicable. But in fact, the handwriting had already been on the wall for some time. In the lecture, below, which I gave on May 12, 2015—two months before Syriza's surrender—I drew upon critical theory á la Adorno and Marx to argue that Syriza's leadership was preparing for capitulation by offering substitute, symbolic satisfactions. Syriza's rhetorical radicalism, undermined by a failure of utopian imagination, was more likely to serve austerity than to reverse it.

I once argued, in another context, that critical theorists often resemble mourners at a wedding. What others applaud—"the Popular Front in France in 1936, the unification of American labor in 1955"—they question. "The motive of such questioning is not hostility but doubt" (Smith, 2009). So it was in this instance. My intent, 100 days after Syriza's victory, was to explain why I doubted that Syriza would fulfill its promises—and yet, despite that failure, would remain popular.

I did not doubt that Syriza might remain in power. But I strongly doubted that Syriza would reverse the wage cuts, layoffs, and service cuts that the eurozone had imposed on beleaguered Greece. All of the proposals put forward before January 2015 by Syriza's key figures were far too modest to undo austerity. Couched in the language of sober realism, they focused narrowly on monetary policy—tweaks to eurozone lending protocols, or (at best) a return to the drachma and economic independence. Although the latter option is preferable to remaining at the mercy of the eurozone's austerity ideologues, it is, in my opinion, far too modest to restore Greece to economic health. The problem is that twenty-first-century capitalism is decreasingly viable and that any attempt to solve its problems by monetary means will fail. If we truly hope to escape from austerity, we must think far outside the box of monetary policy. That, I believe, entails a willingness to take quite seriously solutions that are usually maligned as utopian.

Fuller discussions of this point appear both in the text of my 2015 lecture, below, and in the accompanying 2016 paper, "Outrageous Fortune," which appears at the end of this chapter as an epilogue. The original lecture, which the conference organizers taped and transcribed, has been lightly edited without altering the content. The aim was to capture the immediacy of the moment without the benefit of hindsight.[1] If it appears that my skepticism about Syriza was not unwarranted, readers may also find interest in the perspective that inspired this skepticism.

A word about the unusual format of this paper "Demand the Impossible" was originally a PowerPoint slideshow. Most shows of this kind outline bullet-pointed findings, but "Demand the Impossible" was offered as an illustrated argument. The images were not ancillary but integral to my point. I have a long history of illustrated argument (Smith, 2014, 2015), and PowerPoint makes it possible to present illustrated arguments in person. But given the format of the present book, I can include only a few images here. Hence, I have woven text-only slides into the talk (often, in boxed formats) while other pictorial slides are occasionally mentioned in passing, in ways that I hope capture the point of those slides.

## "Demand the Impossible"

Hi, everyone. I agree with Harry, and my goal now is to act on the premise he enunciated—that is, to apply critical theory to a concrete historical moment, mindful of the gravity that society exerts on thought. Specifically, my aim is to probe what I'm calling "the failure of the utopian imagination" in Greece's response to the eurozone crisis. I know it's a bit early to cry failure. Even as we speak, Greece is meeting with its creditors, so there are many chapters still to be written in this story. But failure, I fear, is on the horizon.

We can skip many details about Syriza's recent history. But one intriguing aspect of the situation is that when Syriza came to power in late January, their inner circle included many remarkable intellectuals. If you look at Solidarity in Poland, the African National Congress in South Africa, and the Workers Party in Brazil, you find other instances where leftist groups came to power. Serious and formidable people were involved in those struggles, and a good many of them were intellectuals. But Greece has a surprising roster of serious and critical thinkers who are at the helm of that struggle, and I am going to call some of their ideas into sharp question.

The intent of my talk is to complicate the idea of possibility and impossibility. Many of you have heard me speak in other sessions so you won't be surprised to learn that I favor the abolition of money. To most people that sounds not only utopian but ultra-utopian. So I want to question what possibility and impossibility mean in the current historical moment. I'll do that through the prism of an interpretation of critical theory which closely resembles the positions taken by Harry, Patrick and Jean, and Christian.

Critical theory as I define it can be found at the crossroads of the *Warenwelt*, that is, "the world of commodities." That word leaps out of the opening sentences of the section in *Capital* on the fetishism of commodities. We live in the *Warenwelt*. *[Points to Christian Lotz:]* You probably recognize the photo in the slide.

Christian: I do! *[The slide shows an Edward Burtynsky photo of shelves with multi-hued boxes, symmetrically aligned, viewed from above in a large grocery store. Christian had spoken on Burtynsky earlier in the day.]*

We live in the *Warenwelt*. This society revolves around the production of commodities to an astonishing, suffocating extent. A "commodity" I will define very simply as a *product* with a *price*. Historically and prehistorically there were many eras when products *had no* prices. Many societies had no money at all. This is not simply a utopian possibility for the future. It's an actual reality from the past.

But the *Warenwelt* is a world in which *every* product has a price. The exercise I'd like to conduct at this point is to ask people to look around the room to see if there is anything in this very richly appointed room that did not at some point have a price. Is there anything here—literally anything—that was not produced to be sold?

*People murmur:* You! Us!

Right, the usual answer is Us. That raises the question of the refinement of our labor power, the cost of our grooming and glasses, and so on; but we can leave all that to one side for now. Suffice to say that, leaving us aside, we live in a world that is almost entirely a world of commodities.

## Critical Theory and the *Warenwelt*

Now, critical theory has a complex relationship to this fact. Harry mentioned Friedrich Pollock; I'll also mention Henryk Grossmann. It happens that the Frankfurt Institute, the matrix from which critical theory was born, was also very active in the analysis of the *Warenwelt* as a system. In 1929, Henryk Grossmann, who had worked for the Frankfurt School for years, published a book in which he became the very first person to analyze the long-term downward spiral of capitalism in terms of the falling profit rate, which is something Marx had said, in Volume 3 of *Capital*, could lead to the ultimate collapse of the capitalist system. Roughly a decade later, Friedrich Pollock, who was also a long-term member of the institute, argued that capitalism could solve all its problems by artful planning. So Pollock and Grossmann were at opposite ends of the spectrum. In some respects, they defined that spectrum.

But critical theorists also analyzed the *Warenwelt* culturally. In a sense, we thus find critical theory at the junction of *Warenwelt* and DisneyWorld, where, in DisneyWorld's slogan, "dreams come true." This is the dream world of commodities. This is as good as it gets.

Or is it? Asking that raises a deeper question linked to the category of utopia. Is there life beyond the *Warenwelt*? Is there life beyond the presence of commodities, the omnipresence of commodities? Can we live *without* commodities? In capitalist society, today, that is the very definition of poverty. Commodities are omnipresent, and yet—paradoxically, for much of humanity, much of the time—they are simply absent. That absence is a life crisis—it means hunger, starvation, and the absence of medicine and health care.

Critical theory, at this level, asks what commodities *mean* to people. What does it mean to work for commodities, to yearn for them? What does it mean to own commodities and to (quote unquote) "enjoy" them? I'm going to look today at the thread in critical theory represented by Theodor Adorno in the 1940s and 1950s, when he was preoccupied with anti-democratic ideology and psychodynamics. Adorno studied culture in a multifaceted way, taking contradictions seriously. Earlier today we discussed his attitudes toward film. A little-known fact is that in mid-1940s Adorno collaborated with Horkheimer and Kracauer on a film script which you can now download from the Max Horkheimer Online Archive.

The title of that film, very appropriately, is "Below the Surface." The hope was to penetrate beneath psychological defenses to the root of prejudice—not just to educate but to strike a nerve. Despite their later criticisms of Hollywood, they sought to enlist Hollywood figures like Elia Kazan and the Dadaist filmmaker Hans Richter to help them. They were serious about this film, and, though it went unproduced, they did complete the script.

## Adorno on TV

About ten years later, while working with a foundation that studied television, Adorno wrote an essay about a sitcom, "Our Miss Brooks." I doubt that any of us saw this show when it was first broadcast, because it went off the air in 1956. But Adorno saw it. *[A slide, titled "Our Doctor Adorno," depicts Adorno inside the frame of a TV set.]* I'm tempted to say that we should think outside the box here. Adorno certainly did. Many critics acidly dismissed TV as a commodified, degenerate medium that was beneath criticism. But Adorno took TV seriously.

He explained that the premise of "Our Miss Brooks" was that the protagonist, Connie Brooks, was an underpaid high school teacher who was pushed around by an oppressive but dim-witted principal. These are not mere details. They are, in fact, the whole point of the show. In Episode 18, which aired on February 6, 1953, Miss Brooks is repeatedly fined for small transgressions, including rapid-fire jokes at the principal's expense. Adorno analyzes this "supposedly funny" premise—I like to picture Adorno sitting in front of a small black-and-white TV, writing the phrase "supposedly funny"—quite acutely. He makes several basic points, which I present on the following slides.

**Slide 8**—*Starving Miss Brooks*

- In this episode, Miss Brooks "is not only underpaid but is incessantly fined by the caricature of a pompous and authoritarian school principal. Thus, she has no money and is actually starving."
- *"The supposedly funny situations consist mostly of her trying to hustle a meal…"*

**Slide 9**—*Levity is the soul of…what?*

- "The heroine shows such an intellectual superiority and high-spiritedness that identification with her is invited, and compensation is offered for the inferiority of her position…"
- Miss Brooks "wisecracks constantly." *The tacit message is evidently this:* "If you are as humorous, good-natured, quick-witted, and charming as she is, *do not worry about being paid a starvation wage. You can cope with your frustration in a humorous way…*"

If you've seen "Our Miss Brooks," or if you watch it on YouTube, you'll quickly discover that the heroine is droll. She is incomparably smarter than the principal. She proves her high intelligence and high spirits with one wisecrack after another. She runs circles around her oafish boss and we, the audience, are invited to identify with her. Adorno thinks that most viewers will find this kind of identification easy, because they, too, are poorly paid and socially subordinate.

Adorno refines this analysis in his discussion of Episode 22, which aired on March 6, 1953. I call this episode *"Cat, Mouse, Money."*

> **Slide 10**—*Be careful what you wish for…*
>
> - In this episode, an old woman wills her worldly belongings to the Madison High faculty. Annoyed, when she dies, to inherit only valueless cat toys, the teachers throw them in the furnace—only to learn that each one contains a $100 bill. *They race—pushing, shoving, conniving—to retrieve the money.* Hijinks ensue.
> - The surface message is cynical, a smiling nod, Adorno says, to the idea that "everybody is greedy and does not mind a little larceny," if they can get away with it. But sadly, for ordinary folk, "getting away with it" is a pipe dream. Greed goeth before a fall, and get-rich-quick schemes are mere fantasies.

> **Slide 11**—*…and be realistic!*
>
> - The deeper message, Adorno says, is this: *"Don't expect the impossible, don't daydream, but be realistic."*
> - "Those who dare to daydream, who expect that money will fall from heaven," are silly, foolish, undignified—they will be sadly disappointed, and, in all likelihood, gravely embarrassed.

The surface message is that everybody is willing to stoop to conquer a dollar or two; that having a little larceny in your heart is normal, but that, in this world, grown-ups adjust and you shouldn't expect to get rich quick—in fact, you can't expect to get rich at all. It's funny seeing people yield to temptation as long as they don't take it too far.

Those who dare to daydream and expect money to fall from the heaven are foolish.

They will be sadly disappointed, and, in all likelihood, embarrassed. Unless you want to be a sitcom buffoon, beware.

Now, you might think that Adorno was reading a lot into two episodes of a single sitcom in 1953—but two years later the most popular sitcom of the 1950s arrived on the scene. This show was originally entitled "You'll Never Be Rich" and starred Phil Silvers as 'Sergeant Bilko,' whose name alone reveals that he's a conniver, with larceny in his soul. No matter what schemes or scams he engineers, he will never be rich. He can't outwit the system. Of course, he's a bit greedy—but aren't we all? And justice is served in the end: the small-fry, who dares to scheme, is punished for his hubris.

It's also worth noting how "Our Miss Brooks" was cast. As Slide 12 explains,

- Our Miss Brooks starred Eve Arden. At first, the producer had wanted Shirley Booth in the role, but he changed his mind when he realized that she took Miss Brook's plight just a bit too seriously... *"All she could see was the downside of the underpaid teacher. She couldn't make any fun of it."*

Ironically, 10 years later, Shirley Booth starred in the most popular sitcom in the early 1960s, playing the maid, Hazel, who routinely outwitted her employer. I guarantee you that Hazel did not expect to get rich. She did not dream, or demand, the impossible.

## DESIRES AND REALITY

The phrase "demand the impossible" was unknown when Adorno wrote his sitcom essay. But in May 1968 that phrase became the slogan of a mass uprising of students and workers in France—and it was clearly meant to be paradoxical. If you demand "the impossible" then (literally speaking) either your demand can never be granted or your goal is *not* impossible. That paradox, that challenge to linear thought, was part of the radical energy of the moment. The aim was to veer to the edge of coherence and call into question what people envision as possible. This was the spirit in which the 1968ers coined another utopian slogan, "Take your desires for reality." In other words, *don't* be realistic. Don't bow to the given, to the *Warenwelt*.

Was this just naivete? Is talk of May 1968 today simply nostalgia? That rarefied moment, after all, was long ago—nearly 47 years to the day. Shouldn't we just forget about Paris, general strikes, and dreamy slogans? That advice, it seems to me, would have been more compelling before Syriza arrived on the scene. But Syriza's rise, for many, conjures images of a new May 1968.

You probably know that "Syriza" is an acronym for "Coalition of the Radical Left." Greece, with just 12 million people, has dozens of left-wing organizations; and now, after years of economic crisis, Greece is on the march. Syriza rose from obscurity to national power, on an anti-austerity platform, just three and a half months ago. This is new, this is fundamental.

The underlying reality is that Europe as a whole is still mired in the global economic crisis that began in 2008. But that fact is obscured by the prosperity of the creditor nations. Since Germany appears healthy, people talk about the "Greek" crisis. But the problem goes far beyond Greece. Unemployment across the 19 nations of the eurozone is over 11 %, and several nations have joblessness rates above 25 %. Germany, as the dominant eurozone power, has suffered vastly less—but only because Germany has offloaded the crisis onto Greece and the other weaker countries of the eurozone. And while the Germans, and the other wealthy eurozone nations, boast about their austere habits and their work ethic, they add insult to injury by demonizing the poorer countries.

Do you know the acronym PIGS? That stands for Portugal, Ireland, Greece, and Spain. The implication of that acronym is that these poor countries are suffering because they're greedy pigs, who have been feeding at the trough rather than showing "discipline." Now they are getting their apparently just come-uppance; they've been forced to tighten their belts, and they will have to tighten their belts still further. That, in short, is what austerity means—and that's important.

If austerity in the USA were equally extreme, many millions of additional people would be unemployed here. Right now, in Greece, *fewer people have jobs than* vice versa. Not all of these people are technically "unemployed," since they include everyone without jobs, including children and pensioners; but still, the scale and impact of unemployment is staggering. Public sector employment has been eviscerated, along with public services. And for what purpose, exactly? Asking minuscule Greece to tighten its belt, to go hungry, might send a handful of euros back to Germany, but it will not solve the crisis. Is it surprising, then, that a powerful Greek anti-austerity movement sprang up almost overnight?

## Resist the Unworkable

At the start of today's talk, I mentioned that Syriza's leadership is top-heavy with intellectuals. The slide, below, shows a pair of headlines that appeared in *The Wall Street Journal* on January 23, just two days before Syriza was voted into office:

- "Syriza's Rise Fueled by Professors-Turned-Politicians."
- "Party in Lead in Greek Election Polls Hones Economic Platform With Cadre of Left-Wing Academics-Turned-Politicians."

That second headline accompanied a photo of Costas Lapavitsas, who until recently taught economics at the School of Oriental and Asian Studies (SOAS) in London.

*[Question:]* Did that story appear on the opinion page or the news page?

The news page. The photo shows Costas Lapavitsas, a very formidable intellectual, talking to steel workers. He was running for office as a Syriza candidate, and he was elected. In the next photo, we see Syriza's photogenic young leader, Alexis Tsipras, on election day. Two days later, on January 27, *The Guardian* reported as follows:

- "Greek PM Alexis Tsipras unveils cabinet of mavericks and visionaries."
- "Tsipras has lined up a formidable coterie of academics, human rights advocates, mavericks and visionaries to participate in Europe's first anti-austerity government."
- "In a taste of what lies ahead, Yanis Varoufakis, the flamboyant new finance minister, said on his way to the government's swearing-in ceremony that negotiations would not continue with the hated Troika of officials representing foreign lenders."

Well, that certainly sounds promising from a critical theory, anti-austerity standpoint. Yanis Varoufakis, the economist whom Tsipras appointed to serve as finance minister, said flatly that negotiations "with the hated troika" (the International Monetary Fund, European Central

Bank, and European Commission) "would not continue." It seemed that, no matter how much the Greeks paid, they were pressured to pay more. So the new finance minister announced that he would break off negotiations. That's where matters stood two days after the election.

John Milios is another major Syriza intellectual. In what follows, I will pay careful attention to what Syriza's leading intellectuals say and write, because I think that gives us a clue to Syriza's likely future. Milios, Varoufakis, and Lapavitsas are my main examples, and Milios, in particular, attracted wide attention at an early stage. Here's what *The Guardian* reported about Milios a month before the election, on December 23, 2014:

- "Syriza's chief economist plots a radical Greek evolution within the eurozone."
- "John Milios's phone rings a lot these days. There are hedge funds and financial institutions and investors, all curious to know what the German-trained professor thinks."

"I am a Marxist, like the majority in Syriza," Milios told *The Guardian*. I don't want to fetishize the word 'Marxist' here, but this suggests that something truly new may be afoot in Greece. My question is the degree to which this is likely to prove true. Will Syriza, in power, embrace a critical vision or a traditional outlook? Asking that question raises another: What aspects of the specific gravity of the situation are exerting pressure on Syriza's thought and action at this fraught moment?

One basic reality, of course, is what the Troika wants and demands. And from the beginning, the Troika's chief negotiator, Wolfgang Schäuble of Germany, has told Varoufakis emphatically: "Not so fast." Schäuble insisted that debt repayment is non-negotiable. So at the start neither side expressed a readiness to negotiate. Photos of Varoufakis with Schäuble soon became symbols of this impasse. In photo after photo, the elderly, glowering Schäuble and the youthful, shaven-headed Varoufakis argue passionately; they point fingers, they lock horns, they bump heads.

Since I wanted a slide that would portray this conflict playfully, with a joke drawn from Shakespeare's *Julius Caesar*, I asked my son Dan, who is an illustrator, for a cartoon. He emailed me back saying, "You know Dad, I'm not really a cartoonist. I paint in oil. Do you mind if I do an oil painting?" So I said, please! Here, then, we have Schäuble, looking fresh and assured, predicting the future for Varoufakis:

# DEFAULT, DEAR YANIS, IS NOT IN THE CARDS...

*illustration by Daniel Smith, May 2015*

Varoufakis predicted a different future, saying, on Twitter (January 27, 2015): "We will destroy the Greek oligarchy system." That's tough talk and typical of him.

## THINK SMALL?

If you follow the news closely, you'll know that, lately, coverage of the Greek crisis has focused obsessively on Yanis Varoufakis. A year ago he was quietly teaching at the University of Texas in Austin, but since then he has catapulted to celebrity. He has received a stunning amount of coverage, much of which dwells on his personality. The media chronicles his every adventure and misadventure, not only by interviewing and filming him at every turn, but by means of cartoons, posters, and more. A quick scan of Google Images yields quite a bounty—Yanis as a masked avenger under the heading "V for Varoufakis," Yanis as a superhero with laser vision, and my favorite, a Marvel Comics-style portrayal of a gaunt, implacable Yanis, ready to single-handedly bring down austerity, silhouetted over the image of a mourning, defeated Angela Merkel.

The actual Yanis Varoufakis is an economist who specializes in game theory. He is also a prolific author whose book on the financial crisis, *The*

*Global Minotaur*, attracted a lot of attention. In 2010, Varoufakis co-authored "A Modest Proposal for Resolving the eurozone Crisis," which is now available in what he and his co-authors (Stuart Holland and James K. Galbraith) call Version 4.0. This proposal is essential reading if we want to know what Varoufakis is likely to pursue as Syriza's finance minister in the coming months. The key, overarching points appear in Slide 36:

> - "Any solution to the crisis must respect realistic constraints on political action. *This is why grand schemes should be shunned.*"
> - "We propose a European New Deal" that would show results "in months." Specifically, they propose an "Investment-Led Recovery and Convergence Program" that would be "co-financed by bonds issued jointly by the European Investment Bank (ECB) and the European Investment Fund (EIF)."

For the tough-talking finance minister of "Europe's first anti-austerity government," this is a remarkably modest proposal: "Shun grand schemes." That appears to mean, don't daydream, don't demand the impossible. Yet on the day that Tsipras appointed him as finance minister, Varoufakis jolted Schäuble and the Troika by calling himself a libertarian Marxist. On another occasion, he identified himself as an "erratic Marxist." But Version 4.0 of the "Modest Proposal," which was circulating in 2014 when Syriza seemed poised to win power, spoke a different language. Shunning "grand schemes," Varoufakis and his co-authors proposed an "investment-led" recovery program that would be financed by Troika-issued bonds.

Could this work? A good argument can be made for modesty in the face of crisis. Varoufakis and many others in Syriza say that, in a moment of humanitarian crisis and trauma, it would be irresponsible to fall short by over-reaching. A phrase that is often heard in defense of moderation is this: *Don't let the perfect be the enemy of the good.* The good is small, but it's attainable. Don't dream too much. Don't aim too high.

On a personal note, I should say that, in many contexts, I sympathize with the argument I just summarized. I believe in fighting to win small victories. Early in this century I spent three years in a difficult campaign to pass a municipal living wage law. I later spent three years campaigning for a Kansas minimum wage law. I'm pleased to say that both campaigns succeeded; but I'm also candid enough to say that these were small victories. Perhaps as many as 25,000 people benefited—which, though far from negligible, is plainly not a major achievement or the result of a "grand" scheme. Currently, for Greece and the eurozone, I believe that grand and even "utopian" schemes are needed. But I am very mindful of the force, the real force, of the argument for small reforms.

What "Version 4.0" proposes is a scheme to raise money. The idea is that private investors would purchase a bond floated by Troika institutions, most notably the European Central Bank. Until now the Troika—the "hated Troika," as Varoufakis called it—has been the architect of austerity. But he and his co-authors seem to think that the ECB, in particular, could now save Greece from austerity—not by providing funding directly, but by floating a bond. Why do they find this credible? Slide 37 summarizes their thinking:

**Slide 37**—*eurozone money?*

- Varoufakis, Holland, and Galbraith want to see banks recapitalized and restructured. And while The ECB "would not seek to buy or guarantee" sovereign debt, it would bankroll a "European Venture Capital Fund" that could play a constructive role with respect to bond purchases and recapitalizations.
- Where will this money come from? Investors: "The world is awash in savings seeking sound investment outlets."
- Holland amplified this point in Varoufakis' blog site: "Bill Gross, head of the PIMCO, the biggest bond investor in the US, stressed that Europe needed to recover growth since there are vast global savings in pension funds and sovereign wealth funds that lack investment outlets."

In other words, the world is awash in speculative money, but many investments now appear subprime. So speculative investors who are reluctant to invest elsewhere (in industry or in other forms of finance) could be enticed into investing in a "venture capital" fund that would, as a side benefit, help to alleviate austerity.

Holland, who advised the president of the European Commission in the 1980s, does not explain in detail how this would work. But he appears to put his trust, not in Syriza or the Greek mass movement, but in the goodwill of the Troika and in the private interest of speculators. The rich, and the ultra-rich, would become the solution, not the problem.

## Do Good to Do Well?

When Engels coined the term "utopian socialism," he was referring to the hope that social problems could be solved by philanthropy. This was the approach taken by reformers who went to the wealthy and powerful to plead, "Please do the right thing." Now, Holland and Varoufakis think that what they propose is *not* utopian because they have a win-win solution, that the wealthy and powerful will do the right thing not for altruistic reasons but because it benefits them.

This brings us to the solution championed by John Milios and his frequent collaborators Dimitris Sotiropoulos and Spyros Lapatsioras. Are there people here who know Milios personally? *(Hands are raised.)* Yeah, that makes sense, Milios is very much our peer. He's written many books and articles on Marxist economics and, like Varoufakis and Lapavitsas, he is well known in the English-speaking world as well as in Europe. In 2014, with his collaborators, he published his own modest proposal:

- *An Outline of a Progressive Resolution to the Euro-area Sovereign Debt Overhang: How a Five-year Suspension of the Debt Burden Could Overthrow Austerity*, by Dimitris P. Sotiropoulos, John Milios, Spyros Lapatsioras. Working Paper No. 819, Levy Economics Institute of Bard College, 2014.

Here is the crux of this proposal. Slide 41—*There is only one true option:*

- "There is only one major and meaningful alternative… to bury austerity and kick-start growth at the EA (Euro Area) level"— namely, *"a major shift in the role of the ECB."*
- "Our main strategy is for the European Central Bank (ECB) to acquire a significant part of the outstanding sovereign debt [and] convert it to [interest-free] bonds. …Debt will not be forgiven."

Later I will discuss the phrase "there is no alternative." But first I want to stress, and underline, that for Milios et al. there is *only one* "major and meaningful alternative" if the eurozone hopes to replace austerity with growth. Not two alternatives, not three—just one. And that solution is a change in the functioning of the European Central Bank.

So again, hope is place in the central bank and the bond market. The solution to Greek problems is not from Greek anti-austerity campaigners but from the very bank that serves as the pivot of the eurozone. Remember, the eurozone is not a state. It is a "zone" defined by a currency and guided by a bank. In a certain obvious sense, the eurozone instantiates the *Warenwelt*. The commodity world *is* a Money World, and the eurozone is Money World for Europe.

What Milios et al. want is thus an adjustment of the *Warenwelt*. Specifically, they want the ECB to buy unsustainable debt and convert it into interest-free bonds. We're in the thicket of finance-speak here. And they flatly reject debt forgiveness. This, one might think, is a curious stance for Syriza's future chief economist to embrace, even if he did not regularly advertise his Marxism. But Milios et al. want to be realistic. Is their plan, in fact, realistic? If austerity is truly to be "buried," will central bankers be the gravediggers?

To assess this question, we need to keep in mind, to start with, that Milios, Sotiropoulos, and Lapatsioras take as their point of departure the "Plan for Politically Acceptable Debt-Restructuring in the eurozone" (PADRE) which had been proposed in January 2014 by two senior financial luminaries, Pierre Pâris and Charles Wyplosz.

What they propose is briefly summarized in Slide 42:

- Pâris & Wyplosz want the ECB to intervene "without limit" to buy "about 4.5 trillion euros" worth of debt.
- *These purchases can be made with money borrowed from the private sector at 3 % interest...* This should work given the reconstituted ECB's financial "firepower" and "tremendous debt management capability."
- If more money is needed, *"our proposal could also include the extra 'emergency' taxation of the European UHNW (ultra-high-net-worth individuals),"* with 30 million-plus euros.

Milios et al. like the PADRE premise—that the ECB should intervene "without limit" to buy debt—but they want to target nations whose debts exceed their Gross Domestic Product (GDP). Of the 19 countries of the eurozone, a good number fall into this category. So what Milios et al. propose is to buy *that* excess debt. They want the ECB to spend enough money to get debt below 50 % of GDP for each eurozone nation. The bank would convert this debt into long-term, discounted, interest-free bonds that would yield meaningful profits when they are ultimately repurchased at their face value. And if even the ECB's "tremendous" financial firepower proves insufficient, that firepower can be supplemented by taxing "ultra-high net-worth individuals."

I can't resist a touch of irony here. You might think that Marxists in a phase of crisis and upsurge would invoke Marx's celebrated line, *"Workers of the world, unite! You have nothing to lose but your chains."* But in fact, quite literally, the proposals I have just discussed amount essentially to this: *"Hedge funds of the world, unite! You have nothing to lose but your bonds."*

Practically speaking, would "ultra-high-net-worth" investor seven *buy* those bonds? Would the European Central Bank dedicate its "firepower" to finding out? I'm doubtful. But that, we now know, is what Syriza's soon-to-be finance minister and soon-to-be chief economist were saying on the very eve of 2015.

## A Better Currency is Possible?

Costas Lapavitsas take a different approach. Like Milios and Varoufakis, Lapavistas has shown a readiness to collaborate with or draw inspiration from left-leaning figures from the upper reaches of the financial world. But Lapavitsas and his collaborator, Heiner Flassbeck, who was once deputy finance minister of Germany, consider it naïve to rely on the generosity of the European Central Bank. The Troika powers have been working against Greek interests. Simply asking them nicely to float a bond will not solve Greek problems, according to Lapavitsas and Flassbeck.

Lapavitsas is a major figure. He published a big book called *Profiting Without Producing* in 2013 and, like Milios, he has been productive for a long time. Not many countries have two figures who are as eminent in the sphere of Marxist economics as Milios and Lapavitsas. But Lapavitsas does not agree with Milios that "a major shift in the role of the ECB" is the only path out of the crisis. Instead, as Slide 47 explains, he and Flassbeck want Greece to break with the ECB.

The underlying problem, they say, is that since the eurozone nations share a single currency, they are unable to restrict imports and stimulate exports in the traditional way—by devaluing their currency. So the solution is to exit the eurozone, replace the euro with the drachma, and devalue the drachma drastically. That would bolster the economy by mak-

> Slide 47—*So long to the euro, hello to the drachma...*
>
> - *Lapavitsas and Flassbeck want Greece to return to the drachma— to leave the eurozone.* They think this will restore Greek competitiveness by letting the drachma fall drastically in value, blocking imports and stimulating exports.
> - They think the European Union has a "moral and practical obligation" to expedite and financially assist Greek exit from the eurozone, and that an "orderly devaluation...*might preserve much better the core idea on which economic integration in Europe was founded, namely, free trade...*"

ing Greek exports cheaper and imports, particularly from Germany, more expensive.

Lapavitsas and Flassbeck say that this bold strategy, which has been dubbed "Grexit," would be cheaper than current policy and more compatible with free trade. But to succeed, Grexit requires an "orderly" devaluation of the drachma, facilitated by the eurozone and what they say would be at most a partial restoration of austerity-slashed wages. So this too appears to be a plea to the eurozone for a monetary, free-trade solution. With help from the ECB, the drachma, but not wages, will be restored.

When critics challenge Lapavistas from the left—saying that restoring and devaluing the drachma would be less effective than a more radical agenda, grounded in mass action—he replies scornfully, dismissing radical alternatives as unrealistic and irresponsible. In other words, Lapavitsas agrees: *Don't daydream. Don't demand the impossible.* Syriza's base, which includes many ultra-*low*-net-worth individuals, should keep their expectations low.

Similar views are widely held outside Greece. The French economist Thomas Piketty, whose bestseller *Capital in the Twenty-First Century*

(2013) called renewed attention to inequality, sharply criticizes the eurozone but, at the same time, he essentially agrees with Lapavitsas and Flassbeck:

- "We may have a common currency for 19 countries, but each of these countries has a different tax system, and fiscal policy was never harmonized in Europe. It can't work. In creating the eurozone we have created a monster. Before there was a common currency, the countries could simply devalue their currencies to become more competitive. As a member of the eurozone, Greece was barred from using this established and effective concept."
- What we need is a "fiscal union" with blended budgets and "a common debt repayment fund for the eurozone, like the one proposed by the German Council of Economic Experts... Each country would remain responsible for repaying its portion of the total debt."
- "...I propose a European parliament for the eurozone [in which] each country would be represented...in proportion to its population... In other words, Germany, with its 80 million inhabitants, would have the largest number of members."

For Piketty, in other words, the path to devaluation has been barred by a "monster," the eurozone. But the answer is not debt forgiveness, or anything specific to Greece, but the creation of a European parliament, with a blended budget in which Germany would have the largest number of votes. Debt repayment would be orchestrated by a "fiscal union" grander, not smaller, than the eurozone as currently constituted. Piketty, in short, wants to *reform* the monster, not defy or destroy it.

## *Warenwelt*, Eurozone

Marx said that, in the *Warenwelt*, production for exchange and profit comes to seem ever more natural and inevitable. People increasingly doubt that society could ever survive on a large scale without exchange or money. It seems that products must have prices; that money is destiny. But my feeling is the reverse. The more I study the *Warenwelt*, the stranger it seems—and the less likely does it seem that society can *survive* on the basis of production for exchange and profit. Money, far from being our destiny, seems like a poison.

Consider this: When we discuss the eurozone, we're talking about an entire continent *which is defined by its currency*. Europe is now a *money* zone. The same is true, of course, for the global economy as a whole—this truly *is* Money World. But the eurozone makes that obvious. Europe, as the euro's afflicted "zone," is representative. Affliction is the rule *wherever* money rules.

An often-cited fact in discussions of inequality is that the world's 80 richest families have as much combined wealth as the poorest *half* of humanity—over three billion people.[2] Think about that for a moment. Now, what form does wealth take in our society? The form of money. So what does it mean to be "poor"? It means lacking money—and plainly, vast numbers of people lack money.

Has anyone here heard of the "Bottom of the Pyramid" theory? This is a current in recent economic thought which calls attention to the fact that there are billions of poor people on the planet. This, for investors, offers a golden opportunity, because even though the poor as individuals have only a few pennies or dollars, collectively they have a lot of money—and they have to spend that money to survive. Bottom of the Pyramid investors treat the global poor as a *market*. They want profits to "trickle up" from the poorest of the poor.

But why are people poor in the first place? I will argue that "poverty" as we define it is a modern phenomenon. Until just a few centuries ago, nearly everyone on the planet farmed for a living. They occasionally suffered droughts, famines, or bad harvests—but they had land, they had livestock. Most families owned farms. We have come to take for granted the idea that people, especially on the remote fringes of the Euro-Atlantic economy, are impoverished; but why do we assume that? Mainstream economists like to argue that, by some indices (vaccination rates, infant mortality, adult longevity), global prosperity has risen steadily, and that we are now nearing the border, at least, of global affluence. But many tens of millions of people are now landless and jobless. Without land, people need money to survive; and without jobs, they lack money. So I question the conventional rags-to-riches story. Moneylessness is a growing global condition; and austerity and recession are making it worse.

Until modern times, enduring mass poverty was rare. Of course, humanity as a whole was poor, in a sense. But grinding, unceasing poverty in what Mike Davis has called our "planet of slums" is historically new. And consider this fundamental fact: *Nothing in nature has caused this poverty.* This is one of the saddest ironies of the *Warenwelt*. Nature offers us its bounty today as before; but without money, we are denied access to nature and its fruits.

If the seven billion people on earth chose to produce as much food as they needed without worrying about money, they could eliminate hunger easily. I repeat: easily. If they chose to stop destroying the global ecosystem, they could do it. Why doesn't that happen? Because it isn't profitable. Don't forget, this is Money World. As the title of a book in Greece explains, "It's Capitalism, Stupid!" There is money to be made in annihilating the environment—but not, sadly, in the annihilation of poverty.

Why do we accept a society in which the presence or absence of money rules our lives? Many societies, and entire historical eras, subsisted without money. Why now do we concede power over society to money? Why do we scoff at the idea that, collectively, we could abolish money and live by sharing rather than by selling?

For critical theory, *money is the problem*. For traditional theory, *money is the solution*. Judged by that criterion, and well aware that I may be premature or unduly harsh in my assessment, I think Syriza represents theory of the most traditional kind. This is not intended as an indictment of Tsipras, Milios, or anyone else in particular. If you've read to the end of *Commonwealth*, you will know that, in the name of "the commons" and "the multitude," Antonio Negri and Michael Hardt deny the possibility of a world of use-values that people simply make, share, and enjoy. They too propose the redeployment and rethinking of finance in a world of commodities, money, and capital. So Syriza's intellectuals are far from unique.

I occasionally suggest in conversation that money could be abolished, and when I do, I usually encounter puzzlement. People say, well, surely, you still want living wages, and pensions? How else would you get by now, or in retirement? And why would anyone innovate or take chances without the hope of gain? In reply, I say, let's take a conceptual leap. Try, literally, to imagine a world with no money—*none at all*. Without the Damocles' sword of money over our heads, without the pressing need to work for profit or wages, we could simply cooperate. We could work to survive and thrive; we could discuss what to make, and cooperate in production and distribution, without taking orders. Discussion, of course, isn't always easy. It can be messy and people would disagree. Cooperation isn't paradise. But rather than suffering and dying for lack of money, we could simply resolve to live, and flourish.

Countless voices admonish us to think positively: Times may be hard, but an uptick will follow. "These things go in cycles. We're in a downturn, but a boom is around the corner. We just have to be patient, just stay the course." Well, maybe not. History often moves by leaps. Assuming cyclical, linear progress may be comforting but it isn't wise. In the long run, *capitalism itself* may be unsustainable. If, in fact, Money World ultimately does fail—if money ceases to make the world go round—should we fail as well? Or should we resolve to live in a new way?

## Resistance as Spectacle

Syriza, it seems, is betting on money and the eurozone. Critics who question the wisdom of this approach were challenged recently by Varoufakis's colleague and "Modest Proposal" co-author, James Galbraith, who defends Syriza on very revealing grounds. Slide 53 captures Galbraith's point:

- *4.7.15:* "What the Greeks have done…in the past few months, is astounding. …They have ended a rather rotten and corrupt previous, two-party duopoly, and they have installed a government of dissidents, activists and professors—including, of course, a Finance Minister who was for years, until very recently, banned and blacklisted from Greek television… That man is now the Finance Minister of the Hellenic Republic. *And the Greek people did this, by the way, in the face of a wall of resistance from their own media…*"

When I first read this, I found it striking that Galbraith places so much emphasis on television and the media. Varoufakis, who once was banned from the airwaves, is now on every channel. Despite media resistance, Syriza has registered "astounding" gains. Very little, of course, has yet been achieved to resolve the humanitarian crisis or roll back austerity. But the "wall" of media resistance has been breached.

Galbraith, in my opinion, is not wrong to stress the media's role in Syriza's progress. But my reasoning differs considerably from his. I contend that Varoufakis has become not only a government minister but, quite literally, a television star, and that in fact he is playing a role akin to that played by Our Miss Brooks and Sergeant Bilko. Who were Connie Brooks and Ernie Bilko? Fast-talking rebels who tweaked authority. They showed that underlings can outwit the boss, that, like The Fonz on *Happy Days,* they can be cooler than cool. They may not get rich, or even get ahead, but they bask in the sunlight of their own cleverness and irreverence.

There are countless photos of Varoufakis online. In a category I call "Yanis and the Suits," we see stiff officials, uneasy in the presence of the carefree Yanis, who wears leather jackets and doesn't even tuck in his shirts, let alone wear ties. Here we see Yanis, shaking hands with his fellow finance ministers. Here he is, *en route* to a meeting on his motorcycle. Here he is, scolding Schäuble; here he is, smiling impishly at central bankers. Many journalists have also stressed that Yanis is a game theorist, often with the implication that he is smarter than his adversaries: "Beware, all ye who enter into negotiations with a Theorist of Games!" Personally, though, I wouldn't bet against people, like Schäuble, who have actually negotiated.

Yanis is a media star. Do you recall the old Gil Scott-Heron song, "The Revolution Will Not Be Televised"? Well, apparently it will be. Go to YouTube and you'll find endless interview clips. In many ways, Varoufakis deserves the attention. He's direct, funny, a breath of fresh air. He cuts right through bureau-speak. He is defiant—and many supporters take pride in that defiance. Varoufakis stands up to the Germans, the Troika, and the bankers. You may have heard recently that he has so inflamed his fellow finance ministers that they won't talk to him. (His seat at the negotiating table has, for now, been taken by his "shadow," Euclid Tsakalotos, who wrote a good book about the crisis a few years ago.)

Suffice to say, Varoufakis is quite literally the embodiment of resistance in Syriza's Greece. But beneath the surface, he is much less militant than his persona. Many of you know the slogan "There Is No Alternative," which is often shortened to the acronym TINA. This slogan was coined by Margaret Thatcher, the former British prime minister, who repeated it over 500 times—and her memorial website lists every single instance! Evidently, Thatcher's disciples are extremely proud of her for having told us all, in the spirit of neoliberalism, in the spirit of the market, that *there is no alternative.* Only the market can keep us free and safe. Obviously, by this logic, *seeking an alternative* is, in effect, demanding the impossible.

Interestingly, in his essay "How I Became an Erratic Marxist," Varoufakis reports that he was profoundly influenced by his experience in Britain in the 1980s when Thatcher was prime minister. He became convinced that she was, for all intents and purposes, right about the folly of seeking a genuinely radical alternative. He calls this an essential part of "Mrs. Thatcher's Legacy." Slide 61 distills his main points on this subject:

- "Instead of radicalizing British society, the recession that Thatcher's govern-ment so carefully engineered...*permanently destroyed the very possibility* of radical, progressive politics in Britain."
- "The lesson Thatcher taught me about the capacity of a long lasting recession to undermine progressive politics is one that I carry with me into today's Euro-pean crisis. *It is the reason I am willing to confess...the sin of choosing not to propose radical political programs...to dismantle the awful eurozone.*"

Rather amazingly—should I say erratically?—Varoufakis had concluded at this early date that the "very possibility" of radical, progressive politics in Britain had been destroyed *forever*. Afraid, further, that recession would lead Greece to a similar fate, he foreswore radicalism *in advance*. His tacit assumption was that the crisis of neoliberal capitalism could be resolved *only* by neoliberal means: *There is no alternative* to the market, to the euro, and to the eurozone. Instead of seeing the anti-austerity movement as a springboard for independent, self-reliant action, he asked the Greek mass movement to accept, in advance, that salvation outside the euro is impossible.

But evidently not all impossibilities are equal. As finance minister, Varoufakis insistently told the Troika, "You can't squeeze blood from a stone"; Greece had already been bled white. But times change. When Schäuble et al. refused to bend, Varoufakis vowed to do the impossible. In a televised interview on March 1, 2015, he pledged: "We shall squeeze blood out of stone."[3]

## What if *Modest* Solutions are Impossible?

Is there an alternative? Varoufakis et al. say that if the Greeks are immodest, if they embrace grand schemes, if they reject the debt, disaster will ensue—default, the collapse of the Greek banks, and ultimately, fascism, which is prefigured by the rise of Golden Dawn, the party of the extreme right. Let's consider that last point. My feeling is that Golden Dawn is not currently a credible threat. Golden Dawn is a Hitlerite party—openly Hitlerite. They are strong only in a region of Greece that was infamous for collaborating with the Nazis. Golden Dawn is *still* pro-Nazi. In Greece, with bitter memories of German atrocities in World War II, this kind of reactionary nostalgia is not a recipe for political traction. And though the threat of fascism should never be taken lightly, the larger reality, on the ground right now, is radical and progressive—a mass, left-wing anti-austerity movement.

What should that movement pursue? Should Greece settle for the good and resist the perfect? For me, that question raises another: Can "the good"—relief from debt and austerity—actually be attained by the means that are proposed? I think the answer is No. Neither bond that has been proposed—by Milios, by Varoufakis—*will actually be floated*. Those bonds are not truly in the interest of the creditor nations and institutions. Imagining that Germany and the Troika powers will risk further losses by floating experimental bonds to help Greece dodge austerity is fanciful. Hoping that global investors like Bill Gross will come to the rescue is fanciful.

What *actually* will reverse austerity and keep fascism at bay? Not, I contend, "realism" *á la* Varoufakis and Tsipras? Let's return to Adorno. In the phase of Critical Theory that I value most, in the 1940s, Adorno was the architect of a fundamental new theory of politically relevant personality tendencies. At one extreme we find personality tendencies that draw people to fascism—tendencies that Adorno and his co-authors called "authoritarian." At the other extreme, we find democratic tendencies. Most people, most of the time, fall somewhere between these extremes. So taking seriously the threat of a pendulum swing to the right is plainly necessary. But that does not mean abandoning all hope for a swing to the left.

If we hope to move the needle toward anti-authoritarianism, we must try to *understand* why people are drawn to authoritarianism. In a 1950 essay called "Democratic Leadership and Mass Manipulation," Adorno argued that democracy cannot be advanced by attempts to trigger automatic democratic responses. Our goal must be to engage people in dialogue about what is truly possible and truly impossible. If the powers-that-be—in this instance, the Troika et al.—won't solve our problems for us, we'll have to solve them ourselves.

Even framing the question as a matter of open and uncertain dialogue will strike some people as utopian. Others might feel that encouraging people to solve their problems outside the box of established institutions can only breed unrealistic expectations and, ultimately, disillusionment and reaction. But which is the more utopian course? To pursue dialogue or refrain from dialogue? To better understand and more effectively oppose authoritarianism or to retreat from the encounter?

## Squeeze Blood from a Stone?

I'm almost finished now, and I appreciate your patience. You will not be surprised to learn that, in this money-mad world, "Demand the Impossible" is now a corporate slogan. SwissQuote, which is a speculative online trading firm, has coopted not only that slogan but Che Guevara's iconic image. It's quite a marketing feat to say that investors should demand the impossible—which is, apparently, a slightly better yield on their investments. Right now, that isn't actually impossible. But it may get harder in the future, if the recent past is any guide.

*[Patrick Murray:]* By the way I think there's a credit card company that uses the slogan "Expect the impossible."

*[Tony Smith:]* Here's what the *New York Times* website said five hours ago: "Greece moves to pay debt, but European finance ministers unsatisfied."

Right, exactly. Here's one last slide, which shows a scene from the recent pro-democracy uprising in Hong Kong. I loved seeing this banner appear at the height of the struggle: *"Soyez réaliste, demandez l'impossible."* So this echo of May 1968 is not only an advertising motto, selling online trading. It is also still a very real hope for young people who have not yet learned, it seems, to seek only modest solutions.

*To conclude:* You'll recall the pun in my earlier cartoon, in which I portrayed Schäuble as Cassius, addressing Varoufakis as Brutus, in Shakespeare's *Julius Caesar:* "Default, dear Yanis, is not in the cards…" The actual quote is this: "The fault, dear Brutus, is not in our stars / But in ourselves, that we are underlings."

Thank you.

## Epilogue

### *Outrageous Fortune: Further Reflections on Austerity, Resistance, and the Utopian Imagination*[4]

David Norman Smith

Athens in July 2015 was the site of the *Democracy Rising World Conference,* a gathering of intellectuals and activists who came together in the afterglow of SYRIZA's triumph in January to consider the future of the radical anti-austerity left. Announced in March, the conference took direct aim at the anti-utopian premises of the austerity ideologues. The conference manifesto opened with these stirring words: "Margaret Thatcher's slogan 'There is no alternative' was a declaration of war that installed the horrors of neoliberal policies...."

> It is now abundantly clear that neoliberalism has accelerated radical inequality and...forced the world to conform to unquestionable, anti-democratic policies, lest even greater disasters befall us. [But] the recent historic victory of SYRIZA brings forth the message that citizens must decide their own future.... In the wake of SYRIZA's victory and the hope it articulates for the world, we propose a conference with academics and activists from the birthplace of democracy, Athens, Greece.[5]

But hope was already fragile by the time the conference opened on July 17th. Just days before, SYRIZA's parliamentary majority had stunned the world by accepting the eurozone's harshest and most stringent austerity plan to date. The anti-austerity sentiment of the national referendum on July 5th was disregarded. SYRIZA's left wing, like much of the Greek public, was incensed, and the controversial finance minister, Varoufakis, resigned. The philosopher and critic Creston Davis, one of the principal organizers of the conference, said that *Democracy Rising* convened amid "riots, fires, and demonstrations... One conference participant said, 'Athens is literally burning, my eyes still sting from the police's tear-gas, and I will be giving my talk in just a few minutes." With a hint of bravado, the speaker added: "This is what a conference on democracy should be."[6]

*Slings and Arrows*

Not everyone was equally sanguine. On July 17th, dissident SYRIZA MP Costas Lapavitsas asked to address the opening plenary session of the conference. His speech was "combustible," one observer wrote, sparking "pandemonium in the lecture hall."[7] Greeted with fierce enthusiasm by an overflow crowd, Lapavitsas was blunt: "The SYRIZA government has just signed up to a new bailout agreement. This bailout agreement is a very bad deal." He went on:

> Inequality will increase because the measures will take away 800 million euros annually from...pensioners, who are typically among the poorest layers of the population. Inequality will also increase because, of course, unemployment will again rise this year and next.

…Taxes have also been increased on enterprises, and they're going to hit small and medium businesses primarily, which are the backbone, still, of the Greek economy. Taxes have also been imposed on agriculture, and they're probably the most severe increase in taxes, doubling the income tax for farmers and imposing a raft of other obligations on them.

…the agreement is also bad because it will do nothing for the national debt. There is no restructuring of the debt. [And] the measures will do nothing for development. There is nothing developmental in these measures. The so-called package of 35 billion Euros doesn't exist. These are monies that already have been allotted to Greece…—there's no new money in this.[8]

In short, Lapavitsas concluded, "The government of the left has signed up Greece to a neocolonial agreement." The agreement is not a rational necessity, a "Brest-Litovsk," but rather "a disastrous capitulation" to neocolonialism as well as neoliberalism.[9]

*A Sea of Troubles*

Why did SYRIZA capitulate? To keep Greece in the eurozone. But this is sheer folly, Lapavitsas argued. Staying in the eurozone subordinates Greece not only to the "Troika" of creditors but to the dominion of the euro. "Allow me a digression on the question of money, since this is an academic audience and…I've spent more than 30 years studying money. …In its purest and simplest form [money is] a thing… Blindly, mechanically, society subjects itself to the thing. We've known that for a long time. Keynes called it the slavery of the yellow metal."

For Lapavitsas, the alternative is obvious—to break the hegemony of the euro. "What we need to do is to withdraw our consent to this agreement [and] to redesign a radical program that is consistent with our values, our aims, and what we've told to the Greek people…all these years. And that radical program is impossible without Euro exit. The only thing that we really need to do is focus on developing a plan for Euro exit that will allow us to implement our program. It is so obvious I'm amazed that people still don't see it after five months of failed negotiations."[10]

The philosopher Costas Douzinas, urging "critical support" for Tsipras and the bailout agreement, was caustic in his response to Lapavitsas. "… Yesterday we were here when the minister for education told us that if we were to leave the euro there would be no water in the islands.[11] And [Lapavitsas], my friend, spoke in the past about rationing food and pharmaceuticals and energy.... Can a left government that [elicits] the hope of the Greek people and the Greek left and the European left, can it take that risk? And my answer, in pure economic and risk theory terms, is that it cannot. It could be, it could be perhaps, I would say, the longest suicide note in the history of the left."[12]

I would argue that, given the terms of this debate, Lapavitsas was clearly in the right at this juncture. SYRIZA's bailout agreement was already the longest suicide note in Greek left-wing history, as bankrupt politically as it was economically. In the short run, only Grexit could have prevented Greece from hemorrhaging further—and that remains true, even now. Each new 'bailout' only deepens the overall Greek debt, and the bailout funds go almost entirely to the banks, including (often) German banks. Reinstating the drachma would permit Greece to devalue its currency and prevent domestic industries from being overwhelmed by Franco-German imports. The risks of Grexit, as Lapavitsas convincingly demonstrates, are modest and limited.[13] The true danger is not exit but failure to exit—addiction to the euro, *incomplete* anti-austerity politics.

*To Take Up Arms?*
The ultimate question, then, is why SYRIZA opted for austerity and dependence rather than exit and autonomy. In "Demand the Impossible," I traced the likelihood of this choice to the Money World fetishism of SYRIZA's leaders. Tsipras, Milios, Varoufakis and the others were clearly unable to think beyond the horizon of the *Warenwelt*—and Tsipras, at least, was well able to calculate the algorithm that would keep him in power even without upholding his anti-austerity promises. But the events after May 12th—the July 5th referendum, the July 13th capitulation, and SYRIZA's re-election on September 20th—require explanation at the level of public opinion. Deceptions and miscalculations by politicians are comparatively easy to understand. But why was the Greek public willing to *settle* for symbolic satisfactions? Why, ultimately, did even militant opponents of austerity pay homage to the euro?

Lapavitsas offered a simple but profoundly mistaken answer to this question when he spoke at the *Democracy Rising* conference: "...the referendum, which said *No* so powerfully, showed...that the euro is a class issue. It isn't some impersonal form of money... And people have instinctively understood it. The rich voted *Yes*, the poor voted *No* in the referendum, period."[14]

If only it were so simple. The reality is quite different, and harder to fathom. Upon inspection, it becomes clear that the deeper underlying reality was neither anti-austerity nor pro-euro sentiment, but rather, both at once—that is, *ambivalence*. And that ambivalence was strongest among working people and the poor. Affluent Greeks, as we will see, were *not* ambivalent in 2015: they were straightforwardly pro-euro and pro-austerity. But working-class and hard-luck Greeks were torn. They wanted, and still want, an end to austerity *along with* the euro and eurozone membership—even when the latter plainly and devastatingly conflicts with the former.

Like Lapavitsas himself—for whom the drachma looms so large—the Greek public dreams the dream of money. Although Greece has been the site of important communal experiments in the recent past, including, beginning in 2011, the sustained occupation and self-management of Vio.Me, a building materials plant in Thessaloniki, it remains difficult, it seems, for the Greek public to envision a future without money.[15] Even the bitter experience of austerity has not been enough to sour them on the euro. Again, the question is why?

*Is the Euro a Fetish?*

SYRIZA, like most political parties, "leads" by following. Founded in 2004 as a coalition of radical grouplets, SYRIZA was a miniature force until May 2010, when, in the desperate aftermath of the global downturn of 2008, the Greek government accepted a rigorous austerity program in return for a eurozone bailout. The fallout was immediate. Until that moment, Greece had been a stable two-party system for almost four decades, since the revival of democracy in 1974 after an interval of military dictatorship. But each of the two major parties, the Pan-Hellenic Socialists (PASOK) and New Democracy (ND), signed off on austerity. A mass anti-austerity movement sprang to life, and the major parties plunged in popularity. SYRIZA's stock rose accordingly, as SYRIZA came to be perceived as the anti-austerity party *par excellence*.[16]

The scale of the Greek anti-austerity movement was little short of astonishing. No fewer than 23 % of the entire Greek public reported participating in protests in 2010. In 2011, the percentage rose to 36 %. The latter is a truly remarkable figure, nearly triple the rate in France in the iconic month of May '68.[17] It should thus come as no surprise that, in the national election held on May 6, 2012, SYRIZA vaulted to prominence on the strength of its anti-austerity reputation. PASOK and ND, the two formerly pre-eminent parties, won a total of just 32.1 % of the vote while SYRIZA won 16.8 %–5.6 % above PASOK and just 2.1 % below ND. But since neither ND nor SYRIZA was able to form a government, a new election was slated for June 17th. In the intervening six weeks, SYRIZA underwent a metamorphosis. The character of that "Ovid-like" change merits scrutiny.[18] According to the political scientists Sofia Vasilopoulou and Daphne Halikiopoulou, SYRIZA became increasingly "incoherent." They point to SYRIZA's "inconsistent" and "ambiguous" stance on the euro in particular—and it is certainly true that Alexis Tsipras was not a paragon of consistency in this phase.[19] When he stressed his opposition to austerity, he voiced skepticism about the euro. When he resolved to remain in the eurozone, he warned against the drachma. But I would argue that what appears to be incoherence in this instance is actually a politics designed to play upon *ambivalence*. Tsipras alternated between positive and negative rhetoric because the public, including opponents of austerity, felt conflicted.

At times Tsipras was blandly reassuring, insisting that austerity could be overcome without exit from the eurozone: "I will keep Greece in the eurozone," he wrote in the *Financial Times*—but the very next day, just four days before the June election, he sounded a very different note, stressing, in a televised interview, that "the euro is not a fetish," to be defended at all costs: "Our priority is to save the country in the euro, not to save the euro in Greece, destroying the Greek society and the Greek people."[20] Since opinion polls already clearly showed that the Greek public wanted to overcome austerity *within the eurozone*, it would have been imprudent for SYRIZA to campaign for Grexit, default, and a return to the drachma. So the nimble Tsipras, in 2012 and afterwards, consistently—and I would argue, *coherently*—steered a course between anti-austerity militancy and pro-euro hesitancy. Like any accomplished politician, he spoke the language of ambivalence fluently.

That was still clear on the eve of the January 2015 election, when SYRIZA's main slogan remained ambiguous: "No sacrifice for the euro, no illusions in the drachma."[21] This was a pledge to end austerity without tears. The euro would be preserved, since restoring the drachma would be worse—and this would be possible *without sacrifice*. This begged the question—What if keeping the euro *required* sacrifice? What if the sacrificial rituals of austerity *could not* be reversed without exit and default? Those possibilities were artfully left to one side. SYRIZA promised to square the circle.

*Political Magic?*

Mixed messages from politicians often mirror the mixed feelings of the public. The mystery is not why Tsipras pandered to ambivalence but why public ambivalence remained so strong—and why, when Tsipras ultimately chose compliance over defiance, his base stood by him. This is not to say that protests have been infrequent since SYRIZA accepted the task of imposing austerity on Greece. Strikes and general strikes, marches, and many other forms of urban and rural protest have been rife. But as recently as May 2016, more Greeks said that they would prefer to keep SYRIZA in power than vote for ND, which is now the main opposition party.[22] "Despite dissatisfaction with the government at 86.5 %, 44 % would prefer to see the coalition continue its four-year term whereas 41 % would like snap elections."[23]

SYRIZA has managed to remain in power despite its chameleon-like oscillations. The secret to this success is that Tsipras has appealed simultaneously to anti-austerity and pro-euro sentiments. By striking a theatrically anti-austerity stance in negotiations with the Troika while reassuring the electorate that Greece would stay in the eurozone, Tsipras and his negotiator-in-chief, Varoufakis, dramatically improved SYRIZA's standing with the public during the early months of 2015. Winning the January election with just 36.3 % of the vote, Tsipras' approval ratings soared in the ensuing months, rising to 77 % in May.[24] Since, in that same month, 78 % of SYRIZA's base firmly opposed 'backing down' in dialogue with the Troika,[25] observers might have guessed that SYRIZA's support would plummet after the reversal of July 13th. The *No* vote of the July 5th referendum had lifted Tsipras to new heights, making his subsequent surrender all the harder to swallow. Yet, even so, when a new election was held on September 20th, SYRIZA won 35.5 % of the vote—a drop of *less than 1 %* since January.[26]

Tsipras, who had once famously said that he was "not Harry Potter," now inspired researchers to wonder, tongue-in-cheek, if he had, in fact, worked a kind of magic.[27] How else could he have been elected in January on an anti-austerity platform, only to be re-elected, eight months later, with undiminished support, after spectacularly reversing course *despite ardent and rising anti-austerity feeling*?

No magic, of course, was involved. But the underlying psychology that yielded this result is no less challenging to fathom. The key fact is that, despite its intense and consistent opposition to austerity, the Greek public has been even more intensely and consistently attached to the euro. While majority opinion has always opposed austerity—55 % in 2010, 71 % in 2011, 63 % in 2012, and 68 % in 2015—support for the euro has been even stronger and more consistent, holding constant from 78 % in 2011 to 79 % in 2012, 79 % in January 2015, and 76 % in September 2015.

The capacity of the Greek public to hold anti-austerity and pro-euro opinions simultaneously was strikingly shown by a poll in June 2015. Asked if they approved of the Troika's two most recent demands, respondents said *No* to pension cuts (90 %) and *No* to the relaxation of rules concerning mass layoffs (82 %). Asked if, given the trend of recent history, they expected Greece to go bankrupt in the near future, 33 % more agreed in June than in February. A slight majority now held negative opinions of the European Union. But when asked about the euro, the answers were again positive. ND and PASOK, predictably, were 96 % positive. But even SYRIZA supporters were significantly pro-euro: 59 % to 35 %.[28] And in fact, over the course of 2015, supporters of *nearly every Greek party* became more committed to the eurozone.

On a scale of 1-to-10, where **one** means "exit" and **10** means "stay," SYRIZA supporters went from 4.11 in January (leaning away from the eurozone) to 7.85 in September.[29] PASOK and ND went in the same direction, 7.23 to 8.57 and 8.12 to 9.11, as did similar, lesser parties. And even the ultra-right supporters of Golden Dawn and the far-left supporters of the Communist Party, who had always strongly resisted austerity, followed the same path, shifting from 3.73 to 5.37 and 2.28 to 3.78, respectively.

In other words, even those who voted for fascists now favor staying in the eurozone!

*The Euro is a Fetish*

What we see, in short, is ambivalence. Opposition to austerity is strong and genuine, but so is reluctance to default and return to the drachma. The pollster Yiannis Mavris had detected this duality as early as September 2011, writing that "Greek public opinion…reveals certain contradictions. …The feeling of outrage still prevails…and yet, at the same time, increased attachment to the euro. Acceptance of the euro…remains high with 63 % expressing a 'positive opinion'…Indeed, [in the past four months, as the protest movement rose to unprecedented levels], the percentage…has risen +5 % [and] the highest increase…is where one would expect exactly the opposite, i.e. among the social strata that have been hit more severely by the crisis and the measures taken."

Support for the euro was up 11 % among workers, 14 % among the jobless, 8 % among voters 25–34, and 11 % among voters 35–44.[30]

The euro, in short, certainly appears to exert fetish-like appeal. Even those who suffer most as a consequence of Money World's austerity policies, and those who favor militant protest to bring austerity to a halt, have been reluctant to risk the experiment of life without the euro. That may cease to be true in the future, perhaps even in the near future—the Greek story is far from over. But to date, ambivalence and euro fetishism have proven stronger than resistance to austerity.

Many of SYRIZA's critics propose solutions of their own to the crisis. I offer a question: How can we explain ambivalence? How can we explain, and counter, the influence of euro fetishism? If we hope to defeat austerity in the future, we need to better understand what stands in our way. Ambivalence is not the least of these obstacles.

## Notes

1. Or footnotes. Specific lines from the texts cited here can be found via keyword searches online, and I have appended a reference list, below.
2. In January, 2016, Oxfam released a report showing that this number has fallen from 80 to 62. In 2010, the equivalent number was over 200.
3. Varoufakis, televised interview with the Associated Press, https://www.youtube.com/watch?v=HaNhxClzfAU
    See also Dalton and Dendrinou, March 3, 2015, below.
4. I offered remarks parallel to those presented here in a talk to the International Social Theory Consortium at Iowa State University in Ames, Iowa, on June 9, 2016. For a video upload of that talk, see https://panopto.its.iastate.edu/Panopto/Pages/Viewer.aspx?id=2c6f3cc4-8d5d-4d83-84a3-05c2ef333193
5. Call for Papers: Global Center for Advanced Studies Conference "Democracy Rising," March 7, 2015: https://gcasblog.wordpress.com/2015/03/07/call-for-papers-gcas-conference-democracy-rising-athens-july-2015/
6. Creston Davis, July 26, 2015, "GCAS' First World Conference, 'Democracy Rising… Just the Beginning." https://globalcenterforadvancedstudies.org/gcas-first-world-conference-democracy-rising-just-the-beginning/

7. Chloe Wyma, August 8, 2015. "Debating democracy in a European debt colony," ROAR Magazine. https://roarmag/essays/democracy-rising-conference-report/
8. See the transcript: July 17, 2015, "Lapavitsas Calls for Exit as the Only Strategy for Greek People," http://therealnews.com/t2/index.php?option=com_content&task=view&id=31&Itemid=74&jumival=14278. See also the live Twitter feed a by Craig McVegas, https://storify.com/CraigMcVegas/costas-lapavitsas-at-the-university-of-athens
9. Brest-Litovsk was the site where the Bolsheviks negotiated a peace treaty with Germany in early 1918. Although this treaty was criticized as a "separate peace," the Bolsheviks defended it on the ground that they need time, and an exit from World War 1, to bring the revolution to fruition.
10. See the transcript, cited above.
11. Wyma (cited above) quotes Aristides Baltas, the Education Minister, as saying that if Tsipras hadn't capitulated to the Troika, "bank closures would have prevented ships from delivering drinking water to the Greek islands."
12. See the transcript, cited above. Douzinas, long a faculty member at Birkbeck College in London, borrowed this phrase from a dissident luminary in the British Labour Party, who, in 1983, famously accused the left-wing party majority of adopting suicidally radical positions.
13. Lapavitsas and his collaborators have argued this position for years. See, e.g., their early and many-sided discussion in *Crisis in the eurozone*, introduced by Stathis Kouvelakis (London and New York: Verso, 2012).
14. See the transcript, cited above.
15. Theodoros Karyotis has several excellent online articles that cogently explain the communal experiments now underway in Greece, and possible on a wider scale in the future.
16. A neo-Nazi party, Golden Dawn, also won a modest anti-austerity following. But Golden Dawn's extremism has restricted its influence. After winning 7 % of the national vote in May 2012, Golden Dawn appeared to many observers to be *en route* to major influence. But in fact, despite all the upheavals of Greek politics in the years after 2012, Golden Dawn's influence, and vote tally, has remained static.

17. These figures are drawn from two texts by Georgios Karyotis and Wolfgang Rüdig: "The Three Waves of Anti-Austerity Protest in Greece, 2010–2015" (2016, unpublished); and "Protest Participation, Electoral Choices and Public Attitudes towards Austerity in Greece," in *The Politics of Extreme Austerity: Greece in the eurozone Crisis*, edited by Karyotis and Roman Gerodimos (London: Palgrave Macmillan, 2015, pp. 123–141). My thanks to Georgios Karyotis for sharing the first of these papers with me.
18. This was the expression used by ND spokesman Simos Kedikoglou to characterize SYRIZA's 'mutations.' See the Athens News Service, 14 January 2013, http://www.hri.org/news/greek/ana/2013/13-01-14.ana.html
19. Sofia Vasilopoulou and Daphne Halikiopoulou, 2013, "In the Shadow of Grexit: The Greek Election of 17 June 2012," *South European Society and Politics*, 18 (4): 523–542. Reprinted in *Protest Elections and Challenger Parties*, edited by Susannah Verney and Anna Bosco. London and New York: Routledge, 2016.
20. Alexis Tsipras, interviewed by Antonis Sroiter May 17, 2012, "Euro is not a fetish and I am not Harry Potter," http://en.protothema.gr/alexis-tsipras-euro-is-not-a-fetish-and-i-am-not-harry-potter/
21. «καμιά θυσία για το ευρώ, καμιά αυταπάτη για τη δραχμή»
22. 22 % favor continuing the present government; 21.1 % say they will vote for ND in the next election. http://greece.greekreporter.com/2016/03/20/latest-poll-shows-71-of-people-do-not-trust-tspiras-greeks-want-change-in-government/#sthash.eM3QV1jG.dpuf
23. http://greece.greekreporter.com/2016/05/28/poll-almost-nine-in-10-greeks-are-dissatisfied-with-the-govt/#sthash.OuyiUl02.dpuf
24. Public Issue, *Political Barometer* 144, May 2015, http://www.publicissue.gr/en/2090/pol-bar-144-may-2015/
25. Yiannis Mavris, 26 May 2015, "Yes to negotiation, no to retreat, no to elections: How the political climate and the parties' influence are shaping up, four months after elections," http://www.mavris.gr/en/654/4-months-after/print/
26. Public Issue, *Political Barometer* 148, Greek General Elections, September 2015, Wave 3: 14-17/9/2015, http://www.publicissue.gr/en/2869/pol-bar-148-sep-2015-3/

27. Georgios Karyotis, Wolfgang Rüdig, Niccole Pamphilis. 2016. "A Kind of Magic? Explaining Syriza's Victory in the September 2015 Elections." PowerPoint, Political Studies Association. 66th Annual Conference, Brighton, 22–23 March.
28. Public Issue, *Political Barometer* 145, June 2015, http://www.publicissue.gr/en/2768/pol-bar-145-june-2015/
29. This was partly, but only partly, because SYRIZA's left broke away to form Popular Unity, which, in September, was slightly less sympathetic to the euro than SYRIZA had been as a whole in January.
30. Yiannis Mavris, September 26, 2011, "The contradictory attitudes of Greeks toward the euro," http://www.mavris.gr/en/22/euro-analysis-2011/

## References and Further Reading

Adorno, T. W. (1950). Democratic leadership and mass manipulation. In A. Gouldner (Ed.), *Studies in leadership* (pp. 418–435). New York: Harper & Brothers.
Adorno, T. W. (1954). How to look at television. *The Quarterly of Film Radio and Television, 8*(3), Spring, 213–235.
Adorno, T. W., Nevitt Sanford, R., Frenkel-Brunswik, E., & Levinson, D. (1950). *The authoritarian personality.* New York: Harper & Brothers.
Bogiopoulos, N. (2014). *It's capitalism, stupid!* New York: Livanis Usa.
Burtynsky, E., et al. (2003). *Manufactured landscapes: The photographs of Edward Burtynsky.* New Haven and London: Yale University Press.
Dalton, M., & Dendrinou, V. (2015, March 3). Greece faces cash squeeze as debt is due. [VAROUFAKIS VOWS TO "SQUEEZE BLOOD OUT OF STONE"]. *Wall Street Journal*, p. A6. Retrieved from http://online.wsj.com/documents/print/WSJ_-A006-20150303.pdf
Davis, M. (2006). *Planet of slums.* London and New York: Verso.
Flassbeck, H., & Lapavitsas, C. (2013). *The systemic crisis of the Euro—True causes and effective therapies.* Berlin: Studien of the Rosa-Luxemburg-Stiftung. Retrieved from https://www.rosalux.de/fileadmin/rls_uploads/pdfs/Studien/Studien_The_systemic_crisis_web.pdf
Flassbeck, H., & Lapavitsas, C. (2015). *Against the troika: Crisis and austerity in the Eurozone.* London and New York: Verso.
Forelle, C. (2015, January 23). Syriza's rise fueled by professors-turned-politicians. *Wall Street Journal.* Retrieved from http://www.wsj.com/articles/syrizas-rise-fueled-by-professors-turned-politicians-1422045127
Galbraith, J. K. ( 2015, April 7). The real thing: An anti-austerity European government. Retrieved from https://www.socialeurope.eu/2015/04/real-thing-anti-austerity-european-government/

Grossmann, H. (1992 [1929]). *The law of accumulation and breakdown of the capitalist system* (J. Banaji, translated and abridged). London: Pluto Press.

Holland, S. (2013, September 22). Hollande and Merkel: Where left is right—Guest post by Stuart Holland in the blog *Yanis Varoufakis, Thoughts for the Post-2008 World*. Retrieved from https://yanisvaroufakis.eu/2013/09/22/hollande-and-merkel-where-left-is-right-guest-post-by-stuart-holland/

Jenemann, D. (2007). *Adorno in America*. Minneapolis: University of Minnesota Press.

Kallman, J. (2006, July 23). Our Miss Booth. Retrieved from http://www.webring.org/l/rd?ring=otr;id=34;url=http%3A%2F%2Feasyace%2Eblogspot%2Ecom%2F2006%2F07%2Four%2Dmiss%2Dbooth%2Ehtml

Lapavitsas, C. (2003). *Social foundations of markets, money and credit*. London and New York: Routledge.

Lapavitsas, C. (2013). *Profiting without producing: How finance exploits us all*. London and New York: Verso.

Lapavitsas, C., et al. (2012). *Crisis in the Eurozone* (S. Kouvelakis, Intro.). London and New York: Verso.

Marx, K. (1976 [1867]). *Capital* (Vol. 1, B. Fowkes, Trans.; E. Mandel, Ed.). London: Penguin with New Left Books.

Marx, K. (1978 [1885]). *Capital* (Vol. 2, D. Fernbach, Trans.; E. Mandel, Ed.). London: Penguin with New Left Books.

Marx, K. (1981 [1894]). *Capital* (Vol. 3, D. Fernbach, Trans.; E. Mandel, Ed.). London: Penguin.

Milios, J., Dimoulis, D., & Economakis, G. (2002). *Karl Marx and the classics*. Aldershot: Ashgate.

Milios, J., & Sotiropoulos, D. P. (2009). *Rethinking imperialism: A study of capitalist rule*. Basingstoke: Palgrave Macmillan.

Nachman, G. (1998). *Raised on radio*. New York: Pantheon Books. ["ALL SHE COULD SEE WAS THE DOWNSIDE OF THE UNDERPAID TEACHER. SHE COULDN'T MAKE ANY FUN OF IT."]

OXFAM. (2016, January 18). *An economy for the 1%—How privilege and power in the economy drive extreme inequality and how this can be stopped*. Briefing Report No. 210. Retrieved from https://www.oxfam.org/sites/www.oxfam.org/files/file_attachments/bp210-economy-one-percent-tax-havens-180116-en_0.pdf

Pâris, P., & Wyplosz, C. (2013, August 6). *To end the Eurozone crisis, bury the debt forever*. VOX, Policy Portal of the Centre for Economic Policy Research (CEPR). Retrieved from http://voxeu.org/article/end-eurozone-crisis-bury-debt-forever

Pâris, P., & Wyplosz, C. (2014, January 28). *PADRE: Politically acceptable debt restructuring in the Eurozone*. Geneva reports on the World Economy, Special Report 3. Geneva and London: International Center for Monetary and Banking Studies, Centre for Economic Policy Research. Retrieved from http://voxeu.org/sites/default/files/Geneva_Special_Report_3.pdf

Piketty, T. (2013). *Capital in the twenty-first century*. Cambridge, MA: Harvard University Press.

Piketty, T. (2015, March 10). Thomas Piketty on the eurozone: 'We Have Created a Monster.' Interview by Julia Amalia Heyer and Christoph Pauly. *Spiegel Online International*. Retrieved from http://www.spiegel.de/international/europe/thomas-piketty-interview-about-the-european-financial-crisis-a-1022629.html

Pollock, F. (1990 [1941]). State capitalism: Its possibilities and limitations. In A. Arato & E. Gebhardt (Eds.), *The essential Frankfurt school reader* (pp. 71–94). New York: Continuum.

Prahalad, C. K. (2009). *The fortune at the bottom of the pyramid, revised and updated 5th anniversary edition: Eradicating poverty through profits*. London: Financial Times Press.

Smith, D. N. (2009). Solidarity in question: Critical theory, labor, and anti-semitism. *Critical Sociology, 35*(5), 601–628.

Smith, D. N. (2013). Review of Michael Hardt and Antonio Negri, *Commonwealth*. Harvard University Press. *International Journal of Comparative Sociology, 54*(1), February, 83–85.

Smith, D. N. (2014a). *Marx's capital illustrated* (illustrated by Phil Evans, 2nd ed., with a new epilogue). Chicago: Haymarket.

Smith, D. N. (2015). The adventures of professor Piketty, in which we meet the intrepid data-hunter Thomas Piketty and hear his startling story: A fantasy, illustrated by Tom Johnson. *Critical Sociology, 41*(2), 325–334.

Smith, H.(2014b, December 23). Syriza's chief economist plots a radical Greek evolution within the eurozone. [MILIOS IN THE GUARDIAN: I AM A MARX-IST LIKE THE MAJORITY IN SYRIZA]. *The Guardian*. Retrieved from https://www.theguardian.com/world/2014/dec/23/syriza-john-milios-greece-eurozone

Smith, H., &Traynor, I. (2015, January 27). Greek PM Alexis Tsipras unveils cabinet of mavericks and visionaries. *The Guardian*. Retrieved from https://www.theguardian.com/world/2015/jan/27/greece-alexis-tsipras-syriza-cabinet

Sotiropoulos, D. P., Milios, J., & Lapatsioras, S. (2013). *A political economy of contemporary capitalism and its crisis: Demystifying finance*. London and New York: Routledge.

Sotiropoulos, D. P., Milios, J., & Lapatsioras, S. (2014, November). *An outline of a progressive resolution to the Euro-area sovereign debt overhang: How a five-year suspension of the debt burden could overthrow austerity*. Working Paper No. 819, Levy Economics Institute of Bard College, Annandale-on-Hudson, NY. Retrieved from http://www.levyinstitute.org/publications/an-outline-of-a-progressive-resolution-to-the-euro-area-sovereign-debt-overhang

Tsakolotos, E., & Laskos, C. (2013). *Crucible of resistance: Greece, the Eurozone and the world economic crisis*. London: Pluto Press.

Vaoufakis, Y. (2011). *The global minotaur: America, the true origins of the financial crisis and the future of the world economy*. London and New York: Zed.

Varoufakis, Y. (2014, January 15). The modest proposal for resolving the Euro crisis explained: An interview with Roger Strassburg and Jens Berger of *NachDenkSeiten*. Retrieved from https://yanisvaroufakis.eu/2014/01/15/4951/

Varoufakis, Y. (2015, February 18). How I became an erratic Marxist. Adapted from a lecture originally delivered at the 6th Subversive Festival in Zagreb in 2013. Retrieved from http://www.theguardian.com/news/2015/feb/18/yanis-varoufakis-how-i-became-an-erratic-marxist

Varoufakis, Y., Holland, S., & Galbraith, J. K. (2013, July). *A modest proposal for resolving the Eurozone crisis*, Version 4.0. Retrieved from https://yanisvaroufakis.eu/euro-crisis/modest-proposal/

Wealth-X and UBS. (2014, November 20). Wealth-X and UBS World Ultra Wealth Report 2014 launched in Hong Kong. Retrieved from http://www.wealthx.com/articles/2015/global-ultra-wealthy-population-hold-nearly-us3-trillion-in-owner-occupied-residential-real-estate-assets/

CHAPTER 9

# The Constellation of Social Ontology: Walter Benjamin, Eduard Fuchs, and the Body of History

*Kevin S. Amidon and Daniel Krier*

## Walter Benjamin, Critical Theory, and the Problem of Sexuality

"Fuchs lacks not only a sense of the destructive in caricature but also a sense of the destructive in sexuality, especially in orgasm." In this sentence, Walter Benjamin encapsulated perhaps the most pointed critique of his subject as he drafted the essay "Eduard Fuchs: Collector and Historian" (Eiland & Jennings, 2014, p. 549; hereafter: Fuchs essay). Nonetheless this striking critical statement did not appear in the published essay, for in the process of his final revision of the proofs, Benjamin struck the sentence (Benjamin, 1977, p. 1356). Benjamin's editorial choice has one clear and well-documented explanation: he had no desire to offend Fuchs. They were personally acquainted in their mutual Paris exile of the mid-1930s,

K.S. Amidon (✉)
Department of World Languages and Cultures,
Iowa State University, Ames, IA, USA

D. Krier
Department of Sociology, Iowa State University, Ames, IA, USA

and they met several times. Fuchs even read and commented upon the essay draft, and Benjamin incorporated some of his suggestions (Eiland & Jennings, 2014, p. 550). From the time in late 1933 or early 1934 that Max Horkheimer, the director of the Institute of Social Research (hereafter: Institute) known to scholars as the Frankfurt School, had commissioned Benjamin to undertake the Fuchs project for the *Zeitschrift für Sozialforschung* [*ZfS*], the Institute's journal-in-exile, it took Benjamin over three years of effort to bring the essay to publication. During this interregnum, while dwelling upon the dissonant relationships of bodies, images and text in Fuchs's work, Benjamin produced some of his most important writings. Benjamin's essay on Fuchs finally appeared, without this provocative and highly critical assessment of Fuchs's understanding of sex and sexuality, in the 1937 volume of the *ZfS* (Eiland & Jennings, 2014, p. 546).

Benjamin's elimination of the sentence hints at much deeper critical stakes. It reveals a constitutive tension that runs through multiple strains of his work, a tension that generates dialectical energy between themes that appear variably conjunct and disjunct across Benjamin's prolific journalistic and scholarly production. This tension places the Fuchs essay even more centrally within the emergence of Benjamin's mature theoretical–methodological constellation than has already been recognized in the voluminous literature. It is the tension between body and image, between the biological–corporeal and the textual–representational. The critical significance of Benjamin's productive resolution of dialectical imagery from an extraordinary range of the material of modern life has occasioned vast and revealing scholarly commentary (Jennings, 1987). The significance of corporeality in his work, however, has not always been reflected in the scholarly literature (Richter, 2002). Body and image saturate Benjamin's writings. Howard Caygill has recognized these issues most clearly in Benjamin's work as a whole:

> Benjamin's resolution of the tension between word and image is often carried through in terms of corporeal rhythms ... in the Baudelaire essay it is resolved into the libidinal rhythms of the orgasm. However the turn to corporeal rhythms is complicated by Benjamin's speculative account of experience which introduced the infinite into experience through the argument that time is not linear but a complex formation of past, present, and future. Accordingly the alignment of concept and intuition in experience was also of extreme complexity, with the patternings of word and image shot through with memories and intimations. (Caygill, 1998, p. 80)

Nonetheless Caygill does not read the Fuchs essay closely. Nowhere, however, more significantly than in the Fuchs essay is it possible to derive a subtler understanding of the relationships between the body, sexuality, imagery, and history in Benjamin's later work. Such a reading can further point onward toward potential forms of critical theory that can fruitfully address emergent social forms and practices in the twenty-first century. The body of Benjamin's theory of history, read through its constellation of texts and images, reveals new paths to the understanding of social ontology.

Most centrally, it is the question of sexuality, and not just of its representation, but also of its elision, refiguration, reinscription, and sublation through Benjamin's critical constellations. The body, together with its socially and materially accreted sexuality, stands at the center of the critical resolution of Benjamin's methodological vision of materialist history in the Fuchs essay. It is at once revealed and hidden, made manifest not directly but obliquely through reflection on and refraction through the pursuit of a practice of history that is recursively constitutive of and coterminous with social ontology. Sexuality manifests itself within Benjamin's thought in the Fuchs essay in unique ways, ways that reveal further the close links between the essay and the work he pursued alongside it in the 1930s, particularly "The Work of Art in the Age of its Technological Reproducibility" (hereafter: Artwork essay). Furthermore, the clear emergence of sexuality into view within Benjamin's critical horizon allows further clarification of the links between the Fuchs essay and the work of Benjamin's interlocutors in the early Frankfurt School at the time, especially Max Horkheimer.

Benjamin constellates sexuality as the vector of biological reproduction, whereby it becomes capable of resolution from and through its commensurate dialectical partner, the technological reproduction of the work of art. This dialectical refraction of the issue of reproduction through both body and work becomes the conceptual fulcrum that allows Benjamin to structure his fully fledged theory of materialist history. The stakes emerge at a central point in the Fuchs essay where Benjamin explores the "biological" quality of Fuchs's understanding of artistic creativity. Benjamin frames this passage, like much of the essay, as simultaneous critique of and engagement with its subject, but always in the service of a more expansive argument about the method and material of history. He begins with a vividly phrased critique of the reductive (and of course heavily gendered) quality of Fuchs's "biological" elision of creativity and sexuality through excess—but at the same time he grants Fuchs a significant level of interpretive innovation:

> Fuchs's notion of creativity has a strongly biological slant. Artists from whom the author distances himself are portrayed as lacking in virility, while genius appears with attributes that occasionally border on the priapic. The mark of such biologistic thinking can be found in Fuchs's judgments of El Greco, Murillo, and Ribera. "All three became classic representatives of the Baroque spirit because each in his way was a 'thwarted' eroticist" ... From different sources, this concept of genius fed the same widespread conviction that creativity was above all a manifestation of superabundant strength. Similar tendencies later led Fuchs to conceptions akin to psychoanalysis. He was the first to make them fruitful for aesthetics. (Benjamin, 2002, p. 272; references hereafter by page number only)

Benjamin's concept of the biological is itself somewhat reductive here, for it resolves as the relationship between the corporeal and the sexual, admixed clearly with recognition of Fuchs's gendered analytical rhetoric. It therefore subtly reinforces the stakes surrounding the conceptual constellation of reproduction as the sublation of the corporeal in the essay.

The section of the essay from which this quotation is drawn culminates in a lengthy discussion of how Fuchs's terms of analysis reveal his heavy investment in the German "Social Democratic doctrines of the period," particularly the ways in which "the Darwinian influence served to maintain the party's faith and determination in its struggle" with Bismarck and the Prussian state apparatus during the 1870s and 1880s (p. 273). Benjamin thereby expands his engagement of the biological to include not just the corporeal-sexual, but also the heavily contested intellectual politics of Darwinism in Germany during the latter half of the nineteenth century and into the twentieth (Gliboff, 2008). Attention to this moment of German social democratic history redoubles Benjamin's critical focus on how the biological dialectically interpolates both the corporeal and the political: German socialists made the Darwinian "laws" of natural selection into a direct correlative of the "laws" of Marxian historical progress and revolution in the later nineteenth century (Kelly, 1981, chap. 7). With this argument about the politics of biology, Benjamin successfully widens his analytical optic to encompass clearly the question of historical materialism as revealed in the history of party-political conflict received and refigured by Fuchs.

The body, in its reproductive capacity, thus serves Benjamin's critical goal of the manifestation of the full historical stakes of the rise of the technological reproducibility of the work of art. As Benjamin achieved stages of completion in the Fuchs and Artwork essays, both of which were written in the midst of his necessarily fragmented and methodologically fracturing Arcades Project, the issue of sexuality became submerged somewhat back into the vast and diverse body of material out of which Benjamin sought to constellate his materialist history. His deletion of the sentence about the destructive power of sexuality in the published version of the Fuchs essay forms the most visible evidence of this process. Benjamin struggled for some three years with the composition of the essay, and the trajectory of the emergence and submersion of the material manifestation of the body's reproductive processes thus forms a conceptual-critical correlative of the flow Benjamin's own intellectual development. The critical exploration of the potential for destruction inherent in reproduction, both that of the artwork and that of the material body, becomes his manifest interest. This central theme in Benjamin's work took its final fragmentary form during his fatal 1940 flight from the Nazi occupation of France in his "On the Concept of History," which derived much from the Fuchs essay. Through Benjamin's method, bodies and artworks are rendered recursively fragmentary through the destructive power of reproduction, particularly where that reproduction is excessive. They thereby become, however, in dialectical constellation with one another, the incipient material of historical representation itself. In Benjamin's optics, the traces of the body devolve through representation into works like the caricatures that Eduard Fuchs so vigorously reproduced and ramified within the vast textual structures of his books. The materiality of the body, and along with it the sphere of sexuality, can therefore appear to vanish within the Fuchs essay, the history of its composition, and its accompanying work. This vanishing is, however, itself an artifact of Benjamin's critical–historical method. His dialectical images remain everywhere saturated with sublated renderings of the body.

## Eduard Fuchs: The Vanishing Mediator of Classical Critical Theory

Fuchs (1870–1940) led a colorful if often, in the words of his two-time scholarly biographer Ulrich Weitz, "shadowy" life as printer, publisher, social democratic (and sometime communist) advocate and agitator, administrator, author, and collector. His books and his marriage made him rich. The two of Fuchs's several profusely illustrated and extensively annotated sets of multi-volume publications that Benjamin analyzed most extensively logically contain the most material related to the body and sexuality, and their pictorial representation: *Illustrierte Sittengeschichte vom Mittelalter bis zur Gegenwart* [Illustrated History of Manners from the Middle Ages to the Present; 6 vols. Originally published 1909–1912] and *Geschichte der erotischen Kunst* [History of Erotic Art; 3 vols. Originally published 1908; 1922–1923] (Benjamin, 2002, pp. 272, 280, 289). These collections, brought together out of Fuchs's own vast personal collection of caricatures, accrete massive amounts of text to the high quality, lithographically reproduced images visible on nearly every page (Bach, 2010).

Fuchs lived in the late 1920s and early 1930s in a Berlin villa designed for a previous owner by the young Mies van der Rohe that he filled with his massive collections (Gorsen, 2006, p. 221). Nonetheless his socialist politics, along with the recurring perception among prosecutors that his books were criminally obscene, brought him a lifelong series of criminal and civil charges, trials, imprisonments, controversies, and clashes with various authorities. Fuchs had been among the prominent Social Democrats who split with the party over its support for the First World War to found the Spartacist League/Independent Social Democratic Party. That party went on to fracture further into the Communist Party of Germany (KPD). Fuchs participated in both of these party-political innovations, though he subsequently broke with the KPD in 1928 (Weitz, 2014). While Benjamin never implies that Fuchs came to take a certain personal pleasure in his adversarial position to the German state, Peter Gorsen calls the lengthy set of conflicts over obscenity in which Fuchs and his publisher, Albert Langen, battled the imperial authorities before the First World War "crafty [*listig*]" (Gorsen, 2006, p. 219). In 1933, Fuchs fled the Nazis for exile in Paris, where he and Benjamin became personally acquainted. Despite much effort his collections were never restituted to him, and were largely auctioned off by the Nazis.

Generally unremarked in the English-language literature is that Fuchs did not happen by chance upon his contacts to the figures of the Frankfurt School, especially Horkheimer. From the initiation of the underlying institutional developments in the early 1920s that led to the Institute's foundation until Fuchs's death in 1940, he was in regular contact with Horkheimer. Likely from its inception, Fuchs belonged to the trustees of the Society for Social Research [*Gesellschaft für Sozialforschung*], the private foundation established in 1922 by Felix Weil with a substantial endowment from his wealthy father to support the Institute that came to share its name (Gorsen, 2006, p. 220; Weitz, 1991, pp. 413–416). The early group of trustees also included additional Weil family members, Friedrich Pollock, Max Horkheimer, Kurt Albert Gerlach, and Richard Sorge (Jay, 1996, pp. 8–9; Wiggershaus, 1995, pp. 20–21).[1] It appears that Fuchs and Weil had originally met in Tübingen when they overlapped for a short time as students there and discovered their shared interests in revolutionary politics. Weil's activities as a student agitator had even led to his legal banishment from Württemberg, and his relationship with Fuchs remained close enough that he apparently even arranged for Fuchs to serve as trustee of some portion of his personal fortune (Weitz, 2014, p. 272). Fuchs's association with the Institute took the form of his establishment in 1924, again with Weil's financial assistance and after discussions with Horkheimer, of a Berlin-based *Sozialwissenschaftliches Archiv* (Archive for Social Research). The primary goal of the Archive was to collect material about the German working class and the political parties affiliated with it (Weitz, 2014, p. 273). For this archive, Fuchs purchased a large amount of material from the newly formed KPD, which at the time was constantly in the sights of the German authorities for its advocacy of revolutionary overthrow of the republic. The Archive attracted notice from significant figures in international communism and brought Fuchs into contact with David Riazanov, the director of the Marx-Engels Institute in Moscow. In October 1925, however, barely a year after the Archive had begun operations, the Prussian police raided it on the suspicion that it formed an illegal archive related to the KPD's treasonous activities. Fuchs was soon being personally investigated for treason by the state prosecutors, though they concluded in March 1926 that evidence was insufficient to charge him (Weitz, 2014, pp. 276–284).

Through his work with the Archive and its materials both before and after its official dissolution, Fuchs was regularly in correspondence with the Institute, especially with Friedrich Pollock, who held a range of responsibility for the Institute's administrative operations (Wiggershaus, 1995). He apparently even regularly visited the Institute's photographic laboratory in Frankfurt in order to assist in the making of photographic reproductions of significant documents and images of the history of Marxism, all the while in regular correspondence with Riazanov (Weitz, 2014, p. 286). Nonetheless the relationship with the Institute had moments of significant friction. In the aftermath of the police raid on the Archive, it came to light that, apparently without Fuchs's knowledge, some of the Archive's employees had been hired at the behest of the KPD. Pollock and the Institute, always concerned that they not become associated with potentially illegal political activities, chose to close the archive and end the employment of the staff effective 31 December 1925. As Pollock wrote to Fuchs, the Institute "has been drawn, due to the lack of conscience on the part of certain employees, into a political affair." Because the Institute "wanted to avoid, under all circumstances, being drawn into the political struggle," it had no choice but to dissolve the Archive (Weitz, 2014, p. 282).

Pollock's language here prefigures conflicts that the leaders of the Institute, especially Horkheimer, would have with other members during the Institute's period of exile in the United States due to concerns that the Institute not cultivate a political reputation too close to Marxism or communism (Amidon & Worrell, 2008; Worrell, 2006). It is therefore no exaggeration to describe Fuchs as having held a central position in the establishment and financing of the Frankfurt School. Fuchs even corresponded with Horkheimer in the late 1930s about the possibility of emigrating to the United States (Weitz, 2014, p. 357). Horkheimer remained circumspect in his extant correspondence and papers about why he wished to have an article about Fuchs written for the *ZfS*, and why he chose Benjamin to write it. There is also no evidence in the correspondence between Benjamin, Horkheimer, Adorno, and Pollock that Fuchs himself felt it necessary to reveal to or discuss with Benjamin his longstanding connections with Horkheimer and the Institute. Fuchs, indeed, always remained the vanishing mediator, the "man in the shadows." Scholarship has revealed, however, that his activities were so closely bound up with the Institute that while he cannot count as one if its inner circle, he must be recognized as standing among its most closely affiliated figures.

## SEXUALITY, PORNOGRAPHY, AND THE REALIZATION OF THE FUCHS ESSAY

When Benjamin's complete draft of the Fuchs essay reached New York, Horkheimer proved to be very pleased with it despite its arduous process of composition and much concern about the result. He wrote an extensive letter to Benjamin on 16 March 1937 with his thoughts and comments about the essay, and introduced it with a statement of strong praise: "I congratulate you on it. I read it with the greatest pleasure. You have solved this task, which for many reasons did not come easily to you, at last in a way that the true theoretical intentions of the *Zeitschrift* are advanced by it" (Benjamin, 1977, p. 1331; trans. Amidon). In introducing his suggestions for (mostly minor) revisions, Horkheimer went on to emphasize the collaborative nature of the work represented in the *ZfS*, stating that the authors of all of the major essays in the volume shared ideas with one another on their pieces, usually in person. The institute's project thus represented a multi-layered form of collaboration. The 1937 issue of the *ZfS* also represented the moment at which Horkheimer's vision for Critical Theory achieved its methodological breakthrough. It contained, along with the Fuchs essay, Horkheimer's essay "Traditional and Critical Theory," which brought together in a fully fledged programmatic statement Horkheimer's long-developing ideas for the Frankfurt School's method of critical interdisciplinary scholarship (Amidon, 2008). While the *ZfS* had published Benjamin's work previously, particularly a French translation of a shorter version of "The Work of Art in the Age of its Technological Reproducibility" in the 1936 volume, the simultaneous publication of the Fuchs essay and Horkheimer's methodological manifesto demonstrates the centrality of Benjamin's intellectual work to the project of Critical Theory at the moment of its crystallization. While Benjamin would occasionally express to others a desire to maintain some distance between his own work and the Institute's greater project, in the later 1930s, his essays became major pillars of the Frankfurt School's emergent scholarly and critical identity (Eiland & Jennings, 2014, p. 388).

In Horkheimer's conclusion to his letter of 16 March 1937, however, he takes up, after six pages of detailed comments on the content of the essay, a theme that foregrounds the core thematic constellation of the essay discussed above: pornography. Pornography brings together in a complex and value-laden genre the constitutive themes of the essay: corporeality, sexuality and the reproduction of images. Horkheimer's comments contrast strongly with Benjamin's choice (likely made later, and without evidence that Horkheimer, Adorno, or others suggested it), to tone down in his critique of Fuchs's understanding of the destructive power of sexuality and the orgasm. Horkheimer suggests to Benjamin that he address the concern, clearly broached in Fuchs's trials on charges of obscenity, that his volumes were received in the market as pornography:

> I found one small thought lacking, which while less than flattering with respect to Fuchs, could be revealing to the matter. Nowhere, namely, is it

indicated, that even despite all the Puritanism, the success of Fuchs's publications in the market can be derived not least the fact that they were sought out as pornography. That he himself never reckoned with this, and in fact was not even capable of reckoning with this, doesn't necessarily do him honor, but belongs nonetheless to the understanding of his livelihood as a writer. I leave it to you whether you want to add a little sentence or a paragraph in which this subject matter is thought about. (Benjamin, 1977, p. 1337; trans. Amidon)

Horkheimer then concluded his letter by explaining that Friedrich Pollock, who functioned as the chief administrator of the Institute, would be arriving in Paris on the same ship as the letter, and that he would trust Benjamin and Pollock to decide how to approach Fuchs with the manuscript of the essay. Horkheimer was not optimistic, expecting that Fuchs would "curse."

Benjamin responded to Horkheimer's comments extensively in a letter of 28 March 1937. Nowhere in this letter, however, did he address Horkheimer's remarks about the perception of Fuchs's publications as pornography. As published, the essay does contain one mention of pornography. Nonetheless, there appears to be no other mention of Horkheimer's suggestion anywhere in Benjamin's later published correspondence. Benjamin thus becomes, in a curious way, doubly silent about sexuality and its visual representation as pornography: not just did he eliminate his critical comment about Fuchs's lack of understanding of it, but he appears to have chosen not take up Horkheimer's suggestion that he elaborate on pornography in the essay itself.

Benjamin's silence here is curious not because it evinces a reticence to discuss or analyze the relationship between pornography and other forms of text and image. Rather, it is curious precisely because Benjamin clearly did consider pornography to belong to the spheres of representation and reproduction that drew his interest in the Fuchs essay. In 1927, he wrote and published in the respected journal *Die literarische Welt* a short essay with the title "A State Monopoly on Pornography." This essay is a reflection upon the banning by the Spanish authorities of a certain class of publications widely available in newsstands. These often included texts by respected authors writing pornographic literature, often under their own names. In it he argues—in a manner striking for its combination of seriousness and irony—that language, by its very nature, contains elements that tend toward the pornographic. Benjamin does not consider here directly the relationships between language, text, and image that became central to the Fuchs essay, but the stakes are similar. He argues that all language is representational, and holds within itself a certain pornographic potential: "In one respect, pornographic books are like other books: they are all based on language and writing. If language did not contain elements in its vocabulary that are obscene in themselves, pornography would be robbed of its best instruments" (Benjamin, 2000, p. 72). This claim develops into an early form of Benjamin's argument for a critical–historical method that pays closest attention not to the beautiful or privileged, but to fragments, detritus, remainders:

> Language in the various phases of its historical development is a single great experiment that is conducted in as many laboratories as there are people … By-products of every kind are inevitable. They include all the idioms and fixed expressions, whether written or spoken, that stand outside normal usage: nicknames, company names, swear words, oaths, devotional expressions, and obscenities. These may be excessive, lacking in expression, sacred, a fermentation of cultic language, or else overexplicit, shameless, and depraved. The waste products of daily usage, these same elements acquire a crucial value in other contexts—in scientific contexts, above all—since there these astonishing linguistic splinters can be understood as fragments from the primeval granite of the linguistic massif. (Benjamin, 2000, pp. 72–73)

Knowledge, for Benjamin, emerges most significantly from objects that, because they are perceived only as waste, are commonly overlooked by disciplinary inquiry. They resist easy subsumption into received forms or categories.

Benjamin draws two conclusions from this set of observations about the inherently pornographic qualities of linguistic representation. The first is that rather than try to banish the obscene from social discourse, society ought to make use of the forces out of which it emerges. Here, he prefigures arguments from the Fuchs essay. Rather than suppressing the obscene, he argues that it represents powerful forces that must be harnessed. He deploys a powerful technological metaphor here: "Just as Niagara Falls feeds power stations, in the same way the downward torrent of language into smut and vulgarity should be used as a mighty source of energy to drive the dynamo of the creative act" (Benjamin, 2000, p. 73). The second is a counter-intuitive idea that must at once be provocative and ironic: "For this reason we call for a state monopoly on pornography.

We demand the socialization of this not inconsiderable source of power" (Benjamin, 2000, p. 73). His conclusion is that doing so would put economic forces into the service of art, because talented authors could be properly remunerated for their expertise. This fascinating heterodoxy in Benjamin's thought—a quasi-capitalist argument in the service of the goal of the "socialization" of the power of a socially disruptive representational form—looks forward to the fully developed critical–historical methods advocated in the Fuchs essay.

## Historical Materialism, Knowledge, and the Remnants of the Corporeal

The Fuchs essay takes the stakes of the argument found in "A State Monopoly on Pornography" and develops them both in breadth, incorporating the representation and reproduction of images as well as texts, and in depth, exploring a controversial but shadowy figure who worked across political, cultural, and intellectual boundaries. The result is a complex and variegated discussion of the political economy of art, out of which Benjamin develops a sophisticated argument about the critical methods of historical materialist scholarship. His argument brings together the material of history, the relationship between text and image, moral psychology, the biological, and the corporeal.

Before the Fuchs essay saw print in the 1937 *ZfS*, however, Benjamin had to contend with a concern on the part of the editorial board, likely led by Pollock, that the essay was too overtly Marxist, and could therefore endanger the Institute's scholarly status—much in the same way that Pollock had scolded Fuchs a decade before for having allowed, even unintentionally, the Institute to be pulled into political controversy through the Archive's links to the KPD. This resulted in a third elision in the process of the essay's realization, alongside Benjamin's removal of his strongest critical statement about Fuchs's deficits and his lack of response to Horkheimer's advice that he address the question of the pornographic marketability of Fuchs's works. In the original published version of the essay, the editors deleted the entire first paragraph, which included the claim that "it is the recent past of the Marxist theory of art which is at issue here ... For unlike Marxist economics, this theory still has no history" (260). Benjamin had little choice but to go along with this decision. The apparent motivation on the part of the editors was that Fuchs's collections, still stuck in Nazi Germany, remained in (ultimately unsuccessful) litigation about their release and potential export, and that reminders of Fuchs's Marxist associations could possibly endanger this process further (Benjamin, 1977).

Benjamin's argument in the first section of the Fuchs essay rapidly develops into a powerful statement of the critical–historical method that not only observes and analyzes the material detritus of modern life, but takes on the hypostasized edifices of disciplinary orthodoxy about historical facts and breaks them up. Just as language tends toward the pornographic, materialist historical cognition tends toward the destructive, even violent:

> The historical materialist blasts the epoch out of its reified "historical continuity," and thereby the life out of the epoch, and the work out of the lifework. Yet this construct results in the simultaneous preservation and sublation [*Aufhebung*] of the lifework *in* the work, of the epoch *in* the lifework, and of the course of history *in* the epoch. (262; emphasis original)

For Benjamin here, "life" carries three valences of meaning, and a fourth that remains a dialectically charged implication. It means, firstly, the life of an individual as biographical history; secondly, the metaphorical sense of the epoch itself being alive, rather than dead; and thirdly, the conceptual sense of life as the object of biological inquiry. The fourth valence is the implied one: if "life" in all these senses forms a locus of historical materialist inquiry, then the question of the embodied qualities of that life is dialectically implicit. In all three of these valences of meaning, the corporeality of the living being is sublated. The body's absence from these arguments recursively generates the possibility of its presence.

The remarkable conclusion here is that a successfully critical–historical materialism renders historical facts not as an eternal, "epic" image of the past, but as a means of linking past, present, and future. Thus, Benjamin argues, adding further layers to the concept "life": "Historical materialism conceives historical understanding as an afterlife of that which has been understood and whose pulse can be felt in the present" (262). The past, therefore, has two lives. Benjamin's motto here could very well be "The past is dead. Long live the past." "Afterlife" here stands dialectically stretched between the prepositional sense of "living past" a given point in time, of surviving and carrying forward, and the nominal sense of a "living past," that the past lives on without bound through its remnants and artifacts. This "living past," however, is what the historical materialist presents through experience: "Historical materialism presents a given experience with the past—an experience that is unique ... The immense forces bound up in historicism's 'Once upon a time' are liberated in this experience ... [Historical materialism] is directed toward a consciousness of the present which explodes the continuum of history" (262). The unity implied here between the nominal and prepositional qualities of the living past requires in turn the unity of the subject and object of historical practice. The body becomes social by living past itself, resolving into the possibility of its own cognition beyond itself in the living past. Experience, then, is the body's journey into historical materiality, but this materiality is always dialectically charged with the body's vanishing into historicity.

Section II of the Fuchs essay focuses on the details of Fuchs's biography. In Section III, Benjamin further develops his critique of what he sees to be the uncritical aspects of cultural history [*Kulturgeschichte*] out of significant thematic elements that he has raised in his treatment Fuchs's "life." Here is found the aphoristic phrase that has emerged from the essay as its most memorable, that "There is no document of culture which is not at the same time a document of barbarism" (267). The context of this statement, however, is crucial to its interpretation. Benjamin embeds it within the elaboration of his thematics of life in multiple ways. First, he links history to life through the concept "lineage," emphasizing the generational flow of the material that becomes history. Here, he emphasizes in particular the ways that traditional disciplinarity renders that material static, even dead, and thereby sunders it from historical cognition. This deadening process further leaves this material indistinguishable from property, and thereby from the processes of alienation that underlie capital accumulation

> Doesn't the study of individual disciplines (once the semblance of their unity has been removed) inevitably coalesce in the study of cultural history as the inventory which humanity has preserved to the present day? [...] Whatever the historical materialist surveys in art or science has, without exception, a lineage he cannot observe without horror. (267)

Then, after the famous phrase about the mutual implication of culture and barbarism, Benjamin redoubles the focus on property and ownership, drawing in his themes of human reproduction and destruction. He initiates the passage with a rhetorical flourish that shows the stakes and demonstrates that claims about barbarism are only a subsidiary point. The passage culminates in a statement that makes clear the distinction between the "survival" of the dead artifacts of cultural history and the living past—afterlife—of the objects of dialectical materialist history.

> Nevertheless the crucial element does not lie here. If the concept of culture is problematic for historical materialism, it cannot conceive of the disintegration of culture into goods which become objects of possession for mankind … The concept of culture—as the embodiment of creations considered independent, if not of the production process in which they originate, then of a production process in which they continue to survive—has a fetishistic quality. Culture appears reified. (267)

This sense of reification captures the process whereby concepts, ideas, and representations—the intangible material that recursively renders into the texts and images of the objects of culture—become property. It is how these objects are separated from the dialectically charged space of experience out of which they emerge and which further allows their capture as forms of capital. Here lies the core of Benjamin's critique of Fuchs: as a materialist and as a historian, he was unable to see deeply enough into these dynamics. Fuchs's studies and collecting practices made materialist historical analysis possible. Fuchs himself, however, never achieved a fully fledged form of historical practice adequate to his material.

The passage that leads into this statement by completing Benjamin's discussion of Fuchs's biography in Section II brings together all of the essay's thematic constituents: the body, sexuality, production, destruction, excess, experience text, even war. This thematic complex then requires a symbolic figuration adequate to the density of the material packed into the argument. That figure, expanded and refigured into the concept traffic [*Verkehr*] in the passage, is perhaps the nineteenth- and twentieth-century technology that captured the greatest symbolic power, because it became the visible figure of the institutional expansion of capital accumulation through public and private finance: the locomotive. Benjamin quotes here both French and German figures who saw the locomotive as "the saint of the future" and as a kind of refigured "angel … since a locomotive is worth more than the nicest pair of wings" (266). Benjamin was furthermore one of the earliest literary critics to recognize the significance of an author whose work explores in great symbolic and figurative depth the nature of *Verkehr*: Franz Kafka (Anderson, 1992). Further, this passage points subtly to the primary means by which the body is sublated into and through capital: through the alienation of labor. The embodied qualities of industrial labor—everywhere manifest in the physical operation of the shrieking, panting, smoking, roaring steam locomotive with its engineer and fireman visible in the cab and illuminated often by the light of the firebox flames—vanish in the experience of the bourgeoisie. Benjamin's words give this dialectics of corporeality, and its links to historical materialist practice, vivid texture:

> It may cause one to ask whether the complacency [*Gemütlichkeit*] of the nineteenth-century bourgeoisie did not stem from the hollow comfort of never having to experience how the productive forces had to develop under their hands. This experience was really reserved for the following century, which has discovered that the speed of traffic [*Verkehr*] and the ability of machines to duplicate words and writing outstrips human needs. The energies that technology develops beyond this threshold are destructive. First of all, they advance the technology of war and its propagandistic preparation. (267)

Here "traffic"—*Verkehr*—must be understood to carry its double load of symbolic meaning emerging from the German concept: *Verkehr* is both traffic in the technological–economic sense, and sexual relations not as an abstract concept, but as the potential physical interaction between bodies. The economy's surplus, which becomes its potential for destruction, thus reveals its close correlation with the potentially excessive moments in sexuality. Destruction thereby begins to reveal its dialectical variegation. Within the entire Fuchs essay, this passage brings out most directly the negative loadings of destruction in Benjamin's thought. Nonetheless it reveals where, using Benjamin's own term, the threshold lies between destruction as violence, exploitation, and alienation and destruction as a constitutive process in the making-manifest of the material of a living, productive, dialectical form of history.

## Prurience, Prudery, and Production: Sexuality and its Representation Under the Condition of Technological Reproducibility

At this point in the essay, the stakes of the statement about the destructive quality of the orgasm that Benjamin excised from the essay have been revealed. He is ready to describe in detail the content of Fuchs's work, and how it relates to the methods and tasks of historical materialism. Benjamin targets his criticisms of Fuchs at several different levels of argument. Foremost among them is Benjamin's exploration of how and why Fuchs's work could at once be seen by the German authorities as prurient to the point of pornographically obscene, but at the same time, Fuchs's own arguments recapitulated forms of bourgeois moralism to the point of prudery. This discussion extends over Sections IV and V of the essay, which further extend the exploration of the themes of dialectical materialist epistemology, creativity, and biological life.

Benjamin begins with a short discussion of Fuchs's career that brings out the tensions and struggles that Fuchs faced: "Those aspects of his work which are likely to endure were wrested from an intellectual constellation that could hardly have appeared less propitious. This is the point where Fuchs the collector taught Fuchs the theoretician to comprehend much that the times denied him" (268). Immediately here, for the first and only time in the main body of the essay, Benjamin raises the question of pornography in relation to Fuchs's work, framing it with a statement about the destruction of traditional disciplinary discourses: "He was a collector who strayed into marginal areas—such as caricature and pornographic imagery—which sooner or later meant the ruin of a whole series of clichés in traditional art history" (268). Fuchs himself, in Benjamin's interpretation, specifically set himself apart from classicistic concepts of art, but in doing so, the qualities of moralistic prudery that his work contains became manifest through a kind of sublimation of the corporeal aspects of artistic representation. Benjamin frames this in an embedded quotation from the first volume of Fuchs's *Erotic Art*: "Fuchs prophesied a new beauty 'which, in the end, will be infinitely greater than that of antiquity. Whereas the latter was only the highest animalistic form, the new beauty will be filled with a lofty spiritual and emotional content'" (269). It is not the stock Marxist rhetoric of "form" and "content" which interests Benjamin here, however, but rather the opportunity to highlight how Fuchs's weaknesses contribute to the advancement of historical materialist understanding. He continues with another of the essay's well-known passages that vividly represents practices of the reception of art as themselves the fragmentary artifacts of cognition that must be sublated into a fuller form of knowledge:

> Of course it would be a mistake to assume that the idealist view of art was itself entirely unhinged. That cannot happen until the *disjecta membra*

which idealism contains—as "historical representation" on the one hand and "appreciation" on the other—are merged and therefore surpassed. (269)

This argument does not denigrate Fuchs's conceptual vocabulary or interpretive practices, or of other theorists of art like Heinrich Wölfflin, whose formalism is compared in this section to Fuchs's practices. Slightly later, Benjamin also dramatically compares Fuchs to the ethnologist Adolf Bastian, whose "insatiable hunger for material" (271) led him to embark on research and collecting expeditions with the same tireless, nearly compulsive enthusiasm that Fuchs showed toward his collecting, writing, publishing, and political work.

This discussion of the ways in which forms of interpretive or disciplinary practice themselves must be understood as the material of historical understanding—an argument that parallels closely Horkheimer's claims differentiating Critical Theory from traditional theory—leads Benjamin toward his first longer discussion of technologies of reproduction in the Fuchs essay. This anticipates not only later passages but also develops parallels with the Artwork essay, composed in the midst of the long process of work on the Fuchs essay. Here it becomes clear that rhetoric of destruction is directed specifically not toward material objects—and most definitely not toward bodies—but toward abstract disciplines and techniques of representation and interpretation that can become captured within processes of technological reproduction. He develops this argument from the outset by distinguishing "the historical object" itself from such disciplinary practices: "The historical object removed from pure facticity does not need any 'appreciation.'" Furthermore, Fuchs was a pioneer because, as Benjamin argues, his work centers around "motifs" that "refer to forms of knowledge which could only prove destructive to traditional forms of art" (269).

Fuchs's failure—the reason that his interpretations have little "destructive force" (270), is because Fuchs did not make this connection between artistic objects, practices of interpretation and representation, and technologies of reproduction. He could therefore default only to largely vacuous interpretive concepts like "mood of the times," which despite his materialist intentions left his thinking undialectical and therefore inadequate to the fullness of history. Benjamin, however, takes this opportunity to make some of his most forceful statements in the essay about the centrality of reproductive technologies to historical understanding. The central point here is how a clearly historical materialist approach can counter the process whereby art and its processes of production, interpretation, and reception can be captured by capital.

> The concern with techniques of reproduction, more than any other line of research, brings out the crucial importance of reception; it enables us to correct the process of reification which takes place in a work of art … For it is precisely historical materialism that is interested in tracing the changes of artistic vision not so much to a changed ideal of beauty [a core argument in Fuchs's texts], as to more elementary processes—processes set in motion by economic and technological transformations in production. (269–270)

Attention to the history and political economy of the many layers of reproduction begins, therefore, to emerge as the most effective epistemology. The dynamics of capitalism tear the work of art from its technical and social field of relation. Historical materialism seeks to restore this embeddedness.

Sections V, VI, VII, and VIII discuss both intensively and extensively Fuchs's ideas about artistic creativity. Benjamin thus returns through two different angles to the issue of the body: through Fuchs's arguments about the embodied qualities of creativity that link it to sexuality, and again through Fuchs's tendency to recapitulate forms of bourgeois moralism in his texts. This two-pronged approach generates the most revealing contrasts and tensions between Benjamin's methods and Fuchs's. It thus makes manifest the reasons why Benjamin struggled with his work on the Fuchs essay: they both make arguments about the relationships between the body, art, and the social, and teasing their positions apart is a not a straightforward task.

Section V contains the most revealing material in the essay on life and the forms of inquiry into it. Here, as introduced above, Benjamin engages with the disciplinary field of biology in his exploration of the flaws in Fuchs's historical approach. He states that "Fuchs's notion of creativity has a strongly biological slant" (272). The meaning of "biological" here only becomes clear in the subsequent discussion, as Benjamin explains how that this refers to how Fuchs saw creativity as a manifestation of sexuality. Without using the Freudian language of sublimation (as significantly as is what Benjamin notes to be Fuchs's closeness to psychoanalytic concepts), Fuchs saw artistic objects as manifestations of erotic energy. Biology therefore becomes, in Benjamin's analytical schema, coterminous with a concept of sexuality as something going well beyond the sphere of the corporeal. While this hardly does justice to the complex politics of the biological disciplines in the early twentieth-century German-speaking world, Benjamin develops the claim into a subtle linking of Fuchs's Social Democratic commitments in the 1890s to his own arguments about historical materialism—and this link itself reveals significant moments of those biological politics. As Benjamin explains, the German Social Democratic Party's commitment to Darwin alongside Marx as a foundational narrative of historical progress meant that "history assumed deterministic traits" (273). What the SPD did with its program of political education, therefore, was to produce a kind of pseudo-dialectics. Where the emergent narratives of large-scale change in dynamic societies or organismal populations that parallel each other in Marx and Darwin contained highly variegated dialectical tools of analysis, the party's making of them into reified forms of political enlightenment evacuated them of their power for historical materialism.

Benjamin goes on to show further—in another exploration of the subtleties of the epistemic field of biology in the late nineteenth and early twentieth centuries—the functioning of a number of sub-disciplinary emanations of nineteenth century biology in the political discourse of the time. Here he appropriates terms from the critic H. Laufenberg that link biological and political–economic categories: "Nevertheless, many were satisfied with the theses which divided historical processes into 'physiological' and 'pathological' ones, or affirmed that the materialism of natural science 'automatically turned into historical materialism once it came into the hands of the proletariat'" (273). Clearly, such naïve political narratives could not carry the power that their original advocates had hoped they would. Benjamin rounds off the section with the conclusion that no matter how much narratives of progress might seem to embody the living past of historical materialism, they usually fail, because they traffic in the evacuation of the dialectical aspects of thought.

Section VII focuses specifically on the question of Fuchs's bourgeois moralism, and how it relates to the reductive historical thinking that led Fuchs to give credence to undialectical progress narratives. Again, of course, Fuchs's collecting and scholarship carry the potential to provide the basis for a genuinely materialist history. But undifferentiated forms of the reception of Marxist thought and theory thwarted this possibility. Revolution was no simple narrative of progressive triumph in sequential class conflicts:

> Not surprisingly the bourgeois moralism contains elements which collide with Fuchs's materialism. If Fuchs had recognized this, he might have been

able to tone down this opposition. He was convinced, however, that that his moralistic consideration of history and his historical materialism were in complete accord. This was an illusion, buttressed by a widespread opinion badly in need of revision: that the bourgeois revolutions, as celebrated by the bourgeoisie itself, are the immediate source of a proletarian revolution. (277)

In Benjamin's reading, bourgeois moralism arose out of this self-congratulatory sensibility, culminating in a "class morality" of "conscience" that served to embed the injustice of property relations built on the basis of alienated labor even deeper into economic relations.

The themes of sexuality, moralism, and creativity are read together in Section VIII, which serves as the first of two full elaborations of Benjamin's thematic constellation. He begins by quoting a statement by Fuchs that clearly shows the tensions in his moralistic rhetoric about sexuality. Here Fuchs deploys the language of the "Lebensphilosophie" of nineteenth-century Germany, and furthermore, in an evacuated form, the vocabulary of "values" that dominated late German neo-Kantian philosophy around 1900, implying obliquely that sexuality drives reproduction, both artistic and biological. Where Fuchs finds sexuality and creativity demonstrably linked, he values them together. Where he sees sexuality essentially only as embodied practice of pleasure, his moralistic revulsion drives him so far as to dub it "evil." Here Benjamin again quotes from the early parts of the first volume of Fuchs's *Erotische Kunst*:

> Concerning sexuality he says: "All forms of sensual behavior in which the creative element of their law of life becomes visible are justified. Certain forms, however, are evil—namely those in which this highest of drives becomes degraded to a mere means of refined craving for pleasure ..." Fuchs never acquired a proper distrust of the bourgeois scorn for pure sexual pleasure and the more or less fantastic means of creating it. (278–279)

In a subtle but clear reference to the medicalizing discourses in late-nineteenth-century European juridico-legal approaches to forms of non-procreative sexuality, Benjamin further notes how Fuchs, in a parallel manner, accepts and deploys arguments about practices seen as being "against nature" and representing "degenerate individuality" (279). Benjamin thereby closes additional links in his thematic constellation between the body, sexuality, reproduction, and historical knowledge.

Fuchs revels in his material undialectically, failing to recognize the moments of excess in commodity reproduction that destructively enable the accumulation of capital. He thereby accretes and recapitulates bourgeois moral forms including the exclusion and disavowal of non-reproductive sexuality, all via speculative detours into reductive biologistic and natural–historical argument. Benjamin insists, rather, that the destructive excess itself becomes the engine of historical cognition. He thereby opens up a space for the emergence of social ontology. Fuchs looks on the surface like a libertine, and the German authorities repeatedly took him for a potentially criminal one. Nonetheless he was not. His short-circuited recapitulation of bourgeois modes of production and reproduction drive him to accept and deploy bourgeois sex morality. He was no libertine.

Benjamin appears here to be defending a kind of pleasure principle-driven practice and understanding of sexuality, but one that remains always in the service of historical materialist cognition. Fuchs liberates the gaze in the service of freeing the proletariat, and focuses it on the body and its accretions (fashion, caricature, political symbol). His underdeveloped theory of history, however, leaves the body subject to the coercive and alienating strictures of bourgeois disciplinarity, just as his techno-reproductive method itself resolved his collections into substantial financial and real property. Benjamin liberates the fragments, remnants, artifacts, and detritus of the body in order to place them in the service of a fully dialectical materialist method that holds promise to give form to social processes. He does so, however, at the expense of requiring a sublation of the body. His method renders and dissolves corporeality into historical cognition.

Here, where Benjamin brings his analysis of Fuchs to its most pointedly powerful critical conclusions, this tension between their respective forms of argument erupts in a telling contrast. This is in the passage where Benjamin specifically explores Fuchs's engagement with the "sexual-psychological problem." At the same time that he praises some of Fuchs's analytical claims, he criticizes Fuchs for a "detour through natural history." He himself, however, deploys an analogous kind of argument in a footnote to this passage, almost as if he wished to demonstrate how his fully developed critical-historical methods could do justice to the material of the past in ways that Fuchs's cannot.

In introducing this argument, Benjamin emphasizes that "it is difficult to clarify the sexual-psychological problem" (279). He continues, however, with a specifically historical–materialist discussion that links bourgeois economic and moral practices, and culminates in simultaneous criticism and praise of Fuchs:

> But ever since the bourgeoisie came to power, this clarification has become particularly important. This is where taboos against more or less broad areas of sexual pleasure have their place. The repressions which are thereby produced in the masses engender masochistic and sadistic complexes. Those in power then further these complexes by delivering up to the masses those objects which prove most favorable to their own politics … Fuchs failed to produce a social critique in this regard. Thus, a passage where he compensates for this lack by means of a detour through natural history becomes all the more important. The passage in question is his brilliant defense of orgies [found in vol. 2 of *Erotische Kunst*]. (279)

Benjamin elaborates on how Fuchs, in this and similar passages, "deals critically with traditional norms" (279). Remarkably, however, and in a way reminiscent of the dialectical irony of his claims about state control of pornography, Benjamin includes a footnote here that itself hypothesizes a straightforwardly natural–historical explanation for human sexual practices, one that centers around precisely the thing that Benjamin thought Fuchs failed to understand: the orgasm:

> Fuchs is on the track of something important here. Would it be too rash to connect the threshold between human and animal, such as Fuchs recognizes in the orgy, with that other threshold constituted by the emergence of upright posture? The latter brings with it a phenomenon unprecedented in natural history: partners can look into each other's eyes during orgasm. Only then does an orgy become possible. What is decisive is not the increase in visual stimuli but rather the fact that now the expression of satiety and even of impotence can itself become an erotic stimulant. (299, n. 70)

Benjamin thus demonstrates that it is not biological explanation itself that he resists in Fuchs. Rather, it is inadequate methods that sunder the links between the past and the present, and make it impossible to link embodied practices to social reality.

With this point, Benjamin has rounded out the critical and methodological framing of the essay. He has not, however, yet fully shown how his own methods can do greater justice to the material of history than can

Fuchs's. This he does in the final two sections of the essay, which explore the cultural figure who most engaged Fuchs as a collector and author: the French artist and caricaturist Honoré Daumier. Benjamin allows his scholarly imagination full flight here, in an imagined rhetorical question linking Fuchs's interpretive work, the language of Darwinistic historical argument including its category "life," the production and reproduction of images, and class analysis, and the passage culminates in a claim about the representation of the body:

> What impressed Fuchs most was the element of strife—the agonistic dimension—in Daumier's art. Would it be too daring to seek the origin of Daumier's great caricatures in a question? Daumier seems to ask himself: "What would bourgeois people of my time look like if one were to imagine their struggle for existence as taking place in a *palaestra*, an arena?" Daumier translated the public and private life of Parisians into the language of the agon. The athletic tension of the whole body—its muscular movements—arouse Daumier's greatest enthusiasm. (281)

Here, the thematic constituents of Benjamin's entire analysis begin to come together in a thorough critical analysis of an artist who made full use of the reproductive technologies of his day. Fuchs recognized the significance of technological reproduction in understanding Daumier and his world, but his methods could not fully carry out the consequences of this recognition (283).

With this discussion, Benjamin completes his constellation of Fuchs's representational world. He can therefore grant Fuchs substantial recognition: Fuchs sought to restore a properly social understanding of art.

> Fuchs belongs in this line of great and systematic collectors who were resolutely intent on a single subject matter. It has been his goal to restore to the work of art its existence within society, from which it had been so decisively cut off that the collector could find it only in the art market; there—reduced to a commodity, far removed both from its creators and from those who were able to understand it—the work of art endured ... Fuchs was one of the first to expound the specific character of mass art and this to develop the impulses he had received from historical materialism. (283)

Thoroughly and successfully understood historical materialism is, therefore, the means to the end not just of countering the dynamics in capitalism that reduces objects to commodities, but also of creating a new form of social ontology that itself successfully resists its own evacuation through the processes of capital accumulation. Only such a form of knowledge production can do justice to the embodied practices of the production of art, to the sexual lives of individuals in their social surroundings, to the detritus thrown off by capital and its processes, and to the understanding of all of the valences of reproduction that affect and constitute bodies, works of art, and social worlds.

## Conclusion: Historical Material, Social Ontology, and Critical Practice Today

Benjamin thus returns, after a thorough exploration of its consequences, to the point he drew at the beginning of the Fuchs essay out of an analysis Engels's discussion, in a letter to Franz Mehring written in 1893, of the fate of thought under the regime of capital. He quotes Engels:

> Ever since the bourgeois illusion of the eternity and finality of capitalist production entered the picture, even the overcoming of the mercantilists by the physiocrats and Adam Smith is seen as a mere victory of thought—not as the reflection in thought of the changed economic facts, but as the finally achieved correct insight into actual relations existing always and everywhere. (261)

The idea that capital dominates the world eternally leads not just to the commodification of bodies and ideas, but also to the evacuation of genuine political–economic understanding. This is a constitutive moment of the trauma in Eric Santner's concept of the "*traumamtlich*": the residual destructiveness present in the institutions and "offices" of the modern economy (Santner, 2015). Economic facts are emptied of social content by the false totality of capital. Capital thereby interrupts social ontology because ideas become disconnected from historical–political practice. Theory also, thereby, runs the risk of becoming uncritical: it becomes disciplinarily dominating, excluding from its closed sphere of explanatory technique the material from which new knowledge might emerge. Materialist historical practice resolves the possibility of the social out of the false equivalences of commodity production and reproduction. Meaningful critical-historical practice thus becomes one with social ontology. Benjamin's materialist history also becomes further congruent with

Horkheimer's Critical Theory, but with an even more subtly explored disciplinary and methodological dynamics: true disciplinarity resolves history as dialectical image in the present, and thus grounds the emergence of potential futures. All disciplinarity, if it is to be the source of genuine knowledge, must therefore recognize its essentially violent destructiveness to be capable of this emergent futurity. Method and material must become emergent in one another.

In pursuing this form of methodological–disciplinary renewal, Benjamin dissolves the problem of the representation of the body and of sexuality into his constellation of a materialist history. The body of—and in—history is thus resolved into the materialist historical process that is revealed through the detritus, artifacts, and *disjecta membra* of social relations. Materialist history is, therefore, social ontology, but it requires a simultaneous understanding of the stakes of the sublation of discrete bodies and sexual relations into the constellation of text and image to become so. This is a lesson that today's critical theory needs to make its own.

Today's undialectical discourses of "disruptive innovation"—seeking the destruction and fragmentation of existing modes of production in the name of new ones that seem, primarily, to concentrate capital accumulation only ever more thoroughly in the hands of the partisans of an apolitical or post-political technology—redouble the stakes that Benjamin identified in the nineteenth century's "bungled reception of technology" (266): that they heighten and thicken the reification of reproductive forces in the service of capital. A thoroughly revived materialist practice of the sort that Benjamin imagined, one that contains within itself the constitutive elements of social ontology, might, however, still hold the promise of attending to the genuine detritus of the contemporary techno-economy, perhaps even including the status of labor as a cast-off artifact of the cycles of capital accumulation through technological recursion. This lesson remains in need of learning and re-learning today.

## Note

1. Neither Jay nor Wiggershaus note that Fuchs was among the original trustees, and this is surely a significant source of the lack of awareness about his participation among English-speaking scholars. It is possible that Fuchs joined at a somewhat later date, and therefore would not have been listed among the founding trustees. It is nonetheless

clear that his involvement was significant. Fuchs's somewhat shadowy involvement could plausibly have been the source of rumors noted by Jay: "To my knowledge however, there is no evidence to indicate any political contributors, although allegations to this effect were made by the Institute's detractors in later years" (Jay, 1996, p. 8).

REFERENCES

Amidon, K. S. (2008). "Diesmal fehlt die Biologie!" Max Horkheimer, Richard Thurnwald, and the biological prehistory of German *Sozialforschung*. *New German Critique, 35*(2), 103–137.

Amidon, K. S., & Worrell, M. P. (2008). ARL Gurland, the Frankfurt School, and the critical theory of antisemitism. *Telos, 2008*(144), 129–147.

Anderson, M. M. (1992). *Kafka's clothes: Ornament and aestheticism in the Habsburg fin de siecle*. Oxford: Oxford University Press.

Bach, U. E. (2010). "It would be delicious to write books for a new society, but not for the newly rich": Eduard Fuchs between elite and mass culture. In L. Tatlock (Ed.), *Publishing culture and the "reading nation": German book history in the long nineteenth century* (pp. 294–312). Rochester, NY: Camden House.

Benjamin, W. (1977). *Gesammelte Schriften* (Vol. II.3). Frankfurt/M.: Suhrkamp.

Benjamin, W. (2000). *Walter Benjamin: Selected writings, Vol. 2, 1927–1935*. Cambridge, MA: Harvard University Press.

Benjamin, W. (2002). *Walter Benjamin: Selected writings, Vol. 3, 1935–1938*. Cambridge, MA: Harvard University Press.

Caygill, H. (1998). *Walter Benjamin: The colour of experience*. London: Routledge.

Eiland, H., & Jennings, M. W. (2014). *Walter Benjamin*. Cambridge, MA: Harvard University Press.

Gliboff, S. (2008). *HG Bronn, Ernst Haeckel, and the origins of German darwinism*. Cambridge, MA: MIT Press.

Gorsen, P. (2006). Wer war Eduard Fuchs? *Zeitschrift für Sexualforschung, 19*(3), 215–233.

Jay, M. (1996). *The dialectical imagination: A history of the Frankfurt School and the Institute of Social Research, 1923–1950*. Berkeley: University of California Press.

Jennings, M. W. (1987). *Dialectical images: Walter Benjamin's theory of literary criticism*. Ithaca, NY: Cornell University Press.

Kelly, A. (1981). *The descent of Darwin: The popularization of Darwinism in Germany, 1860–1914*. Chapel Hill, NC: UNC Press.

Richter, G. (2002). *Walter Benjamin and the corpus of autobiography*. Detroit, MI: Wayne State University Press.

Santner, E. L. (2015). *The weight of all flesh: On the subject-matter of political economy*. (K. Goodman, Ed.). New York, NY: Oxford University Press.

Weitz, U. (1991). *Salonkultur und Proletariat*. Stuttgart: Stöffler und Schütz.

Weitz, U. (2014). *Der Mann im Schatten: Eduard Fuchs*. Berlin: Dietz.

Wiggershaus, R. (1995). *The Frankfurt School: Its history, theories, and political significance*. Cambridge, MA: MIT Press.

Worrell, M. P. (2006). The other Frankfurt School. *Fast Capitalism, 2*(1), 48–72.

CHAPTER 10

# The Body Ontology of Capitalism

*Daniel Krier and Kevin S. Amidon*

INTRODUCTION

This chapter locates the body in a critical social ontology operative on the triple planes *socio–psyche–soma*. While critical social theory powerfully negates symbolic structures of political economy (and imaginary projections of ideological culture), it never quite knows what to do with corporeal bodies. We begin with Marx's account of the body ontology of capitalism in his post-1859 writings (especially *Capital, Vol. 1*), in which value (on the ontic plane of abstract labor) appears as a sublime substance absorbed during the labor process. Psychoanalytic social theory takes up the body where Marx left off, and we analyze the congruent body ontologies of Marx and Jacques Lacan. Lacanian social theory analyzes imaginary (sublime) ideologies as ontically shifted projections of structurally wounded bodies (Žižek, 1989, 1992). For Zizek, sublime ideological objects complete and unify reality for subjects whose wounded bodies are violently installed within capital's symbolic order (Žižek, 1999). The prevalence of wounded body fantasies in the cultural productions of late capitalism, including those that

D. Krier (✉)
Department of Sociology, Iowa State University, Ames, IA, USA

K.S. Amidon
Department of World Languages and Cultures,
Iowa State University, Ames, IA, USA

© The Author(s) 2017
D. Krier, M.P. Worrell (eds.), *The Social Ontology of Capitalism*,
DOI 10.1057/978-1-137-59952-0_10

feature reanimated corpses (undead) and incorporation of the body into technological structures (cyborgs). These fantasy projections sustain the subjectivity of workers whose embodied drives are disrupted upon installation within the structural–symbolic order of capitalism, generating fantasies of wounding, energy-streaming and perforation of bodily boundaries. We will argue, with Marx, that body ontology is necessary to comprehend and critique capital in its symbolic and imaginary forms.

## Marx's Body Ontology of Capital

Like murderers in classic detective fiction, critical theorists of capitalism never quite know what to do with the body. Political theorists have investigated the "two bodies," imaginary and symbolic, of kings and democratic peoples, while largely ignoring the corporeal, organic bodies of political power (Kantorowicz, 1997; Santner, 2012). With important exceptions (Agamben, 1998, 2016; McNally, 2011; Reich, 1949; Santner, 1996, 2015; Theweleit, 1988, 1989), bodies are invisible in critical and social theory. Corporeal bodies of laborers in capitalist industry were everywhere implicated in Marx's post-1859 writings, especially *Capital, Volume 1*, in which narration of workers' bodies was sometimes so dense and detailed that the pages seemed saturated with sweat and blood. In a close reading of Marx's *Capital*, the first body encountered is the "physical body of the commodity itself" (1867/1977, p. 126). Bodies, especially laboring bodies, sporadically walk in and out of Marx's text as he guides the reader through the various metamorphoses of the commodity in capital, the circulation of capital, the transformation of money into capital and the general formula of capital and its contradictions. Bodies begin to pile up and accumulate beginning with the chapter, "The Sale and Purchase of Labor-Power," where laboring bodies are analyzed as organic bearers of the entire symbolic system of capital.

Marx's explanatory strategy generated significant ontological stakes by shifting between the three planes of *socio–psyche–soma* as he related the dynamics of capital, commodity and labor. Labor in capital is "objectified" in commodities, and thus shifts from the ontic plane of embodied, organic existence into the ontologically imaginary world of products and the ontologically symbolic-social world of value. Labor-power, or the capacity for labor, is unique among commodities as the only "commodity whose use-value possesses the peculiar property of being a source of value, whose actual consumption is therefore itself an objectification of labor, hence a creation of value" (1867/1977, p. 270). Laboring lies at the ontic intersection of psyche–soma: "labour-power ... the aggregate of those mental and physical capabilities existing in the physical form, the living personality, of a human being, capabilities which he sets in motion whenever he produces a use-value of any kind" (1867/1977, p. 270).

Within the capitalist mode of production, the concrete labor of the worker is transformed into the ontologically symbolic category of "abstract labor." Labor time, quantitatively equivalent across various categories of concrete labor, lies at the ontic intersection of *soma–socio*: "the proprietor of labor power (the worker who possesses his labor-power as 'his own property') must always sell it for a limited period only ... a definite period of time, temporarily" (1867/1977, p. 271). The intersection between the ontic planes of *soma–socio* is fundamentally implicated in the value of the "peculiar commodity" labor-power whose value is determined "by the labor-time necessary for the production and consequently the reproduction of ... labour, a definite quantity of human muscle, nerve, brain, etc. is expended, and these things have to be replaced" (1867/1977, pp. 274–275). The value of labor-power included "natural needs, such as food, clothing, fuel, and housing" as well as historically contingent social needs that varied based upon the "historical and moral" development of society (1867/1977, p. 275).

In Marx's writings, the body ontology of capitalism was bound up with the historical structure of the social. The double ontology of soma–socio determined sex itself: because workers in capital aged and died, procreation was subsumed within the value of labor-power. "The labour-power withdrawn from the market by wear and tear, and by death, must be continually replaced by, at the very least, an equal amount of fresh labour power" (1867/1977, p. 275). The content of cultural education and disciplinary training were also subsumed within the value of labor power (1867/1977, pp. 275–276). The body of the worker, then, bore the burden of social–historical development since:

> The value of labour power can be resolved into the value of a definite quantity of the means of subsistence. It therefore varies with the value of the means of subsistence, i.e., with the quantity of labour time required to produce them. (1867/1977, p. 276)

The body of workers set the "ultimate or minimum limit of the value of labour-power" equivalent to the "value of the commodities which have to be supplied every day to the bearer of labour power," embodied workers in order to "renew" their "life-process" (1867/1977, pp. 276–277).

The density of body analysis in *Capital* accelerates through Part III: "Production of Absolute Surplus Value," whose five chapters chart the course whereby laboring bodies are installed in the system of capitalist production that absorbs their expended labor congealed in commodities, whose exchange realizes surplus value, such that their embodied vital forces register effects on all three ontological planes (*soma, psyche, socio*). Chapter 11: "The Working Day" is among the bloodiest passages in Marx's work that sweats with muscular expenditure that depletes organic vitality. "The Working Day." In Part IV on the "Production of Relative Surplus Value," Marx again works through the body ontology at the base of capitalism, with chapters on relative surplus value as a concept, cooperation, division of labor and machinery. In this part of *Capital*, the laboring body appears as a negative, as a thing that capital seeks to obsessively avoid, to reduce to a minimum the socially necessary labor time (value) of production.

Capitalism as a social system (ontologically symbolic) is rooted in the natural powers of working bodies (ontologically somatic). "Labour is, first of all, a process between man and nature [that] … sets in motion the natural forces which belong to his own body, his arms, legs, head and hands, in order to appropriate (seize) the materials of nature in a form adapted to his own needs" (1867/1977, p. 283). The teleological nature of human work (*poiesis* in the Aristotelian sense), activity piloted toward a specific end-in-view lifts work out of pure body ontology into the psychic and social plane. While "a bee would put many a human architect to shame by the construction of its honeycomb cells," the teleological nature of work/*poiesis* is what "distinguishes the worst architect from the best of bees" because the architect "builds the cell in his mind before he constructs it with wax" (1867/1977, p. 284). Work, the production of commodities (utilities with value) is, to Marx, an ontologically tripled activity implicating *socio–psyche–soma*.

Workers and their organic bodies are the "instruments of labor … those of a mechanical kind … the bones and muscles of production" (1867/1977, p. 286). The creative potential, the life activity of the worker is deployed during labor but is burnt up in the process. Marx writes that labor, the ontologically somatic being, "is extinguished," dying into the thing produced, simultaneously producing an ontic shift such that "labour has become bound up in its object: labour has been objectified … the worker has spun, and the product is a spinning" (1867/1977, p. 287). Already dead labor (constant capital, as well as *dying* labor, the variable component!) buries itself in the commodities and capital it produces: it terminates in the body that emerges from the process as a product. This sacrificial death of the body is constitutive of capitalism, because no capital, fixed or constant, or natural material can produce value, only embodied workers. The powers of the laboring body magically transcend the ontologically-somatic to generate effects in the symbolic-structural order of value:

> living labour must seize on these things, awaken them from the dead, change them from merely possible into real and effective use values. Bathed in the fire of labour, appropriated as part of its organism, and infused with vital energy for the performance of the functions appropriate to their concept and to their vocation in the process, they are indeed consumed, but to some purpose. (1867/1977, p. 289)

The body ontology of capital—the activity of the living laborer—animates the corpse of dead labor that was previously "extinguished" as capital, which "incorporates labour, as a living agent of fermentation, into the lifeless constituents of the product" (1867/1977, p. 292). Marx theorizes ontological splitting into *socio–psyche–soma* and its reunification in commodities and capital as the essential secret of capital: "During the labour process, the worker's labour constantly undergoes a transformation, from the form of unrest into that of being, from the form of motion into that of objectivity" (1867/1977, p. 296). Capital is that perverse social substance that has the unique capacity to absorb the vitality and biopowers of living labor into itself, growing in the process. Capital reduces concrete energies of laboring bodies to the symbolic unit "average labor" and the "quantitative universal of labor-time:" "by being soaked in labour, the raw material is in fact changed into yarn, because labour-power is expended in the form of spinning and added to it; but the product, the yarn, is now nothing more than a measure of the labour absorbed into the cotton" (1867/1977, pp. 296–297). The "swollen" value of commodities is the symbolic index of "quantities of crystallized labor time." Attention to Marx's verbs reveals this: production "absorbs" labor, products have labor *absorbed, crystallized, congealed* or *objectified* within them, all alchemical/philosophical terms that reference fundamental changes of state or ontological shifts.

Capital absorbs living labor (ontologically somatic) and congeals/crystallizes/objectifies it into commodities (ontologically psychic as an object of desire), then through the process of realization, the absorbed labor undergoes another ontological transformation into money value (ontologically symbolic). Valorization (the symbolic increase of value from M to M') requires that the labor power absorbed by capital in commodity production exceed the value of laboring power. The worker is forced to work longer than necessary to recover the value of his laboring power. This of course is the great secret of the apparently "self-generating" monstrous quality of capital that Marx illustrates with the famous quotation from Goethe's *Faust*:

> by incorporating living labour into their lifeless objectivity, the capitalist simultaneously transforms value, i.e., past labour in its objectified and lifeless form, into capital, value which can perform its own valorization process, an animated monster which begins to "work," "as if its body were by love possessed." (1867/1977, p. 302)

The fundamental ontological break in the production process occurs through the doubling of concrete, qualitatively distinctive, embodied labor into "abstract social labor" measured quantitatively as "labor-time" to measure the quantum of labor absorbed by capital in production (Marx, 1867/1977, p. 30; see also Postone, 1993). Marx's description of this ontological shift uses spiritual (alchemical) metaphors:

> While productive labour is changing the means of production into constituent elements of a new product, their value undergoes a metempsychosis. It deserts the consumed body to occupy the newly created one. But this transmigration takes place, as it were, behind the back of the actual labour in progress. (1867/1977, p. 314)

The term "metempsychosis" is important here: the transmigration of souls from one body to another, especially one of an entirely different species/form. "Behind the back" of workers, their laboring bodies, ontologically somatic bearers of value, are burnt up as a "consumed bodies," releases value as a soul/spirit (ontologically symbolic) that haunts the thing produced. In capitalism, production is the perpetual burning up or sacrifice of the somatic whose soul (value) refreshes and reanimates the dead labor of capital (1867/1977, p. 322). Surplus value, whose acquisition constitutes the telos of capital, is "merely a congealed quantity of surplus labour-time" (1867/1977, p. 325).

The body ontology of capital sets limits to the rate and extent of capital accumulation. The laboring body has physical limits and temporal limits: "the vital force must rest, sleep ... to feed, wash and clothe himself ... [as well as certain] moral obstacles ... intellectual and social requirements ... conditioned by the general level of civilization" (1867/1977, p. 341). The ontological phase-shifting continues as capital's "voracious appetite for surplus labour" reduces labor to "nothing more than personified labor time" (ontological move from somatic to imaginary bearer of the symbolic) (1867/1977, p. 352). The body of the capitalist is also reconfigured as "capital personified" (an ontological move from the somatic to imaginary bearer of the symbolic), a body post-metempsychosis, possessed by capital itself (compare the spirit of capitalism that possesses businessmen in Weber, 1920/1958):

> His soul is the soul of capital. But capital has one sole driving force, the drive to valorize itself, to create surplus-value, to make its constant part, the means of production, absorb the greatest possible amounts of surplus labor. Capital is dead labor which, vampire-like, lives only by sucking living labour, and lives the more, the more labour it sucks. (1867/1977, p. 342)

This is one of the most powerful phrasings of the body ontology of capital in all of Marx's writings. Capital requires violent, sacrificial destruction of the somatic enroute to its own symbolic expansion (on moral ordering of sacrifice and expiation in societies, see Durkheim, 1915/1965; Freud, 1918). Marx describes the body-ripping qualities of capital using folkloric terms: "werewolf-like hunger for surplus labor" (1867/1977, p. 353) and the "vampire thirst for the living blood of labour" (1867/1977, p. 367). Workers were overworked into a "stone like torpor" (1867/1977, p. 35), suffering "degenerescence" due to complete absorption of the time of life as labor time (1867/1977, p. 355). Marx describes the bodies of bakers' journeymen depleted by shifts that begin at 11 p.m. and last overnight, requiring workers to make a bed by sleeping atop their own rising dough (1867/1977, pp. 359–360). Marx further describes a "motley crowd of workers of all callings, ages and sexes, who throng around us more urgently than did the souls of the slain around Ulysses, on whom we see at a glance the signs of over-work," milliners and blacksmiths who suffer "death from simple overwork" and whose lifespan is reduced by an average of 13 years (1867/1977, p. 364). He describes "stunted, short-lived and rapidly replaced" working bodies that were "plucked, so to speak, before they were ripe." (1867/1977, p. 380). The sacrifice of the ontologically somatic enroute to surplus value is explicit when he writes that "children were quite simply slaughtered for the sake of their delicate fingers just as horned cattle are slaughtered in southern Russia for their hides and fat" (1867/1977, p. 406).

Marx triples his optics across the ontological shifts in capital: from the material, concrete world of productive processes (ontology of soma–psyche) into depth consideration of the immaterial, symbolic, abstract and weightless world of valorization (symbolic ontology). Marx maintains contact with all three ontic levels as he drills down to the process of valorization:

> as soon as we view the production process as a process of valorization … the means of production are at once changed into means for the absorption of the labour of others. It is no longer the worker who employs the means of production, but the means of production which employ the worker … inversion, distortion … the relation between dead labour and living labour, between value and the force that creates value, is mirrored in the consciousness of the capitalist. (1867/1977, p. 425)

## Marx's Body Ontology, Division of Labor and Machine Production

Under modern industrial organization, with detailed division of labor and specialization, the body ontology of capital changes: "a worker who performs the same simple operation for the whole of his life converts his body into the automatic, one-sided implement of that operation" (1867/1977, p. 458). The combination of large numbers of specialized workers generates a "collective worker," an assemblage technically limited laborers unable to perform production on their own but require large combines. The degradation of the worker is inverted and doubled as the enhanced power of capital: "the one-sidedness and even the deficiencies of the specialized individual worker become perfections when he is part of the collective worker" (1867/1977, pp. 468–469).

The detailed division of labor in industry "seizes labor-power by the roots" and rips apart the bodily capabilities of workers:

> It converts the worker into a crippled monstrosity by furthering his particular skill as in a forcing-house, through the suppression of a whole world

of productive drives and inclinations, just as in the states of La Plata they butcher a whole beast for the sake of his hide or his tallow. Not only is the specialized work distributed among the different individuals, but the individual himself is divided up, and transformed into the automatic motor of a detail operation ... Unfitted by nature to make anything independently, the manufacturing worker develops his productive activity only as an appendage of that workshop. As the chosen people bore in their features the sign that they were the property of Jehovah, so the division of labour brands the manufacturing worker as the property of capital. (1867/1977, pp. 481–482)

The division of labor in modern industry, on the surface an efficient machine for the production of commodities (ontologically psychic/imaginary), it appears "simply [as] a pretext for profit-making ... [factories] are there to absorb surplus labor" (1867/1977, p. 373), to perform the magical ontological sacrifice of the somatic, "crippling of body and mind" (1867/1977, p. 484), to generate symbolic-spiritual value. Industrial production in machino-factories intensifies and "filling up of the pores" of labor time (1867/1977, p. 534). The worker in modern machine production becomes an organ or part of a larger body, an industrial–machinic organism on a vast scale, a massive engine "the parts of which are men" (1867/1977, p. 483). The worker becomes a virtual cyborg: "the machine makes use of him ... it is the movements of the machine that he must follow ... a lifeless mechanism which is independent of the workers who are incorporated into it as its living appendages" (1867/1977, p. 548). The body ontology of capitalism now includes tortuous excess, damage that is not sacrificed into value but dissipates as an unvalorized destructive somatic excess:

Factory work exhausts the nervous system to the uttermost; at the same time, it does away with the many-sided play of the muscles, and confiscates every atom of freedom both in bodily and in intellectual activity ... Owing to its conversion into an automaton, the instrument of labour confronts the worker during the labour process in the shape of capital, dad labour, which dominates and soaks up living labour power. (1867/1977, p. 548)

The manifold body sufferings of workers often fail to be sacralized into value: "Every sense organ is injured by the artificially high temperatures, by the dust-laden atmosphere, by the deafening noise, not to mention the danger to life and limb" (1867/1977, p. 552). The excess somatic damage to workers bodies was catalogued by Marx with great detail: boys in matchmaking factories dipped their hands in "melted phosphorous, whose poisonous vapour rose into their faces" (1867/1977, p. 606), and workers were disciplined with extraordinarily corporeal forms of punishment: beatings, ear clippings, brandings and other carceral punishments were deployed against working bodies to direct flows of human energy into colonies, enclosures and systems of wage labor (see also Federici, 2014).

Marx's body ontology of capital also included the consuming body of the worker, whose poor diet, bad housing, overcrowded and unhealthy "negation of all delicacy, such unclean confusion of bodies and bodily functions, such exposure of animal and sexual nakedness, as is rather bestial than human ... a baptism into infamy" (1867/1977, p. 813). Marx relates accounts of working families forced to relieve themselves by defecating into chest-of-drawers emptied once a week, and other accounts of bathroom, bedroom and other embodied living arrangements (1867/1977, p. 844).

## Marx *avec* Lacan: Marx's Body Ontology and Psychoanalytic Theory

Our close reading of *Capital* reinforces the view that Marx's social ontology of capitalism is triadic: labor, commodity and capital are triple-determined by all three ontic planes:

- *socio*, or the symbolic structure of value, language and law;
- *psyche*, or imaginary objects of commodified desire and ideological productions; and
- *soma*, or embodied energies and organic drives of workers (and to a lesser degree, capitalists).

In Marx's body ontology, the *soma* remains forever conjoined or tethered to *psyche* and *socio*. In Marx, bodies and organic drives of real workers are material bearers of value. Bodies of workers and their organic drives are structurally wounded upon installation in the capitalist mode of production. Enroute to commodity production the valorization of capital, bodies are depleted, damaged and their organic drives thwarted. Some, but not all, "body consumption" is productively absorbed by capital and crystallized in labor products. Capitalism produces not only material products, but also imaginary cultural productions for ideological ends. Ideology in capital, especially sublime objects (see below), is crafted to facilitate the bodily installation of workers within the production system and to *keep them there once installed*. In Althusser's famous formulation, the embodied subjects of ideology are interpolated within the structural–symbolic order of capital. Hence, the social ontology of capital is always already a body ontology: even ideological productions of capital are constructed to keep working and consuming bodies "in position" within capitalism's structural order. The body ontology of ideology is analyzed below with a special focus upon widespread fantasies wounded bodies, in the historical figures of Zinzendorf and Schreber, and in contemporary vampires, zombies and cyborgs.

Readers of psychoanalytic critical theory will recognize in Marx's triple ontology the Imaginary–Symbolic–Real triadic structure developed by Jacques Lacan (2006, pp. 318–333; see also Dolar, 1996; Žižek, 1989). Table 10.1 maps the correspondence between the body ontologies of Marx and Lacan. The table overlays Lacan's realm of the real with Marx's somatic plane, Lacan's imaginary realm with Marx's psychic plane and Lacan's symbolic realm with Marx's plane of *socio*. Labor is located in the real–soma–labor column, commodities in the imaginary–psyche–commodity column, and money, or more precisely, the money form of value, in the symbolic–socio–capital column.

**Table 10.1** Body ontology of capitalism: Marx *avec* Lacan

| *Real*–soma–*labor* | *Imaginary*–psyche–*commodity* | *Symbolic*–socio–*capital* (*money form*) |
|---|---|---|
| • Material body and organic drives <br> • Qualitative and singular | • Fantasy <br> • Mirror specular doubles <br> • Spectral semblance <br> • Totemism and fetishism | • Structural, <br> • Quantitative, <br> • Abstract, <br> • Immaterial, <br> • Weightless–oppressive |
| • Concrete use-value <br> • Concrete labor | • Doubling of use-value (relative singular) and its particular equivalent <br> • Commodity form of value Value small *a* | • Money = quantum of value <br> • "Comes and goes" in flash of realization <br> • Money form of value <br> • Value big *A* |
| • Concrete capital (constant/variable) <br> • Technical composition of production <br> L+L' | • Commodities swollen with labor absorbed by capital during production <br> • Organic composition of capital <br> C+C' | • Self-valorizing value <br><br><br><br> M+M' |

In the real–soma–labor column, we position singular workers whose material bodies and organic drives are deployed in concrete labor and whose survival depends upon the consumption of concrete use-values. These concrete workers are installed within concrete capital, productive workplaces that produce use-values as a side activity to the absorption of labor. The progressive development of more powerful productive forces capable of absorbing ever larger quantities of labor time constitutes the technical composition of production (Labor + Labor') (Marx, 1894, n.p.).

In the imaginary–psyche–commodity column, we situate commodities and workers (reduced to purveyors of labor time) facing each other as specular "doubles" or particular equivalents. In this realm, commodities are spectres (sublime objects) of fantasy that are fetishized, even totemized, as semblances radiating power, fascination and triggering desire. Commodities face each other in the marketplace as particular equivalents (commodity form of value), mirroring the double reflection of fetish (display) value and congealed labor (value small $a$, or imaginary value). At this level, the telology of capital appears as the acquisition of surplus commodities (congealed labor) and the accumulation of productive technologies (dead labor) in the organic composition of capital (commodities + commodities').

In the symbolic–socio–capital column, we locate money as the universal equivalent, quantitatively abstracted from particular commodities. Capital in this form is both immaterial–weightless and oppressive, as the often-unconscious, structuring power of capitalist modernity. The money form of value is a symbolic marker of quantums of value, a structural force that "comes and goes," retroactively determining quantums of value realized in exchange (value big $A$). Money, as a purely symbolic form of value, weighs and registers the abstract labor resulting from the entire circuit of capital. It is the monster of self-valorizing value, of money begetting money (money + money').

Marx's critique of political economy and psychoanalytic critical theory map the body ontology of capital in congruent ways. In capitalism, bodies expend labor that is absorbed by means of production, congealed in products of labor that emerge later as commodities upon dispossession and realization through process of exchange and realized in exchange: all of the major categories of capital, even those situated in imaginary and symbolic orders, are ontologically borne by the "real" corporeality of bodies. Wounded body fantasies have become prevalent within the cultural productions of late capitalism, including those that feature reanimated corpses (undead) (McNally, 2011) and incorporation of the body into technological structures (cyborgs, armored subjects) (Haraway, 1991; Worrell and Krier, 2012). These cultural products, like all fantasies, "flesh out" the symbolic order to subjects whose bodies bear the burdens of capital. With Marx and Lacan, we conclude that body ontology is necessary to comprehend and critique capital in its symbolic and imaginary forms.

## References

Agamben, G. (2016). *The use of bodies: Homo sacer IV(2)* (A. Kotsko, Trans.). Stanford, CA: Stanford University Press.
Agamben, G. (1998). *Homo sacer: Sovereign power and bare life*. Stanford, CA: Stanford University Press.
Dolar, M. (1996). The object voice. In R. Salacel & S. Zizek (Eds.), *Gaze and voice as love objects* (pp. 7–31). Durham/London: Duke University Press.
Durkheim, E. (1915/1965). *The elementary forms of the religious life*. London: Routledge.
Federici, S. (2014). *Caliban and the witch: Women, the body and primitive accumulation*. Brooklyn, NY: Autonomedia.
Freud, S. (1918). *Totem and taboo*. New York: Moffat, Yard and Co..
Haraway, D. (1991). *Simians, cyborgs and women: The Reinvention of nature*. New York: Routledge.
Kantorowicz, E. H. (1997). *The king's two bodies: A study in mediaeval political theology*. Princeton, NJ: Princeton University Press.
Lacan, J. 2006. *Ecrits* (B. Fink, Trans.). New York: Norton.
Marx, K. (1894). *Capital: A critique of political economy* (Vol. 3). Marxists.org. Retrieved from https://www.marxists.org/archive/marx/works/1894-c3/ch08.html.
Marx, K. (1867/1977). *Capital* (Vol. 1) (B. Fowkes, Trans.). New York: Vintage.
McNally, D. (2011). *Monsters of the market: Zombies, vampires and global capitalism*. Chicago: Haymarket Books.
Postone, M. (1993). *Time, labor, and social domination: A reinterpretation of Marx's critical theory*. Cambridge: Cambridge University Press.
Reich, R. (1949). *Character-analysis, 3rd enlarged edition* (T. P. Wolfe, Trans.). New York: Orgone Institute.
Santner, E. (1996). *My own private Germany. Daniel Paul Schreber's secret history of modernity*. Princeton: Princeton University Press.
Santner, E. L. (2012). *The royal remains: The people's two bodies and the endgames of sovereignty*. Chicago: University of Chicago Press.
Santner, E. L. (2015). *The weight of all flesh: On the subject-matter of political economy*. (K. Goodman, Ed.). New York: Oxford University Press.

Theweleit, K. (1988). *Male fantasies, Volume 1: Women, floods, bodies, history* (S. Conway, Trans.). Minneapolis: University of Minnesota Press.

Theweleit, K. (1989). *Male fantasies, Volume 2: Male bodies: Psychoanalyzing the white terror.* (E. Carter & C. Turner, Trans.). Minneapolis: University of Minnesota Press.

Weber, M. (1920/1958). *The protestant ethic and the spirit of capitalism* (T. Parsons, Trans.). New York: Charles Scribner's Sons.

Worrell, M. P. and Krier, D. (2012). The imperial eye. *Fast Capitalism, 9*(1). Retrieved from https://www.uta.edu/huma/agger/fastcapitalism/9_1/worrellkrier9_1.html

Žižek, S. (1989). *The sublime object of ideology.* London: Verso.

Žižek, S. (1992). *Everything you always wanted to know about Lacan (but were afraid to ask Hitchcock).* London: Verso.

Žižek, S. (1999). *The ticklish subject: The absent center of political ontology.* London: Verso.

CHAPTER 11

# The Morality of Misery

*Tony A. Feldmann*

### INTRODUCTION

More than 60,000 individuals protested on April 15, 2015 for a $15 minimum wage. The protests occurred in 230 cities across the USA and involved students, union members, and low-wage workers. These protestors want to "end poverty wages" and "challenge the 1 % corporate agenda" (Watson, 2015, np). The movement has a preliminary goal of raising the minimum wage, but they also have a broader goal to "challenge the 1 percent's domination of economic and political system and change the balance of power in our society" (Watson, 2015, np). Though this movement is worthy of investigation in its own right, I am interested in the mass of workers who do not have the same sentiments as the $15 Now campaign. Indeed, there are many workers, including low-wage workers, who are hostile to the goals of this movement. How could they be hostile to a movement that supports their own interests? What is the nature of this hostility? And, where does it originate?

In an article posted on theblaze.com, Matt Walsh outlines his opposition to the movement. The article is titled "Fast Food Workers: You Don't Deserve $15 an Hour to Flip Burgers, and That's OK," and it has been shared over 1.1 million times on various social media websites. To Walsh,

T.A. Feldmann (✉)
Department of Sociology, University of Kansas, Lawrence, KS, USA

it is delusional for someone to "consider [themselves] *entitled* to close to a $29,000 a year full-time salary for doing a job that requires no skill, no expertise and no education." He argues that this is an issue of fairness and cites his own personal experience to illustrate his point. Walsh started working his first minimum-wage job as a teenager, and he worked hard, moved from position to position, and eventually, at the age of 26, he was hired for a position which paid around $40,000 a year. His current position requires more skill, which is why, he claims, it pays more. Raising the minimum wage to $15 an hour would put someone who is "pushing buttons on a cash register at Taco Bell" in the "same ballpark as biologists, auto mechanics, biochemists, teachers, geologists, roofers and bank tellers." Walsh asks, "Does that sound fair?" He emphasizes that he does not believe that people in themselves are worth less, but the value of the position they hold reflects the amount of skill required to perform that position. "Your job isn't worth 15 bucks an hour. Sure, as a human being, you're priceless ... But your job wrapping hamburgers in foil and putting them in paper bags—that has a price tag, and the price tag ain't anywhere close to the one our economy and society puts on teachers and mechanics" (Watson, 2015, np). He recommends they work hard, improve their skill set, and find a job with a higher wage.

Walsh's anti-$15 minimum wage stance is familiar to the recent "surf and turf" welfare policy campaigns that have been proposed and, in some states, implemented. For example, Missouri Republicans are looking to restrict what welfare recipients can purchase at the grocery store by banning them from buying "cookies, chips, energy drinks, soft drinks, and seafood or steak" (Ferdman, 2015). The Republicans argue that such items are "luxury food" and that it is an "abuse" of social programs for welfare recipients to enjoy such "luxury." Rick Brattin, the congressman who is proposing the legislation, states, "When I can't afford it on my pay, I don't want people on the taxpayer's dime to afford those kinds of foods either." Like Walsh, Brattin is appealing to a certain conception of fairness here. Let us consider the matter more closely.

## The Morality of Misery

What are we to make of this moral sentiment of fairness? Is this not a rather odd expression of a moral "ought"? For, what is being posited here is that we ought to distribute resources in a particular manner. Yet, the sentiment is not a positive claim about their allocation; it is not that people have a right to a certain bundle of resources. Rather the sentiment is that certain people ought not to have access to a particular amount of resources. The sentiment seems to be expressing an inverted sense of fairness, or fairness in the negative. It is this negative fairness that I call the *morality of misery*.

Fairness often seems to represent equality in justice. That is, we are all subject to justice in the same manner. Usually, this conception refers to both distributive and procedural justice. Distributive justice refers to the perceived correctness of the allocation of resources, or, in other words, the bundle of resources each person has is just. Procedural justice refers to the perceived correctness of the rules used to allocate resources, or, in other words, the way in which we go about deciding who gets what is just. Thus, the distinction is between the actual allocation of resources versus the rules used to attain that allocation. The moral sentiment being considered here appears to be only concerned with distributive justice. The negative fairness of the morality of misery claims that certain individuals ought not have access to certain resources. However, the sentiment also has a relationship with procedural justice; in the examples above the individuals feel that there is a violation of the rules of allocation. *Thus, the morality of misery refers to the perceived correctness of the suffering engendered by existing social practices.* Essentially, individuals feel like certain forms of existing suffering are just, and attempts to sidestep such suffering are immoral. The allocation of resources is at the same time the allocation of suffering, and the morality of misery refers to the perceived correctness of sufferings distribution. It is the dialectical underside of distributive justice.

The morality of misery is a very odd moral stance because it is commonly formulated in such a way as to use suffering to justify suffering. Its most prevalent manifestation is in the following principle: Because x suffering has occurred, it is fair that y suffering occurs. For example, Walsh justifies his opposition to the minimum wage because he had to endure years of working low-paying jobs. "When you stomp your feet and insist you should be handed what some of us worked decades to earn, that's when it becomes time for, as the kids would say, real talk" (Walsh, 2015). Walsh is arguing that because he, as well as many others, have suffered through low-paying jobs, it is fair that McDonalds employees suffer as well. Brattin justifies his strict welfare policy by arguing that because he cannot afford certain "luxury food," then it is only fair that welfare recipients do not get to enjoy them.

It may be asked, "If the morality of misery and distributive justice are two sides of the same coin, then what is its value as a concept? For, when we are discussing one are we not already discussing the other?" Yes and no. Let us consider Walsh's argument opposing the raising of the minimum wage. Walsh does argue that some businesses may have to reduce payroll, and he points out that the overall effect on the economy is uncertain. However, he is not arguing that these individuals are taking from the deserving, thus violating distributive justice. Rather, he claims that the position they hold should not provide a "comfortable" living, "as if 'comfort' is a human right" (Walsh, 2015, n.d.). Walsh believes these individuals should suffer: "You should stop trying to make this job comfortable, and start trying to make it an uncomfortable rung on a ladder to a better place" (Walsh, 2015, n.d.). Walsh is not concerned with the positive allocation of resources. He is concerned with allocation of suffering, and raising the minimum wage would allow individuals to avoid the suffering they deserve.

It may also be asked, "Why should we care about the morality of misery? Couldn't it be the case that some forms of suffering are just?" The main concern I have with regard to the morality of misery is when it is employed to justify unnecessary forms of suffering. For, there is no guarantee that the suffering engendered by existing social practices is morally just. Indeed, it often seems as if such suffering never is. So, what are the origins of the morality of misery? How is it implemented in our contemporary circumstances? In the following sections I look to provide some resolution to these questions.

## Commodity Exchange and the Morality of Misery

"The wealth of societies in which the capitalist mode of production prevails appears as an 'immense collections of commodities'; the individual commodity appears as its elementary form" (Marx, 1990[1867], p. 125). Here we have the famous first line of Marx's *Capital*. Yet, the significance of this sentence could not be overestimated. We live in a world of generalized commodity production. In our world, the means of production, labor, and the means of consumption are all separated by property rights and brought together by commodity exchange. Commodity exchange is foundational to the day-in and day-out experiences people have in our social world. Indeed, the experience of the ethics of commodity exchange substantially impacts how people think about a range of moral issues. Thus, it is important that we possess a clear understanding of the commodity form, the capital–wage relationship, and the dynamics of capitalism in general.

Let us begin with the commodity, the "elementary form" of wealth in our social world. The commodity has a twofold nature; it is both an object of utility and a value. As an object of utility the commodity possesses certain qualities which satisfy human needs. As an object of value the commodity is rendered equal to another commodity quantitatively. Thus, "as use-values, commodities differ above all in quality, while as values they can only differ in quantity, and therefore do not contain an atom of use-value" (Marx, 1990 [1867], p. 128). When we consider a commodity as a value we are not concerned with the concrete "material constituents and forms which make" a commodity useful (Marx, 1990 [1867], p. 128).

When we consider commodities as values we are reducing them to some common substance, and it is Marx's position that this substance is human labor. However, the concrete human labor which produces a given commodity is not what is reflected in the commodity's value. For, all forms of labor are qualitatively different in their concreteness. The physical movements involved in weaving are qualitatively distinct from the physical movements involved in tailoring. Rather, when we exchange commodities we are considering them as representations of labor in general, or as the crystallization of abstract labor. Thus, labor also has a twofold nature in capitalism: As an activity which, in its concreteness, creates useful objects and, in its abstractness, acts as the social status of commodities (Marx, 1990 [1867], p. 137). This point about the nature of labor within capitalism is crucial; indeed, Marx saw it as his most important insight (Marx, 1990 [1867], p. 132).

> "Not an atom of matter enters into the objectivity of commodities as values; in this it is the direct opposite of the coarsely sensuous objectivity of commodities as physical objects. We may twist and turn a single commodity as we wish; it remains impossible to grasp it as a thing of value. However, let us remember that commodities possess an objective character as values only in so far as they are all expressions of an identical social substance, human labor, that their objective character as values is therefore purely social. From this it follows self-evidently that it can only appear in the social relation between commodity and commodity." (Marx, 1990 [1867], p. 138)

The value of a commodity is its *social status* as socially necessary abstract labor. This "status" is not a cultural definition, but the result of "the lived intentionality of commodity producers" (Smith, 2001, p. 57). Thus, value is not derived from the concrete labor expended in a commodity's production.

Now, let us consider the value-form or the form of appearance of value in the exchange relation. Value is a social status, and as such it is not directly perceivable. Rather, value can be perceived only in the exchange relation, and in the exchange relation there are two forms of appearance of value. Let us use Marx's famous example of 20 yards of linen = 1 coat. In this value relation there are two value-forms: The linen is the *relative value-form*, and the coat is the *equivalent value-form*. Thus, the coat is *the form of appearance of the value of linen* in the equation above. The value of linen cannot be expressed in linen; it can only be expressed in another commodity. Thus, the relative and equivalent value-forms are mutually exclusive poles of the value relation. When the weaver brings his/her linen to the market, the value of the linen appears to the weaver in the form of one coat. When the tailor brings his/her coat to the market, the value of the coat appears to the tailor in the form of 20 yards of linen. Now, once the universal equivalent of money is introduced the value-form becomes a number, and 20 yards of linen = \$30.00.

The value-form has an important consequence for how people experience commodity exchange. Specifically, people often *misperceive* the value of a commodity as reflecting some inherent quality of the commodity in itself, and it is this misperception which Marx calls the fetishism of commodities. Importantly, it is not that people do not see the social labor that goes into the production of commodities which generates this misperception. Rather, it stems from the value-form itself. When people participate in commodity exchange, they are seemingly putting two objects in a relation with one another; thus, the social quality of exchange appears to be between objects and not people. This exchange experience lends itself to the fetishism that the value of a commodity reflects the concrete properties of the object. The consequences of this are far reaching.

Value negates utility. Within capitalism, in order for people to gain access to an object's utility they must realize its value first. Thus, within capitalism price tags possess commodities in a ghostly manner, overriding their corporeality via an unperceivable social force, but people experience commodities as possessing price tags (e.g. "The coat's price is \$30.00"). How do people come to possess the money needed to realize the value of the means of consumption? For the majority of people, they do so through the exchange of the only commodity they possess: Their ability to work, or in other words, their labor power. As Marx notes, the sale of labor power has two necessary preconditions: First, the owner of labor power must be the sole proprietor of it, and second, the owner must be compelled to sell it (Marx, 1990 [1867], pp. 271–272). The only way for most people to get access to the resources they need is through the sale of their labor power. Importantly, labor power and labor are not the same. Labor power refers to the *capacity* to work, whereas labor refers the *activity* of working. This distinction is crucial because the wage contract lends itself to the same fetishism as all other forms of commodity exchange.

When workers sell their labor power, they often *misperceive* it as the sale of their labor, and this misperception is the result of the form of appearance of the value of labor power. When workers engage in the wage relationship, the value of their relative commodity, labor power, appears to them in the form of an equivalent commodity, a wage. Furthermore, the wage is tied to a duration of work time. Thus, workers misperceive the wage as a reflection of the laboring activity they engage in during that work time. The fact that workers get paid after they have expended their labor power contributes to this misperception, and this confusion is another example of commodity fetishism.

Now, the value of labor power is not solely determined by socially necessary abstract labor time. Unlike all other commodities, the value of labor power also "contains a historical and moral element" (Marx, 1990 [1867], p. 275). In other words, the value of labor power is also significantly determined by social expectations. It is from this twofold nature of the value of labor power that stems the contradictory quality of attitudes toward wage rates. On the one hand, the $15 Now movement is pushing for a shift in the expectations regarding the minimum wage. On the other hand, Walsh is arguing that the minimum wage reflects the skill of the concrete labor performed in minimum wage positions.

It is at this point that the morality of misery comes into play. Essentially, Walsh has fallen under the spell of commodity fetishism when it comes to wage labor. He falsely believes that the spectrum of wages reflects the spectrum of skills needed for different positions, or that concrete labor has value. To Walsh, wage labor is an exchange of equivalents between the expenditure of a certain quantity of labor for a certain quantity of money. Thus, the amount of resources one has and the amount of suffering one experiences are the result of an equal and just exchange. Raising the minimum wage, to Walsh, violates this equal exchange as it deviates from the "real" value of such work, and it allows people to unnecessarily avoid just suffering.

A similar dynamic is occurring with the "surf and turf" welfare policies. Those who receive welfare benefits are perceived to be violating the equal exchange of wage labor. They are getting access to the means of consumption without giving up their time and energy. This point helps to explain why certain items are considered "luxury items" by the advocates of this policy. If someone who engages in wage labor cannot afford such items, then someone who does not engage in wage labor definitely should not get such items. A welfare recipient getting to eat seafood or steak becomes an egregious violation of the ethics of commodity exchange.

Let us lay out the place of the morality of misery in the social world of commodity exchange more explicitly. Commodity exchanged is experienced as an exchange of equal objects, and this equality marks the principle of capitalism's procedural justice. Furthermore, the equal exchange of commodities justifies the outcomes of that exchange or capitalism's distributive justice. Commodity exchange determines the allocation of resources as well as suffering. Thus, suffering is experienced as deserving when it is perceived to be the result of commodity exchange. Workers falsely believe that the reason they get is because they give. What do they give? Their time and energy. What do they get? Commodities. Thus, if someone does not have commodities, it must be because they do not give in a manner deserving of such commodities. If the undeserving want to enjoy some commodities, then they need to follow Walsh's advice: "Tuck in your shirt. Plaster a fake smile on your face. Go to work." Just as the dutiful Christian who has been born into sin must be redeemed and baptized in the Holy Spirit if he or she is to enjoy heaven, the undeserving can someday enjoy the "heaven" that is consumerism, but only after they have been redeemed through a baptism in the alienating spirit of wage labor. Perhaps the "iron cage" of commodity exchange (Weber, 1958 [1920]) is still held together by a search for moral redemption through a life dedicated to work, and perhaps those who must dedicate their life to work can redeem their loss by infusing their "cage" with moral worth.

## The Morality of Misery and the Politics of Inequality

So far I have restricted my analysis to the relationship between the morality of misery and attitudes toward the minimum wage and welfare policies, but the morality of misery may relate to beliefs and attitudes regarding equality in other realms of our social world. In this section I will explore the way in which the morality of misery relates to gender and racial inequality. I do not seek to reduce such inequalities to being the product of commodity exchange. Rather, I seek to show how the experience of commodity exchange in modern society contributes to conceptions of fairness in these realms. Finally, I seek to demonstrate that Marx provides a theoretical portal through which we can explore how his theory of capitalism relates to race, gender, and culture, and it is this point that I would like to explore first.

Marx's lack of attention to gender and race in *Capital* has brought about many discussions of how his theory relates to these other forms of domination. Some have argued that Marx's theory suffers from a fundamental bias that leaves it unable to properly address cultural factors. For example, Chakrabarty (2000) argues that Marx's concept of "abstract labor" is a product of European Enlightenment thought which blocks Marx's theory from properly addressing the dynamics of capitalism in a non-European context. Nancy Hartsock (1985) has engaged in a productive discussion of how one might employ Marxian theory to understand gender inequality in modern society. Hartsock points out that in *Capital* Marx is primarily concerned with wage labor and does not discuss the non-commodified realm of household work, which is a feminine arena. I think Hartsock is on the right track for attempting to bring Marxian concepts to bear on the gendered nature of domination, but I will argue that Marx offers a theoretical moment for how consideration of cultural aspects of domination can be brought into his theory.

As I have already discussed, Marx argues that the value of labor power has a twofold nature. It is determined by the labor time required to reproduce the worker as well as an "historical and moral element" (Marx, 1990 [1867], p. 275). It is the second moment where a discussion of culture can be brought into Marx's theory. The social construction of masculinity and femininity influences the valuing of male and female labor power, and vice versa (Mandel & Semyonov, 2014). The privileging of masculine traits over feminine traits devalues the work women perform. Furthermore, the classification of household labor, which only generates use-values, as feminine and wage labor, which generates use-values and value, as masculine reinforces the devaluing of femininity. The fetishism of commodities leads individuals to believe that the wage they receive reflects the quality of the labor they perform. If the labor of women is not of the same quality as the labor of men, then it is not worthy of the same wage or social recognition, and if the labor of women does not get the same recognition as that of men, then the morality of misery argues that it is due to it being unworthy of equal status.

The logic of this argument can also be extended to racial inequality. Martin Gilens (1999) in his empirically rich book, *Why Americans Hate Welfare*, comes across this same dynamic. He finds that Americans are generally reluctant to dedicate more resources in order to address poverty because they are concerned that undeserving people may get those resources. Importantly, the American image of the "undeserving" has been racialized, and many Americans have come to believe that African Americans are lazy and the primary recipients of welfare benefits. Americans are obsessed with ensuring that welfare is only used as a temporary measure, and that those who use the program are on their way to having a self-sustaining job. Indeed, Americans overwhelmingly support policies that require welfare recipients to participate in work or educational programs. For instance, 97 percent of Americans support requiring "welfare recipients to work in exchange for their benefits" (Gilens, 1999, p. 186). Furthermore, this dynamic applies to what Roediger (2007 [1991]) called the "wages of whiteness." Roediger found that identification of slavery as black labor and wage work as white labor undermined anti-capitalist sentiments and made the white working class more accepting of their subordination. Again, if the quality of black labor is less than that of white labor, then black labor does not deserve the same compensation, and if black labor does not receive the same compensation as white labor, then the morality of misery argues that it is due to it being unworthy of equal status.

The morality of misery may resonate with more general political attitudes like right-wing authoritarianism (RWA). Such a relationship is important as RWA has a strong correlation with various types of prejudice (Altemeyer, 1998). RWA is a syndrome consisting of the willingness to submit and the willingness to dominate (Adorno, Fenkel-Brunswik, Leveinson, & Sanford, 1950; Altemeyer, 1988, 1996, 2007; Fromm, 1965 [1941]). Commodity exchange perpetuates various inequalities, and so it provides several opportunities for those who score high in RWAs to express their sadomasochism. Those who score high in RWAs identify with traditional norms, values, and beliefs, and they divide the world between us (the good) and them (the evil) (Altemeyer, 1998). In the context of the commodity world, the submission to wage labor is fundamentally a part of the existing/traditional social order. To RWAs, the "good" are those who submit, and the "bad" are those who avoid/cheat the existing order. The demonological anti-semitism witnessed in the twentieth century can in part be understood as an attempt by workers to comprehend the "havoc that capital wreaks" (Smith, 2006) by projecting it onto an evil other (Postone, 1993; Worrell, 2008). RWAs might be the most ardent supporters of the morality of misery, as it wraps their own submission to wage labor in a blanket of moral worth while allowing them to blame existing inequalities on the moral failings of disadvantaged groups.

## The Morality of Misery and Critical Theory

In this last section I seek to place the Morality of Misery in the context of critical theory. In order to do so I will discuss how the argument in this paper relates to the works of Lukács and Postone. I have selected Lukács and Postone because, to my mind, each leans too far in their analysis with Lukács being overly optimistic and Postone being too pessimistic. Finally, I will argue that the analysis of the experience of wage labor in this paper identifies a rift that sits at the center of critical theory.

In *History and Class Consciousness* (1971 [1922]), Lukács argues that the standpoint of the proletariat lends itself to a critique of reification and capitalism. Lukács argues that the fetishism of commodities is dispelled once the proletariat comes to understand themselves as commodities. Once the worker's consciousness becomes "the *self-consciousness of the commodity*" the worker recognizes that his or her status as a commodity is due to his or her participation in certain social relations (Lukács, 1971[1922], p. 168). Once such self-consciousness is achieved the worker will then recognize that the only reason commodities have value is because of their position within a particular set of social relations. The abstract mental category of value is the result of a social process, and is not reflective of the qualities of objects in themselves. From here the working class can begin the process of liberating themselves from capitalist domination as the social qualities of the system become increasingly apparent.

However, the morality of misery indicates that, if anything, the opposite is more likely to happen, and for the very same reason that Lukács emphasizes. When workers recognize their social status as a commodity, there is no guarantee that they will not simply apply commodity fetishism to themselves as well. In fact, this is where the morality of misery stems from—the misperception that a wage reflects the quality of the labor being performed. Indeed, there is a general tendency for workers to view themselves as possessing some inner qualities, for example, moral worth, which gets reflected in their income (Lamont, 2000). They then go on to believe that if a group gets paid less it is due to their lack of these inner qualities. In this sense, Lukács is overly optimistic in his argument that the experience of wage labor lends itself to a revolutionary consciousness.

Moishe Postone seems to lean on the more pessimistic side. In *Time, Labor, and Social Domination* (1993) Postone offers a reinterpretation of Marx's theory, and in his analysis he argues that we should no longer view working class consciousness as a source of radical anti-capitalist consciousness. Postone claims that when workers assert their political interests they almost always do so in a manner that does not challenge the system itself. Thus, working class politics tends to be "capital-constituting, rather than capital-transcending" because "proletarian labor does not fundamentally contradict capital" (1993, p. 371). However, Postone seems to skirt aspects of wage labor which lend themselves to a revolutionary consciousness. Workers do identify with wage labor and fall under the spell of commodity fetishism, but they also actively debate the "historical and moral" aspects of the value of their labor power. Workers in the $15 minimum wage movement argue that they should not work 40 hours per week and still live in poverty. Postone is correct in that this is not a capital-transcending movement, but the logic of the movement is. When workers demand better pay they are necessarily questioning the structural dynamic of capitalist relations. Capital demands that workers submit to the abstract law of value, and these workers are refusing while at the same time demanding that how they participate in our economic institutions and how they are compensated ought to be negotiated. Demanding that wages are something to be consciously negotiated is only a step away from demanding that the institutional relationships are also something to be consciously negotiated.

## Conclusion

Robert Antonio (1981) correctly identifies the core of critical theory to be a theoretical analysis of modern domination with an eye for liberating openings. Furthermore, the primary question that critical theory was originally concerned with was the nature of working class consciousness (Jay, 1996 [1973]; Worrell, 1998). In this chapter I have attempted to bring this question back into the discussion by emphasizing how the very experience of wage labor can contribute to workers' self-subordination. However, wage labor can also be a source of undermining fetishism and reification. It is important to keep in mind working-class consciousness is two-sided and contradictory. Workers may recognize the injustices of the system and promote their interests, but they may also find moral worth in "aggressive and assertive stereotyping and negation of those whose difference presents a challenge to their identity" (Knights & Willmott, 1989, p. 549). Even though the self-liberation of the working class is not an historical inevitability, critical theory will be missing an important insight if it ignores the liberating potential already present in working class consciousness and where that potential comes from.

REFERENCES

Adorno, T. W., Fenkel-Brunswik, E., Leveinson, D. J., & Sanford, R. N. (1950). *The authoritarian personality*. Oxford, England: Harpers.
Altemeyer, B. (1988). *Enemies of freedom: Understanding right-wing authoritarianism*. San Francisco, CA: Jossey-Bass Inc..
Altemeyer, B. (1996). *The authoritarian specter*. Cambridge, MA: Harvard University Press.
Altemeyer, B. (1998). The "Other" authoritarian personality. *Advances in Experimental Social Psychology, 30*, 47–92.
Altemeyer, B. (2007). *The authoritarians*. Retrieved January 4, 2016, from http://home.cc.umanitoba.ca/~altemey/
Antonio, R. J. (1981). Immanent critique as the core of critical theory: Its origins and developments in Hegel, Marx and contemporary thought. *British Journal of Sociology, 32*(3), 330–345.
Chakrabarty, D. (2000). *Provincializing Europe: Postcolonial thought and historical difference*. Princeton, NJ: Princeton University Press.
Ferdman, R.A. (2015). Missouri Republicans are trying to ban food stamp recipients from buying steak and seafood. *Washington Post*. Retrieved January 5, 2016, from http://www.washingtonpost.com/blogs/wonk-blog/wp/2015/04/03/missouri-republicans-are-trying-to-ban-food-stamp-recipients-from-buying-steak-and-seafood/
Fromm, E. (1965 [1941]). *Escape from freedom*. New York, NY: Hearst Corp.
Gilens, M. (1999). *Why Americans hate welfare*. Chicago, IL: The University of Chicago Press.
Hartsock, N. C. M. (1985). *Money, sex, and power: Toward a feminist historical materialism*. Boston, MA: Northeastern University Press.
Jay, M. (1996 [1973]). *The dialectical imagination: A history of the Frankfurt school and the institute of social research, 1923–1950*. Berkeley: University of California Press.
Knights, D., & Willmott, H. (1989). Power and subjectivity at work: From degradation to subjugation in social relations. *Sociology, 23*(4), 535–558.

Lamont, M. (2000). *The dignity of working men: Morality and the boundaries of race, class, and immigration*. London: Harvard University Press.

Lukács, G. (1971 [1922]). *History and class consciousness: Studies in Marxist dialectics*. The Merlin Press Ltd.

Mandel, H., & Semyonov, M. (2014). Gender pay gap and employment sector: Sources of earnings disparities in the United States, 1970–2010. *Demography, 51*, 1597–1618.

Marx, K. (1990 [1867]). *Capital vol. I: A critique of political economy*. New York, NY: Penguin Books.

Postone, M. (1993). *Time, labor, and social domination: A reinterpretation of Marx's critical theory*. Cambridge: Cambridge University Press.

Roediger, D. R. (2007 [1991]). *The wages of whiteness: Race and the making of the American working class*. New York, NY: Verso.

Smith, D.N. (2001). The spectral reality of value: Sieber, Marx, and commodity fetishism. In P. Zerembka (Ed.), *Marx's capital and capitalism: Markets in a socialist alternative* (pp. 47–66). Bingley, UK: Emerald Group Publishing.

Smith, D. N. (2006). Authority fetishism and the Manichaean vision: Stigma, stereotyping, and charisma as keys to 'pseudo-orientation in an estranged society.'. In L. Langman & D. Kalekin-Fishman (Eds.), *The evolution of alienation: Trauma, promise, and the millennium* (pp. 91–114). Lanham, MD: Rowman & Littlefield Publishers, Inc..

Walsh, M. (2015). Fast food workers: You don't deserve $15 an hour to flip burgers, and that's OK. Retrieved from http://www.theblaze.com/contributions/fast-food-workers-you-dont-deserve-15-an-hour-to-flip-burgers-and-thats-ok/

Watson, B. (2015, April 17). Snapshot of the movement—The fight for $15 in 7 major cities. *15Now.org*. Retrieved from http://15now.org/2015/04/snapshot-of-the-movement-the-fight-for-15-in-7-major-cities/

Weber, M. (1958 [1920]). *The protestant ethic and the spirit of capitalism* (2nd ed.). New York: Scribners.

Worrell, M. P. (1998). Authoritarianism, critical theory, and political psychology: past, present, and future. *Social Thought & Research, 21*(1–2), 1–33.

Worrell, M. P. (2008). *Dialectic of solidarity: Labor, antisemitism, and the Frankfurt School*. Boston, MA: Brill.

# Index

A

abstraction, 12, 19, 80, 85, 86, 93–5, 98, 99, 101, 102, 115, 123, 132–5, 142, 175, 180, 185, 187
abstract labor, 13, 80, 83, 94, 95, 98, 101, 126, 133–6, 263, 265, 274, 281, 283, 285
Adorno, Theodor, 12, 34, 54, 56, 57, 60, 64, 115, 174, 178, 180, 181, 183, 185, 186, 196, 199–2, 217, 226, 242, 243, 286
aesthetics, 12, 90, 174, 176, 177, 179, 186, 188, 192, 238
alienation, 3, 8, 9, 19, 36, 37, 51, 54, 60, 65, 77, 80, 85, 90, 93, 94, 99, 103, 108, 248, 250
Amidon, Kevin, 5, 12, 13, 235–61, 263–75
anti-austerity politics, 12, 221
anti-utopian complex, 12
Aristotle, 16, 25, 28, 29, 32, 41n12, 42n14, 55, 127
artifice, 10, 47–71
asset bubbles, 11, 148, 150, 161–2, 164, 168n1
*aufheben*, 99
austerity, 12, 195, 196, 202–4, 206–10, 213, 214, 216–27, 228n16, 229n17
authority, 21, 77, 81, 83, 101, 113, 215

B

background, 6, 76, 88, 124, 158, 188
Bataille, George, 109
bearer, 83, 85, 86, 94, 101, 264, 266, 268, 269, 272
Benjamin
 "Eduard Fuchs: Collector and Historian," 13, 235
 "work of art in the age of technological reproducibility," 12, 237, 243

---

Note: Page numbers followed by "n" denote notes.

Benjamin, Walter, 12, 13, 174, 235–61
Berger, Peter, 5
*Bildung*, 33
body fantasies, 13, 263, 274
body ontology, 13, 263–75
body wounding, 264
bourgeois, 56, 77, 81, 88, 90, 99, 102, 104, 107, 124, 126, 136, 140, 185, 191, 250, 251, 253–9
  horizon, 124
Brecht, Bertold, 174, 180
Buchananism, 113
bureaucracy (bureaucrats), 62
Burtynsky, Edward, 12, 177, 186–92, 198

### C
calling, 7, 107–16, 197, 206, 218, 269
Cambridge Social Ontology Group (CSOG), 4
capital (Marx), 5–13, 36, 37, 47–71, 75–116, 125, 127–9, 131–2, 134–5, 139–42, 145, 148, 151–68, 168n2, 169n3, 169n5, 169n7, 170n10, 170n11, 170n13, 170n14, 173–92, 198, 207, 211, 213, 248–50, 253, 256, 259, 260, 263–75, 280, 285, 286, 288
capitalism, v–vi, 3–13, 34, 36, 37, 48, 49, 51–3, 56–8, 60–6, 70n6, 71n7, 76–8, 84, 86, 88–103, 106, 110–13, 124, 126, 128, 129, 132, 135, 137, 145–9, 153, 154, 156–8, 160, 161, 166, 170n14, 173–6, 181–3, 185, 189, 196, 198, 199, 213, 214, 216, 253, 258, 263–75, 280–2, 285, 287
capitalist, vi, 3, 9, 10, 33, 34, 37, 48–50, 52, 56–65, 68, 75–9, 85, 86, 88, 89, 92, 93, 98–100, 102, 104, 106–8, 110–12, 124, 125, 127–9, 131, 133–6, 140–2, 146, 151–7, 159–2, 165, 167, 170n13, 173, 174, 176, 181, 185–7, 192, 199, 246, 259, 264–6, 268–70, 272, 274, 280, 286–8
  societies, 9, 49, 50, 56, 58, 60, 124, 125, 127–9, 131, 135, 186
capital personified, 269
cheese powdered, 104–6
China, 146–8, 150, 159, 163, 164, 169n4, 169n6, 169n9, 188
circuits, 7, 11, 103, 153
civilization, 10, 48, 55, 60, 269
Clarke, Simon, 125
class, 10, 13, 33, 56, 62, 75, 77, 79, 87, 88, 90, 92, 99, 102, 104, 111–13, 132, 140, 141, 153, 174, 176, 186, 221, 222, 226, 227n4, 230n32, 241, 244, 254, 255, 258, 286–9
cognition, v, 16–23, 25, 27, 28, 42n17, 247, 248, 251, 256
cold war, 54
collective
  consciousness, 77, 90, 95, 96, 98
  intentionality, vi, 4–6, 30, 31, 281
  worker, 85, 94, 98, 113, 141, 167, 270
commodity(ies), 75, 77, 79–81, 84, 85, 87–90, 93, 100, 101, 107, 124, 128–37, 139–42, 152, 153, 162, 169n3, 184, 191, 198, 199, 213, 259, 264–8, 271–4, 280–5, 287
  circulation, 84–90, 131, 137, 138, 140, 141, 184, 185
  dual nature of, 10
  exchange, 13, 113, 138, 174, 280, 282–6
  fetishism, 7, 54, 60, 65, 87, 191, 283, 287, 288
communism, 112, 241, 242

communist party, 225, 240
Comte, Auguste, 76
concrete labor, 80, 94, 95, 98, 101, 133, 134, 152, 265, 273, 274, 281, 283
constructivism, 30–2, 128
corporeal, 12, 13, 236, 238, 243, 246–51, 253, 256, 263, 264, 272, 274, 282
Coughlinism, 113
credit, 8, 11, 132, 146–9, 152, 154–61, 163–7, 168n1, 168n2, 169n6, 195, 197, 202, 217, 220
  money, 147, 148, 152, 157–9, 161, 165
critical
  judgment, 19, 22, 24, 32, 34, 36, 38
  methods, 13, 246, 251, 253, 256–8
  realism, 11, 181–3, 192
  social ontology, 9, 16, 19, 24, 25, 31, 32, 34, 37, 38, 263
  theory, vi, 9, 10, 12, 13, 15–43, 47–71, 78, 84, 93, 114, 115, 174, 180, 185, 196–200, 204, 213, 217, 226, 235–9, 243, 252, 260, 273, 274, 287–9
critical–practical rationality, 16, 22, 34
critique, vi, 3, 8–10, 12, 13, 15–43, 47–71, 80, 84, 100, 125, 179, 181–3, 186, 189, 226, 235, 237, 243, 248, 249, 257, 264, 274, 275, 287
CSOG. *See* Cambridge Social Ontology Group (CSOG)
currency, 83, 146, 148, 150, 156, 164, 208, 210–12, 221
cyborg, 13, 264, 271, 273, 275

# D

Dahms, Harry, 9, 47–71
Dante, 140

dead labor, 191, 267–9, 274
debt, 11, 83, 145–70, 204, 207–9, 211, 216, 217, 220, 221
debt-based capital, 11
deleveraging, 149, 164–6
"Demand the Impossible," 12, 195–230
desire, 39n3, 66, 68, 75, 99, 100, 104, 109, 202–3, 235, 243, 268, 272, 274
devaluation, 78, 79, 88–90, 93, 100, 101, 107, 111, 156, 157, 162, 165, 166, 169n5, 210, 211
dialectical theorizing, 9
dialectics, 7, 86, 199, 250, 254
Dickens, Charles, 123, 137, 138
disenchantment, 10, 75, 77, 86, 87, 90
division of labor, 49, 109–11, 114, 125, 185, 266, 270–2
Durkheim, Emile, 4–6, 8, 51, 53–5, 76, 77, 81, 84–6, 93, 95–8, 104, 115, 269
dynamics, 25, 32, 40n6, 58, 183, 199, 249, 253, 258, 260, 264, 280, 285

# E

ECB. *See* European Central Bank (ECB)
ecology (environment), 40n7, 68, 167, 187, 213
economic crisis (2008), 12, 202
economic transformation, 9
enlightenment, 15, 18, 55, 60, 64, 191, 254, 285
entitlements, 60, 174, 188, 201, 278
epistemic refraction, 22
epistemology, 16, 60, 251, 253
euro (currency), 208, 210–12, 216, 220–6, 229n20, 230n28

European Central Bank (ECB), 206–10
eurozone, 12, 195–230
exchange value, 10, 78, 79, 88, 92, 101, 111, 125, 137, 139, 185
exploitation, 12, 84, 85, 87, 94, 104, 107, 108, 110, 158–60, 163, 250

## F

fact (facticity), 6, 8, 11, 12, 17, 26, 27, 32, 36, 40n8, 41n12, 48, 51–3, 55, 58, 59, 63, 70n4, 76, 77, 83, 84, 86, 87, 89, 94, 96, 98, 102, 103, 108, 112, 133, 140, 142n2, 154, 157, 160, 179, 183–7, 196, 198–202, 209, 212–15, 224, 225, 228n16, 244, 257, 267, 283, 287
fancy pants, 107
Fast food, 277
*Faust*, 268
Federal reserve, 158, 159, 162, 170n12
Feldmann, Tony, 13, 277–89
fictional (fictitious) value, 79, 82
film (cinema), 11, 12, 141, 174, 176, 177, 199, 200
finance, 59, 79, 83, 162, 195, 204, 206–10, 213–16, 219, 249
financial
  bubbles, 11, 148, 168n1
  crisis, 150, 155, 161, 167, 206, 209, 210
  sector, 11, 146–8, 151, 156, 161, 162, 167
financialization, 147, 161
force, 20, 51, 55, 67, 69, 83, 96, 107, 154, 156, 160, 189, 207, 222, 227, 252, 269, 270, 274, 282
forgetting, 151, 183–7, 190, 191

Foucault, Michel, 100, 103
Frankfurt School (Institute for Social Research), 9, 13, 47–71, 94, 98, 112, 226, 236, 237, 240, 242
Freud, Sigmund, 5, 8, 47, 79, 93, 97, 99, 269
Fromm, Erich, 8, 98, 114, 226, 230n32, 286
Fuchs, Eduard, 12, 13, 235–61

## G

GDP, 147, 149, 160, 169n7, 170n11, 170n12, 209
gender, 4, 125, 139, 169n3, 284, 285
general formula for capital, 10, 75–116
Germany, 49, 50, 59, 63, 65, 146, 150, 202–4, 210, 211, 217, 226, 227, 228n9, 230n32, 238, 240, 246, 255
global
  capital, 12
  imbalances, 148–50, 162–4
globalization, 9, 12, 70n6, 160, 165, 175, 187, 190, 192
Goethe, 109
Gould, Carol, 5, 40n8, 107, 108
Great Recession (post 2008), 147–9, 161, 164–6
Greece, 12, 195–230
Grossmann, Henryk, 198, 199
growth, 11, 68, 147, 150, 151, 153, 154, 158, 160, 162, 164, 170n11, 207, 208

## H

Habermas, Jurgen, 9, 20–2, 48, 174
Hayek, Freidrich, 5, 138
Hegel, Georg, 5, 8, 9, 18, 19, 21, 23, 25, 27, 28, 30, 33, 36, 37, 38n1,

39n3, 40n5, 40n6, 42n14, 42n15, 42n17, 56, 77, 92, 93, 96, 103, 109–11, 114, 115, 138
hegemony, 10, 77, 220
Hilferding, Rudolph (Finance Capital), 59
historical
  change, 9, 53, 190
  materialism, 8, 238, 246–51, 253–5, 258
history, 4, 9, 11–13, 28, 38n2, 56, 57, 63, 68, 104, 109, 125–9, 134, 146, 147, 158–60, 163, 167, 168, 177, 181, 197, 214, 221, 225, 235–61, 287
Hitler, 226
Hobbes, Thomas, v, 16
Honneth, Axel, 9, 42n17, 48
Horkheimer, Max, 13, 48–50, 52, 56–60, 64, 65, 76, 84, 199, 226, 230n31, 230n32, 236, 237, 240–4
housing bubble, 148, 151, 161, 162

## I

Ice Capades, Smirnoff, 77
imaginary, 6, 8, 13, 81, 82, 86, 94, 95, 101, 102, 263, 264, 269, 271–5
IMF. *See* International Monetary Fund (IMF)
immanence, 5, 18, 20, 24, 25, 31–4, 38n1, 40n6, 151
individual consciousness, 95–7
infraliminal, 10, 75, 78, 89, 90, 92, 98–100, 103, 113
International Monetary Fund (IMF), 12, 170n10, 204
irrational (irrationality), 52, 93, 113, 115, 155, 157, 162, 186

## K

Kant, Immanuel, 17–20, 92, 97
Keynes, 161, 220
KPD (Communist Party), 240–2, 246
Krier, Dan, v–vi, 3–13, 77, 109, 112, 161, 235–61, 263–75
Kuhn, Thomas, 11, 145

## L

labor, 11–13, 20, 30, 35–7, 49, 76, 77, 79, 80, 83–90, 92–5, 98, 99, 101–3, 105, 107–14, 124–7, 129, 132–6, 138–41, 152–6, 158, 159, 162, 166, 169n3, 169n6, 170n14, 173, 174, 184–8, 190, 191, 196, 198, 230n32, 250, 255, 260, 263–74, 280–8
  markets, 11, 155, 170n14
Lacan, Jacques, 263, 273
Lapavistas, Costas, 210
late modernity, 15
Lawson, Tony, 5
lifeworld, 20, 33
living dead, 86, 100, 109
Locke, John, v, 17, 128
logic of capital, 47–71, 89
Lotz, Christian, 11, 12, 131, 173–92, 198
Luckmann, Thomas, 5
Lukacs, Georg, 5, 11–13, 30, 41n11, 54, 60, 103, 107, 108, 174, 176, 177, 179–83, 189, 192, 287, 288
luxury goods, 13, 146

## M

Macaroni and cheese, Kraft, 104
magic, 103, 109, 113, 184, 224–5, 229n26
Marxheimian sociology, 8

Marxism, vi, 8, 10, 12, 60, 64, 75–8, 83, 84, 93, 99, 100, 102, 108, 110–12, 114, 129, 136, 209, 241, 242
Marx, Karl, 4, 5, 7–10, 13, 18, 19, 21, 23, 25, 27, 30, 33, 35–7, 39n4, 40n8, 42n15, 47, 51–7, 59, 60, 62, 75–90, 92, 94, 95, 98, 101–3, 111, 112, 123–7, 129–41, 142n2, 142n3, 146, 151, 152, 154–7, 159, 164, 167, 168n2, 173–5, 184, 185, 196, 198, 211, 241, 254, 263, 264, 266–75, 280–3, 285
Marxology, 75–116
materialism, 4, 8, 10, 76, 77, 86, 124, 238, 246–51, 253–5, 258
Mauss, Marcel, 8, 92, 115
mediation, 92, 115, 186
Merkel, Angela, 206
metaphysics (metaphysical), 17, 19, 20, 38n1, 41n13
metempsychosis, 268, 269
methodological, 10, 13, 77, 174, 184, 236, 237, 243, 257, 260
Milios, John, 12, 204, 208–10, 213, 217, 221
mimesis, 12, 173–92
minimum wage, 206, 277–80, 283, 284, 288
modern society, 9, 50–6, 58–60, 65–9, 70n4, 129, 135, 180, 285
monetary system, 11, 153, 158, 162, 169n3, 170n10, 196, 204, 210
money, 4, 5, 8, 10, 11, 83–5, 87, 88, 90, 92, 101, 123, 125, 128, 131–5, 137, 139, 140, 146–8, 150, 152, 153, 155–9, 161, 162, 165, 168n1, 170n10, 173–5, 184, 185, 192, 197, 198, 200, 201, 207–9, 212–14, 218, 220–2, 226, 227, 264, 268, 273, 274, 282, 283

monopoly (monopolies), 60, 63, 65, 244–6
capitalism, 60, 63, 65
monsterization, 94
moral
failures, 287
sentiment, 13, 278, 279
morality of misery, 13, 277–89
Murray, Patrick, 10, 123–42

## N

national innovation systems, 11, 160, 169n7
Nazi (National Socialism), 63, 94, 217, 228n16, 239, 240, 246
negation, 32, 34, 36, 79, 89, 99, 107, 110, 181, 185, 272, 289
neoliberal (neoliberalism), 100, 215, 216, 219, 220
Neumann, Franz (Behemoth), 63–5
Nietzsche, Friedrich, 93, 97, 102, 104, 114, 115, 184
normative (norms), 9, 11, 15, 17–19, 29, 32, 67, 68, 87

## O

objective structures, 24, 25
objectivity, 10, 20, 22, 39n3, 75, 78, 136, 137, 267, 268, 281
ontic drift, 77
ontic plane, 263–5, 272
ontologically
-psychic, 266, 268, 271
-somatic, 266–71, 273
-symbolic, 264–6, 268
ontological plane, 86, 266
ontology, v–vi, 3–13, 15–43, 108, 109, 235–61, 263–75
Our Miss Brooks, 200, 201, 215
overaccumulation, 154–7, 160
overexertion, 154, 164

## P

paradigms, 11, 145, 147–9
pathological sociality, 36
pervert's gaze, 94
Peter and Paul, 81
photography, 12, 173–92
Piketty, Thomas, 211, 213
Plato, 8
Plight, 56–66, 70n6, 202
*poiesis*, 115, 266
political
   economy, 5, 7–9, 11, 13, 34,
      47–71, 82, 124, 125, 142n1,
      166, 184, 246, 253, 263, 274
   failures, 150–1
politics and the political, v, 5, 7–9,
   11–13, 16, 17, 24, 47–71, 82,
   103, 110, 111, 124, 125, 138,
   142n1, 150–3, 156, 157, 166,
   167, 169n7, 170n13, 173, 176,
   179, 181–4, 187, 189, 203, 206,
   209, 216, 217, 221–4, 227,
   228n16, 229n17, 229n19,
   229n24, 229n26, 238, 240–2,
   246, 252–4, 256, 257, 259–61,
   263, 264, 274, 277, 284–8
Pollock, Friedrich, 49, 57, 59–66,
   71n7, 198, 199, 241, 242, 244,
   246
pornography, 242–6, 251, 257
*post-human*, 10
Postone, Moishe, 13, 60, 65, 70n5,
   71n6, 71n8, 71n10, 75, 107,
   108, 129, 136, 268, 287, 288
power, 8, 10, 12, 13, 15, 19, 21–3,
   27, 28, 31, 32, 36, 37, 40n6,
   40n7, 49, 55, 61, 62, 65, 67, 69,
   82–90, 92, 94, 96, 99, 102,
   105–7, 111–13, 127–9, 133–5,
   138–41, 151, 152, 154, 155,
   157, 158, 160, 167, 168n2,
   169n3, 170n14, 176, 183, 191,
   196–8, 202–4, 206, 207, 209,
   210, 213, 217, 221, 224, 226,
   229n26, 239, 243, 245–7, 249,
   254, 256, 257, 263–71, 274,
   277, 282, 283, 285, 288
pragmatist (pragmatism), v, 19–21,
   32, 37
primitive, 108
process, 10, 11, 21, 23, 28–30, 33,
   41n13, 53, 55, 56, 58, 59, 61,
   63, 64, 66, 68, 69, 70n4, 79, 85,
   86, 88–90, 92–4, 98, 99, 102,
   103, 105, 115, 133–6, 138, 140,
   142n1, 146, 154–6, 168n2,
   169n7, 170n14, 173, 176,
   178–80, 184–6, 188, 191, 235,
   239, 242, 246–50, 252, 253,
   260, 266–8, 270, 271, 287
profane, 6, 10, 75–116
psyche, 100, 114, 263–7, 270, 272–4
psychoanalysis, 238
purely social, 10, 80, 125, 126,
   135–40, 142n3, 281

## Q

quantitative easing, 83, 165

## R

race, 4, 201, 285
rates of investment, 146–7, 157
real
   abstraction, 19, 80, 85, 86, 93, 94,
      98, 99, 101, 115, 123, 134,
      135, 142, 175, 187
   community, vi, 5, 16, 30–4, 49, 123
realism, 4, 10–12, 75–116, 173–92,
   196, 217
reason, v, 15, 16, 18–24, 29, 36, 38,
   38n1, 39n4, 42n17, 52, 54–6,
   60, 62, 69, 76, 79, 82, 90, 126,
   161, 163, 175, 181, 216, 218,
   245, 252, 284, 287

redneck, 106
reflection (mirror), v, 28, 35, 42n17, 89, 99, 106, 127, 174, 176, 186, 188, 212, 237, 244, 259, 274, 283
reification (reified), 6, 19, 22, 23, 36, 37, 54, 60, 65, 90, 183, 249, 253, 260, 287, 288
relational (relations), 4, 21, 24, 26–30, 33–5, 40n7, 42n14, 173
repossession, 103–7
reproduction, 12, 46, 84, 94, 154, 167, 168n2, 179, 237–9, 243, 244, 248, 252, 253, 255, 256, 258, 259, 265
resistance, 69, 169n6, 191, 214–16, 218–27
revolution, 59, 94, 102, 111, 112, 125, 181, 215, 228n9, 238, 254, 255
Robot Marxists, 108
Rousseau, 33

S
sacralized, 271
sacred, 6, 10, 75–116, 245
sacrifice, 87, 110, 114, 223, 268–71
*sacrifice of the intellect*, 114
Santner, Eric, 259, 264
Schreber (Judge Daniel), 273
Schuler, Jeanne, 10, 123–42
science, v, vi, 3, 4, 16, 19, 39n4, 47–52, 54, 57–9, 62, 64, 81, 86, 95, 106, 114, 115, 123, 125, 127–9, 135, 137, 142n1, 188, 242, 248, 254, 255
Searle, John, vi, 4–6, 30, 31
Sekula, Allan, 12
sexuality, 4, 235–40, 242–4, 249, 250, 253, 255, 256, 260
Shakespeare, 107, 136, 204, 218

slavery, 87, 108, 220, 286
slaves, 108
Smith, Adam, 4, 147, 259
Smith, David N., 12, 84, 195–230, 241
Smith, Tony, 6, 11, 145–70
social class, 13, 140
social constructionism, 6
social fact (social realism), 8, 76, 77, 86, 89
social forms, 4, 11, 21, 22, 32–4, 50, 52, 99, 124, 126–32, 135, 136, 237
socialism, 60, 61, 63, 111, 112, 124, 181, 182, 207
socialist movement, 127
sociality, 10, 16, 17, 19–24, 26, 27, 29–38, 123–42
social ontology, v, vi, 3–13, 15–43, 235–61, 263, 272, 273
social pathologies, 9, 34, 36, 151, 159
social relations of production, 5, 11, 16, 26–8, 30, 31, 34, 37, 40n7, 77, 80, 94, 124, 154, 158, 159, 166, 167, 173, 176, 184–6, 260, 287
socio, 9, 48, 50–4, 58, 59, 64, 66, 68, 70n3, 71n8, 166, 263–7, 272–4
sociological, 3, 4, 6, 8, 41n10, 75–116, 123–5, 127, 138, 181
sociology, 3, 4, 6, 8, 49–53, 70n3, 76, 95, 97, 125
*socio-psyche-soma*, 263, 264, 266, 267
soma, 263–7, 270, 272–4
specter, 10, 218
speculative (speculation), 4, 21, 97, 108, 132, 148, 150, 155, 161, 162, 164, 168n1, 207, 218, 236, 256
speculative realism, 4, 97
Spinoza, 25

spirit, 5, 9, 10, 21, 38n2, 54–6, 60, 84, 85, 87, 97, 177, 195, 202, 215, 238, 268, 269, 284
splitting (doubling), 79, 82, 89, 267
state capitalism, 60–6, 71n7, 199
stereoscopic conceptualization, 10, 78
stimulus, vi, 164, 210, 257
subject-substance, 7, 80, 87, 101
sublime (sublimation), 7, 13, 92, 100, 103, 115, 188, 263, 272, 274
sublime object of ideology, 13, 263, 272, 274
substance, 4, 7, 17, 25–8, 30, 32, 35, 40n6, 40n8, 75, 78, 80, 87, 89, 90, 92, 95, 101, 123, 132–4, 136, 137, 196, 267, 281
substantial (substance), 26, 56, 78, 160, 241, 258
supraliminal, 10, 78, 92, 99
supra-sensible, 125, 130, 140
surplus value, 11, 85–8, 94, 99, 107, 113, 124, 127, 131, 132, 140, 153, 154, 170n14, 184, 266, 268–70
symbolic, 13, 86, 111, 196, 221, 249, 250, 263–75
Symposium for New Directions in Critical Social Theory, 3, 90
Syriza, 12, 195–7, 202–4, 206, 207, 211, 213, 219–25, 230n28

## T

technology
  paradigm, 153
  trajectory, 153
*telos*, 27, 29, 30, 37, 127, 129, 268
theft (steal), 103–6
Thompson, Michael, 9, 15–43, 182, 183
time, 6, 8, 9, 19, 27, 28, 30, 39n4, 51, 55, 58, 59, 62, 65, 67, 69, 70n5, 81, 84, 93, 96, 98, 99, 101–4, 106, 107, 115, 123, 127, 132–5, 153, 154, 158, 160, 161, 165, 166, 168n1, 176, 189, 190, 196, 199, 210, 217, 219, 220, 225, 228n9, 236–9, 241, 247, 248, 251, 254, 256, 258, 265–9, 271, 274, 278, 279, 283–5, 288
total debt, 145, 146, 211
traditional theory, 52, 66, 213, 252
triple ontology, 273
Trumpism, 113
Twinkies, 76

## U

unconscious, 8, 76, 274
undead, 13, 100, 264, 274
undeserving poor, 13, 284, 286
United States (US), 49, 59, 62, 65, 79, 83, 104, 105, 113, 128, 145, 148, 157–9, 162–4, 169n4, 169n9, 190, 203, 207, 242
US. *See* United States (US)
use value, 6, 7, 11, 81, 82, 101, 127, 131, 139, 140, 152, 153, 160, 264, 265, 273, 281
utility (use value), 61, 82, 101, 281, 282
utopianism, 12

## V

valorization process, 11, 92, 155, 268
value
  fetishism, 7, 78, 79, 82, 86, 87, 90, 107, 138, 142n3, 184, 273, 282, 283, 285, 287, 288
  form, 10, 137, 139, 184, 282
vampire, 269
Varoufakis, Yanis, 12, 195, 204–8, 210, 213–19, 221, 224, 227n3

Veblen, Thorstein, 5, 130
visual art, 12
votes and voting, 195, 196, 203, 211, 221, 223–6, 228n16, 229n21
vulgar materialist, 96

## W

wage labor, 13, 86, 127, 135, 170n14, 272, 283–5, 287, 288
Walsh, Matt, 277–80, 283, 284
Warenwelt, 198–200, 202, 208, 211–14, 221
Weber, Max, 5, 9, 47, 51, 53–5, 84, 86–8, 102, 107, 109, 112, 114, 115, 123, 146, 269, 284
welfare
  benefits, 283, 286
  policies, 283, 284
  programs, 13
werewolf, 269
western philosophy, 17, 60
Whitman, Walt, 98, 102
*Wizard of Oz*, 7
work, vi, 4, 5, 12, 13, 36, 37, 58, 59, 62–6, 68, 79, 84, 85, 90, 98, 106, 108–11, 113–15, 127, 130, 131, 147, 154, 168n1, 173, 175, 177–9
working bodies (laboring bodies), 266, 269, 272
Worrell, Mark, v–vi, 3–13, 75–116, 242, 275, 287, 288

## Z

Zinzendorf (Count Nicholas), 273
Zizek, Slavoj, 13, 99, 100, 108, 263, 273

www.ingramcontent.com/pod-product-compliance
Lightning Source LLC
Chambersburg PA
CBHW070129030225
21296CB00005B/223